Russia's Dangerous Texts

Russia's Dangerous Texts

Politics Between the Lines

Kathleen F. Parthé

Yale University Press

New Haven and London

Set in type by The Composing Room of Michigan, Inc.
Printed in the United States of America.

Library of Congress Cataloging-in-Publication Data

Parthé, Kathleen.
Russia's dangerous texts : politics between the lines / Kathleen F. Parthé.
    p.   cm.
Includes bibliographical references and index.
ISBN 0-300-09851-0 (cloth : alk. paper)
1. Russian literature—Political aspects.   2. Politics and literature—Russia.
3. Politics and literature—Soviet Union.   4. Politics in literature.   5. Nationalism in literature.   I. Title.

PG2987.P58P37 2004
891.709′358—dc22   2004042031

A catalogue record for this book is available from the British Library.

The paper in this book meets the guidelines for permanence and durability of the Committee on Production Guidelines for Book Longevity of the Council on Library Resources.
10 9 8 7 6 5 4 3 2 1

Contents

Preface

This book examines the ways in which writers unnerved and irritated the country's authoritarian rulers both before and after the Revolution, and gauges the cumulative impact of literary-political tensions on Russian national identity. Attempts to silence nonconforming voices absorbed considerable resources, but despite all these efforts, the production, distribution, and discussion of texts outside official channels never ceased. Respect for truth-telling artistic works existed even within the government departments charged with suppressing those truths: state power may have infiltrated the literary world, but literature infiltrated state power in turn. The writers' resolve to create daring texts remained strong, critics turned the review article into an ideological genre, and the reading public found subversive messages, whether they had been inserted or not, in artistic works. Along with tragic stories from modern Russian history of lost manuscripts and repressed authors, the record also shows an unbroken thread of political discourse through art.

I arrived at the idea for this book from several different starting points. During the Brezhnev years I regularly taught a seminar on the

Soviet dissident movement, focusing on politically and artistically provocative works from the USSR, on criminal cases that the government constructed against literary figures, and on writers' memoirs of prison and exile. The study of this now historical subject provided vivid contrasts of treachery and courage, venality and righteousness, mediocrity and artistry, and offered compelling tales of precious manuscripts, risk-taking authors, and grateful readers.

A second stimulus was my book *Russian Village Prose: the Radiant Past.*[1] My original intent in writing that monograph was to construct a canon according to primarily artistic criteria. Since the mid-1950s, rural writers (*derevenshchiki*) had behaved neither like toadies nor dissidents; instead, they were given limited permission to differ on rural policy and literary style. But as the book took shape, the Soviet Union began to change profoundly and rapidly, and some of my writers mutated into awkward activists whose basic political achievement was to cause a reevaluation of their works as stimuli for the rise of chauvinism. I was both fascinated and horrified as I watched the texts I had studied for years called a danger to the nation. *Russian Village Prose* was published in 1992 while that situation was still very much in flux. A dozen years later, in a political and cultural atmosphere that has moved beyond the period of acute crisis, an analysis of the disparate readings of rural prose illustrates some deeply held assumptions about the political power of writers in Russia.

As I studied the Russian press and mapped out the bizarre Red-Brown (Communist-nationalist) worldview, I saw that this research had to be placed in the larger context of a post-Soviet Russian society in which literature had been cut adrift from state control and state support. How did this newly free and newly poor literary-critical world react while the nation cast around for values and ideas to guide it through uncharted and very rough waters? My work during the second half of the 1990s as a consultant to the Librarian of Congress on a Russian identity project brought me into contact with Russians who were working successfully to build a new society. The fact that they shared a referential world rooted in literary traditions led me to speculate that perhaps the legacy of dangerous texts supporting alternate values could be seen, among other places, in the spirit and energy that these pioneers were bringing to post-Soviet Russia. I wondered to what extent the links in this chain could be traced, or at least suggested. This is the present book's third point of origin.

I begin by identifying ten historically powerful beliefs about the relationship between literature, politics, and national identity in Russia. The list is my own, and while it may be incomplete, it is, hopefully, not subjective. The rest of this chapter is devoted to a close look at the paths taken in the struggle between texts and the state over the centuries in an archetypal Russian contest of *kto kogo?* (who will prevail over whom?). Did this contest change in any substantive way after the Revolution, or was the pattern in place long before 1917? In the second chapter I describe a paradigm for the political reading of literary texts in Russia and demonstrate how the paradigm's existence is confirmed by its reflection in parody. Aksenov, Voinovich, Sinyavsky/Tertz and other writers both lived through and laughed at the excesses of their text-centered, authoritarian nation. The third chapter charts the stages in the reception of Village Prose over the course of four decades; frequently changing and sharply differing interpretations of post-Stalinist rural literature show how texts can lose their specificity as they become *pre*-texts for debate.

In the fourth chapter I examine how the canon came to be perceived as national territory, property to be defended not so much from external threats as from aliens within. The periodic coming together of spatial and cultural components of national identity with hyperethnicity affected the reading, and at times the fate, of writers and texts that fell outside the borders of the "textual nation." In the chapter that follows I focus on the powerful cult of righteousness and suffering in the literary-political sphere and ask what the tribulations of a writer or a text have to do with literary value. In both these chapters it is striking to see that what is conventionally called "political" in Russia is so often spiritually based. As the tsar's saintly aura and the church's intercessional role declined, authors took up these mantles and acquired a potentially dangerous political and spiritual power. Russia's greatest writers stood for the nation, as well as standing between the government and its oppressed subjects.

In the sixth and final chapter I look back on the now historical nexus to see whether the ten beliefs about the literature-state relationship and the paradigm hold up to the closer scrutiny that these case studies provide, or whether there are counterexamples that lead to a more comprehensive view. The belief, strongly voiced by some of Russia's most revered writers, that to preserve the integrity of creator and text all contact with the state must be avoided undergoes the most extensive reexamination. In judging the behavior of individual literary figures, keeping a distance from the state was not the only culturally sanctioned option. I also ask in this chapter whether it is possible to write a coherent and acceptable history of the twentieth-century canon now that the long-separated strands of Russian literature have finally come together. The chronology and politics of creation, transmission, and reception present formidable problems for the cultural historian of this period.

Jacob Neusner, the prolific scholar of classical Judaism, confronts challenges of reception in his own field by distinguishing between "description, that is, the text; then analysis, that is, the context; and finally, interpretation, that is the matrix, in which a system has its being." Neusner explains that by "system" he means that which "forms a statement of a social entity, specifying its worldview and way of life."[2] He says that systems are described "from their end product, the writings," and if we are to produce accurate descriptions we cannot lose sight of individual documents and the canon that they form, to which we have given such explanatory power.[3] In the case of Russia, where literature is thought not to have just explained the nation to itself and to the world, but to have helped shape its political history, it is important to trace with great care the steps by which this is said to have happened.

The title of the present book is ambiguous in ways that should be addressed at the outset: how do I define "text," and to whom might a text be "dangerous" because of its relationship to the "politics" of the day or to sacred national beliefs and values? A variety of written texts enter into this discussion, artistic and nonartistic, published and unpublished, complete and fragmentary, attributed and anonymous. Osip Mandelstam muttered and whispered poems that were preserved in the memories of those closest to him, but his words materialized into a dangerous text in the hands of the secret police.[4] Irina Ratushinskaya wrote poems on bars of soap but washed or scraped away the lines as soon as she memorized them, while Alexander Solzhenitsyn used a specially-made set of prayer beads as an aide-mémoire in the gulag.

Forms and categories of texts cannot be rigidly defined or else we risk losing the thread of a very interesting and instructive story. Not all self-published literature (*samizdat*) was either artistic or dangerous, and not all officially published works (*gosizdat*) fully supported state ideology or policy. Successive Russian governments turned their attention to different kinds of writing, including books, journals, and letters that came into Russia from other countries. In the age of Nicholas I, every kind of printed paper from abroad, including candy wrappers, posters, and sheet music for patriotic songs, was subject to careful examination for subversive messages. Between 1832 and 1857 under the chairmanship of Alexander Krasovsky, the government's Foreign Censorship Committee even examined music without words and looked closely at paper with no visible printing on it for the possible presence of "incendiary Polish slogans written in invisible ink." Emigré publications in Russian might look harmless enough on the outside only to have radical leaflets pasted between the covers. "The wrapping paper in which publications were received also came under suspicion, since it was often newsprint, and newspapers might contain harmful material. That too was to be examined, along with other packing debris brought from the Customs offices; great piles of rubbish apparently accumulated in the committee quarters."[5] In the Warsaw office of the Imperial Foreign Censorship every available space was piled high with dusty, mildewed forbidden texts, and chairs were stuffed with packs of newspapers that had been refused distribution.[6] Mikhail Bakhtin may have smoked some potentially dangerous texts; nineteenth-century censors sat on them.

It is true that in constructing any set, including the set of dangerous texts referred to in this book, the choice of elements seen as relevant to an argument takes us halfway towards our answer; opening up that set of objects could "yield more satisfying interpretive results—greater simplicity, expanded scope, [and] enhanced predictive power."[7] Of the many thousands of texts that could be brought to this study, I have chosen those which have helped me see more clearly and explain more successfully the literary-political process, both from a critical distance and in illuminating close-up shots. And in doing so I hope that I do not fit one Russian critic's generic profile of a "rosy-cheeked American Slavist, for whom every combination of cyrillic letters looks like Russian literature."[8] A number of the documents I discuss are not strictly literary, but they were in some way linked to the potentially dangerous artistic word.

What kind of politics did writers and critics who fell under suspicion advocate? It is easier to describe the attitudes with which they viewed the surrounding reality: irony, indignation, nihilism, antinihilism, and at times a quiet hopefulness. They presented themselves as witnesses to the truth of history, as the nation's spirit and its conscience, and as a reminder that Russians must live "not by lies," as Solzhenitsyn was fond of saying. No document that expected to have an above-ground life could afford to be very explicit, and even Chernyshevsky's influential novel *What Is to Be Done?* sketched out new social arrangements in detail, while leaving the time frame vague, and giving no idea of how Russians would maneuver successfully around the tsar and the secret police to bring about the sea-change he described. Underground literary works more openly opposed the status quo, but their proposals for alternative arrangements were vague or highly impractical. Readers knew all too well the world they must abandon, and had a vision of the distant realm towards which they must strive, but were given few pointers on how to get there and what to do when they arrived.

The political platforms and actions that arrested writers were accused of advocating had, at best, little relation to their writing, and in Stalin's time often none at all, as the wildest schemes for wrecking, espionage, and assassination attempts were attributed to literary and nonliterary figures alike. There were some cases, Mandelstam's being the most obvious, where the text really did give the writer away, but mostly what we see is the government's ritual, coded indictment of a writer for having given some signal in his work that the state of the nation was not good, and that centralized authority (*vlast'*) was not wisely or justly exercised.

Which qualities of the writer and text could become politically marked, engendering a debate that took on a life of its own? It could be any of a number of things, some intrinsic (genre, theme, character, setting, narrator, ethos, style, use of metaphor and inference, the work in its entirety, or even a very brief passage from it), others extrinsic (the writer's background, including ethnic identity, friendships, oppositional behavior outside of literature, the ideological profile of the literary movement with which the work was identified, events within the country or elsewhere that coincided with its appearance). The text in question might have been published in Russia after having gone through the state's extensive screening process, or it might have appeared abroad, in underground and unofficial publications, or it may never have circulated beyond a group close to the author. During the discussion of library "cleansing" in 1923–24 the relativism of the evaluation process was freely admitted. There were no completely "bad" or "good" books. There were, instead, "*comparatively* bad and *comparatively* good books . . . they are bad or good in one regard or another, *for one goal or another*."[9]

When these three elements stand together—writer/text/politics—what at first glance appear to be transparent connections belie a more complex situation. Discussions of politics and texts in Russia grounded themselves in the premise that the state acted out of an impulse towards self-defense when it saw in certain works of literature alternative political values which posed a short- or long-term challenge to central authority. Sensing a rival or an enemy, it struck first. Archival materials from the years 1917–53 that were made available after 1991 show how in the policing of literature every writer's file was assumed to be a criminal case in preparation. After looking at the state's substantial preemptive investigative process, the resonance of a novel like Tertz's *The Trial Begins* (*Sud idet*, 1959), is that much greater. Yevgeny Zamyatin suggested in the early 1920s that only fantastic realism could capture the spirit of this new age, and Sinyavsky/Tertz concurred, but the observation that the atmosphere in Russia was profoundly bizarre was not new. Dostoevsky, another advocate of fantastic realism, experienced firsthand the absurdity of official Russia. In the mid-1870s, when his progovernment views were known and he was highly regarded by the imperial family, officials in the town of Staraya Russa, where Dostoevsky stayed with his family for months at a time, still kept thick files on his activities. The police did reassure his wife that they were for the moment satisfied with Dostoevsky's behavior and hoped that the ex-prisoner would not give them trouble in the future. Official surveillance appears to have ceased shortly after that, but the writer did not learn that it had ended until 1880, a scant half-year before his death.[10]

Government reactions notwithstanding, the actual danger that writers and works posed never lay in divulging secret information that could weaken the country's defenses or harm its reputation abroad, nor in rousing a restive population to civil war, and, given the many-layered censorship, there was little opportunity to offend public morality. Joseph Brodsky was more of a problem to Soviet authorities when news of his sentence for parasitism won him support at home and abroad than when he was writing poetry for a small but appreciative audience, and Vladimir Bukovsky was just one more teenager drawn to the world of literary *samizdat* until the state taught him the power of the true subversive.

After Sinyavsky and Daniel were put on trial, they finally did become a threat to the state. The writers' fearlessness and quiet dignity on the stand sent a powerful message of self-liberation to the nascent democratic movement, a message that far exceeded the impact of their underground works *The Trial Begins* and "This is Moscow Speaking." The artistic texts posed an indirect danger in that their self-confident irony tempted a rigid and unimaginative state to react harshly and in ways that strengthened the post-Stalinist civil rights movement. The trial transcript was the genuinely dangerous text, as "tens of thousands of cigarette-paper-thin sheets began to circulate from hand to hand, bearing a type-written text that was barely legible—the 'last words' of Sinyavsky and Daniel at their trial."[11]

In their stories, Sinyavsky/Tertz and Daniel/Arzhak challenged Socialist Realism's right to control art; on the stand they challenged the state's right to lie about its citizens and to bully Russians into lying about themselves. Their influence was maximized by a network of supporters who undermined the government's attempt to close the trial to the outside world. When Sinyavsky and Daniel defied the state in that courtroom the Soviet Union was diminished, as it was in its encounters with Solzhenitsyn. Throughout the history of dangerous texts in Russia, there have been numerous "moments of witness," when people stood up for the truth and communicated it to others, and epochal change became a greater likelihood.

A poignantly forthright scene in Mikhail Bulgakov's *The Master and Margarita* reminds us that it was not every writer's fate to play a publicly heroic political role. In one of the final chapters it is announced that the tormented Master's novel has been read and that Woland should reward him with peace. "'And why don't you take him with you into the light?' 'He has not earned light, he earned peace,' Levi answered sadly.'"[12] The struggle to be an honest writer has shattered the Master's nerves, but his devotion to the truth has encouraged a fellow mental patient, the poet Ivan Ponyrov, to carry on this work. It was not given to everyone to openly oppose the state, but many people contributed in other ways to the fabric of literary resistance.

Along with letting the reader know what I hope to do in this book, it is probably wise to explain what I will not attempt. This book is not an exhaustive history of the government's control of writers and texts through censorship, trial, imprisonment, exile, expulsion, and by other means, nor is it a complete survey of oppositional writing, whether encoded in published works or more openly expressed underground or abroad. Valuable books and articles on these and related subjects already exist and archival research will give us more material for analysis in the future. This book approaches significant paradigms both conceptually and by looking at specific aspects of literature that were given a political valuation in Russia's highly charged atmosphere. With different angles of vision, different phenomena come into view. In his study of Russian social and political myths Michael Cherniavsky defended his methodology by saying that he was not offering "a comprehensive collation of all the material" because a statistical presentation of minority and majority opinions would be "meaningless." Instead he would "illustrate the possible uses of the myths, the meanings that could be assigned to them, the tendencies with which they were applied."[13] That seems a sound approach and one that I seek to emulate in a book which combines synthesis with original analysis.

To the question about what kinds of texts and authors were politicized, I have added a related question that intrigues me: can the politics "between the lines" of poetry and prose be connected to the decline of the Soviet Union and the political life of post-Soviet Russia? A paradigm that operated through 1990 virtually disappeared from view in the years that followed, and the apparent disjuncture between past and present is not a trivial matter. When Gorbachev gave literature its freedom, did state officials and politicians abandon the cultural sphere as a source of support except on ritual occasions? Did writers celebrate their liberation into an unsupervised professional life by choosing to disconnect from the political interests of the nation? Were readers so exhausted by the avalanche of formerly banned texts and by the demands of a less predictable economic life that they began to reach for detective stories and the remote control instead of thick journals and serious novels? Given the central role of artistic texts in the formation of Russian identity and in the gestation of political issues, what would the effect of disengaged readers and writers be on the evolution of Russian culture, politics, and national identity? Will future influences on national consciousness be diffuse, eclectic, and only peripherally cultural?

The early glasnost years brought euphoria about a culture that was newly free and yet still politically active, while the 1990s saw widespread pessimism about the future of both serious literature and genuine democracy. At this juncture in Russian history, at the beginning of a new age that will come to exist in its own right and not only as a postscript to the preceding epoch (post-totalitarian, postcommunist, post-Soviet), it is appropriate to examine common beliefs about the power of Russian writers and texts to move history, the responsibilities that went with this power, and how what we call "politics" formed in the miasma of a stagnant authoritarian society. Taking the biological metaphor a bit further, we can ask whether the politics of post-Soviet Russia represents new growth on an established plant, a mutation, a transplant from abroad, an entirely new species, or perhaps all of the above, juxtaposed in a typically messy, typically Russian way. If we accept that the literary sphere was a highly-charged space for at least a hundred and sixty years, with government authorities, critics, writers, and readers believing in its considerable power, then can we explain in a convincing way what it is that happened because literature was written and read politically that would not have happened otherwise? If there is no discernible effect on post-Soviet politics writ large, could this tradition perhaps account for the rapid growth of private publishing, or the unexpected strength of civil society initiatives?

By reexamining some of the key premises behind the literary-political connection as it has been traditionally articulated, I am at no point questioning the writers' willingness to take risks for truth-telling art, nor do I minimize the government's willingness to bring its considerable might down on their heads. In the uncertain world of writer-regime relations, to intend to be courageous was to be courageous, since neither the effectiveness of the gesture nor the reaction of the authorities could be predicted with any accuracy. Osip Mandelstam's death in the gulag is a vivid reminder that there were poets who gave up their freedom and sometimes their lives rather than renounce their verse. Sinyavsky and Daniel spent months in jail and years in the camps, but they lived long enough to see that at least some of the important battles they fought had been won. This book is an attempt to further clarify the writer/state nexus by distilling the most common assumptions about this relationship, and then looking at it from new angles to see if this changes our sense of how the paradigm worked, what happened when it ceased to function, and what analyzing all of this tells us about Russia and Russianness past, present, and future.

Acknowledgments

During the early stages of this project I received support from a number of sources, which I gratefully acknowledge. A Fellowship for University Teachers from the National Endowment for the Humanities funded my research during a sabbatical, and the International Research and Exchanges Board provided two Short-Term Travel Grants for trips to Moscow. Following my presentation of a research paper as part of the Columbia University Slavic Seminar Series, I was encouraged to apply for a University Seminars Publications Grant, which helped bring this book into the world. The Kennan Institute for Advanced Russian Studies, under Directors Peter Reddaway and Blair Ruble, has over the years given me a Research Scholar Grant, several short-term grants, and the opportunity to attend many stimulating lectures which did much to broaden my perspective on Russia, and it is with gratitude and pleasure that I have served on the Advisory Council.

To the Library of Congress I owe the same debt as all scholars who have been fortunate enough to do research in that splendid collection and magnificent setting. But I wish to extend my particular thanks to

Dr. James Billington for inviting me to work with him on a project devoted to tracking and analyzing post-Soviet Russian national identity. The three Russian colloquia at the New Jerusalem Monastery, in Tomsk, and in Moscow, which I helped organize and preserve in lengthy conference reports, were some of the most satisfying and enriching experiences of my professional life to date. I put the manuscript of *Russia's Dangerous Texts* aside for several years as a result, but when I returned to it I had a deeper understanding of contemporary Russia, better questions and, hopefully, better answers.

Caryl Emerson and Leonard Babby played the same critical roles as they did for *Russian Village Prose* and I owe them my sincere thanks. Colleagues in the United States and abroad responded to earlier versions of these chapters and among them I especially wish to mention Anna Maslennikova and Cathy Nepomnyashchy, who gave the manuscript an especially careful reading, Cynthia Whittaker, Robert Belknap, Robin Feuer Miller, Josie Woll, Ambassador Heyward Isham, Leon Aron, Daniel Rancour-Laferriere, John Givens, Brenda Meehan, Arnold McMillan, Gary Saul Morson, Natalia Ivanova, Lev Anninsky, David Gillespie, Peter Rollberg, Valerie Nollan, Marina Balina, Alla Bolshakova, and Erika Haber.

Representative Curt Weldon (R-Pa.), an expert on Russian-American relations, has shared his ideas on the many areas—including culture—where cooperation with post-totalitarian Russia is possible and desirable. Economist Anders Åslund, whom I came to know through the Kennan Institute, challenged the literary scholar's assumption that cultural dissent was a primary factor in the decline of the Soviet Union. It is true that Lenin deported both economists and literary scholars on the "philosophers' ship" in 1922, judging them to be equally dangerous to the still fragile RSFSR. While I am not willing to yield too much territory to the economists, Russian specialists must look beyond the data and conclusions of a single discipline if our work is to have explanatory power and long-term credibility.

William Scott Green, Dean of the College at the University of Rochester and a scholar of religion and Judaic Studies, helped provide a more conceptually rigorous framework for this monograph through his teaching on theories of religion and his writing on the authority of the text under conditions of powerlessness. Dean of the Faculty Thomas LeBlanc was generous in his support of my research and inquired about the progress of the book on a regular basis, even during fire drills. My department chair, Thomas DiPiero, willingly offered both scholarly opinions and his considerable technical skills, and students in my "Dangerous Texts," "Secret Nation," "Politics of Identity" and "Russia

Now" courses have been enthusiastic and imaginative in their own work on this and related topics. Jonathan Brent, Editorial Director of Yale University Press, whom I first met in Richard Gustafson's Tolstoy seminar at Columbia, deserves deep respect and appreciation for his major contributions to the field of Russian studies, and my personal gratitude for his scholarly example, his editorial energy, and his infinite patience.

Finally, to the many Russian writers who took considerable risks for their "dangerous texts," I dedicate this book. They were *podvizhniki,* "heroic figures" in the truest sense. One of the most talented and fearlessly honest of these heroes was Yevgeny Zamyatin, jailed both before and after the Revolution and later ostracized by some of his fellow exiles in Paris. In a 1923 essay Zamyatin said that heretics were the sole remedy against the entropy of human thought, and an absolute necessity in any society. Just two years later, in 1925, the Stalinist period began in earnest and politically edged satire was banished from public view for decades. But the year 1925 also saw the birth of Andrei Donatovich Sinyavsky, who did much to revive literary heresy and political satire. The artistic depth of so many works and the high moral ground occupied by numerous authors are legacies in which both Russians and those of us privileged to teach and analyze their culture can take great pride.

A NOTE ON TRANSLITERATION

For bibliographical references and Russian words in the text this book follows a modified Library of Congress system of transliteration. Russian names in the text modify this system further by using standard English forms (Alexander vs. Aleksandr), eliminating soft signs, and substituting "ya," "yu," and "y" for "ia," "iu," and "ii/yi."

Chapter 1 Literature
and Politics in Russia

Over the course of a century and a half from Pushkin's time until the late Soviet period, intense interaction between literature and state power became a distinctive feature of Russian civilization. Both the government and those who opposed it believed that the artistic text could be a powerful force for good or ill and for that reason gave it serious and sustained attention. By the 1860s, Dostoevsky feared that despite the empire's watchful eye, Russia was being undermined by a progressive ideology widely supported in the literary world, although an official censor felt that books were "merely thermometers of ideas already present in society. To smash the thermometer does not mean that one changes the weather, but only that one destroys the means of keeping track of its changes."[1] Seven decades later, the ever vigilant Communist government wondered whether reissuing Dostoevsky's own *Notes from Underground* and *Demons* would weaken support for Soviet authority. Both regimes feared their writers and both regimes eventually fell, reinforcing the widespread belief in the power of texts to move history.

After Stalin's death in 1953, the official attitude towards nonconforming writers and their works provided both Russians and outside observers with a reliable way of monitoring the general political atmosphere in this secretive state. Our own estimate of Soviet Russia's capacity for civilized behavior rose and fell according to the treatment of Boris Pasternak, Joseph Brodsky, Andrei Sinyavsky, Alexander Solzhenitsyn, and other key cultural figures. Since Pushkin's time, the hypertrophied literary-political nexus in Russia has generated powerful myths that have served as articles of faith and as thresholds for the analysis of both literature and politics.[2] To examine these myths and beliefs is not to deny their truth-value or their impact; it is simply to hold them up to the light of a different age, one in which they are, thankfully, no longer matters of life and death.

TEN COMMON BELIEFS ABOUT THE CONNECTION BETWEEN LITERATURE AND POLITICS IN RUSSIA

1. The Russians read more than any other people

From the 1930s onward, the Soviet people were proclaimed to be "the most avid readers in the world" (*samyi chitaiushchii v mire narod*).[3] This statement appeared on posters and billboards, reminding citizens to buy newspapers, magazines, and books.[4] The superlative *samyi* is linked to an active participle, *chitaiushchii* (reading), and both words lend an aggressive character to *narod* (the people). Virtually everything in Russia had to be bigger, better, and more vigorous than anywhere else, as the USSR competed with the West on all levels, including in literacy rates and the amount of reading done by its citizens. At the same time, the government reminded itself that if in fact there were many millions of enthusiastic readers, then what they had access to counted.

While the tsarist and Soviet governments constantly monitored the reading practices of the intelligentsia, they were also worried about text-inspired ideas that might reach a larger number of people, some of whom were capable of translating ill-understood plans for change into action. Despite these concerns, during the 1960s and 1970s the print runs of novels, story collections, and literary journals were frequently very high, and as a result there was a substantial supply of affordable reading material, albeit of varying quality.[5] The widespread popularity of the printed word in the age of television was something in which the Soviet Union could take pride, and it was an undeniable legacy of the universal literacy campaign carried out in the 1920s.

The devotion of the Soviet intelligentsia to texts continued traditions established more than a century earlier. Russians came to be known as a people who read broadly and deeply, who could memorize vast quantities of poetry and were able to recognize from "half a hint" a politically daring subtext.[6] This long chain of subtexts formed a liberating "hidden transcript" for a captive people.[7] In artistic literature Russians encountered the heroic figures and absorbed the national values that had helped the country to survive. Among educated people, belief in the centrality of writing, reading, and analyzing literature showed the cumulative effect of legends of impassioned discussion groups (*kruzhki*) in the nineteenth century, devotion to writers who had dared to address the nation's burning questions both before and after the Revolution, and memories of an intense, often costly attachment to literature that endured after 1917.

The encouragement of writing and reading as ways of fulfilling one's obligations to the state occurred at key moments in Russian history: the conversion in 988, the early eighteenth-century transformation by Peter I of a faith-centered kingdom (*tsarstvo*) into a more secular empire (*imperiia*), the nurturing of a better-educated elite by Catherine II, the disciplined reinforcement of the triadic values of Orthodoxy-Autocracy-Nationality after 1825, the reform agenda of the 1860s, the formation of the world's first socialist state, and in the wake of the Nazi invasion. A few years after Stalin's death, Khrushchev was asking writers to support de-Stalinization, and in the mid-1980s Mikhail Gorbachev hoped that the literary world would use glasnost to support perestroika. Along with a tradition of writers who answered the state's summons (or somehow worked around it), a parallel antigovernment tradition of writing, reading, and discussion arose among individuals and groups unhappy with the status quo, who found in texts a place to retreat and plan, however impractically, for change. Taking texts seriously was a national habit and a civic duty, whatever kind of Russia one envisioned.

Before 1985, a cadre of determined Soviet readers had engaged in the risky and exhausting practice of copying, distributing, and reading works in *samizdat*. Suddenly, these materials became available to a wider audience, along with volumes of light reading from entrepreneurs in the newly legal world of private publishing. "Employees worked multiple shifts. . . . An edition of a hundred thousand sold out in two weeks. . . . Libraries were rifled, reprints and reeditions were made of everything that had ever been in demand, no matter what or where."[8] When publishers ran out of Russian works for the mass reader and reprints of previously translated foreign books, there was a push to quickly translate more works from abroad, especially from America and England.

By the 1990s, this post-totalitarian reading frenzy seemed to have subsided. The nostalgia that surfaced during this decade included a sense that Russia's great attachment to reading had vanished, perhaps forever. Critics lamented that "we were always a literature-centered society, and now we're not."[9] Literary newspapers still asked people involved in the cultural sphere what they had read most recently and which journals they found most interesting, but looking at the results, their correspondents complained that "once upon a time in Rus there was a WRITER WHO READ (*CHITAIUSHCHII PISATEL'*)" but that time had passed.[10] The "reading-est" nation, including its formerly well-read authors, had other pressing concerns, other interesting opportunities, and other forms of entertainment.

2. Literature is where the formation of politics, prophecy, and national identity took place in Russia

> Aside from literature, there was nowhere to go.
> —*the narrator of* Notes from Underground[11]

> Literature carried out a lofty mission, and a critic, when speaking about literature, was part of that mission.
> —*Alexander Ageev*[12]

The Russian intelligentsia, modern Russian literature, and modern Russian national identity took shape simultaneously during the last quarter of the eighteenth century, and everything was in place for Alexander Pushkin's genius to bring these processes to maturity a few decades later. The evolution of the intelligentsia, secular literature and a more supple written language between the 1780s and 1820s coincided with the waning tradition of the sanctified ruler. While the masses maintained their belief in the power of a "true tsar" to intercede for them, their primary attention devolved to the saints of old and to the righteous ones among them, and their "cognitive map" included real and legendary holy places on Russian soil, as well as Constantinople and Jerusalem. The Europeanized intelligentsia, whose philosophical, and, subsequently, ideological orientation ranged from ultraconservative and nationalist to radical, increasingly put its faith in the creative writers' and later the critics' ability to speak for the nation. A growing number of journals and newspapers gave voice to the more educated members of the population; the government paid great attention to these publications since their potential reach went far beyond elite circles.

Among the literary intelligentsia, whose ranks swelled in the 1840s with people not of gentry status (*raznochintsy*), the artistic text became the basis of their religion and their politics. The rise of nationalism had brought with it hopes and expectations about the ways culture might strengthen national identity and pride. At the same time, the Russian empire had grown large and ambitious, and its ruling apparatus was impatient with anything that opposed state power, including the voices of a newly confident culture. While accepting the responsibility of being witnesses and advocates for the people, writers felt the weight of the center's goals and restrictions. The poet Gavriil Derzhavin "spoke truth to power," but he did it with respect and wit; Alexander Pushkin took the negotiation of the uncertain territory that lay between power (*vlast'*) and the people (*narod*) a stage further. In their own self-images, Russia's writers ranged from witty courtiers to aesthetic nihilists. The author acted not as an openly political person, but as someone with the right and the duty to speak for more than himself in his art.

Readers began to matter, and their approbation or condemnation, their buying or not buying works, came to be important during Pushkin's lifetime. One goal in the publishing world was to encourage those accustomed to reading French literature to take a greater interest in Russian journals, but Pushkin, although labeled a literary aristocrat, planted the seeds for a larger and less elite audience to come to belles-lettres. He helped to establish literature as the focal point for the expression of Russian national identity, and one aspect of his monumental legacy is that more than any other author, Russians have felt that to read Pushkin's verse was to read the nation.

Politics and Prophecy

In his *Atlas of the European Novel*, Franco Moretti illustrates how French, German, and British ideas "acquire symbolic momentum" as they head eastward and into the Russian nineteenth-century novel, where they become a "genuine threat to all that is most deeply Russian."[13] As this once-powerful tradition waned in the early 1990s, there were spirited discussions of how politically aware literature had evolved.[14] In 1855, Nikolai Chernyshevsky had spoken of writers acknowledging "the direct duty" of expressing the "entire intellectual life" of the nation. Dmitry Pisarev (1861) saw "the whole sum of ideas about society . . . concentrated in fiction and the criticism of fiction," which made writers out of would-be politicians, and moved artists towards journalism. In the 1880s, the Vicomte de Vogué found in Russia poetry and fiction a shelter for important ideas, and almost a century later George Steiner found it still to be true that "all of Russian literature is essentially political." Texts were written, examined for publication, and read in a tightly controlled political context.

Artistic texts and review articles were often "the only public forum for . . . important political and social issues."[15] However much literature was subject to censorship in the nineteenth century, it was still less suspect than writing that directly addressed the nation's problems. The beginnings of a serious critical press in the 1830s coincided with Romanticism's elevation of the poet and the growth of national consciousness; critics informed the writers of responsibilities to their fellow Russians, and reacted negatively when these sacred obligations were not met. But when writers went too far in addressing contemporary problems they ran into roadblocks from the state. A balance had to be found between two fundamentally different sets of political requirements if a writer hoped to be published without being attacked soon afterward.

The public airing of political questions had nowhere else to go, so it flowed into the only available vessels, literary and critical texts. In pre-Petrine Russia, the church had been "the main, if not the only source of political thought." Now a sacred status and spiritual power were transferred to modern secular literature.[16] Writers were seen as political figures and modern-day prophets who addressed the nation and the ages. Alexander Radishchev's narrator used a prophetic voice in *A Journey From St. Petersburg to Moscow* (1790), warning that the accumulated anger of the serfs would eventually manifest itself in a bloody attack on their masters. The longer it took to alleviate the injustices of serfdom, the more serious would be the resulting vengeance. "This is no dream; my vision penetrates the dense curtain of time that veils the future from our eyes. I look through the space of a whole century."[17] In *The Captain's Daughter* (1836) Pushkin's hero, recalling the after-effects of the Pugachev rebellion on his family's estate, sounds a similar note in predicting that any Russian revolt will be "senseless and merciless."[18] The perceived martyrdom of Radishchev, Ryleev, Pushkin, and many other writer-saints lent their political and prophetic statements an even greater authority.

Dostoevsky's "Pushkin" speech both captured and improved upon this paradigm. According to Dostoevsky, Pushkin could see "the national spirit of our future, already concealed in our present and expressed prophetically," and he was able to explain the divine purpose behind the Petrine revolution, which was to create a Russia that could serve as a universalizing force, capable of resolving all of Europe's contradictions. "For what is the strength and spirit of Russianness if not its ultimate aspirations toward universality and the universal brotherhood of peoples? Having become completely a national poet, Pushkin at once, as soon as he came in contact with the force of the People . . . senses the great future mission of this force. Here he is a visionary; here he is a prophet."[19]

Yevgeny Zamyatin's essays and his novel *We* warned readers about the entropy of human thought, whose unmistakable signs he saw all around him at the beginning of the 1920s. Literature must be "a sailor sent aloft" who reports below on what tomorrow will bring. A writer may be judged a heretic in his own time, and punished as such, but his "harmful literature" will prove to be right "150 years later."[20] Radishchev and his work were quickly removed from circulation, and the section of Pushkin's *Captain's Daughter* devoted to unrest on the estate was first published only in 1880. Zamyatin's essays slipped through in the early 1920s, and then disappeared from view for sixty years. Eventually, though, these and many other voices were heard.

Alexander Herzen, a mid-nineteenth-century expatriate writer and editor, felt strongly that poets were prophets and that "they utter . . . what is unrecognised, what exists in the dim consciousness of the masses, what is already slumbering in it."[21] James Billington has summarized persuasively the arguments for seeing the nineteenth-century writer as more a prophet who provides inspiration than a political leader with a precise agenda.[22] This coincides with views of the Russian canon as a remarkably spiritual form of secular text and not a textbook for governance. Dostoevsky's tribute to Pushkin in 1880 and Solzhenitsyn's Nobel lecture ninety years later praise Russian literature for using beauty to bring harmony to a troubled world. Pushkin had claimed in 1830 that he had more influence than "an entire ministry."[23] In Solzhenitsyn's novel *The First Circle*, Innokenty Volodin, defending literature's distancing of its voice from the state, said that a great writer "is, so to speak, a second government. That's why no regime anywhere has loved its great writers, only its minor ones."[24] This is the affirmation of a tradition that was already more than a century old.

Donald Fanger describes a trajectory that ran from Nikolai Gogol's admonition about talent carrying a responsibility "to elevate Russian readers morally and inculcate a shared sense of the country's destiny," through Turgenev's "Hannibal oath" to oppose serfdom, Dostoevsky's changing, but always passionately espoused, ideological stances, Tolstoy's radical idea of transforming not just the government apparatus but every single person in Russia, through the serious political responsibilities and resulting perils faced by oppositional writers in the twentieth century all the way up to Solzhenitsyn.[25] Gogol clearly had in mind the literary world as a support system for an autocratic, nationalistic, divinely sanctioned government, while Solzhenitsyn's hero Innokenty referred to a fearless and vigilant literature that held the leadership accountable for their actions. Opposition writers in Russia, both before and after the Revolution of 1917, were treated, and came to act, as if they fell somewhere along the spectrum between a British "shadow cabinet" and a French "fifth column."

National Identity

A study of Russian national consciousness over the centuries shows the land/people/holy-image triad evolving into a land/people/text model with the rise of modern Russian literature in the 1820s. A Russian who turned to Tolstoy's *War and Peace* would find a powerfully articulated sense of the land and its people, not just in the stirring battle scenes and the depictions of Kutuzov, Bagration, and Prince Andrei, but also in Natasha's authentic Russian dance after the hunt, when she understands the Russianness of the peasants and embodies it flawlessly and instinctively. And while Natasha had been taught all the French dances (indeed the dancing master is part of the Rostov household), the movements described in this scene were "inimitable and unteachable Russian ones."[26] True Russianness cannot be taught. Tolstoy shed his habitual irony to create a moment in which a unified Russian identity is made manifest: Natasha, her rustic "Uncle," and his serfs share a feeling for the nation, less than a year before Napoleon's invasion would put Russia to a terrible test. The Rostovs, Bolkonskys, and Pierre Bezukhov not only reflected Russian identity; they became, like the characters from a number of literary works, some of its constituent elements.

While Russianness cannot be taught, it can be chosen. During the second half of the nineteenth century, Jews in the empire's Pale of Settlement were increasingly drawn to the Russian language and its literature, which, they felt, "made us Russian."[27] They entered a tradition in which writers spoke for the land and its people, whether from a pro- or antigovernment position. The durability of this belief, and the unexpected forms it sometimes took, can be seen from a 1915 diary entry by the Russian-Jewish writer S. Ansky, who traveled with the imperial army into newly conquered territories in order to distribute humanitarian aid to the stricken Jewish communities. As he walked around the ruins of a town he noticed that "in every corner of the burnt street, on the walls and on the destroyed houses, there were newly affixed signs on which street names were written in Russian letters. The Russians had given all the streets new, highly literary names: Pushkin Street, Gogol Street, Lermontov Street, I think there was a Turgenev Street, too."[28] There are many ways that victors impose their identity on lands won in battle, and Ansky, who placed a high value on both Russian culture and the lives of Jewish war victims, saw in the choice of identity markers an implied cynicism and an insult to the memory of Russia's greatest writers, which in his eyes raised the act to the level of sacrilege.

Texts that spoke only for themselves or for an apolitical art rather than for the nation as a whole may have been important in the literary sphere but not in national consciousness. Geoffrey Hosking has emphasized the nation-forming role of the canon, and with a nod to Benedict Anderson, observed that "Russia's 'imagined community' was fashioned by literature more than by any other factor."[29] The Pushkin celebrations of 1880 did much "to crystallize literature as the bearer of national identity," a process that had been going on for half a century.[30]

The rise of literacy and of popular publications for new readers led to discussions both before and after the Revolutions of 1917 as to how the Russian canon could help bridge the gap between the intelligentsia and other literate members of the population, and how it could nurture the growth of a national identity independent of tsar and church. "The widespread adoption of the classics of Russian literature and their authors as emblems of national identity was a victory for radical and liberal publicists and a defeat for tsarist authorities, who had long considered Russian belles lettres subversive."[31]

One could say without exaggeration that well into the 1990s, many Russians saw themselves as a people whose character was largely defined by their greatest authors, among them Pushkin, Lermontov, Gogol, Tolstoy, Turgenev, Dostoevsky, Chekhov, and Akhmatova. Russians could see that as a nation they gave birth to these writers, provided them with character types (e.g. a Natasha-like woman, a man with a touch of Dostoevsky in him), settings, images, and narrative ideas, learned about them in school, and, more importantly, read them on their own. In the twentieth century, there are specific writers one associates with every historical moment: the Revolution, the organization of the Soviet state, the purges, the blockades, the siege of Leningrad and the battle of Stalingrad, the post-Stalin thaw and the beginning of glasnost and perestroika. There are also writers we associate with the everyday life of cities, villages, and even prison camps.

Russian identity has been so closely linked to the national literature that on a "cognitive map" of significant locations in Russia we can find real places linked to writers' lives and imaginative locations from their texts (thus: Tolstoy's Yasnaya Polyana and Pushkin's Mikhailovskoe, as well as Goncharov's Oblomovka, the Rostovs' Moscow house on Povarskaya, Raskolnikov's neighborhood in Petersburg, and the basement apartment of Bulgakov's Master). Literature provided Russia with a significant portion of its spiritual and cultural geography.[32] In the chapter on Russian ultranationalism, I will explore what happens when the concept of literature as identity-forming mutates into the much narrower idea of literature as a genetically based achievement and a means of ethnic defense, which in the Russian case leads to the closing of the cultural borders to outsiders, primarily Jews.

The Text as Locus for Faith, Community, and Values

Any student of nineteenth- and twentieth-century Russia is aware of the substantial space that the literary text occupied in national life. The implications of this text-centeredness can be better understood by looking at examples from the life of the Jewish people. It has been said of the diaspora that "in the absence of the temple and its Holy of Holies, the scroll and its writing became for ancient rabbis primary repositories and conveyors of social legitimacy, cultural authenticity, and religious meaning," and that "in order to be 'Israel,' Jews had to invest themselves in scripture."[33] In his *History of the World*, H. G. Wells referred to Judaism as a "literature-sustained religion."[34] Peretz Smolenskin, a writer from the Pale of Settlement, said in 1877 that for the Jewish people, Torah was the "foundation of its statehood" and even "took precedence over its land and over its political identity. . . . Our Torah is the native land that makes us a people."[35]

Jews in the Russian Empire who were "russified, secularized, then politicized" immersed themselves in Russian Realism and civic criticism, and brought to their reading of texts, especially the more radical ones, "specifically Jewish cultural and religious terms."[36] In the words of Chaim Zhitlovsky, Jews studied "in Chernyshevsky's *kheyder*"; the author of *What Is to Be Done?* was their *rebbe* and they were his followers.[37] Even as the twenty-first century began, Russian-Jewish immigrants in Israel were maintaining a distinctive identity that included a strong affinity for the literature and culture of the country they had left behind, as if they had exchanged a spiritual diaspora as Jews in Russia for a cultural exile as Russians in Israel.[38]

The philosopher Ivan Ilin, who was expelled from Russia in 1922, instructed others who fled or were deported after the Revolution to hold on to their sense of a homeland and of Russianness (*russkost'*), and to pass it on to their children. They could do this by going to the texts of their beloved, sacralized native literature: "He who seeks a path to Russia, let him go to her geniuses and her prophets. . . . most of all and forever—go to Pushkin."[39] Ilin credited some of his fellow émigrés with literally "writing Russia," keeping alive the identity of a country which seemed to many in exile to have, like ancient Israel, an existence only in faith and memory.[40]

Alexander Solzhenitsyn's Nobel Lecture emphasized the role that literature has played in "reconciling" and coordinating different scales of values; like Dostoevsky, Solzhenitsyn conflated the Russian with the universal. Party-line critics in the USSR complained about works and trends that ignored the Soviet value system, like Village Prose, which reintroduced peasant mores into literature. Later on, conservative nationalists, alarmed by the rapid spread of Western ways, advocated a literature infused with Orthodox spirituality as a guide to correct individual and national behavior.

In the preface to the first collection of Sinyavsky/Tertz works published in Russia (1992) Vladimir Novikov said that whether important literary works can make someone a better or kinder person is an open question, but at the same time Novikov acknowledged Sinyavsky/Tertz as proof that a writer's word (*pisatel'skoe slovo*) can make a reader feel bolder and freer than ever before.[41] At the end of the 1990s a high school teacher of Russian literature with forty-five years' experience talked about the Russian classics as providing much-needed support for Russia's youth: "To help them to grow strong, to make sense of life, and to get their bearings—that's the goal when we teach literature in school today. And the Russian classics are there to help us." [42] One of his students explained that Chekhov's longing for spiritual supports and genuine values made sense "today, when foundations and basic supports are crumbling."[43] This analysis of the attitudes of Russian high school students towards the classics appeared not in a pedagogical magazine or a newspaper but in *Novyi mir,* the best-known of the thick journals.

If in the pre-Revolutionary era writers and critics predicted, yearned for, or feared major alterations in the structure of the state, in the immediate post-Revolutionary period many literary figures concentrated on understanding and adjusting to the realities of the new age. Within a few years one branch of literature was living very much above ground, where some writers mutated into virtual cheerleaders. Other branches survived underground and abroad until they could begin to surface publicly in Soviet Russia, a process that began slowly after Stalin's death in 1953 and took almost four decades to complete. One literature welcomed the radiant future, while among other literatures, the witness narratives in particular were rightly seen as personal statements that when taken together had a potentially explosive impact as they contradicted and disproved official state accounts. Literature could provide a support for the existing political order, a check on its excesses, an attempt to rally opposition, an alternative politics, or a retreat from politics altogether, which in the Stalinist period was itself a provocative and risky act. In 1992, one critic described how "we used to take refuge as readers," echoing Dostoevsky's Underground Man for whom there also seemed to be nowhere else to go except towards the next sheltering text.

Whether the message between the lines looked like politics, prophecy, an assertion of national identity, or a statement of faith, whether it took the form of a poignant recollection, a challenge to the status quo, or a bold prognosis, literature was seen as a medium that could have a strongly positive or negative effect on the nation. The text was—by any of a number of accepted and overlapping definitions—a potentially dangerous instrument in the wrong hands. That the message was being presented in an imaginative or abstract form made the decoding of texts by readers, critics, and state authorities an important stage in what Russians came to refer to as the "literary process." It was an activity that was fraught with tension and of compelling interest to all parties involved.

3. One text would be on everyone's mind at a given time

> The glossy journals—that sought-after unified field. . . . it is here that from morning till night a search for the long-desired national accord is taking place.[44]
> —Alexander Ageev

The "one text" phenomenon refers to what happened when virtually all serious readers would focus on a single work for a given period of time, to be replaced at some point by another work in a chain of politically provocative "best-sellers." This might be a piece of *samizdat* making its way through the urban intelligentsia, or an unusually bold example of *gosizdat* championed by some critics and attacked by others. From Ovechkin's "District Routine" (1952) to Sinyavsky/Tertz's *Strolls with Pushkin* (1989), and from Pomerantsev's article "On Sincerity in Literature" (1953) to Erofeyev's "A Funeral Feast for Soviet Literature" (1990), paraliterary space was rarely empty for long.

The decade preceding glasnost (1975–85) has been described as a time when the intelligentsia ignored the lame remnants of officially sponsored Socialist Realism and avidly consumed "Pikul on Rasputin, Voznesensky's experimental prose and a photocopied Nabokov . . . as if it were a single text."[45] To the two eternal and cursed Russian questions "Who is to blame?" and "What is to be done?," commentators added a third: "What are you reading?"[46] The Gorbachev years saw an exhausting procession of "one texts," as censorship was eased and the "desk drawers" of Russian literature all seemed to open at once.

"From late 1987 into 1989, everyone on the metros and buses seemed to be reading the same thing at the same time. One month it was *Doctor Zhivago*, the next it was *Life and Fate*. It was a civic, as well as literary, explosion."[47]

"One text" is also a useful term for characterizing an ongoing discussion which links a piece of literature to critical commentary as well as to the government's views as expressed in everything from review articles to trial transcripts. In the Russian context both meanings of "one text" apply, with a third connotation added in the Gorbachev era when the three main branches of post-Revolutionary Russian literature—Soviet, underground, and émigré (*gosizdat, samizdat,* and *tamizdat*)—were reunited in "one text," and, potentially, in one literary history.

By the 1840s, the Russians were already a "textual community" that devoted enormous energy to the discussion of both published and unpublished works, with certain texts and their authors gaining attention and legitimacy, but all in the context of powerlessness, because even those writers who cooperated fully with the regime had "more power, but not real power."[48] They never came anywhere near to state power (*vlast'*). There was consistent, serious attention to texts and their meaning for the nation, and on many occasions a single text evoked not just intellectual but deeply emotional responses. To mention just one example, the critic Nikolai Strakhov remembered that "only *Crime and Punishment* was read during 1866, only it was spoken about," and not just in terms of literary qualities and shocking murder scenes, but also because of the obvious ideological resonance to the events of the day.[49]

In the process of writing *War and Peace* Tolstoy decided to refrain from scoring political points against other works of literature or factions in Russian society, to step back from the literary process. In doing so "the political novel that he originally envisaged eventually metamorphoses into a psychological and moral work more congenial to him."[50] *War and Peace* might be central in the minds of readers as their "one text," but if so it would be in a self-contained way and not tied to a particular current event or issue. Tolstoy intended that his work not have an immediate and ephemeral political impact, and to this end he wrote in a draft for an introduction that he made no promise that having begun the work, he would bring it to a conclusion, and that "no idea is being put forward in it; nothing is being proved."[51] What Tolstoy avoided in the turbulent 1860s was wholeheartedly embraced by Dostoevsky, who saw what in more modern terms could be called a symbiotic relationship between a given critic and a writer, with "every important Russian critic . . . devoting himself to one author and developing his own thoughts in this context."[52] In the "one text" setting, not only do the barriers fall between commentary and text, but also between works by different authors, so that the protagonists of Dostoevsky's *Demons* were read as "Turgenev's heroes grown old."[53]

The reasons for such an intense focus have to do with the association of literature with belief, not so much in abstract theological concepts, but in the idea of a God-chosen Russian people, the holy Russian land, and sacred texts. Russian culture had a primary literary model in the *zhitie* (saint's life), a closed or "faith" narrative where there is only one path for events to follow, since it is by definition an exemplary tale of a life lived for the Orthodox Church and for the glory of Russia. A society that focuses its attention on and invests its faith in texts will generally spend a great deal of time in a careful and consequential exegesis. Gary Saul Morson says that the act of interpreting a work endows it "with a past, a future, or both: one imagines a history or projects a destiny. Books are treasured or burned not for what they 'are,' but for what they have done or may do."[54]

This hermeneutic process links the original work to successive interpretations and counterinterpretations to form what can be seen as a single, open-ended document. In Soviet Russia, the active involvement of writers, readers (including critics), and the state came to be called the literary process. "Our culture was like a well-lived-in [*obzhitoi*] home, in which for every word there was either support or rejection. Remember how when you got to work someone would ask right as you came through the door: Did you see the new film? Were you at the premiere? Have you read that novel? It was shameful to say you hadn't! 'What, you really don't know about it?' Everyone, the whole society, lived on literature and art."[55]

Discussion of the "text of the moment" took place in the apartments of the urban intelligentsia, and in lecture halls throughout the nation where Party operatives regularly spoke and organized conferences on the ideological significance of both officially and unofficially published works. This sequence of events has been characterized as "Get it! Read it! Gasp with delight or horror! Talk about it at every stage of the social pyramid!"[56] Sergei Chuprinin marveled at how the rumor of a text that challenged the status quo spread quickly, as did news of its author and of journals that skillfully maneuvered texts past the formidable barriers erected to keep them away from the public. Readers looked forward to the next work "that would bring us together in genuine unanimity around the question: Have you read it?"[57] A new link in this chain was "a national event" because "literature truly meant everything to us."[58] One aspect of such a "textual community" is that its "map" comes to be populated not only by one's own writers (*svoi pisateli*), but also by "others," those whose words fall outside the "national" text, and consequently outside the nation.[59] Writers and critics in Russia stood in perpetual danger of failing to meet the expectations either of the reader or of the state.

4. *In Russia, poets get shot*
5. *But manuscripts don't burn*
6. *Although they can cause fires*

These three maxims are conceptually linked in ways that help establish a broader context for the political reception of literature in Russia, where writers suffered but carried on, where texts were always vulnerable but often indestructible, and where the concept of state power prevailed while regimes fell. The maxims may appear to contradict each other, but as anyone who has studied Russian proverbs can confirm, a nation's collective wisdom is not a perfectly organized, logical system but a juxtaposition of all the elements that have resonated sufficiently to be passed down.

Osip Mandelstam, an incontrovertible authority on suffering for one's text, was said to believe that "poetry was nowhere valued so highly as in Russia: there people were shot for it" (*nigde stikhi ne tseniatsia tak vysoko, kak v Rossii—zdes' za nikh rasstrelivaiut*).[60] An examination in the late 1980s of KGB archival material on repressed writers revealed in greater detail than before the fascinating and chilling stories of some of the approximately fifteen hundred literary figures who perished during the Stalinist purges.[61] Solzhenitsyn described post-Revolutionary Russian literature as a forest in which a few trees were left after all the devastation; he mourned not only stories that were lost but ones that were never written because of the deaths of writers in the gulag.[62]

Bulgakov's *The Master and Margarita*, a work written between 1928 and 1940, but only published in censored form in Russia in 1966–67, offers a more reassuring assessment of the artistic text's powers of endurance. In one of the most frequently quoted sentences in the entire Russian canon, Woland reassures the distraught Margarita that the Master's novel still exists despite its apparent fiery end because "manuscripts do not burn." But it also exists because the Master knows every word of his book by heart; it was invulnerable and indestructible all the time. Secret police files reveal that while a number of confiscated manuscripts may have been destroyed or mislaid, they were for the most part stamped with the words "to be preserved forever" (*khranit' vechno*); virtually everything was viewed as evidence for a possible future arrest.

Like the Master, writers and their friends sometimes burned texts in a moment of panic, but manuscripts were also successfully preserved in hiding places all over the country. In post-Stalinist Russia, unofficial works were copied, circulated, and where possible sent abroad, to appear openly only after 1985. Many writers believed that their texts, like the Biblical "nonburning bush" (*neopalimaia kupina*), could survive fires that ought to have consumed them, and could actually cause some fires of their own. In the spring of 1862, not long after the publication of his novel *Fathers and Sons,* Ivan Turgenev returned to an arson-plagued St. Petersburg. "See what *your* nihilists are doing!" said an acquaintance he ran into on Nevsky Prospekt. "They're setting Petersburg on fire!"[63] One group of revolutionaries made the explosive power of the word real with bombs encased in dictionaries.[64] In 1886, on the twenty-fifth anniversary of the radical critic Dobrolyubov's death, a thousand young people, among them Lenin's brother Alexander Ulyanov, staged a demonstration at the Volkovo cemetery. Lenin and many others in his generation credited the novel *What Is to Be Done?,* written by Dobrolyubov's collaborator Chernyshevsky, for inspiring them in their decades-long struggle. It seemed that the written word had set fire to people's minds and in 1917, they knew what had to be done.

7. *Writers must avoid all contact with* vlast' *(power)*
8. *The burden of a political function weakened art*
9. *Censorship stimulated the imagination of Russian writers more than freedom*

Literacy and religious books came to Kievan Rus through its rulers, and, centuries later, the support and the themes for secular texts also came from court circles. This situation changed in the age of Alexander I, as writers turned away from composing odes to their godlike sovereigns and began to take literature outside the imperial court to country estates and their own circles.[65] The relationship between writers and power, which already began to show strains in the late eighteenth century with the cases of Nikolai Novikov and Alexander Radishchev, suffered ambiguities and tensions ever after. In the 1820s, Alexander Pushkin and Petr Vyazemsky were said to have formed a "literary aristocracy," whose members "do not solicit the protection of gentlemen," being gentlemen themselves. Vyazemsky said that for a writer, the "the Tsar's caress" was "a tempting shore, who leads us into sin and distracts us from our lawful obligation."[66] Unlike Faddei Bulgarin, the aristocrats did not have to earn their living from writing and were in a position to keep literature from becoming "a kind of state service, a branch of the police, or what is even worse, a department of the Ministry of Education. Independence is the power we should serve."[67]

The arguments in print over the aristocratic party lasted until 1830, but the December 1825 uprising and its aftermath showed that all writers would have to deal with a center that feared independent minds and pens. State power was, in all senses, the great leveler. After the implementation of censorship policies and structures, which the Soviets later made more comprehensive and effective, a fundamental question confronting the writer in Russia was whether to appear in print or not, rather than simply circulate works privately, because under both tsars and commissars this decision involved securing permission from the state and making changes where asked. Vladimir Bukovsky, one of the most important dissidents of the Brezhnev period, describes the process by which a writer interested in getting published "agrees to cross out a line here, add a paragraph there, change an ending, remove one of the characters, revise the title," by which time the "whole point" is gone. But the writer still claims that on certain pages there are hints at a deeper, more daring message "and the villain says almost *everything*" only to be reformed and renounce his bold words.[68]

Nineteenth-century writers railed against the absurdity of the restrictions, worked around them to the best of their ability, and suffered when—despite taking precautions—they ran afoul of the authorities. In the post-Revolutionary period the stakes were much higher, and a more punitive state apparatus engendered both more obedient and more rebellious literary figures. Osip Mandelstam, a powerful voice in a fragile body, divided "all the works of world literature into those written with and without permission. The first are trash, the second—stolen air."[69] Yevgeny Zamyatin spoke of critical essays as falling into "God-save-the-Tsar" (*Bozhe tsaria khrani*) and "non-God-save-the-Tsar" (*ne-Bozhe-Tsaria*) categories.[70] In the end, Soviet controls over literature proved to be porous by design as well as by accident, but it is fair to say that anything that appeared officially in print in the Soviet Union was, in Mandelstam's terms, permitted to appear. Looking from the outside, it might seem a reasonable inference that nothing but praise of the system would have been approved for publication, but any close examination of artistic and critical literature from the Soviet era, especially after Stalin's death, reveals a much more nuanced picture that includes among the published works what might be called "licensed critics" and "permitted anomalies."[71] This easing of restraints had begun in earnest by December 1953, with the *Novyi mir* publication of Vladimir Pomerantsev's essay "On Sincerity in Literature," and it continued, with many freezes and thaws, until the dismantling of the censorship system itself in the second half of the eighties.

Aside from the practical and immediate question of whether to submit work for government approval, the notion that politics weakened art was more prevalent among poets than writers of prose. Was a political orientation forced upon a nascent Russian realism by Belinsky and his heirs? Were writers waiting and working for the day when they could give up contemporary problems and get back to art on a full-time basis? In comparing, somewhat spitefully, Dostoevsky and Gleb Uspensky, Tolstoy said that "Dostoievsky went in for politics and coquetted while Uspensky is more simple and sincere"; Dostoevsky "learnt to think" from the Fourierists, among others, "and afterward all his life long he hated them."[72] Tolstoy saw Dostoevsky as being driven by the realization that like some of his own characters "he had served a cause in which he did not believe."[73] Tolstoy's preference was for art that was neither political nor pure, but served broad philosophical, ethical, and pedagogical goals.

Tolstoy experienced difficulties of his own when he began to compose *War and Peace* as a political novel, which Kathryn Feuer tells us meant "undertaking a kind of writing alien to him" about which he had strong reservations.[74] As Feuer charts his progress from 1856 through the mid-1860s, we see Tolstoy's increasing unwillingness to take sides on some of the most important questions of the day, especially serfdom, where he found himself disagreeing with those landowners who stubbornly opposed emancipation as well as with those who thoughtlessly supported it. This extended to a refusal to become part of the literary process by writing fiction that could be employed in debates already in progress: Tolstoy did not intend his work to be part of a linked discussion, but to be a unique text, without literary "fathers" or "sons." Was this an aristocrat's disdain of the *raznochintsy*-dominated critical establishment? Or was it a desire not to have his work used to advance one argument and attack another?

That the work's wholeness and integrity (*tsel'nost'*) was central to Tolstoy's intentions can be shown by his comment in "Some Words about *War and Peace*," that the book "is what the author wished and was able to express in the form in which it is expressed."[75] Tolstoy struggled mightily to write a novel in which critics could not find politically provocative statements, which would have destroyed the unity and clarity that were so important to the author's design. As big as it was, *War and Peace* was meant to be swallowed in its entirety.

The desire for *War and Peace* to be read as an indivisible whole does not mean that Tolstoy objected to cuts demanded by the censorship. Letters to Petr Bartenev, the editor of the journal *Russkii arkhiv*, reveal a surprisingly flexible attitude, with Tolstoy giving the editor "*carte blanche* to cross out everything that seems dangerous to you. You know better than I what is possible and what isn't."

Two days later Tolstoy wrote again to say that as he approached the end of the work "I am becoming afraid that the censorship or the printers might give us some nasty trouble. I place my only hope about these two matters with you."[76]

The more politicized fiction and nonfiction Tolstoy wrote in the 1860s, like *The Contaminated Family*, as well as that of later decades, like the novel *Resurrection*, is almost universally judged to be of minimal artistic interest.[77] By the time Tolstoy entered the literary-political arena his art had changed profoundly and he had little interesting company, since virtually everyone else who had taken part in the noisy debates of the 1840s to 1870s was dead or otherwise silenced. He had the stage almost to himself and his international fame protected him, as did his too obvious desire to be a martyr. To the end, Tolstoy operated on his own terms and according to his own timetable.

That Russia had a literary process rather than simply a literature seemed to some to be a sign of weakness rather than of strength. And yet it has often been observed that many talented artists wrote more interesting stories, whether for *gosizdat* or the drawer, under communism than they did in emigration or in postcommunist Russia. One is left to make what one can of this observation. Is it the accumulated strain of years of oppression, the disorientation and the loss of focus that came with enforced exile, emigration, or, for those who stayed, with the dissolution of the country around them? In the early 1980s, Hungarian dissident Miklos Haraszti came closer than most analysts to understanding the artistic fate of formerly oppressed writers. The truth was that "untouchable taboos, unlivable lives, unspeakable utterances, unformable forms, the perpetual abortion of unthinkable thoughts do not make us aesthetically sterile. The edifice of art is built out of the very barriers put before it by the state. We skillfully reshuffle the furniture around the walls of the house of art. We learn to live with discipline; we are at home with it. It is a part of us, and soon we will hunger for it because we are unable to create without it."[78]

10. Writers undermined the authoritarian state until it collapsed. In the end, the most dangerous Russian writer/text of them all was _____ [fill in the blank]

> It seemed to a lot of people that a major Russian writer could record and explain everything that concerned the country and its people. . . . genius made the classic writer all-powerful, able to perform any task better than any other person.[79]
> —*Olga Slavnikova*
>
> Twentieth-century Russian literature existed in opposition to dictatorship.[80]
> —*Vitaly Shentalinsky*

A number of names have been suggested for the honor of being Russia's most dangerous writer: Alexander Radishchev, and nineteenth-century authors from Pushkin to Tolstoy. Leon Trotsky spoke of Belinsky as "the leader of society in his day," and said that if Belinsky could be transported to the USSR, he would probably be a member of the Politburo.[81] Lenin admired the way that the critic Dobrolyubov used *Oblomov* "to agitate for freedom, action, and revolutionary struggle," and *On the Eve* to issue "a revolutionary proclamation, written in such a way that till this day it has not been forgotten."[82] Joseph Frank, the great chronicler of Fedor Dostoevsky's career, makes a case for Nicholas Chernyshevsky's *What Is to Be Done?*, the text which supplied the growing network of active protorevolutionaries and their passive sympathizers with a positive, if wildly impractical, blueprint for a new society, and with a writer whose long imprisonment gave him the crown of martyrdom. Chernyshevsky's ideas were not only accepted *on* faith, but *as* faith. "No work in modern literature, with the possible exception of *Uncle Tom's Cabin,* can compete with *What Is to Be Done?* in its effect on human lives and its power to make history. For Chernyshevsky's novel, far more than Marx's *Capital,* supplied the emotional dynamic that eventually went to make the Russian Revolution."[83]

After 1917, there is a new gallery of dangerous people and works from which to choose: Mandelstam with his grotesque description of Stalin; the heretic Zamyatin, who recognized and described the mind-numbing potential of a Soviet system still in its formative stages; Anna Akhmatova, whose "Requiem" is surely the most lyrically powerful indictment of the Terror; and Bulgakov, who showed that even the devil himself was no match for the mediocrity and vindictiveness of Soviet society. Or was the most revolutionary of them all Abram Tertz, the subject of a lengthy KGB manhunt ending in a trial no less fantastic than the works that inspired it? The choice of one writer over all the others, when made, is expressed in absolute terms that brook little argument. "In Grossman's two major works, *Life and Fate . . .* and *Everything Flows. . . .* we find one of the most damning indictments of Stalinism ever likely to appear, and in the case of *Everything Flows* the systematic annihilation of the Lenin cult. This alone would make *Everything Flows* the most subversive piece of literature ever to have been penned by a Soviet writer."[84]

Yevgeny Yevtushenko claimed a key role for himself as the first rebellious poet to surface after Stalin's death, understandably not mentioning a pro-Stalin poem of his written before 1953. "When I began writing my poem *Zima Junction,* the first truth-seeking poetry after so many years of official lies, there was no Solzhenitsyn, no Sakharov, no novels by Pasternak, Grossman, or Dudintsev, there were no dissidents, no abstract artists, no film *Repentance*. Akhmadulina and Voznesensky had not started publishing their poetry, the word 'jazz' was banned, and there was no private travel abroad for Soviet citizens. In 1953 I was all the dissidents rolled up into one."[85] Explaining that he began his career with a poem that criticized border restrictions, Yevtushenko points out that he tackled anti-Semitism in "Babii Yar" (1960), and the threat of a return to oppression in "The Heirs of Stalin" (1962), poems which became monuments to victims of the Nazis and the Communists. He claims that even his love poems championed the rights of the individual against the collective.[86] As if that were not enough, he is "proud to be responsible for the repeal of Soviet-era censorship laws."[87]

Outside Russia, Solzhenitsyn has often been given pride of place as "the most dangerous writer of them all." The extraordinary campaign mounted against him in the Soviet Union, records of which were released by Yeltsin in 1992 and published in Russian the following year and in English in 1995, make it clear that the state saw him as a serious opponent, worthy of continued attention.[88] At home, the importance of his role in the downfall of the regime began to be questioned even before his return in 1994, although a survey in St. Petersburg that year found 48 percent in favor of his becoming president of Russia, as opposed to 18 percent for Yeltsin.[89] Solzhenitsyn understood the ambiguity of his legacy on the eve of his return.

> There are those who weep for communism, and consider me its main destroyer. . . . Secondly, the mafia understands that if I wasn't going to make peace with the KGB, I certainly would not with them. Third, there are those who believe in myths—for example, that I will return and become head of Pamyat or head the right wing. They cannot understand that I want nothing to do with power or any political position. Finally, there are the powers-that-be themselves. I do not avoid critical comments. . . . I speak out sharply and will continue doing that."[90]

Solzhenitsyn rejected any possibility of entering politics, and, as to whether writing *Gulag* had been his most dangerous individual antigovernment act, he deferred to Varlam Shalamov and the vast nation of *zeks* (prisoners), for it was through a powerful collective rather than individual memory of the Gulag that he wished to discredit the Soviet system. To paraphrase Sinyavsky, Solzhenitsyn saw himself as a voice for the chorus, and not simply from it. Miklos Haraszti says that Solzhenitsyn's novels would have eventually been published, "but with *The Gulag Archipelago* he proved that he was not interested in influencing policy but only in destroying the state."[91] Some would juxtapose him to other writers whose contribution was not to the destruction of the system, but to the much more complicated problem of a dignified and worthy survival within it. "But if Alexander Solzhenitsyn helped to destroy the Soviet system, Okudzhava helped the intelligentsia to survive within the system. His life was a lesson in honest and honourable living . . . and in that he was arguably more important than Solzhenitsyn. . . . Okudzhava was what separated us from dishonour."[92] This entire category involves the linked understandings (a) that a truth-telling work of literature is a mighty weapon against an evil state; (b) that a writer's suffering makes a work even more powerful than it would have been otherwise; and, finally, (c) that history is changed by both collective and cumulative efforts, and through the work and works of extraordinary individuals.

The common thread in this set of maxims about Russian literature and state power is the idea that literature (fiction and other artistic prose, poetry, and criticism) has a high status, and was potentially dangerous because it was thought capable of influencing Russian hearts and souls, of moving the people towards or away from the state. Those with a gift for uttering powerful words found that much was demanded of them both by those who were in power and by those who were not. Everything about this literature was outsized (*velikaia*), from the length of some novels to the role given writers, especially those whose texts were considered so truthful as to be dangerous.

While upholding the myth of the "literary wife and widow," protecting Mandelstam's legacy with every line she wrote, Nadezhda Mandelstam sought to deconstruct several other literary myths. The attempt to portray Maxim Gorky as having made valiant attempts to save Gumilev, and having been so upset by the news of the poet's execution that he reportedly coughed up blood, was just so much fantasy as far as the redoubtable Nadezhda Yakovlevna was concerned. "Ehrenburg and Chukovski imagined they were defending the good name of literature by describing how writers went to the rescue of their colleagues. . . . In this they were trying to keep alive the cult of literature and the writer. But literature had so thoroughly disgraced itself that such attempts to salvage its honor were of little use. This kind of cult is typical of our times . . . of which even the most minor figures may be the object in our country."[93]

Could this entire construct of a Most Dangerous Text and a Most Courageous Author be just another case of Russian exceptionalism? After all, Russia is by no means the only nation where artistic texts have played a political role or where writers have suffered, and certainly if one expands the definition—as the government certainly did—to include nonliterary texts, then the list of examples from other cultures grows very large indeed. Is there any text more dangerous than the 1916 Easter Monday Proclamation of the Irish Republic, whose seven signatories knew that they would pay with their lives?[94] And yet there is a very strong perception that texts and state power in Russia were involved in an especially intense relationship for 150 years. The state acted as if texts mattered, leaving writers little choice but to agree. When the state stopped paying close attention to artistic and critical writing around 1990, the official political frame around literary works began to disappear, and no amount of agonizing by writers and critics over their loss of importance has brought it back. Political power games had moved on to another field.

TEXTS AND THE STATE: WHO WILL PREVAIL?

If we were to juxtapose Kievan Rus in the time of Vladimir and his son Yaroslav the Wise and the Russian Empire of Nicholas I—historical periods separated by eight hundred years—we would see a striking contrast in the state's attitude towards texts, going from the very positive and nurturing to the very negative and punitive. One could easily come up with a list of reasons for this fundamental shift in cultural-political behavior, the most obvious being that Kievan Rus fell to foreign invasion and its own disunity. As a result of this trauma, vividly reflected in the chronicles and other sources, and the influence of Tatar governing strategies, Muscovy and later the Russian Empire took care to ensure the survival and strength of the nation by requiring a high degree of uniformity and loyalty, an expectation which covered texts both public and private. And yet along with the significant differences between the atmosphere in Kievan Rus and Nicolaevan Russia, there is an equally significant constant, that of the state as a major partner and sponsor in culture as a whole and in verbal culture and the production and distribution of texts in particular.

As Russia grew, the power at its center sought the full cooperation and control of a far-flung population in order to be able to govern and defend its territory. The rulers and bureaucrats of each age inherited the accumulated memories of previous "times of trouble," and new disorders reinforced the belief that the first line of defense was the one against internal sedition, especially in written form. The general explanation sketched out above is well known and not unique to Russia; the way in which the "dangerous text" paradigm in Russia evolved, however, is a story in itself.

In Russian folklore, and later in nationalist writings, the very words "Kiev," "Novgorod," and "Rus" came to stand for a golden age in which texts apparently enjoyed a high status. The Primary Chronicle tells of the great reverence for books among the early rulers of Kievan Rus, when "Vladimir took the children of leading families and gave them over to book-learning. The mothers of these children wept bitterly over them, for they were not yet strong in faith."[95] Vladimir's son Yaroslav, who became Grand Prince of Kiev in 1016, is said to have had an especially strong attachment to books, not only devoting many hours to reading, but also commissioning translations from Greek into Slavonic for his collection, and depositing many volumes in the Kievan church of St. Sophia, which he had built. "His father Vladimir plowed and harrowed the soil when he enlightened Rus' through baptism, while this prince sowed the hearts of the faithful with the written word, and we in turn reap the harvest by receiving the teaching of books."[96]

Books came into Rus with Orthodoxy as the primary carriers of "correct praise" (the literal meaning of the word for Orthodoxy, *pravoslavie*). They were introduced to an often uncomprehending and fearful population, whose spiritual world was based in nature and the agricultural cycle and whose folk wisdom was handed down orally from one generation to the next. To counteract the old beliefs, the Chronicles extolled book-learning in Kiev not merely as the means by which the newly Christian nation would meet its need for rapid instruction in matters of faith, but as the fulfillment of divine prophecy. Books are called the "springs of wisdom," and their depth is said to be "immeasurable." "He who reads books often converses with God or with holy men."[97] Bishop Ilarion explained that one wrote not for the ignorant, "but for them that have feasted to fulfillment on the sweetness of books."[98] Books were one of the acquisitions necessary to make Kievan Rus a legitimate Christian nation.

Words and texts in Russian civilization were never entirely free; they always had both a value and a price. The written language was introduced as the principal means of conveying a state-sponsored faith whose adoption was simply announced to the population as a fait accompli. The design of an alphabet for the Slavs had been ordered a century before by a Byzantine Empire that was in competition with Rome for the bodies and souls of Eastern Europeans. The Kievan chronicler believed that God had led the Eastern Slavs to Orthodoxy, but it was the Grand Prince who carried out God's plan, and to do so he needed literate monks to copy texts that would help priests spread the message as widely and as quickly as possible. The written word was controlled by the state through people of faith for the purpose of growing that faith, but the ultimate authority was always the secular ruler rather than the metropolitan or patriarch.

The same chronicler who recorded the loving reception of the holy books from Byzantium, also recorded a warning to Vladimir about books that came from untrustworthy sources. "After Vladimir was baptized, the priests explained to him the tenets of the Christian faith, urging him to avoid the deceit of the heretics by adhering to the following creeds. . . . Do not accept the teachings of the Latins, whose instruction is vicious. . . . After the seventh council, Peter the Stammerer came with others to Rome and corrupted the faith, seizing the Holy See. . . . His partisans disturbed all Italy, disseminating their teaching in various terms. . . . Avoid their doctrine."[99]

If there were dangerous "countertexts" for the Kievan period it is difficult to reconstruct them, since these were probably oral compositions or documents not likely to have been recorded or preserved by the monk-chroniclers. We can get a good sense of the pagan view of the new faith, however, in the folklore that has come down to us, rarely in its pure form, more often mixed with Christian beliefs; we can see shadows of it in the Paterikon's "lives" of the monks and in *The Igor Tale.* Dual faith (*dvoeverie*), the amalgam of Orthodox and pagan beliefs and rituals, was deeply irritating to church and state, which made vigorous efforts well into the nineteenth century to root it out. The more subversive folk genres—superstitious tales, charms, and songs likely to offend public morals—remained submerged in the countryside.

Hundreds of years after the Baptism of Rus, Tsar Alexei moved to expel folk entertainers (*skomorokhi*) to the north of Russia so that their words and music could not pollute the minds and souls of Muscovites during a very tense period in Russian urban history. The epic tradition survived far away from Moscow's watchful eyes and the songs (*byliny*) were passed down from memory to memory and generation to generation until they were discovered and recorded for posterity by a group of politically active nineteenth-century Russians exiled to the north. No longer considered dangerous, epic songs and folk tales became a valued part of the national heritage and remained so, even during Soviet times. Ivan the Fool (*Ivan durak*), the peasant hero of countless folk narratives who invariably won out over the rich and powerful, provided not only a vicarious sense of satisfaction for the listener, but also a strategy for survival under any regime. Members of the Russian intelligentsia described playing *Ivan-durak* to avoid being recruited by the KGB without penalty.[100]

Another type of noncanonical oral behavior, holy foolishness (*iurodtsvo*), was deftly woven into Russian civilization, and it is not only described but celebrated in texts that have come down to us. During his stay in Muscovite Russia, Giles Fletcher was amazed to see wild-looking figures with long hair and chains accepted "as prophets and men of great holiness, giving them a liberty to

speak . . . without any controlment" even against the ruler himself. He witnessed the reverence paid in the newly built church on Red Square to the miracle-working remains of Vasily the Blessed (*Blazhennyi*), who had criticized
Ivan the Terrible. Fletcher observed that the people liked holy fools (*iurodivye*)
because they can "note their great men's faults that no man else dare speak." But
he did warn that "it is a very hard and cold profession to go naked in Russia,"
and that those who were not true prophets but merely imitated this behavior in
order to speak their minds against the government were likely to be "made away
in secret."[101]

Texts played a powerful role in paganism and dual faith. *Zagovory* (charms)
existed in both oral and written forms; written charms were common in Muscovite Russia and were associated by church and state with sorcery and *porcha*
(spoiling) so that "any scrap of paper, and even more so, a letter or a notebook"
became suspect and could be used as evidence in judicial cases.[102] "However
widespread, the possession or knowledge of charms was extremely dangerous. . . . Also common were talismans, which supposedly protected the wearer
from harmful sorcery; these often took the form of written charms combined
with special grasses or roots into amulets (*nauzy*)."[103]

A folk narrative from Ryazan tells of a baby of mysterious origins who grows
up to become a monk-bookbinder, and then uses that position to insert alien
material into the Gospels which convinces a bishop that it is permissible for the
monastic clergy to marry (in Russian Orthodoxy priests could marry but not
monks). A lector uncovers the demonic identity of the bookbinder just in time;
locked inside the church during the services—religious services generally being
unbearable to evil spirits—the demon monk is whisked up to the cupola and
flies away. "Now the bishop was convinced what sort of monk he was. He
dropped the idea of getting married and ordered the very same book that had
led him into error to be burned."[104]

Common to both belief systems is a strong faith in the magic power of words
to call forth either sacred or demonic forces. The devil was said to use written
contracts in his efforts to trick human beings into committing sins. A scroll was
placed in the hands of a deceased person, requesting forgiveness of sins and entry into heaven as a Russian Orthodox believer. The English ship's captain
Richard Chancellor noted in 1553 that "this writing or letter they say they send
to Saint Peter, who . . . reads it by and by and admits him to heaven" with a
higher rank than other Christians.[105] Texts cost and texts counted all through
this intertwined pagan-Orthodox cultural history. Giles Fletcher's account of
his diplomatic journey to Muscovy in 1588–89, which he called *Of the Russe*

Commonwealth, contained so many negative observations that the English merchant community successfully petitioned their government to suppress the book so as not to endanger trading privileges with Russia. Their fears of what might have happened were borne out centuries later in 1848, when Nicholas I seized the first Russian translation of Fletcher and punished the officials who had allowed its publication.[106]

Indicative of sixteenth-century Muscovite culture is the decision to gather together all existing types of holy images and texts (icon patterns, chronicles, saints' lives), as well as the rules governing society (*Domostroi*) into large volumes. This was done not in the manner of Renaissance artists and scholars, who studied antiquity as a basis for creating something new, but was done so that there would be no need for change, only for copying; the textual nation was complete, and a border could be drawn around it. Fletcher observed that the level of literacy was relatively low amongst the clergy, and the church hierarchy warned Russia's rulers that to allow any "novelty of learning" to come in from the outside world would "breed innovation" and endanger the state.[107] A generalized fear of texts was gaining ground by this point, touching not only materials that might corrupt Muscovites, but also correspondence carried on by foreigners in Russia, which could weaken the country in more immediate ways.[108]

A century earlier, when Constantinople had fallen to the Ottoman Turks, Moscow declared itself to be the Third Rome, which could be taken to mean that both history and the further production of texts would come to an end. One merely had to check that traditions were remembered correctly and observed properly in what was to be a civilization based on faithful copies. When printing presses began to appear in Muscovy in the second half of the sixteenth century, with the tsar's support but not without controversy, they were intended for the printing of religious materials and primers. For prints (*lubki*), fables, songs, spiritual poetry, and many prayer books, "such ancient methods of reproduction as hand copying and woodblock printing were widespread and thriving" in the seventeenth century.[109] To the majority of Muscovites, who read little or nothing, the humble woodcut (*lubok*) sent out its own popular and at times subversive message, and as a result its production and distribution were subject to church pressure and state control.[110]

The textual standstill to which Muscovite Russia had come was shattered in the mid-seventeenth century when a religious revival in the decades following the Time of Troubles coincided with a wider use of printing presses. Patriarch Nikon decided that prayer books could not be printed from existing mistake-ridden manuscript copies and chose to consult Byzantine—instead of Russian—sources for a correct version from which to proceed. This may have been a sound editorial decision, but Nikon still wound up with a flawed text, and the nation was spiritually rent asunder during the schism that followed. "To both sides, the fate of the Russian church would be resolved around the formulation of the prayer books."[111] The split between the official church and the *staroobriadtsy* "Old Ritualists" or, more commonly, "Old Believers" was about much more than the spelling of Jesus' name (the traditional *Isus* versus the more correct *Iisus*); the schismatics, whose numbers came to include a sizable segment of the population, firmly believed that to change this spelling was to lose God and embrace the Antichrist, so every letter counted.

Nikonian texts were seen as demonic by the Old Believers, and texts that the *staroobriadtsy* produced were, in turn, anathema to church and state. As Gary Marker points out, the printing presses gave the church the ability to produce large numbers of corrected prayer books, but this was not an unalloyed advantage, since it "contributed to popular awareness of the changed texts and, inadvertently, galvanized resistance to them."[112] Even after Nikon overplayed his hand by encroaching on state power and was deposed as patriarch, Tsar Alexei continued to suppress schismatics and their writings. Years earlier, his *Ulozhenie* (Law Code) of 1649 had introduced as its first provision a "new category of crimes, political crimes."[113] A 1674 government report on Old Believers at the Solovetsky Monastery makes it clear that the best protection from interrogation was illiteracy, since an illiterate monk was less susceptible to a text-borne heresy.[114] Two hundred years later, a visitor to Solovki was told by a monk-gardener that "literacy was not required. Fewer temptations; our ways here are simple."[115] To avoid both evils—accidentally reading a Nikonian text or being found in possession of Old Believer material—one schismatic, Vasily Volosaty, advocated a program "for the destruction of all books and the launching of a penitential fast unto death," while another movement forswore all speech except the word *net* (no).[116] Under Nicholas I, Minister of Education Uvarov similarly wished that "literature might be abolished altogether."[117]

The oppression of the schismatics led their charismatic leader to compose the first modern Russian autobiography, a spiritually conservative yet stylistically progressive work known to us as *The Life of the Archpriest Avvakum*. Avvakum and his closest associates were imprisoned and eventually executed, but even from their northern prison cells (roughly dug pits) they smuggled texts to their followers in hollowed-out wooden crosses. By 1840, Herzen reports, the schismatics were only intermittently persecuted—for example, when a temporary excess of zeal would cause the Synod or the Ministry of Home Affairs to raid an Old Believer hermitage or community. But the visionary and yet highly practical Old Believers by then had agents in Petersburg to warn them of impending danger, at which point they would hide their books and icons and buy drinks for the local priest and police officials, and the danger would pass.[118] It was not until 1861 that the state felt it was safe to permit the printing of a limited edition of Avvakum's life story, which, coming when it did, was an important influence on Fedor Dostoevsky and other writers, and continued to have an impact on literature well into the 1980s.[119]

The harshest treatment of religious dissidents and their writings coincides with the beginning of the Petrine period; the pattern we see in Tsar Alexei's reign of simultaneous progressive and repressive moves was repeated by those who came after him. Like Grand Prince Vladimir, Peter the Great had urgent and specific book needs; in Peter's case this meant textbooks on shipbuilding, navigation, and other practical matters. Because of the urgency, he increased government use of printing presses which until that time had been primarily in the hands of the church. Peter announced a new civil orthography in 1701 for secular books, which differentiated them visually from the old alphabet still employed in religious texts.[120] In spite of a thirst for change that required greater literacy and more books, Peter still felt a Muscovite suspicion of texts as a means of spreading unrest. The first tsar to travel to Europe and the person who worked most vigorously to modernize and westernize this still medieval country also prohibited the writing of letters behind closed doors; a law of 1717 obligated anyone who was aware of such an act, even if ignorant of the letter's content, to report its existence to authorities, codifying in law the patriotic *donos* (denunciation) we associate with Soviet Russia.[121]

Peter's daughter, the Empress Elizabeth, was justly renowned for her taste in palaces, her patronage of the arts, and her love of fashion and entertainment, but she punished even the suspicion of intrigue at court with a cruelty worthy of her father. An indiscreet letter from the aristocratic lover of a banished count hinted at criticism of the Empress and a plot to restore the imprisoned Ivan VI. The investigation led to a punishment designed to truly silence those involved, the removal of their tongues.[122] There is a striking contrast between Russia's military, economic, and artistic development, and the increasing need to control the written and spoken word, a pattern of progress achieved not in spite of control, but because of it.

In the second half of the eighteenth century, Catherine II moved beyond the practical and technical goals of the early Petrine years, and sent young men abroad to study law and to bring the fruits of the Enlightenment back to her empire. At the same time she invited important European thinkers to come to Russia. The well-read Princess Dashkova was asked to head the Academy of Sciences, and members of the educated upper class, freed from compulsory government service during Peter III's brief reign, were encouraged not only to read seriously but also to write. Catherine's model of the European intellectual was transformed on Russian soil into someone more anguished than witty, and more likely to criticize the sovereign than to praise her. A class of educated Russians, somewhat detached from reality but passionately interested in the fate of their embattled nation, was forming into what would eventually be called the *intelligentsiia,* a group that came to dominate the mind, conscience, and literary life of Russia.[123]

Catherine II founded several journals and wrote for them under a transparent pseudonym. The journalist, publisher, and Freemason Nikolai Novikov took up her offer to engage in a friendly debate about the present and future of Russian society in their respective journals, but the moment Novikov assumed the tone of an equal or even superior intellect, abandoning the gentle social satire suggested by the empress for direct criticism, the exchange of opinions came to an end. Eventually Catherine had Novikov arrested; his prison term ended four years later in 1796 only because of Catherine's death and Paul I's contempt for his late mother. Forbidden to resume his publishing activities, Novikov spent the remaining twenty-two years of his life on his estate. He would have appreciated the irony of an 1850 edition of Catherine II's correspondence with Voltaire being banned by Catherine's grandson Nicholas I, and this ban being discussed in a Soviet article published during the Stalinist purges.[124]

An even more dramatic case is that of Alexander Radishchev, another of the bright young men sent to Europe to get the best education the age could offer, and finding on their return to Russia that there was no meaningful role for educated people. After working on a number of plans for reform, some officially commissioned, Radishchev wrote *A Journey from St. Petersburg to Moscow,* which used the popular device of lightly fictionalized travel writing to mask a withering attack on serfdom and other forms of oppression. Private printing presses were permitted after 1793 as long as they were registered with the government, so when Radischev could not find a printer for his *Journey,* he printed it on his own, anonymously, in 1790.[125] The censorship, in one of the most dramatic cases of oversight in Russian history, skimmed the beginning, saw yet another example of fashionable travel literature, and passed on it.

It was not long afterward that the book reached Catherine II, who wrote on the margins of her copy that Radishchev was "worse than Pugachev," the leader of a popular Russian rebellion from 1773 to 1775; the events of 1789 in France were also fresh in her mind. Although Radishchev escaped execution, he was sent to Siberia and freed, like Novikov, upon Paul's accession to the throne. At the optimistic beginning of Alexander I's reign, Radishchev was engaged in drafting a republican constitution for Russia, but he lost his nerve and committed suicide in 1802. Living in exile, Alexander Herzen published Radishchev's *Journey* in 1858, but it was 1905 before it appeared again in Russia. Martyr to a revolutionary text, Alexander Radishchev was one of the first figures whom the Bolsheviks honored with a statue after the Revolution.

The articles of the censorship statute of 1804, were, according to the Minister of Education, "in no way intended to restrict freedom to think or write, but are only proper measures against abuse of that freedom."[126] Despite that reassurance, it was stipulated that every work printed and/or offered for sale in Russia had to be examined by a censor. During the last years of Alexander I's reign, under the oppressive influence of Count Arakcheev, there was evidence of an increasingly restless society in an increasingly immobile state. Alexander Griboyedov's satirical play *Woe from Wit* (*Gore ot uma*) could neither be printed nor performed in the 1820s, but nevertheless it became well known in society through the *samizdat* system of that day. Thought and text were evolving beneath the surface in the years leading up to the Decembrist rebellion. William Mills Todd has shown that from the later eighteenth century up to 1825 the "familiar letter"—while seeming to talk about foreign lands—was a commonly used means of exchanging ideas about Russian society and governance.[127] But, as Todd points out, letters were intercepted and read, and if submitted for publication, were subject to censorship.

In the Russia of Nicholas I (1825–55) almost all the elements of the literary-political nexus, including an organized censorship apparatus and the notorious Third Section, fell into place between 1826 and 1839. There were freezes and thaws along the way in reaction to events in Russia such as attacks on the tsar, and to upheaval in Europe, but basically the same system was still in place in 1905. In 1826, as part of the pretrial investigation of the December 1825 uprising, imprisoned Decembrists were given a survey to fill out, in which two of the seven questions revealed an underlying suspicion that books might have led the primarily upper-class traitors to commit their heinous act. In the tsar's mind, it was important to discover the titles of the guilty volumes, since this was understood to have been a well-read, articulate group of rebels.

6. Did you audit special lectures in addition to your regular schooling? If so, in which subjects, when, and with whom and where? Indicate the textbooks used in studying those subjects.

7. When and where did you acquire liberal ideas? From contact with others or from their suggestions, or from the reading of books or works in manuscript form? Which ones specifically? Who helped to reinforce these notions in you?[128]

The defendants did not reveal Russian sources, blaming the evolution of their ideology primarily on the French, except for Alexander Bestuzhev, who admitted that he had read Denis Fonvizin on the necessity of the rule of law and verses by Pushkin but blamed no particular person for his ideas, which he said were shared by a third of the Russian gentry. That kind of information could only serve to reinforce the tsar's resolve to take any manifestation of free thinking, especially when it was committed to paper, as a serious threat.[129]

The expulsion of the Decembrists from Russian society, not just by the execution of the five leaders, but also by the long terms in prison and exile given many other conspirators, and the ban on mentioning their names in print, gave special resonance to the Romantic trope of "distant friends" in the epigraph to Pushkin's "The Fountain of Bakhchisaray" (1822) and then in the final stanza of his novel in verse, *Evgenii Onegin* (1823–31). Of those friends to whom the first stanzas of the novel were read, the poet says "some are no more, while others are even further away" (*inykh uzh net, a te daleche*). Vladimir Nabokov explains that this quote from the Persian poet Sadi was chosen for "The Fountain" before the insurrection, but it received a provocative retrospective reading not only as a result of the events themselves, but also because Evgeny Baratynsky highlighted this line in a survey of Russian literature in 1827, and then borrowed it for a poem of his own. "When in 1832 Pushkin published Chapter Eight of *EO* separately, readers had no difficulty deciphering the enriched allusion."[130]

In the first section of Alexander Herzen's memoir *My Past and Thoughts,* the reader follows Herzen's life in Russia from 1812 until he left the country permanently in 1847; it is a litany of imprisonment, exile and police supervision. Finally, he saw no alternative but to remove himself to Western Europe, where he was able to write, edit, set up a Russian printing press, and send back to Russia numerous issues of his provocative newspaper *The Bell* (*Kolokol*) and journal *The Pole Star* (*Poliarnaia zvezda*). Like Solzhenitsyn's *The Oak and the Calf,* the Herzen memoir examines ways in which the writer proved a danger to the state, even when forced to leave Russia and operate from abroad.

Questioning the degree of attention given Pushkin's flighty and superficial hero Onegin, Herzen said that the Decembrist was more typical of his time and more "splendid," but if this character shows up at all in literature, it is as reflected in Chatsky, the hero of Griboyedov's *Woe from Wit*. Chatsky was the kind of smart and restless young man who would have been at the very least sympathetic to the uprising. Because of suspicion about his own sympathy for the rebels and their cause, Griboyedov himself was imprisoned and then sent to the war-torn Caucasus where he was killed while on a diplomatic mission in 1829.[131] *Woe from Wit* circulated unofficially during the author's lifetime; it was published in a censored form in 1833, and in a fuller version in 1861. "[The Decembrist] could not be dealt with by Russian literature for all of forty years," complained Herzen, but he insisted on the doomed rebels' importance as a powerful character type. When the Decembrist finally did appear in literature, it was, among other places, through the portraits of the proto-Decembrists Pierre Bezukhov and Prince Andrei's son Nikolai on the final pages of *War and Peace*.[132]

In one of the most dramatic episodes of *My Past and Thoughts,* Herzen describes the fate of even moderately irreverent authors and texts, using the example of a Moscow University student of his acquaintance named Alexander Polezhaev, whose parody of *Onegin* was passed around in student circles. An informer brought this to the attention of Nicholas I in 1826, shortly after the punishment of the Decembrists and the tsar's subsequent coronation in Moscow. Polezhaev was summoned from his room in the middle of night and brought to the tsar himself, where he was presented with an elegantly written-out copy of his poem which he was forced to read aloud. Nicholas saw Polezhaev's parody as evidence of residual Decembrist sentiments that must be cut off at the root; while the Minister of Public Instruction was able to save the young man from the severest punishment, Polezhaev was still forced to join the army as a common soldier and died in 1837. Censored versions of some of his works appeared in Russia; uncensored editions were later printed abroad by Herzen. Much of Polezhaev's writing remained in secret police custody until it was finally published during the Soviet period.[133]

The decades from the 1848 Revolution in France until the assassination of Tsar Alexander II in 1881 saw a Russian society under such pressure that it generated the kind of odd figures that make a historical account read like parody. Herzen recalls his friend Savich, a retired Guards officer who lived abroad after a brother was arrested for political reasons in 1849. Savich gave lessons to support himself, for which he needed calling cards, but he was so paranoid that he refused to put his name on them. When he applied to the Russian Embassy for an amnesty following the death of Nicholas I, the confused officials could find no file on Savich and gave him a passport.[134]

Attempts to stifle political discourse of any kind affected not only Russians who traveled abroad and wished to bring texts home with them, and émigré and expatriate Russians who sent their Russian-language publications back home, but also travelers to Russia whose printed recollections were generally critical and rarely welcome. The work of the Marquis de Custine, who saw deeply into the cult and culture of secrecy in the Empire, "was so strictly forbidden . . . that a bookdealer is fined five thousand rubles for the first copy he sells, ten thousand for the second, and for the third he is exiled to Siberia. Because of this strict ban the book has been disseminated everywhere; in fact good breeding demands that one have read it."[135] It is hardly surprising that the elder George Kennan's articles on Siberian prisons, first published in *The Century* between 1888 and 1891 and much admired by progressive Russians living abroad, were also banned.

Nicolaevan Russia offers abundant case studies of the treatment of texts and their authors as threats to the official triumvirate of tsar, church, and nation. A survey of this period reveals the expected cases of partial or complete censorship of texts and the exile of editors for letting dangerous works slip through the controls into print (e.g. Nikolai Nadezhdin after Petr Chaadaev's "Philosophical Letter" appeared in *Teleskop* in 1836; the censor in this case was merely fired), along with the jailing of censors for similar negligence (Glinka after an article by Ivan Kireevsky appeared).[136] One can find mediocre literary figures willing to act as informers (Faddei Bulgarin, who alerted the government about what was written between the lines of published material); the treatment of an errant author as a madman (Chaadaev, confined to his house for a year, where he was subjected to daily medical harassment, and never allowed to publish again); the assumption by the tsar of the role of "first reader" of a leading writer (Alexander Pushkin), imprisonment or exile as a punishment for having written memorials to fellow writers who died (Lermontov, for his poem about Pushkin; Turgenev, for an essay about Gogol); and long, harsh sentences for taking part in a political discussion group at which a controversial document, Vissarion Belinsky's letter to Gogol, was supposedly read aloud (Dostoevsky and the Petrashevtsy group).

The church had its own concerns about sedition; having long wished to control the distribution of cheap, noncanonical prints, in 1851 "all hitherto uncensored wood blocks and plates were ordered destroyed by the authorities."[137] But despite the suppression of texts for the masses and the elite, the seeds of skepticism, irony, and outright rebellion planted by Radishchev, Pushkin, Griboyedov, Chaadaev, Mikhail Lermontov, and the lost generation of the Decembrists began to take root. In terms that Radishchev had used a half-century before, and Andrei Voznesensky would echo 120 years later in his poem "Leaves and Roots" ("Krony i korni," 1960), Herzen sensed that around 1840 a great historical shift was beginning to make itself felt. "A scarcely perceptible change by which the doctor discerns, before he can fully account for it, . . . that the patient's strength, though very weak, is reviving—there is a different *tone*. Somewhere within, in the morally microscopic world, there is the breath of a different air, more irritant, but healthier. Outwardly, everything was death-like . . . but something was stirring in the consciousness and the conscience."[138]

In a context of "external slavery," literature was providing a means of "inner emancipation."[139] The changes Herzen describes could be seen not only in literary circles and among the intelligentsia as a whole, but also in milieux closer to the center of power. A Baltic aristocrat who returned to the Guards barracks in the capital after an absence of several years discovered to his surprise less discipline at the dinner table, increased criticism of government decisions, unhappiness with Nicholas, and a sense "that *Nihilism* had been born between the cheese and the pears."[140] One sign that the "horror had lost its edge" was the sound of laughter, "which is a bad companion for any religion, and autocracy is a religion."[141] It is no wonder that the censors were always on guard for evidence of irony, satire, or parody in the works they examined.

As Herzen describes it, beginning in 1837 a kind of graphomania took hold not only of Russian society but also of the government, which developed "great literary pretensions," and added to the many periodicals already in existence a network of provincial newspapers and official publications for government departments. "We have journals relating to mining, to dry-salting, French and German ones, naval and military ones. All these are published at government expense; contracts for literary articles are made in the ministries exactly as are contracts for fuel and candles. . . . After monopolising everything else, the government has now taken the monopoly of talk and, imposing silence on everyone else, has begun chattering unceasingly."[142] Texts were multiplying, above and below ground, and, after Herzen left Russia, not only individual works infiltrated from abroad, but eventually multiple copies of heretical newspapers and journals, which generated a steady and passionate response in the form of letters from fellow Russians. Herzen recalled that "each one wrote whatever came into his head: one to blow off steam, another to convince himself that he was a dangerous fellow."[143]

It is not surprising that issues of Herzen's *Kolokol* were treated as dangerous—as well as sacred—objects, and reading, or just possessing, one or more of them was a sine qua non of any *intelligent*. Satiric references in such works as Dostoevsky's *Demons* (*Besy*, 1872) and Fedor Sologub's *Petty Demon* (*Melkii bes*, 1907) to particular periodicals as badges of one's liberalism give some indication of the status of unsanctioned publications in nineteenth-century Russian society. The passages at the beginning of *Demons* about the life of Stepan Verkhovensky amount to a parodic biographical sketch of a man of the forties who ever after fancied himself a political exile, constantly under government supervision because of an article published in a liberal monthly and an allegorical play that briefly circulated in *samizdat* before being published abroad.[144] The elder Verkhovensky's attraction to radical texts was more than matched by his deep fear of punishment.

Stepan Verkhovensky's paranoia was vindicated to some extent by the raid carried out by the governor's assistant Blum, using a catalogue of forbidden works supplied by Peter Verkhovensky's demonic lackeys. The skeptical governor, hearing that this list included the Decembrist Ryleev and all of Herzen, exclaimed that "everyone has those books," but the raid proceeded according to plan. As Stepan Trofimovich later explained, Blum "didn't arrest me, only books," but this still unsettled his mind. Imagining the severe punishment ahead, he visited the governor, whose sanity has been undermined by the mysterious events unfolding around him. [145] Whatever Dostoevsky's purpose in including this material in the narrative, it is an accurate indication of the widespread distribution of illegal texts, and of the vulnerability of anyone possessing them should the government choose to take notice, not unlike the situation that would later prevail in the Soviet Union.

Decades later, the deliberately repulsive hero of Fedor Sologub's novel *Petty Demon* swears that he has never actually read *The Bell*, but he does have in his possession books by Pisarev and copies of the progressive *Notes of the Fatherland*, which was shut down by censors in 1884. When Peredonov realizes that these texts may get him into trouble, he takes swift measures to hide them.

> Earlier Peredonov had kept these books on display in order to show that he held liberal opinions even though in actual fact he held no opinions whatsoever. . . . Moreover, he merely kept the books, he didn't read them.

. . . "What are you carting off there, Ardalyon Borisych?" Prepolovenskaya asked.
"Strictly forbidden books," Peredonov replied without stopping. "People will denounce me if they see them."[146]

To the other aspects of the literary-political nexus whose roots lie in nineteenth-century Russia, one must add the notion of *riskovannost'* (the willingness to engage in politically risky behavior), including the possession of the wrong books and periodicals, which became a principled choice for some and a fashion statement for others.

Alexander II's reign provides another case study of a progressive ruler who nevertheless kept relatively tight controls on texts and had few illusions about even conservative Slavophile writers being entirely dependable. When Minister of Education Kovalevsky suggested that poet Fedor Tyutchev, then head of the committee on Foreign Censorship, and others from the literary world be included in a far-ranging discussion of government control over the printed word, the tsar responded: "Oh, your writers! One cannot rely on a single one of them!"[147] Analyses of this period emphasize the easing of regulations in 1865, which brought an end to prepublication censorship "for the periodicals of editors in good standing" as "authority for the press shifted from the censors to the courts."[148] But the mechanism, and the principles behind it, remained intact and it was easy to tighten the screws after the first attempt on the tsar's life in 1866.

During the first half of the 1860s, as reforms disoriented society from above, there was widespread unrest from below, some of it spontaneous and some the work of agitators, among them a peasant Old Believer and a sympathetic clergyman teaching at an ecclesiastical academy. Along with others, they spread the word that the emancipation manifesto announced in 1861 was false "and that the Tsar would ultimately send the 'true' manifesto, granting the peasants much more land. . . . Elsewhere in the empire, peasants became convinced that the manifesto was false because the 'true' manifesto would have been written in letters of gold." Joseph Frank describes "a veritable blizzard" of pamphlets of unknown origin that hit Petersburg and Moscow, the best-known of them being "The Great Russian," "To the Young Generation," and "Young Russia."[149]

Another manifestation of postemancipation unrest was arson both in the countryside and by 1862 in St. Petersburg itself; even Dostoevsky believed that there was only the most tenuous connection between the pamphlets, arson, and university students, although his efforts to say so in print were stopped by the censorship. Dostoevsky was nonetheless shocked by the presence of these leaflets, stuck behind the door handle of his apartment, some of which advocated violent solutions to Russia's problems.[150] Over a century later, Vladimir Voinovich borrowed the device of the shocking arrival of a revolutionary text—moving the narrative forward to the days following Alexander II's assassination in 1881—as a premise for "Skurlatsky, Man of Letters" (1972), his brilliant parody of revolutionary fervor and the kind of risky behavior fashionable among the literati.

Sometimes the line that separated the world within the text from the reality outside it disappeared, and the work no longer enjoyed the somewhat protected status of an artistic creation. A writer's politically charged figures began to scurry from one plane to the other, causing no end of trouble for the author, as Turgenev found out in the 1860s. Pavel Annenkov had warned him in a letter written prior to the publication of *Fathers and Sons* that "it will cause a great stir—you can expect that. It will not raise the question of talent and artistic merit but rather whether its author is the historian or ringleader of the party. . . . I have heard that Countess Lambert [Turgenev's friend] is dissatisfied with the novel. . . . The world into which you led her is so terrible that she has confused its hideousness with the hideousness of the creative work."[151]

Fedor Dostoevsky was so highly attuned to changes in the political atmosphere that he sensed the appearance of new historical types and incorporated them in his works before the public was fully aware of their existence, to the extent that even he became confused about which had come first, his creation or the real-life figure. Early in the same month that the first installment of *Crime and Punishment* appeared in *The Russian Messenger* (January 1866), a Russian student murdered a moneylender and a servant in a strikingly similar way.[152] Joseph Frank points out that Stepan Verkhovensky's tragicomic gesture of "going to the people" at the end of *Demons* was mirrored two years later in the ludicrously unsuccessful 1874 move to the countryside by radical youth.[153] Russians who read *Demons* during the purge years of the 1930s, or when Khrushchev began denouncing Stalin's crimes in 1956, were frightened by the extent to which Dostoevsky's devils had come to life in Stalinist Russia.[154]

Turgenev and Herzen both got "burned" during the arson scare of the turbulent 1860s, the former for having brought the nihilist Bazarov to life, thus giving an impressionable public a dangerous new hero. The government spread rumors that the incendiaries were students under the influence of Herzen and Chernyshevsky. Herzen's unrelated use of "fire" imagery in his essays for *The Bell* confused the issue, as did his refusal, on principle, to openly disassociate himself from the arsonists or from the anti-Russian insurrection in Poland. The result was a serious loss of support at home for his expatriate journal. "The slander grew and was quickly caught up by the press and spread over the whole of Russia. It was only then that the denunciatory era of our journalism began. . . . The literature of disclosures quickly shifted its weapon and was twisted at once into a literature of police perquisitions and calumniation by informers."[155] A Russian acquaintance in London organized a fifth anniversary party for *The Bell* and urged Herzen to send messages to Petersburg through another Russian traveler. One of the partygoers telegraphed the news to officials at home, and, as a result, the letters were seized, many people were arrested, and Herzen's ties to progressive forces were further eroded.[156]

The most dangerous text of the 1860s is widely agreed to be Nikolai Chernyshevsky's *What Is to Be Done?* (1863), written in answer to *Fathers and Sons,* and itself followed a year later by *Notes from Underground,* Dostoevsky's powerful contribution to this spirited and historically significant discussion.[157] Chernyshevsky, the editor of the influential progressive journal *The Contemporary* (*Sovremennik*) was arrested in July 1862 in connection with the unrest in Petersburg and because of the critical tone his journal had taken towards the provisions of the Emancipation. While in jail, he was not allowed to write political essays but was granted permission to write a novel, which he managed to complete in the space of only four months. The first section of the novel was sent to Prince Golitsyn, the head of the commission looking into Chernyshevsky's case; seeing nothing alarming or directly "political," Golitsyn passed it on to the regular censors who assumed that it had been thoroughly vetted and forwarded it to *The Contemporary.* Nekrasov, the journal's new editor, carelessly left the manuscript in a cab but was able to recover it with the help of an advertisement in a police newspaper.

Following what Joseph Frank calls "the most spectacular example of bureaucratic bungling in the cultural realm during the reign of Alexander II," *What Is to Be Done?* appeared in three installments in *The Contemporary* beginning March 1863; the rest, literally, is history.[158] The government reacted after the fact, giving Chernyshevsky a lengthy sentence which effectively removed him from public life, but this only heightened the aura that surrounded the text. One of the most significant reviews of *What Is to Be Done?* was written by Dmitry Pisarev, a critic who had also been jailed in connection with the radical pamphlets flooding the capital; he, too, was allowed to write and publish. The government thought it was containing the spread of radical thought by jailing writers, but from time to time it played an unintentionally helpful role in disseminating the prisoners' incendiary texts.

Dostoevsky experienced the harsh justice of the Nicolaevan era during his ten-year term of prison and exile for a youthful involvement with utopian socialism; beginning in the 1860s, he was concerned with counteracting the effect of radical texts on the younger generation. But he found that as a former political prisoner he was marked as a security threat in perpetuity. His own writing and the journals he edited were constantly running afoul of the censors; sometimes the reasons seemed patently absurd, as in 1860 when the St. Petersburg Censorship Committee felt that some sections of his *Notes from the House of the Dead* described prison conditions so positively that it might prove an incentive rather than a deterrent to potential criminals.[159]

Dostoevsky's mail was read, he was watched while abroad, and searched thoroughly at border crossings. The authorities did not seem to study closely or take seriously the increasingly conservative, nationalistic, antinihilist tone of his work; Dostoevsky was not just insulted, but also genuinely alarmed at the thought of a bureaucracy that could not tell a reformed utopian socialist from a rising nihilist, despite the excellent paper trail. In the summer of 1868 he complained in a letter: "Fools, fools! Involuntarily, one pulls back from serving them. How many guilty among us they do not notice, but a Dostoevsky is suspect!"[160] Warned that he would be searched again at the border when he returned home in 1871, Dostoevsky burned drafts of *The Idiot, Demons,* and *The Eternal Husband.* Despite that precaution, it was only his infant daughter's loud crying that saved him from a lengthy examination of the remaining texts in his possession at the Russian border.[161]

In his capacity as editor of the conservative weekly *The Citizen* (*Grazhdanin*), Dostoevsky wound up spending an additional two nights in custody after inadvertently publishing an article that quoted Alexander II without the permission of palace authorities. Dostoevsky gives a self-censored account of the June 1873 incident in the *Diary of a Writer* for 1876. He was amused to see a court-appointed lawyer skillfully try to get him off even though he had in fact broken the regulation in question. "I was convicted, of course: literary men are judged harshly." He paid a fine and spent two days in jail, "where I passed the time most pleasantly, and, to some extent, even usefully, becoming acquainted with certain people and certain things."[162] Even an anecdote about running afoul of the arcane censorship laws is told in a coded way, although with a certain tongue-in-cheek air.

The Foreign Censorship Committee, all the way up to the Revolution of 1917, was instructed to pay close attention to works about Jews; even the mention of the centuries spent in the diaspora, persecution of Jews, or the fact that

Rothschild and Jesus were both Jewish, was forbidden.[163] Within the Pale of Settlement Jews were experiencing a time of upheaval, and texts that were judged progressive and beneficial by one segment of the community were seen as extremely dangerous by others. In an autobiographical sketch called "The Sins of Youth" (1910), writer S. Ansky (Solomon Rappoport), recalls how he left his home in Vitebsk in 1881 for the town of Liozno ostensibly to find work as a tutor, but mainly to spread the Jewish Enlightenment to local youth. A book he loaned to one of his pupils was discovered by a yeshiva student, and although Ansky was able through a clever ruse to save the original volume, the townspeople, frightened by the external threat of pogroms and the internal challenge of radical Jewish texts undermining their way of life, decided as a protective measure to bring all the secular books they could find to the courtyard of the synagogue and burn them.[164]

The early Russian Zionist Ahad Ha-Am found it difficult to get essays about the "Jewish idea" past Russian censors, who would not tolerate criticism of the semiofficial Pan-Slav ideology. To get around this obstacle he took the same issues he would have discussed in connection with Dostoevsky's writing and analyzed their sources in Nietzsche, in whom he was also very interested.[165] When conditions in the Pale forced Jews to leave Russia, they took the familiar literary-political paradigm with them: in *To The Other Shore,* Steven Cassedy explains that Russian Jewish intellectuals emigrating to America between 1881 and the 1920s "never abandoned their faith in the ultimately political function and supreme power of literature and literary criticism."[166]

A basically stable literary-political paradigm operated from the first organized censorship regulations of 1804 until the Revolution of 1905; the censorship apparatus succeeded in delaying or preventing many readers from gaining access to texts critical of Russia, but obviously this tactic did not impede the rise and ultimate success of a revolutionary movement. James Billington observed that "the imperial government committed itself to the difficult reactionary position of simply preventing the questions from being asked."[167] The state authorities never asked themselves "what exactly *is* a dangerous idea?" Close attention was paid to such issues as religion and preserving the reputation of Russian royalty while at the same time ideas that proved themselves to be highly dangerous snuck past the borders and entered Russia.[168]

Despite all the levers and levels of control, much that was forbidden reached at least some readers. Russians who traveled abroad were able to read what they wished in Europe, to meet with leading European radicals, and to bring a sampling of books and journals back with them. Some foreign texts—especially theoretical approaches to economics and history—which passed the censor's examination turned out to contain genuinely provocative ideas that found a ready audience in Russia. Karl Marx's writing, for instance, was permitted in a French edition as early as 1848 because the work was judged to be accessible to only a small percentage of the population and because "the subject of the work cannot be applied to Russia and presents rather abstract speculations."[169] The censor's analysis was ultimately correct—Marxism did not work very well in Russia—but it took a long period of experimentation to prove that point.

As the censors themselves noted, anything could be obtained in Russia if you knew where to look, and the ideas the authorities were trying to stifle were being widely discussed anyway. The system was punitive, but with some generous exceptions. It sent a young radical named Ivan Krasnoperov to a Kazan prison in the 1860s, while allowing him to continue his study of the leading questions of the day while he was there. He was able to borrow books by progressive European thinkers from the university library and even to leave the prison accompanied by a guard to buy more reading material from a local foreign bookseller before returning to his cell.[170] Russia was, in the end, open to new ideas, which arrived with the added cachet of being forbidden fruit.

Beginning in the 1880s, the literary-political paradigm operated on a much-reduced scale until it was revived with a vengeance four decades later, after the Revolution. There are a number of literary and political reasons for this. Among the literary factors are the end of the golden age of Russian Realism after the deaths of Dostoevsky and Turgenev and Tolstoy's career-altering "crisis," and the predominance of politically disengaged Symbolist poetry during the ensuing silver age of literature. Chekhov, easily the greatest talent of his day in prose fiction and drama, was much more successful in evoking the waning of an imperfect past than in indicating the path to a more perfect future. In contrast to Chekhov, the cultural avant-garde so openly embraced artistic and political revolution that there was nothing left to look for between the lines. The imperial government never fully gave up its practice of censoring culture, and ecclesiastical censors were very active on questions of morality, but in the years between 1905 and 1917 Russia faced far more serious threats to its well-being than those presented by writers and critics.[171] With the assassination of Alexander II by radicals in 1881, politics came out from under the cloak of literature and literary criticism, and Chernyshevsky's *What Is to Be Done?* was the most important—sometimes the only—work of fiction on the revolutionaries' reading list. It is at this period that we begin to see proto-parties and eventually fully defined political groups.

The literary world was, on the whole, comfortable with the results of the February Revolution, especially when the censorship system basically ceased to function, although one conservative government spokesman cautioned that "the people do not need books in general, but good books; for bad books, like rotten provisions, are transformed from food into deadly poison."[172] The Provisional Government appeared to promise what the artistic intelligentsia had been lobbying for over the past century: the end of an oppressive, biased, and corrupt state, and the introduction of representative structures and artistic freedom.

The Bolshevik coup eight months later was markedly less welcome to writers, and the exodus began, not just because of a fear of censorship or economic hardship but because of the possibility of Bolshevik-sponsored class warfare that would affect many of the producers and consumers of belles-lettres. Some, like Ivan Bunin and the young Vladimir Nabokov, left almost immediately; others waited until developments like the mass expulsion of intellectual leaders in 1922 made it quite clear what lay ahead. The waves of emigrating Russians took their cultural-political traditions with them to Berlin, Paris, and other destinations, and created not just a literature in exile, but a second literary process.[173] But this was the vestige of a paradigm; the real literature-power relationship was reestablished, and its cruelty refined, on Soviet Russian soil.

The Bolshevik wing of the Social Democrats intended all along to exercise control over texts and public discourse once in power, but they had other pressing issues to attend to between October 1917 and the end of the Civil War. While they were loathe to fund the avant-garde to any great extent, there was no deep concern that the population would be led astray by nonrepresentational art and Futurist poetry. The Acmeist poet Nikolai Gumilev was shot in 1920, but his fate had much to do with his ties to the Whites and his openly disdainful attitude towards the new government, and less to do with any belief on the part of the Bolsheviks in the political power of his verse.

The Soviet state inherited two ideologically driven policies for literature, both of which subordinated culture to state interests. To the imperial demand that writers support state power, the state-sponsored belief system, and the dominant nationality was added an internationally minded Marxist ideology that demanded class consciousness and unquestioning support for the Party's plan to transform Russia. Power was still a very concentrated force field in a quickly reconstituted empire. In 1924, Yevgeny Zamyatin saw that life for a heretical writer like himself was remarkably similar under both regimes. "Thus far, I have been in solitary confinement only twice, in 1905–6 and in 1922; both times on Shpalernaya [Island] and both times, by a strange coincidence, in the same gallery [of the prison]. I have been exiled three times, in 1906, in 1911, and in 1922. I have been tried only once, in the Saint Petersburg District Court, for my novella *At the World's End*."[174] By June 1931, Zamyatin saw that things had gotten much worse. "Regardless of the content of the given work, the very fact of my signature has become a sufficient reason for declaring the work criminal."[175] Having received what he considered to be a "writer's death sentence"—in that his works could be neither published nor staged—he asked and received permission from Stalin to leave.[176]

The year 1925 was crucial for the life of texts in Russia because it was then that Stalin solidified his hold on power within the Party, and the consequences began to be felt in cultural circles; poet Sergei Esenin's 1925 suicide may have resulted from other causes, but in Mayakovsky's view, such events were also a comment on the general way of life. Mikhail Bulgakov observed that during the first half of that year he was able to publish his ironic and satiric stories, while during the second half they were suddenly unacceptable. By 1926 the situation had dramatically worsened, and his apartment was searched and his diary and several works, including *Heart of a Dog* (*Sobach'e serdtse*), were taken into custody. They were returned to him several years later after repeated requests to the government. Bulgakov burned the diary soon afterward, but a secret police copy resurfaced four decades later. *Heart of a Dog* was not published in Russia until 1987.

While artistic texts were traditionally seen by the government as a highly effective way of influencing people, nonartistic texts were no less subject to scrutiny in the Soviet Union, especially if they had cultural-political significance. Early in the Soviet period, the intelligentsia was weakened by post-Revolutionary flight, the harsh conditions of the Civil War years, and the mass expulsions of 1922. That same year brought a remarkable plan for cleansing libraries of objectionable volumes and, in the case of larger libraries and museums, creating special archives of "removed books." In each banned volume on display there would be a review of its contents and an explanation of its fate.[177]

As the Stalinist period began, there were still active intellectual circles, one of which included the young Dmitry Likhachev. He and his Leningrad friends began to meet on a weekly basis in 1927, calling themselves the "Cosmic Academy of Sciences" and trying to outdo each other in the wit and erudition of their presentations. Likhachev, then twenty-one years old, prepared a half-joking, half-serious paper on the superiority of the old, sacred orthography over what he called the demonic new Soviet Russian alphabet. Members of the Cosmic Academy were arrested on February 8, 1928; Likhachev's paper was confiscated during the ensuing search and was one of the reasons for the five-year sentence that he received. Sixty-four years later, in 1992, when his conviction had been expunged from the record, Likhachev was allowed to see his file and was given a copy of the orthography paper.[178] From the lengthy, mocking title on it is clear how risky this text would have been in 1928; it supported the faith that was under assault, saying that the old orthography reflected the Orthodox core of Russian culture. Likhachev was dismissive about the new orthography, which he claimed had lowered the cultural level in order to reach the masses; rather than evolving organically, this alphabet revision had been forcibly introduced by the reigning Antichrists.[179]

Dmitry Likhachev was sent north to the Solovki prison camp because of texts that revealed a worldview hostile to Bolshevism. The monks on Solovki had been correct about the dangers of literacy. At first, some prisoners continued to lead a comparatively rich "text life" in Solovki. They recited poetry, read, and wrote, both officially and unofficially. Likhachev's first scholarly publications appeared in *The Islands of Solovki* (*Solovetskie ostrova*), which was available by subscription throughout the USSR. Texts led the Russian people to prison, and texts kept their minds alive while in prison. The existence of a government-sanctioned Solovki journal could, however, give the impression that this was not a killing place, which it was. Likhachev's diary and subsequent written recollections are eloquent supplements to the extensive material on Solovki collected by Alexander Solzhenitsyn for *The Gulag Archipelago*.[180]

In imperial Russia, the controls over literature were meant to prevent core beliefs and structures from being subverted in a way that could eventually endanger the tsarist regime as a whole. In Stalinist Russia, the official goal was to have literature cultivate a new set of values in Soviet society through the Writers' Union established in 1934 and the prescribed artistic method of Socialist Realism, but over the years, preventing the erosion of these values became no less important a goal. In return for writers' cooperation, the USSR would provide financial support for the literary world to an extent not even dreamed of in other countries.

Given the state's agenda, what constituted a "dangerous text" during the Soviet era? In the mid-1920s it could be a biting satire on the awkward first years of the new society, or an expression of fears for its future. Ten years later, after the satirists and the avant-garde had been silenced, it might be a realistic work that failed to embrace the radiant future with sufficient enthusiasm, or the unwritten work of an author who thought silence was preferable to producing an unconvincing lie. In spite of all the perils, "even in the fiercest years, 1936–1938, there were small groups of intellectuals that passed around within the group typed literature that was forbidden or not publishable."[181] The "dangerous" category frequently changed, and in the late 1940s, when Communism co-opted elements of Russian chauvinism, artistic and critical writing had to pass ideological and ethnic loyalty tests, making the chance of failure that much higher.

Stalin's death in 1953 lessened the severity of those loyalty tests and the punishment for failing them, but political controls over culture, and the traditional literary-political nexus, remained in force. One major difference was that the fate of at least some writers became known outside of Russia, and the seemingly impenetrable walls that cut the country off from the rest of the world were breached by texts moving in both directions. Another change was that censors focused on keeping politically unacceptable ideas out of published works, rather than on making sure that the positive agenda outlined in 1934 was present. The state began to allow the publication of artistically interesting works from the past to satisfy readers so weary of canonical Socialist Realism that they were tempted to seek out reading matter among manuscripts that appeared abroad or were distributed unofficially in Russia. Two writers whose works benefited from this change in policy were Ivan Bunin and Mikhail Bulgakov.

Still, there were dramatic episodes: the campaign against Boris Pasternak after the publication abroad of *Doctor Zhivago;* the trial and punishment first of Brodsky, and then of Sinyavsky and Daniel; and the hounding of Alexander Tvardovsky, the intrepid editor of the thick journal *Novyi mir,* and of his most famous author, Alexander Solzhenitsyn. Writers were imprisoned, exiled, expelled, pressured to leave; editors and critics were silenced; and the press runs of journals were increased or decreased depending on their political usefulness or injuriousness. Although the dangers to texts and writers had decreased and the variety of acceptable styles and subjects had expanded by the mid-1980s, paraliterary space had not disappeared and the controls and repressive measure were there to be applied as needed.

Texts judged to be dangerous for the mass reader could occasionally be permitted reading for a smaller audience, and a necessary source of information for an even more select group, whose commitment to Party and state was considered an inoculation against the possibility of infection. The state that sought to quash alternate lines of thought among the population still realized the need for party and security organs to know what was going on in politics, culture, and other spheres in the Soviet Union and abroad. According to Roy Medvedev, "green" or "blue" Tass reports were fairly accessible, while the uncensored "White Tass" news digests were available only to highly placed officials, and "Red Tass" only to those at the very top.[182] "One idiosyncrasy of the Soviet system, aimed at keeping higher circles well-informed without contaminating the minds of ordinary citizens, is the production of 'special editions' of significant and politically sensitive foreign books. . . . they are numbered individually, like highly classified documents in the West, so that no one can get away with a copy without a record of where it is and who is responsible for it."[183] Possibly controversial Russian texts under consideration for publication, like Solzhenitsyn's *One Day in the Life of Ivan Denisovich,* might be copied and sent around government circles for comment. Texts confiscated during searches were sometimes copied for purposes of constructing a criminal case, and for a very special list of insider readers.

The mid-sixties marked the change from an almost exclusively literary "awakening" of society to a movement for civil and human rights as "poets and readers were being sent away in deadly earnest to absolutely real labor camps."[184] At the trial of Andrei Sinyavsky and Yuli Daniel in February 1966, the prosecution insisted that, legally speaking, no line could be drawn between the fictional characters in question and the writers. Sinyavsky and Daniel were not only Tertz and Arzhak (their pseudonyms for publications sent abroad); they and their characters were all actors on the historical stage, and none were out of reach of the Soviet legal system. In his final plea, Andrei Sinyavsky said that by repeating the same objectionable quotations from their works again and again, the prosecution had itself created the fantastic atmosphere of works by Arzhak and Tertz. "It is the atmosphere of a murky anti-Soviet underground hidden behind the bright faces of . . . Sinyavsky and . . . Daniel, who hatch plots, nurture plans for *putsches,* terrorist acts, pogroms, assassinations. . . . It really is very strange that literary images suddenly lose their make-believe character and are interpreted by the prosecution literally—so literally that these court proceedings merge into a literary text as a natural sequel to it."[185]

Adding a short digression on the nature of literature in general and satire in particular, Sinyavsky concluded by saying that he was not an enemy, not an "other" in terms of Soviet society. He confused the issue somewhat by equating himself with the hero of his story "Pkhentz," a stranded visitor from another universe, who wonders why people feel the need to curse him just because he is different.[186] In a similar tone, Sinyavsky complained in a 1990 interview that "no one has read all of *Strolls with Pushkin,* only those five pages," referring to the excerpt of the book whose appearance preceded full publication in Russia.[187] Given the explosive reaction to this extract, one can see how Abram Tertz lived outside the law under two different regimes.

The so-called *shestidesiatniki* (people of the sixties) had been emboldened by the state-declared de-Stalinization campaign that began in the mid-1950s, and they kept it going when the state retreated a decade later. They were stimulated by the World Youth Festival of 1957–58, which was for many a first point of contact with the contemporary West, and by the dedication of a statue to Vladimir Mayakovsky during the summer of 1958 which gave them a rallying spot for unofficial poetry readings.[188] They inserted ever bolder critical and ironic notes into their published works, knowing that readers would not fail to notice these attempts to widen the area of free expression that began to open up soon after Stalin's death in 1953.

Eventually some of the *shestidesiatniki* were framed by their texts, becoming increasingly unpublishable and even untenable in the USSR. A relatively small number were tried and incarcerated, but the government's preference was to simply deny them direct access to the Soviet reader, and to make it possible and desirable for a number of figures with serious support abroad to leave. The production, without permission, of eight copies of the literary almanac *Metropol* in 1979 was one of the final echoes from the *samizdat* world energized by this group, but it also marked a new stage, since it did not hide underground but announced itself in public.[189] The *shestidesiatniki* and their texts were allowed back into the Soviet Union during the Gorbachev era only to find their fortunes sag once again, this time not because of the absence of freedom, but due to its presence. One begins to understand the very specific political and social conditions in which this group could flourish: a declining totalitarian state which had given up most of the instruments of terror but not of censorship, and whose better-educated readers welcomed imaginative and boldly ironic young writers.

With much less finesse, several former *derevenshchiki* (Village Prose writers) began to incorporate one side of a political debate into their fictionalized exposes of collectivization that appeared in the second half of the 1980s. Critic Igor Dedkov saw that the transitional literature of the glasnost period had to carry an especially heavy "historical burden," but that novels like Vasily Belov's *On the Eve* (*Kanuny*) and Boris Mozhaev's *Peasant Men and Women* (*Muzhiki i baby*), both from 1987, drove the ideological point home too hard. The artistic side of the work disappeared and only the political material was visible, but this time it was the author's doing, not the state's: in a sense, the author framed himself. "In such instances, the author's ideas are torn from their artistic foundation and interact as ideas with other, similar ideas that are current nowadays. Some ideas conflict with others, and the dispute continues over the Russian rural commune, over the 'rightists' and Trotskyism, over our national dignity, over the perfidy of non-Russians. . . . Meanwhile, the novel's heroes, the peasant men and women . . . remain below, on the ground, under the obscure clouds of these disputes."[190] Dedkov was shocked that in the epilogue to Mozhaev's novel the author calmly explained that there was no main character "since all of them were rather secondary." What is primary, lamented the critic—who, in a reversal of traditional roles, was now less politically aroused than the writer—is the author's "polemical competition."[191]

Solzhenitsyn was not the only prominent author who approached glasnost with some skepticism. It cost the Soviet government very little to publish a long-dead writer or a third-wave émigré whose works were no longer seen as a threat. *The Gulag Archipelago* was a more serious test, since it left few of the remaining illusions intact. *The Red Wheel* reached even further back, attacking Leninism at its source and the Bolshevik state from the moment of its inception. After a false start in 1988, *Gulag* finally appeared in the August 1989 issue of *Novyi mir*, the same journal that had introduced Solzhenitsyn to the nation twenty-seven years earlier in November 1962 with *One Day in the Life of Ivan Denisovich.*[192] The late eighties, an unsettled time in which the Russian canon was coming together in some places while unraveling in others, presented a classic moment of closure. If the government of the USSR had agreed to the publication of this work, then the only thing that could ever threaten writers and texts again would be a return to the old-style totalitarianism and censorship. As if on cue, with the Soviet empire in Eastern Europe deconstructing as well, Francis Fukuyama's first article on "the end of history" appeared during that same month of August 1989.[193] One stage in the history of the political control of literature in Russia had come to an end, and *The Gulag Archipelago* was evidently the last dangerous text.

For Russia's writers, both those who had remained in the USSR and those who were beginning to return in person or through their works, this would have seemed to be a time full of promise. They could have reasonably expected to be honored by a grateful nation for their past services, for keeping literature alive. Literature and politics could reach an amicable divorce and go their separate ways. Art could stop being a forum for alternative politics, and politics could shed its artistic concerns in the new context of open political discussion.

Throughout *Russia's Dangerous Texts,* but especially in the final chapter and the afterword, I will keep this reasonable expectation from the late 1980s in mind as I attempt to explain why, as at nearly every utopian moment in Russian history, things did not work out exactly as expected, and what this has to do with the kind of "politics" that had filled the interstices in the literary text during the past century and a half.

Chapter 2 The Disappearing Text: Reading Subversion Between the Lines

. . . by the word *tree* a constitution will be understood . . . by the word *arrow*, the autocracy.
—*Pushkin*

Any action was impossible, even a word must be masked, but, to make up for this, great was the power of speech.
—*Herzen*

Having identified core beliefs about the state's encounter with writers and texts, and having followed the historical patterns of this relationship, we are ready to construct a paradigm and to see how its existence is confirmed in the mirror of parody. The dangerous message— whether there by authorial intention or the echo of material deleted by the censor, whether an invention of the state, the wishful thinking of a disenfranchised reader, or the partially hidden agenda of a social critic—is not immediately visible. Pushkin feared that the state would read too much into artistic texts, turning poetic trees and arrows into political weapons, while Herzen saw oppression giving birth to a powerful message encased in art, in which words wore masks that hinted at the significance of what lay beneath them. Politicized readings of artistic texts shaped the evolution of Russian literature as they shaped the lives of Russia's writers and the hopes and expectations of the reading public. Russian texts came to inhabit a distinct "paraliterary space," a term used by Rosalind Krauss in her analysis of western Poststructuralism. In the writings of Derrida and Barthes she saw how the normal differences between literature and criticism disappeared, and "criticism finds itself caught in a dramatic web of many voices, citations, asides. . . . what is created . . . is a kind of paraliterature. . . . The paraliterary space is the space of debate, quotation, partisanship, betrayal, reconciliation; but it is not the space of unity, coherence, or resolution that we think of as constituting a work of literature."[1] It cannot be the space of "unity, coherence, or resolution" in part because it is rare that author, reader, critic, and government agree on the existence, precise content, or import of an implied message.

Paraliterary space is where literature encounters, and sometimes becomes, politics, so it is not surprising that the artistic text often disappears in the fray as the controversial ideas that are said to lie "between the lines" become the most prominent feature of the work, and the pretext for a much broader discussion. Fedor Dostoevsky, whose post-Siberia works were widely criticized in liberal journals, questioned whether his critics had even read the ending of *The Idiot,* so eager were they to find fault with his politics.[2] The same can be said of the conservative nationalists and their Communist fellow-travelers in 1990, when the publication of a brief excerpt from Sinyavsky's *Strolls with Pushkin* turned out to be more than enough to stimulate heated arguments and serious accusations.[3] In a 1999 postmortem on the literary process, one critic derided the kind of tendentious criticism that arose in the mid-nineteenth century that "didn't give a damn about the literary work" (*na tekst bylo naplevat'*). "That kind of criticism for the most part didn't analyze the writer, but sat in judgment over him. . . . The writer and his work just provided the excuse for a statement on current issues. . . . For example, Chernyshevsky didn't write about 'Asya,' but about a type of Russian liberal; Turgenev's story just provided the material."[4]

When the Politburo gathered in January 1974 to decide what to do about Alexander Solzhenitsyn after *Gulag Archipelago* had been published abroad, Leonid Brezhnev mentioned that an anti-Solzhenitsyn press campaign was being prepared, adding matter-of-factly that "nobody has read this book yet, but its contents are already known."[5] The leadership understood that they could judge Solzhenitsyn's potential for mischief without reading his work in its entirety, and that the danger to Soviet society came not only from the book's contents, however explosive, but also from the author's open example of self-liberation and his determination to shatter all lies. What was most important was to stop the writer's influence at home from spreading any further.

In the same year that Solzhenitsyn was deported, Andrei Sinyavsky said that communicating with the government was like trying to get people on the television screen to listen. Books were incomprehensible and superfluous to the authorities, but not to those outside the power structure.[6] Sergei Chuprinin pointed out that for years the story of the unexpected publication of a daring work "flew all around the country in an instant, way ahead of, or often in place of an actual acquaintance with the text."[7] The drama *of* the text easily outweighed the drama *in* the text.

At the hearing where his poems were called "disgusting and anti-Soviet," Joseph Brodsky challenged his accusers to come up with a specific title or a one-line quotation to prove their case. The judge's response was that "I will not allow any quotations," which showed an appreciation for the context in which the criminality of the text is assumed, not proven. The defending counsel pointed out that "not one of the prosecution witnesses knows Brodsky, or has read his poems; the prosecution witnesses have testified on the strength of some unauthenticated documents of mysterious origin or have simply expressed their opinions, making accusing speeches."[8]

When we juxtapose the Brodsky and Sinyavsky/Daniel cases we get a clearer idea of how the text/author/state relationship functioned. The paradigm could be activated either through a judgment made about the author or about the text. Brodsky came to the negative attention of state authorities and they decided to make a general example of him. His poems were basically irrelevant to the case and reading them in court unnecessary; his un-Soviet way of life was held up as a danger to society, especially to its youth, and as a result his texts became dangerous as well. Once the process was set in motion, both prior and subsequent texts succumbed to guilt by association, as Zamyatin had discovered decades earlier.[9] In a letter to Stalin, Zamyatin complained that even a story he published a year before the Revolution was later criticized as "a travesty of the revolution in connection with the transition to NEP."[10] According to the government's line of reasoning in the 1960s, Joseph Brodsky's self-assured non-participation in daily Soviet life infected his poems, which became literary parasites, living off the rest of the canon and threatening to sicken the reader.

The folk concept of *porcha* (spoiling, danger) could all too easily be transferred from writer to text or from text to writer, so that they quickly came to infect one other. This is to be expected when artistic works are treated as faith texts. The icon painter prayed before taking up the brush and was expected to lead a holy life, not unlike the writer of Torah scrolls. In the latter instance, the sanctity is based not so much on the content, or whether the scroll was read, "but rather on how and by whom it was produced. . . . A scroll of heretics or sectarians, after all, was not inspected for accuracy but was simply condemned to burning on the a priori grounds that its producers were untrustworthy."[11]

The literary critic Sinyavsky and the translator Daniel led relatively quiet lives; however, the stories they sent abroad behaved in a much more rambunctious manner, transferring their criminal associations to the writers who had presented them to the world under pseudonyms. It took a surprisingly long time for the state to determine the writers' true identities, but when they were found out it made no difference to the court that these two men were in most other ways responsible citizens. Unlike the Brodsky hearings, their trial featured abundant quotations from the dangerous texts because that was the most compelling evidence of all. There was to be no separation between the voice of the writer and that of the fictional character: the word on the page leaped into their creators' bodies and issued forth from their lips. A favorite government tactic, from the time of Nicholas I through Stalin, was to have the writer read his own dangerous words aloud during the interrogation. Mandelstam, who had not committed his poem about Stalin to paper, was made to recite, and then write out, the definitive version of these verses, because his recitation differed from an informant's copy.[12]

Krauss warns us that in "paraliterary space" what is left is "drama without the Play, voices without the Author, criticism without the Argument."[13] There is no argument or evidence as such, and what is normally on the margins can take center stage, as a passage from "The Used-Book Dealer," one of Varlam Shalamov's Siberian prison camp stories, illustrates. A former NKVD criminal investigator with special training in literature explains how he approached a given text.

> "When reading books I would first of all turn to the notes, the comments. Man is a creature of notes and comments."
> "What about the text?"
> "Not always. There is always time for that."[14]

This echoes with unintentional irony the words of Osip Mandelstam who directs our gaze away from the center to what is inscribed on the margins of manuscripts.[15]

The practice of examining the spaces between the lines and around the texts had been in place for more than a century before the Stalinist purges. Scholarly investigations and memoir literature on pre-Revolutionary censorship provide ample evidence of the scrutiny given all kinds of documents in the search for subversive traits. The liberal-sounding 1804 statute on censorship included among its forty-seven articles one that recommended that "in case of a doubtful passage having a double meaning, it is better to interpret it in the way most advantageous to the author, than to prosecute him." The 1826 censorship law, which formed the basis for the definitive 1828 statute, fundamentally revised this: "Do not permit passages in works and translations to be printed if they have a double meaning and one of the meanings is contrary to the censorship laws."[16] Ambiguity had officially become suspect. One hundred and thirty years later, Vladimir Bukovsky discovered that the state was threatened by "ambiguous jokes, parodies, and lampoons" in a high school literary magazine. There was "no politics in it, and the whole menagerie roars, up to and including the Central Committee."[17] When Bukovsky realized what the state feared the most, he knew what path he must take to prevent a return to Stalinism.

Stanislav Rassadin began in the late 1950s to write about the art of reading, using a coded language for kindred spirits who were "grateful for any hint, for even a meager allusion."[18] In analyzing the 1960s, critics Peter Vail and Alexander Genis describe the complex metaworld (*metamir*) created by the Aesopian system, in which a work was not completed until a well-versed reader filled in the blanks. While Aesopian language could be seen as allowing a level of political discourse, however limited, irony had the opposite effect, and could even be seen as an "obstacle on the path towards social progress," since it questioned the possibility of any goal other than destruction. "The blasphemous nature of irony is in its emptiness. It is a mask under which there is no face."[19]

Under the tsars, the Foreign Censorship Committee was alert to the possibilities of irony and other subversive devices in the works of European writers, especially concerning five basic subject areas—government, royalty, religion, morality, and the social order—both in general and as applied to Russia. Ironic passages might be simply inked out and pasted over, or the entire work could be banned for a particular audience or for everyone in the country. In written accounts of embarrassing moments in Russian history, like the palace coups that killed Peter III and Paul I, no mention could be made of the location or the suddenness of their deaths because that implied an in-house murderer even if nothing else were said.[20] In this context, silence also spoke volumes.

In a real sense, Vissarion Belinsky and his successors cannot be accused of reading more into a work than the government, but he did make certain "that the political resonances of the early Russian novels would not go unnoticed."[21] In his famous letter to Gogol from 1847, Belinsky highlighted the sections of *Selected Passages from a Correspondence with Friends* that he found politically objectionable, remarking that the volume "is now better remembered for the articles which have been written about it than for the book itself."[22] Alexander Herzen said of Belinsky that "the book he was reviewing usually served him as a starting-point, but he abandoned it half-way and plunged into some other question. . . .What fidelity there is to his principles, what dauntless consistency, what adroitness in navigating between the shoals of censorship, what boldness in his attacks on the literary aristocracy."[23]

Belinsky's genius was to simply claim that a literary work suggested something that he himself wished it to suggest; it is not an exaggeration to call him the natural father of a surrogate political child. More than any other Russian critic, Belinsky was responsible for creating a progressive political framework and a politicized critical code for literature that paralleled the reactionary frame that the government already had in place. This code used whatever came to hand to score the necessary political points, and its strategies and style were carried over into the Soviet period, by which time Belinsky himself was banned from the general collections of some libraries during periods of particular militancy.[24]

Typology was an integral part of the "literary process" in Russia from the beginning, and a strategically placed label could identify a work as reflecting the views or advancing the agenda of one or another ideological camp. Belinsky found typology essential in presenting progressive writers and texts to the public. He had to show that Russian society was not a seamless whole and identifying literary types was one way to do this; in 1843, he complained that people were constantly speaking of "a view of Russian literature" and "the state of Russian literature" as if this were a singular entity, something he had been trying to disprove since the mid-1830s. "This is a habit which it is time we gave proper attention to and dropped. We have *several* literatures; by compounding them under the term 'Russian literature' and clothing this term in various epithets we often commit the fault of ascribing the properties of one literature to another which would gladly do without them."[25] Belinsky named four categories: *kopeechnaia literatura* (penny literature; sordid and cheap), *promyshlennaia literatura* (commercial, but of a slightly higher quality), *starcheskaia literatura* (literature of the elders, which looks nostalgically on a simpler past and rejects all change, especially from "a decaying and perverted West"), and an untitled "new" literature which held some hope for the future.[26]

Belinsky and his critical offspring offered a guide to the correct reading of contemporary belles-lettres, indicating the types of texts and characters worthy of the public's attention. Russians had to be trained to identify and prefer the new writing as part of their consciousness-raising; when this happened, they would be naturally linked to others who had read and thought similar things. In a stagnant and repressive society, Belinsky believed that change was inevitable and desirable, and that a new linkage based on moral, spiritual, and intellectual concerns could have a unifying effect on a society divided by disparate classes. He looked between the lines for hints of *progress;* and found ways to make frequent use of this word, defending it as a foreign term for which there was no equivalent in Russian.[27] He described *progress* as that which comes from within a nation, even if the term itself came from abroad, and explained that his yearly summaries of Russian literature in *The Contemporary* were a way of gauging how much *progress* had been made. In the life of a nation and of a literature change might not be immediately perceptible to everyone, but a critic could see deeper and further than others and was called on to share his insights.

These nineteenth-century critics provided a language for talking about authors and works that was picked up and further refined (or is "coarsened" more accurate?), particularly the negative epithets, during the Soviet era. In Bulgakov's *Master and Margarita* (1928–40) the hero recalls with a shudder that after part of his novel was published, he was accused in print of "Pilatism," of being an enemy and a "militant Old Believer." He was amused, then amazed, and finally frightened. "There was something uncommonly fake and uncertain in every line of these articles, despite their threatening and self-assured tone. I kept thinking . . . that the authors of these articles weren't saying what they wanted to say, and that this was why they were so furious."[28] Belinsky himself had berated "literary Old Believers" in his "Survey of Russian Literature in 1846," but by the second half of the 1920s, the authentic rhetorical fervor of the 1840s had mutated into the language of ritualized Soviet-era indictment.[29]

It was not unusual in the pre-Revolutionary period for a novel to be given negative, mutually exclusive political readings by camps that stood in stark opposition to each other. Ivan Turgenev was castigated by some for having killed off his nihilist hero Bazarov, and by others for having brought him to life in the first place. Nihilist and antinihilist writers alike wrote their texts into the discussion that *Fathers and Sons* stimulated. Dostoevsky's problem was somewhat different; criticized by the Left for having turned against his youthful progressive leanings, he realized that, paradoxically, no matter how much he moved to the patriotic right, he was in some official quarters marked forever as an ex-radical and ex-political prisoner, a citizen of what Solzhenitsyn would later call the nation of *zeks* (convicts).

Within this paradigm, the original text and the author's biography disappear as primary objects of analysis, while the supposed "hidden text" becomes the stimulus for discussion and, at times, for official action. At the very least, critical commentary could achieve equal or even superior status to the original work, and it tended to merge into one document, which if not seamless, was still hard to separate back into its component parts. Dostoevsky saw how Dobrolyubov's critical essays became part and parcel of Alexander Ostrovsky's career as a playwright, not just influencing public perception of the plays, but affecting Ostrovsky's understanding of his own work: "Perhaps Ostrovsky himself really never became aware he was showing a Realm of Darkness, but Dobrolyubov *prompted him well*, and it fell on fertile soil."[30] Dobrolyubov's essay "What is Oblomovitis?" is credited with having influenced Turgenev to write a new ending for his 1856 novel *Rudin,* now sending his feckless wanderer to Paris to die on the barricades.[31] Critics were not shy about letting writers know what they wished to see in that increasingly valuable space between the lines.

THE PROOF IS IN THE PARODY

The literary-political nexus, as it functioned historically, had such a deep and lasting impact on all parties that it began to take on a life of its own in works by Vassily Aksenov, Sinyavsky/Tertz, Vladimir Voinovich, and many others. They exposed to laughter the politicized treatment of literature, often specifically mocking Socialist Realism at the same time, in texts that are as much parody as satire. For example, an early version of Voinovich's comic sketch "Skurlatsky, Man of Letters" was embedded in a biography of Vera Figner in the "Flaming Revolutionaries" (*Plamennye revoliutsionery*) series. This series of biographies by relatively liberal writers itself became a factor in the increasingly fractious paraliterary world of the 1970s.[32] A rival publishing project called "Lives of Remarkable People" (*Zhizn' zamechatel'nykh liudei*) used biographies of Ivan Goncharov, Alexander Ostrovsky, Nikolai Gogol, and others as a platform to launch nationalist attacks—between the lines—not on the patriotic Russian communism of the present, but on the cosmopolitan (i.e. Jewish) Bolshevism of 1917.

In the 1920s, the forced inclusion of members of the proletariat in the literary process was a move that proved especially ripe for comic treatment, because the Revolution elevated the Russian worker to be not merely the symbolic locus of Soviet power but also a producer of a new Soviet literature. Trotsky expressed serious doubts about the latter goal in his 1924 essay "Proletarian Culture and Art." He saw the proletariat as unprepared to transform culture; they would have to master already existing art before they could become what he called "culture-bearing."[33] Creating their own works was a long way off, and rushing the process would lead to what Trotsky characterized as "a jumble of concepts and words out of which one can make neither head nor tail."[34] He added that there was no need to turn the proletariat into critics à la Belinsky, because the progressive, politics-building function of Belinsky-type criticism was now the work of society as a whole.[35]

Trotsky's misgivings were ignored and "reader's criticism"—particularly by workers—was encouraged. Even if the proletariat had failed to generate artists, Soviet authorities still found them useful as critics. Questionnaires were distributed among miners, metalworkers, and other groups, and manuals were prepared to help conduct "evenings of worker criticism," with special instructions on how to keep these workers' discussions focused.[36] The workers' alleged dissatisfaction with a literary text or other cultural artifact was justification for suppressing it and criticizing its author. The impractical idea of a rapidly established proletarian art was further debased and ritualized by the use of workers in a censorship function. When attacks by the critics demonized Zamyatin and cut off his access to the public, he decided to employ the regime's own methods to improve his situation. In a June 1931 letter to Stalin, Zamyatin said that on May 15, 1928, his tragedy *Attila* had been read at the Leningrad Bolshoi Dramatic Theater to assembled representatives from eighteen factories, who declared the play to be ideologically acceptable and of high artistic quality.[37] The playwright then quoted directly from the minutes of that meeting.

> The representative of the Volodarsky Plant said: "This is a play by a contemporary author, treating the subject of the class struggle of ancient times. . . . Ideologically, the play is quite acceptable. . . ."
> The representative of the Lenin Factory noted the revolutionary character of the play and said that "in its artistic level, the play reminds us of Shakespeare's works. . . . It is tragic, full of action, and will capture the viewer's attention."
> The representative of the Hydro-Mechanical Plant found "every moment in the play strong and absorbing," and recommended its opening on the theater's anniversary.[38]

Despite this evidence in its support, the play, which was already in rehearsal, was banned. The worker-as-critic strategy was meant to operate in favor of

Party-approved writers, not to validate free spirits, and six months after writing this letter Zamyatin left the Soviet Union forever.

The process of involving workers in the task of cultural oversight also affected the operation of the State Jewish Theater, whose director from 1929 until 1948 was the great Yiddish actor Solomon Mikhoels. The actor's daughter Natalya recalled the 1937 production of Goldfaden's *Shulammite,* which was popular with the public but was criticized in official circles because of its historical and biblical theme.[39] Mikhoels was required to take time out of his rehearsal schedule for meetings about the play with workers. "These discussions took place at factory conferences, a Soviet innovation, where a metalworker or a plumber was allowed not only to share his personal impressions, but to also give instructions to the director and the actors, and to composers, scientists, and artists. In a word, democracy Soviet-style. These discussions and meetings took up a great deal of time and energy, not to mention what they did to one's nerves."[40] With the deliberations dragging on for days, the company wound up having to rehearse late at night and sleep in the theater.

The twentieth anniversary of the State Jewish Theater in 1939 brought tributes from many individuals and groups, including the workers of Clock Factory No. 2. Mikhoel's daughter could not recall precisely why the clock factory was involved, "but those were the 'rules of the game' under the slogan 'take theater to the masses!' And the masses did go to the theater to mark its anniversary."[41] Along with their congratulations, the factory hands brought alarm clocks which they presented to each member of the company. "Many years later you could still find in each actor's apartment a strange wooden object with a clock face lying on one side or even turned upside down. This was the gift of Clock Factory No. 2. In a normal standing position nobody could get it to work."[42] Could one find a better metaphor for the artificially induced and awkwardly executed proletarian role in culture than these semifunctional clocks?

During the March 1964 Brodsky court hearing, proof of his harmful influence on society was supplied in part by a pipe layer and self-described "representative of public opinion," who expressed indignation over Brodsky's verse despite the fact that he had never actually seen the poems and only knew about the poet from the newspapers. "Why doesn't he work? . . . as a worker I am not satisfied by Brodsky's activities." A pensioner who claimed that his son was harmed by exposure to this poetry said that "Brodsky is not merely a parasite. He is a militant parasite."[43] The prosecutor Sorokin described the defendant as belonging to a "set of people who greeted the word 'labour' with satanic laughter."[44] Lidiya Chukovskaya recalled that the newspaper *Evening Leningrad*

(*Vechernyi Leningrad*) published a selection of letters to the editor from workers who wanted Brodsky exiled.[45] Stanislav Rassadin calls this kind of militant reader (or nonreader) "a little grand inquisitor."[46]

In January 1966, the newspaper *Izvestiia* published letters condemning Sinyavsky and Daniel from "agronomists, milkmaids, steelworkers, and deer breeders," among others.[47] When the campaign against Alexander Solzhenitsyn began to intensify, government-sponsored lecturers who knew his work poorly, if at all, went into workplaces, speaking at closed meetings in factories, schools, and other venues throughout the country; they spread the message that the writer and his books were criminal, and that he was both pro-Nazi and secretly Jewish.[48] The Solzhenitsyn file from the Politburo archives, declassified and released in 1992, includes numerous instances where the wrath of workers was made part of the case against the writer. After word came of the release of *The Gulag Archipelago* in the West, letters arrived at the Central Committee from lathe and sewing machine operators, machine tool designers, fitters, metalworkers, collective farmers, tractor drivers, and mill operators.[49] There is a strong statement from the leader of a coal-mining team in Donetsk, who was also a deputy to the Ukrainian Supreme Soviet. "The miners at our mine have always despised Solzhenitsyn's writings. . . . miners call Solzhenitsyn among themselves nothing less than scum and a traitor. . . . The Donets miners like literature and have deep respect for literary expression. . . . But as far as such 'authors' as Solzhenitsyn are concerned, we have always despised them and will continue to do so. . . . His place is among those people without a name and without a motherland. He deserves this shameful fate because of his anti-Soviet scribbling."[50]

These incidents highlight some of the more ludicrous aspects of the evaluation of artistic texts based on their supposed appeal to the proletariat. Vasily Aksenov showed the humorous side of the hypertrophied Soviet literary process in a story from 1965, "The Steel Bird." On a stroll around his Moscow neighborhood, a successful young writer named Ahmed Samopalov learns that people have been talking about his new book at "lightning readers' conferences" in schools, toy factories, at the local pensioners' council, among engineers, truck drivers, and divers repairing a local bridge. In fact, all work has come to a halt in order to devote time to weighty literary questions. A surgeon explains to Ahmed how operating rooms have turned into literary seminars:

"You know, Ahmed, during an operation today we got to arguing about literature. We opened up an abdominal cavity and somehow we got talking. Well naturally we remembered your *Look Back in Delight*. The surgical nurse was reading it in the operating room and she said she was wild about it. I gave you your due too, Ahmed, although I confess I did criticize certain shortcomings. Our anesthetist was completely on your side, but the patient we were operating on said that the book might well be interesting but it was harmful."[51]

A decision is made to perform the operation in two stages so that the patient would have more time to gather the citations necessary to strengthen his argument.

In his 1985 study juxtaposing elite and popular literature, the critic V. Kardin treated with humorous disdain the ignorance in the literary establishment about what people were really reading, appearances to the contrary. He mentions the regular staging of meetings between writers, critics, and the "public," and the publication in literary periodicals of photographs of writers conversing with oil workers, toolmakers, machine operators, cotton growers, and especially weavers and milkmaids. "But the other side of this relationship is not captured in a photo. Are the combine operators, oil workers, programmers, and milkmaids actually reading stories and poems by the writers visiting them? Maybe they're reading something entirely different?"[52]

Aksenov, Kardin, and others focused a satiric eye on the institutionalized practice of drawing authors into debates which were centered on concerns of the proletariat. In "Graphomaniacs," Sinyavsky/Tertz threw some satiric light on the writer's own working conditions; the state's steady gaze made being an unconventional author both risky and prestigious, leading to widespread writing frenzy that functioned far from the daylight world of socially useful work and public scrutiny, burrowing deeply into the Soviet literary underground. Galkin, one of the story's frustrated writers, says that the state's policy of censorship gave him the right to see himself as an unappreciated genius; this self-anointed genius painstakingly produces his own books in editions of one copy.

Walking around Moscow at night, the narrator looks with interest into ground-floor and basement apartments, and everywhere he sees the same familiar scene. "It was late evening—the graphomaniacs' favorite hour—and in every hole accessible to my eyes someone was writing. I had the impression that the town was seething with writers, all of whom, great and small, were moving their fountain pens over paper. . . . In the midst of this writing fraternity I was perhaps the only true writer."[53] The narrator seems less obsessive than some of his literary acquaintances until he reveals that several nineteenth-century Russian novelists stole material from him. The need to produce an original piece of writing drives characters into seclusion and sometimes out of their minds. Bulgakov's Master flees into a basement to complete his manuscript, but he makes the mistake of emerging long enough to submit it for publication, and the ensuing attack on his novel shatters his nerves and undermines his sanity forever.

A print run of one copy seems minimal enough, but Vladimir Voinovich goes one step further in his satirical dystopia *Moscow 2042* (written 1982–85), where state authorities allow writers to compose texts which will never appear on screen, let alone in print, which means that the public will not be in danger of succumbing to their influence, and there will be less demand for paper. The writer-narrator, transported through time to a disintegrating future Russia called Moscowrep, is told that "preliminary literature" (meaning the original artistic text) is no longer needed by most citizens, because they can study summaries of a book's "ideological and artistic content" instead, leaving the reading of actual texts to a much smaller number of citizens.[54] The government has become the editor of all written work, so a "one-text" society has been realized in fact; Voinovich's fantasy echoed the sense among some critics that with so many levels of censorship and editorial oversight, the Soviet government had in a real sense become the "co-author" of all written work.[55]

Opposition writers in Moscowrep are provided with keyboards to record their thoughts, but there are no screens and no printers, and what they produce is called "papless literature." Establishment writers, on the other hand, use word processors that feed into a central machine which edits and coordinates their work into one continuous text about their leader, the Genialissimo; this is the only "pap" literature. In a further practical move, newspapers are printed in the form of toilet paper rolls, reflecting the use to which papers were often put in the Soviet era.[56] Soviet émigrés of the narrator's present also suffer from logorrhea. Sim Simych, the Solzhenitsyn-like character in *Moscow 2042*, works fourteen hours a day on his epic *Greater Zone*, which when completed will consist of sixty volumes that the deliberately archaic Sim insists on calling "slabs."[57]

Graphomania is an indigenous disease of paraliterary space. Svetlana Boym distinguishes between the medical condition of "obsessive writing" in a nontotalitarian context, and "cultural illness," which in Tertz's famous example combined a type of psychic and creative malfunction that prevailed in Russia and Eastern Europe.[58] The situation was not so different in emigration, which poet Naum Korzhavin has called "the realm of graphomania."[59] Vladimir Nabokov's *Glory* (*Podvig*, 1933) offers a tragic and fantastic narrative of a *grafoman manqué*. The young hero, unable to write a book of his own in the text-obsessed community of Berlin, and inspired by a painting that hung above his bed before and after fleeing Soviet Russia, substitutes another kind of glorious deed. He secretly crosses the Soviet border and disappears, as it were, onto a different plane of existence.

The ending of *Glory* honors the willingness, even eagerness, of some Russians to give their lives in the cause of creativity and antitotalitarianism. Devoting one's energies to further the Russian revolutionary cause elicited a markedly different response from Nabokov, as we see in the mocking pseudobiography of Nikolai Chernyshevsky that Nabokov placed in the center of his Berlin novel *The Gift* (*Dar*). The book was published serially in the Paris-based *Contemporary Notes* (*Sovremennye zapiski*) in 1937–38, but without the Chernyshevsky chapter, which did not see the light of day until 1952. In the second half of the 1930s, there were still émigrés who retained their youthful illusions about progressive art in the service of mankind; Chernyshevsky and his novel occupied a sacred place in the martyrology they had constructed.[60]

In Richard Borden's masterful analysis of Valentin Kataev's *The Little Iron Door in the Wall* (*Malen'kaia zhelezhaia dver' v stene*, 1964), he explains how a parodic biography of Lenin was scattered throughout this supposedly serious narrative about the pre-Revolutionary years in European exile.[61] Borden calls the novel a work of "surpassing ambiguity," although perhaps it "proved too elusive" so that readers were likely to abandon it after a few pages and only a handful of critics grasped the hidden irreverence towards this most hallowed of subjects. "Lenin does not merely drown in Kataev's verbiage. As the cumulative effects of Kataev's strategies accrue, Lenin is set up to stand out like a dull, absurd sore thumb against the variegated riches of the phenomenal world. If Lenin is the text, the real story lies in the contrasting texture."[62] Borden shows how Kataev used both parody and a parodic juxtaposition of passages that in a different context could have been read at face value. For example, in a passage that ought to have alerted more readers to the author's game, Kataev claimed to see a resemblance between the handwriting of Lenin and Alexander Pushkin.

Pushkin himself is the most striking example of how the writer's own biography—where he lived, how he suffered for his texts, how he died—occupied a crucial place in the literary-political paradigm. The life of an important writer was inscribed on the cultural map and on the cultural calendar of Russia, and entered the official national biography or the unofficial cultural martyrology. And, as with Pushkin, everything about the writer's life is subject to being read politically, and the political readings themselves are subject to parody. Especially in the case of Pushkin, each commemoration of the writer's birth or death was shaped by the political needs of the age in which it took place, and in turn reinforced the paradigm. The real life Alexander Pushkin would have been amazed to meet the Pushkin of 1899, 1937, 1949, 1987, and 1999. In "Exegi monumentum" (1836), the poet anticipated that his texts, which he called statues "not made by human hands," were his true legacy, but in state terms, the patriotic frame that could be placed around Pushkin has counted far more.

In *A Measure of Trust* (*Stepen' doveriia*, 1973), Voinovich's biography of the revolutionary Vera Figner, we find the story of a certain Skurlatsky, a hanger-on in the intense literary-political world of Russia in the year 1881. Having failed to produce any texts of his own, the utterly superfluous Skurlatsky claims credit for the authorship of a radical pamphlet that someone slipped under his door in the perilous days following the assassination of the tsar; he understands that the aura around the text is what counts, and he stubbornly believes that it is better to die for what are in reality someone else's words than to live any longer without his own.

Voinovich later reworked this dramatic, if peculiar, vignette into the brilliantly comical sketch, "Skurlatsky, Man of Letters." He removed a passage in the middle of the chapter about the arrests of genuine revolutionaries in March 1881, while at the same time adding a parodic frame. The new introduction claims a Gogolian ignorance of the true facts of the case, and then shows Skurlatsky at his self-delusional best. In the book, the Skurlatsky tale ends with his being sent to a mental hospital where he makes a profound impression on the other patients. In the stand-alone sketch, the narrator describes in greater detail Skurlatsky's effect on his new acquaintances who come to the conclusion that they, too, were members of the Executive Committee of the People's Will movement, at which point they begin to make bombs out of the only materials available to them in the hospital, tin cans and kasha. Voinovich generously offers his readers both the paradigm—where even a spurious connection to radical texts leads to an arrest—and the parody, in this narrative of a politically ambitious *grafoman* with a lively imagination but a permanent case of writer's block.[63]

In these comic examinations of the literary process in Russia we have seen a writer-protagonist producing one meticulously handwritten copy of his work, writers with a keyboard but no printer, and pseudo-authors with no text at all except in their imagination. For real life writers and readers, the challenge and the satisfaction in one sense lay in the riskiness (*riskovannost'*) of the business itself; to set foot in this space at all was to take part in what sometimes was played as a parlor game, while at other times escalating into a blood sport. In the absence of open political debate, this was one of the only games in town.

A study of Russian literary history reveals numerous qualities of a text or writer's life that could be read politically. A work could adopt an inappropriate literary style, it could be too Russian or not Russian enough, it could portray the wrong kind of heroic action or take place in an inappropriate setting, or the values of the text could be judged incompatible with the government-sanctioned ethos. In this and in subsequent chapters I will look at categories which have received less attention than others in scholarly literature and yet were consequential, especially in twentieth-century Russia. Looking at such categories illuminates, rather than upsets, the paradigm and the common beliefs about the interaction between literature and power in Russia. The best place to begin is with the inimitable Sinyavsky/Tertz, who observed most rules only in the breach.

SINYAVSKY AND TERTZ IN
PARALITERARY SPACE

The critic Sinyavsky and the writer Tertz were forever landing in the literary-political zone, in "paraliterary space." Tertz's Pushkin "ran into great poetry on thin erotic legs and created a commotion."[64] Andrei Donatovich Sinyavsky entered the public sphere through the side door of literary reviews and prefaces and by holding up one corner of Pasternak's coffin.[65] Abram Tertz ambled onto the paraliterary landscape in the late 1950s when his stories were published abroad and passed around at home; he was unmasked only in 1965. As in the case of Yevgeny Zamyatin, a politicized space surrounded Sinyavsky wherever he went. At a 1981 conference on "The Meaning of Dissent," he addressed the recurring controversy over his works. "There, in the Soviet Union, I was an 'agent of Imperialism'; here, in emigration, I am an 'agent of Moscow.' Meanwhile I have not changed my position, but I have said the same thing: art is greater than reality. A threatening retribution is following me from various corners—for one and the same books, for one and the same statements, for one and the same style, for one and the same crime."[66]

The following year, Sinyavsky spoke about this phenomenon in somewhat darker tones. "After Soviet justice . . . there is émigré justice—and the same evidence. Of course, they do not throw you into a concentration camp. But a camp is not the most frightful thing in the world. . . . even pleasant compared to emigration, where they say you have not been in a camp at all, but that you were sent 'on an assignment' to destroy Russian culture."[67]

By "the same evidence" Sinyavsky meant the same lack of evidence, the same

use of a text read superficially not merely as proof of a crime, but as the crime itself. Questions were asked about the "softness" of his incarceration, since, after
all, he was able to use that time to write the blasphemous *Strolls with Pushkin,*
hardly a Dostoevskian act of repentance before the Russian people.[68] Those
who raised the question were indulging in a bout of "competitive suffering," according to which the persecution of Sinyavsky had to be downgraded in order
to advance that of his aesthetic and ideological rivals.[69] Suffering is a powerful
myth and a condition that is easily utilized in evaluating texts and their creators.

Among the politicized literary categories that affected the reception of
Sinyavsky/Tertz are: style, characterization, ethos, theme, suggestive ambiguities, place or manner of publication, and the author's choice and use of a pseudonym. Sinyavsky realized as early as 1955 that the manner in which he wrote
"had no place in Soviet publishing at that time . . . it simply did not fit the existing traditions and circumstances."[70] His Tertz manuscripts would have to be
spirited out of the country, however perilous a trip that might be. Two years after Stalin's death, and a year before the Twentieth Party Congress and the beginnings of de-Stalinization, the logic and sheer audacity of Sinyavsky's decision are obvious.

When *Strolls with Pushkin* (*Progulki s Pushkinym*) appeared in the West,
Solzhenitsyn described Sinyavsky's writing as "aesthetic nihilism," linking him
to others of his generation and to the members of the revolutionary avant-garde
who had shown a cavalier disregard for the Russian classics.[71] Sinyavsky and
Solzhenitsyn were in basic agreement that it was Tertz's style, broadly defined as
the combination of ethos with voice, that was more a problem than the ideology. Donald Fanger noted that a daring countertradition that freed the writer
to experiment and even blaspheme had been championed by Sinyavsky/Tertz,
but that this anomaly only served to reinforce the primacy of a politically
loaded Realist tradition.[72]

The author did not see his manner of writing as being a threat to Russian literature, let alone to Russia itself, and the atmosphere he created was much
more playful than nihilistic. About *Strolls,* he remarked that it was "simply
amusing to write a scholarly monograph on Pushkin while in a labor camp. But
some things I simply broke first, the way you break a toy, and glued them back
together a new way." In the same interview he said: "I only find it interesting to
write if there is a prohibition, a taboo."[73] In his mind he was writing *for* the creative freedom of the Russian author, and not simply against prevailing norms.

Igor Shafarevich's strongly negative reaction to *Strolls with Pushkin* emphasized the harm he felt this work could do to an unstable Russia; he praised the Islamic world for refusing to tolerate Salman Rushdie's similarly blasphemous *Satanic Verses*.[74] In contrast to the traitorous flight of the early Tertz stories from the USSR, *Strolls with Pushkin* was seen by its detractors as a text that had invaded Russia from abroad, so alien were the pseudonymous author and his approach to a sacred national subject. Shafarevich's reaction serves as an example of how style in Russia could be read as politics, how it could have an ideological resonance. The periodic resacralization of Russian Realism and demonization of the avant-garde are important aspects of this line of thinking.

The government's case against Sinyavsky/Daniel, as revealed in the 1966 trial transcript, focused on the aid and comfort given enemies of the USSR when such anti-Soviet works were published outside the country, on the fifth column that marched between the lines of these stories. In this and many other ways Sinyavsky was judged to have failed as a Soviet writer; in emigration and in the late 1980s in Russia, he was said to have failed as a Russian writer as well.[75] In both cases Sinyavsky was accused of having undermined the strength and mocked the greatness of the Russian people, acts that can be summarized as crimes against national identity.

At their simplest, the aesthetic requirements for a Russian writer were: to embrace a Realism free of ambiguities, to reject modernism as alien, and to acknowledge the political, philosophical, social, and spiritual roles and responsibilities of literary texts and their authors in Russia. Taken to an extreme, the ideology of Russianness demanded ethnic purity, but more commonly it required honoring and serving Russia no matter what the writer's ethnic background might be. To use a pseudonym in order to be protected from political reprisals was bad enough, to hide Jewish roots was understandable, but to mask one's true Russian identity was an inexplicable gesture with negative connotations. For Andrei Sinyavsky, an ethnic Russian and an Orthodox believer, to have taken the name Abram Tertz, a legendary Jewish criminal from Odessa, was "so discordant within the 'mythology' of Russian and Soviet culture that it becomes 'unreadable' or rather elicits multiple readings."[76]

Sinyavsky not only broke cultural-political codes, he rendered them virtually inapplicable to his work. If we attempt to use the ultranationalists' own critical categories based on notions of the legitimacy and illegitimacy of Russian writers, we have to decide whether to call Sinyavsky a pseudo-Russian (*lzhe-russkii*), and whether Tertz is a pseudo-Jew (*lzhe-evrei*) or even a pseudo-Sinyavsky (*lzhe-siniavskii*).[77] The writer himself explained that he wanted to choose a name less "beautiful and significant" than pseudonyms like Bely and Gorky, and to reverse the normal process of Jewish writers choosing Russian surnames.[78] To him, bandits and Jews were emblematic of the writer's daring, noble, and precarious position in Soviet Russia. His insistence on projecting two different ethnic identities also violated the nationalist principle of *tsel'nost'* (wholeness, integrity) which links the people's unified ethnic and cultural identity to state security.[79] The author's crimes against national identity went much deeper than using the wrong pseudonym, an inappropriate place of publication, and creating a non-Realist, mocking narrative. His actions were not misdemeanors, but felonies.

In the post-Soviet period, the literary and political devaluation in some quarters of "the sixties generation" (*shestidesiatniki*) eventually encroached on Andrei Sinyavsky's reputation. In a 1994 interview, the writer Dmitry Prigov offered an analysis of the literary legacy of the 1970s, a time when he himself was known only in narrow circles.

> In those years, to the outside world the status of unofficial writer seemed to be taken over by Solzhenitsyn, Vladimov, Sinyavsky—all the names you know, the political and social writers. . . . My circle was a kind of aesthetic opposition. . . . And, believe me, the powers were no less disgusted with our offense than with the attempt of the dissidents to create an opposition in their own, more traditionally elevated literary language. But, as you see, in the long run my circle, my sort, turned out to be in opposition not only to Soviet power but to dissidents as well. Our position was to deconstruct an attempt to create a myth or a grand theory."[80]

Prigov brushed aside the government's often harsh treatment of these "political and social" dissidents, while telling us that his own type of aesthetic dissidence brought on official wrath.[81] But even a cursory reading of *Strolls with Pushkin* shows that the author's intent was not to create or reinforce myths or theories, but to save Pushkin's texts from the state-sponsored cult of Pushkin. Prigov was not alone in his opinion that writers who were published in the Soviet Union before the Gorbachev era could be seen as a single opportunistic group; in a similar maneuver, many of those who were not published widely in Russia until after 1985 were also reduced to a single category of dissident political and social writers, for whom aesthetics is said to have been a secondary consideration. To collapse the state's interpretation and the author's intent into a single phenomenon erases distinctions which are crucial to an accurate reading of the past 175 years of Russian literature. In competing for a retroactive role in Russian dissident culture, Prigov tried to move Sinyavsky and Solzhenitsyn to the list of what he calls "superannuated literary figures," which allowed him to declare his own circle both true artists and the most genuine kind of opposition.

The ambiguity of paraliterary space lies in the fact that a primarily aesthetic choice made by a Russian writer could very easily be reread as a political act because of the text's subsequent publication history, its reception, or the hint of liberation it carried with it. Sinyavsky was accused of sending Tertz's irreverent and stylistically challenging words over to the other side of the barricades to be used by enemies of the USSR during some of the hottest years of the Cold War. The author entered the Soviet courtroom in 1966 primarily as an advocate of artistic freedom, but his defense of the artist's rights had a deep political impact.[82] He left the court as an important political force, a person whose case, along with that of co-defendant Yuli Daniel, helped forge the various dissident elements into a more coherent and effective civil rights movement. He understood the phenomenon of secondary politicization, of the workings of paraliterary space, admitting that even the "pure poetry" of Akhmatova and Pasternak found itself in conflict with the state.[83]

Of necessity Sinyavsky became an astute political actor, one of the writers who most clearly defined what creative freedom meant to him and where he stood politically, not just between the lines in veiled references to bold thoughts, but openly at the 1966 trial, after the 1993 uprising in Moscow, and during the 1996 presidential campaign, among other occasions. He countered nationalist attacks on *Strolls with Pushkin* in the mid-1970s, when it appeared in Western Europe, and in the late 1980s when it was published in Russia, asking: "What diabolical faith in your own sanctity do you have to have in your soul to allow you to deny other people the right to love their homeland, just because they don't agree with you?"[84]

The early nineties brought significant changes to Sinyavsky's relationship with Russia, especially after the appearance of a two-volume set of his works, the first such edition to be published in his homeland.[85] Sinyavsky had openly supported glasnost and perestroika and the changes in government policy that, among other things, allowed him to return to Russia both in print and in person. And what he had said of the ultranationalists in emigration he later repeated about those holding similar beliefs back in Russia. A 1990 visit to Moscow brought to mind Russian Orthodox nationalists he met in the camps who had expressed a visceral hatred of Jews and other minority groups living in the USSR. Such intolerance put him on his guard: "At that moment I understood all the depth and the danger of Russian nationalism, and I still find all this very painful."[86]

In the mid-1990s Sinyavsky reasserted the right to love his homeland as he saw fit, this time not against the Communist Party or Russian chauvinists, but against those who cheered the government's attack on the Russian White House in October 1993. This included liberal members of the intelligentsia, and such prominent conservative nationalist writers as Viktor Astafiev and Alexander Solzhenitsyn. Sinyavsky felt that writers should courageously defend themselves and others from the state, and must never gravitate towards an alliance with a "party of power."[87] He had said that "poetry and power in Russia very often find themselves if not in direct conflict, then in a complicated relationship."[88] Writers and the rest of the intelligentsia should stay away from openly supporting a government which could easily suck them in, to the detriment of both talent and conscience.[89]

Given his understanding of the perils of a mutated national pride and of aggressive righteousness, how is it that Sinyavsky wound up visiting the offices of the newspaper *Zavtra* (the ultranationalist/Communist successor to the infamous *Den'*) in the months following the government's October 1993 assault on the Russian parliament building and the subsequent street fighting in which many people were killed? What shocked this seemingly unflappable former *zek* was not just the assault, but the way that members of the intelligentsia, in the name of saving democracy and the freedoms it guaranteed, approved this violent action and called repeatedly for the closure of newspapers and journals that spread the "red-brown" message.

Sinyavsky immediately sent a letter of protest directed both at the government and the intelligentsia. In retrospect, he seemed at this traumatic moment to have lost his sense of humor, especially that life-saving irony described in the essay *On Socialist Realism* as "the faithful companion of unbelief and doubt [which] vanishes as soon as there appears a faith that does not tolerate sacrilege."[90] Having described how "irony was replaced by pathos" both in eighteenth-century literature and in Socialist Realism, Sinyavsky appeared to have undergone a comparable transition in October 1993.[91]

What was a stake for Andrei Sinyavsky at this point? Why, after October 1993, did he describe the post-Soviet period as the bitterest years of his life?[92] Why did his talent for irony finally fail him? What was the faith that did not tolerate sacrilege? What kind of politics had he hoped would evolve, and was what actually happened a violation of some specific political value or was it simply *ne to* (not right)? It is clear that Sinyavsky believed in the intelligentsia, especially his fellow "men of the sixties," and knew full well the abuses of the Soviet period, but his irreducible faith was not in any group of people, but in a virtually unrestricted freedom for minds, voices, and texts. Having once been called an enemy of the state, he understood that one sure sign of a healthy democracy and an open society was that it allowed for an opposition, in fact it required one.

What Sinyavsky said about the intelligentsia's reaction to the shelling of the White House is very close to his 1990 remarks about ultranationalists. In both cases he saw an example of what theorists of religion call a failure of charity, that is, a refusal to know and understand opposing views, accompanied by a tendency to demonize the "others," to deny them not only a voice, but to question their right to exist.[93] That he was sensitive to the status of *otherness* is clear from "Pkhentz," the story from which Sinyavsky drew a quotation in his eloquent final plea to the court in 1966: "Just think, if I am simply different from others, they have to start cursing me."[94] As Sinyavsky, and even more so as Tertz, he argued throughout his career for freedom of the imagination as the first freedom; and he imagined that a dialogue with *Zavtra* could be useful. Unlike many of his fellow writers and the intelligentsia as a whole, he was able to hear a wide range of "voices from the chorus" that were making themselves heard in post-Soviet Russia.

After October 1993, Sinyavsky became more publicly attentive to national identity and to Russianness, and the interviews published in *Zavtra* provide ample evidence of that change. In the Russian cultural-political context, the place of publication often counted for or against a writer's reputation, and sometimes even cost him his freedom. Andrei Sinyavsky's several appearances in the most widely read publication of anti-Yeltsin, antidemocratic chauvinists, the very camp that a few years back had castigated him for *Strolls with Pushkin*, forces us to rethink some of the cultural-political truisms that were operative in the 1990s.

In 1994 *Zavtra* published, with permission, the transcript of an appearance at IMLI (the Gorky Institute of World Literature) by Sinyavsky and his wife Mariya Rozanova during which they spoke about the need for the intelligentsia to always function as an opposition.[95] Both were candid about their disagreements with *Zavtra*, as well as where the couple parted company with the liberal intelligentsia. Both Sinyavsky and Rozanova made it clear that members of the intelligentsia, in their indiscriminate and unseemly support of Yeltsin, had ceded to *Zavtra* and its supporters the right to form an opposition.

Later in the same year, Sinyavsky and Rozanova appeared again in *Zavtra* at a roundtable led by Vladimir Bondarenko which included the newspaper's editor Alexander Prokhanov, Lev Anninsky, General Pavel Filatov, Stanislav Kunyaev, Vadim Kozhinov, Father Dmitry Dudko, and others. This time the topic was "Why Are the People Silent?"[96] Bondarenko said that the goal of the forum was to have different political viewpoints represented, but that many writers feared the impact that even coming to *Zavtra's* offices would have on their reputations. Mariya Rozanova spoke about the couple's recent travels around Russia and the hardship they had witnessed, and she suggested that *Zavtra* drop the nonsense it printed about international Jewish conspiracies and start focusing on the real and pressing needs of the Russian people.

Sinyavsky began by expressing his misgivings at coming to any event organized by a newspaper that loudly proclaimed its patriotism and stubbornly concentrated on finding all sources of evil outside of the ethnic Russian population. But he also rejected the intelligentsia's fear of the people, which had led to their approval of the government's violent measures the previous year. He said that he had met ignorant, violent, anti-Semitic types in the Gulag, but he never had the urge to destroy them. "The intelligentsia," he said, "has to some extent lost its sense of compassion."[97]

After Sinyavsky's death in 1997, Bondarenko wrote a warm, respectful article, accompanied by a 1995 photo of him visiting Sinyavsky and Rozanova in their Paris home.[98] Bondarenko's message, a highly unusual one for his newspaper, was that Andrei Donatovich had earned the right to tell the truth as he saw it because of the way he had lived. Bondarenko admitted that there were many arguments and unresolved differences between *Zavtra* and Sinyavsky, who was quoted as saying that it was terrible to find yourself agreeing with your old enemies and watching your own group behaving badly. *Zavtra* editors found him resistant to pressures to change his opinions, but added that each side respected the other's love for Russian literature and for Russia itself. In an equally generous spirit, the memorial article in the liberal *Nezavisimaia gazeta* mentioned the writer's visit to *Zavtra* and decided that "all his life Sinyavsky was more of a democrat than today's superdemocrats."[99]

Yevgeny Zamyatin and Andrei Sinyavsky both gave voice to the "other," irrespective of the current regime, or of whether they were living in Russia or abroad. In an autobiographical essay, Zamyatin ironically recited his own criminal record in both tsarist and Soviet Russia. For Zamyatin, the only honorable role for a writer was as a heretic and a "Scythian" who would never settle into a cozy relationship with the state, and he was disdainful of the writers who quickly turned into commissars after 1917. "Harmful literature" was not to be shunned, because in the end it would prove to be "more useful than useful literature."[100] Of the French Revolutionary Babeuf, guillotined in 1797 because he dared remember the reasons for which the Revolution had been fought, Zamyatin observed that he was "right 150 years later."[101]

Sinyavsky's openness to certain aspects of *Zavtra*'s argument can be seen as one early indication of what was to become a widespread move in Russia in the second half of the 1990s towards a centrist nationalism, strongly statist but with the expectation of a vocal opposition, and pro-Russian but without a return to the old chauvinist ways. Andrei Sinyavsky never set out to be either exemplary or political, preferring the roles of stylistic highwire artist, honorary Jewish gangster, and former *zek*. Yet, when something important was at stake, he showed the same fearless imagination in the political sphere that he displayed in his fiction and criticism. To help keep debate alive and art and its creators honest, again and again he stepped boldly and knowingly into paraliterary space.

Chapter 3 The Dangerous
Narrative of the Russian Village

During the Thaw, at a time when traditional rural communities had all but vanished from the Russian landscape, they put in a strong appearance on the pages of prose fiction. Of all postwar literary movements, Village Prose (*derevenskaia proza*) was the largest, the longest-lasting (1956–80), and the one most often subject to political readings. The village and its inhabitants achieved a higher profile in Soviet literature after 1953 than did cities and urban dwellers, factories and their workers, or battlefields and soldiers. Writers of canonical *derevenskaia proza* enjoyed an immediate legitimacy because of their rural background, and they used that authority to raise social and political issues at the level of metaphor, character, setting, and dialogue. Critics, along with some of the writers themselves after 1985, often used the same metaphors as ideological stepping stones.

What was so provocative about Village Prose? What did it threaten in Soviet and post-Soviet society? Why was it subject to so many fervently held, factually challenged, and mutually exclusive interpretations of its ideological content and its power to influence the course of events? Like most other aspects of the literary process, the "codes" for reading artistic works were subject to change, and between the mid-fifties and the end of the 1990s it is possible to identify five distinct approaches to Village Prose.[1] In each of these codes we can see the functioning of the paradigm sketched out in preceding chapters; in examining these different readings we gain insight into the evolution of politics, culture, and national identity in Russia during the second half of the twentieth century.[2]

AN UNSCHEDULED STOP ON THE ROAD
TO REFORM (1952–1959)

The first steps that eventually led to the appearance of Village Prose were taken with the encouragement of the Party, and if these early works were a threat, it was to the corrupt and inept officials in charge of the agricultural sector and to the sycophantic writers of kolkhoz literature. In the early fifties, the state wanted to generate enthusiasm and energy for the revival of the depopulated and impoverished postwar countryside, but the rural theme was still dominated by some of the most barren examples of Socialist Realism, such as Simeon Babaevsky's *Cavalier of the Golden Star* and Galina Nikolaeva's *Harvest*. Valentin Ovechkin's "District Routine" (1952) and the flood of reform essays (*ocherki*) that followed were an obvious change for the better to most readers. Ovechkin was no dissident; he worked well within the "space" of the collective farm (*kolkhoz*) and the parameters of Communist Party directives, while lobbying for improvements in agricultural administration and calling for a more accurate and lively depiction of the countryside in literature.[3]

Vladimir Pomerantsev shattered the relative quiet of this early stage with his bold 1953 essay "On Sincerity in Literature." Pomerantsev's goals were to simultaneously expose the bankruptcy of the kolkhoz novel, and encourage those writers, above all Ovechkin, who were trying to portray rural life more honestly and effectively. Essays by Fedor Abramov, Sergei Zalygin, Efim Dorosh, Vladimir Tendryakov, and others offered witty, forceful commentary on the shortcomings of kolkhoz narratives, while at the same time warning writers that to replace the *rozovaia kraska* (rosy colors) of court bards with investigative reports would not by itself improve the quality of literature. Experienced literary figures advised younger colleagues to study the best available stylistic models; the list of suggestions was full of pre-Revolutionary names, some of whom (Aksakov, Bunin, Leskov, and Dal) were being republished in the mid-fifties. By ignoring or denigrating Soviet prose and at the same time praising examples of tsarist-era culture, Thaw-era literary criticism undermined Socialist Realism aesthetically while appearing to uphold its ideological goals.

The Party looked to writers to help publicize the existence of abuses and the need for reforms in collective farm management and to encourage the all-important human "levers"—an image popularized in a controversial 1956 story by Alexander Yashin—to carry out changes on the local level. For these reasons, there was a degree of official tolerance, even enthusiasm, for the new rural essay. However, the countryside was not a place where the Party's control of either literature or agriculture could be seriously challenged, and when the suggestions for change were too bold, or the tone too sarcastic, editors were reprimanded and writers either had to recast their works or were unable to get them passed for publication. This was typical of official responses to Thaw literature; critical comments were permitted, but only within definite, and frequently changing, limits.

After a few years had passed, writers who had been focusing on the problems of collective farms began to migrate towards the village and depictions of the traditional way of life they knew from childhood and from family stories. These writers moved from an examination of the surface of contemporary rural life to roots deep in the past. Dorosh's *Rural Diary* (*Derevenskii dnevnik*), works by Tendryakov and Yuri Kazakov, and Vladimir Soloukhin's *Vladimir Country Roads* (*Vladimirskie proselki*) helped to shift the locus of action from the postwar Soviet countryside back to the Russian village, a major change in chronotopes, and from young agronomists full of innovations to old peasants full of memories.

The essays and stories of the later 1950s, in particular Kazakov's "The Old Woman by the Sea" ("Pomorka," 1958), and Abramov's first novel *Brothers and Sisters* (*Brat'ia i sestry*, 1958) prepared readers for Solzhenitsyn's "Matryona's Home" ("Matrenin dvor"), a work that was written during the fifties, but which did not appear until January 1963. The state-supported initiative to energize the collectivized countryside wound up improving the quality and effectiveness of Soviet rural prose which rapidly mutated into a movement with broad popular appeal, substantial critical backing, and all the wrong values. At the Twentieth Party Congress, writers were asked to help tell the truth about history "and that's what Abramov, Mozhaev and others did, openly, honestly, and without distortion."[4]

Yitzak Brudny, in his study of Russian nationalism from Stalin's death until the end of the USSR, takes this early period very seriously.[5] What began as a "broad anti-Stalinist alliance" around the journal *Novyi mir* soon began to split along liberal, anti-Stalinist and conservative, pro-peasant lines. Members of the young urban intelligentsia were energized by such events as the 1957 World Youth Festival in Moscow, one more "identity-threatening culture shock" for village-born writers, who were new to the city, western influences, and intelligentsia circles.[6]

Khrushchev aided and abetted the reemergence of "politics by culture" in several ways.[7] The Twentieth Party Congress in 1956 of course opened up a widespread discussion of the Stalinist legacy. Khrushchev encouraged a revival of the thick journal, the traditional location for culturally grounded political debate, some of which contained criticism of government policies in agriculture. The merging of small collective farms into larger enterprises that began in 1957 was a particular shock to rural writers because they knew that it would further weaken the Russian village: "In the small kolkhoz, the peasants had been able to preserve to a large extent the sense of intimacy and solidarity of the old village that had helped them to survive the difficult war and postwar years."[8] Attempts by Khrushchev to further weaken Russian Orthodoxy by closing monasteries and churches drove religious activity underground, and stimulated an above-ground architectural preservationist movement. Rapid and often careless industrial growth gave rise to environmentalism. The village-centered literature that began to develop during the second half of the fifties took up the plight of peasants, nature, churches and other historical monuments with energy and imagination.

FROM THE SOVIET COUNTRYSIDE
TO THE RUSSIAN VILLAGE (1960–1984)

Literature on rural themes moved from the kolkhoz back to the village, from the Soviet Union back to Russia, and from planning for the future to nostalgia for the past. The responses, positive and negative, to "Matryona's Home," Abramov's "Round and About" ("Vokrug da okolo") and Yashin's "Vologda Wedding" ("Vologodskaia svad'ba"), all published at about the same time, set the tone and the agenda for critical discussion of the new rural literature.[9] It is easy to see what a Party-line critic would object to in the characterization and ethos of Solzhenitsyn's story: the positive hero is an old peasant woman working outside the kolkhoz framework, while the narrator is a former political prisoner returning after 1953 to a countryside that has also fallen victim to Soviet policy. In "Matryona's Home," the reader could see what was wrong with post-

Revolutionary society that had been right about Russian village life. The ethos was bad enough, but the style was problematic as well, not only in Matryona's authentic rural speech, but in the narrator's elevated rhetoric, reminiscent of the rebellious seventeenth-century Archpriest Avvakum, in the final passage about the righteous ones like Matryona who keep the nation from perishing. Preserving the Soviet Union from harm was the duty of the Party, the military, border guards, censors, customs officials, and the secret police, not the responsibility of elderly peasants.

One of the liveliest literary-critical battles of the 1960s was waged over what name to give the new rural prose. As writers began to embrace village settings and themes, and longer stories and novels appeared, "Ovechkin-style" sketch and "rural" essay no longer fit. In the politics of typology, distinctions made within Socialist Realism raised concerns because they gave the lie to the myth of a unified culture that supported agreed-upon goals for the country; it would mean that the great Soviet cultural project had failed or had been forced to make a tactical retreat. The rules of discussion eased up enough after 1953 to allow for a more sophisticated taxonomy appropriate to a literature that was developing along a number of lines, only one of which was Socialist Realism as it had been defined two decades earlier. The new writing that focused in a detailed, often lyrical, way on village life was too widespread a phenomenon not to be discussed as a whole, even if it was only to condemn the trend while praising more conventional works about collective farm life.

The critical term that eventually prevailed was, of course, "Village Prose," but not without a protracted fight that illustrates how ideological messages could be read not only between the lines of a text but also within the terms used to describe literary movements. Of those who objected to the final choice, some felt that it marginalized talented writers as simply literate peasants, while others feared the increased attention and authority these backward-looking writers would get when given their own distinctive label. "A whole pleiad of critics . . . entered the literary process with articles about 'village prose,'" which became not so much an object of literary-critical study as "an occasion for argument about the most important contemporary problems."[10]

The number and variety of responses is not surprising, given that contrary to the tenets of Socialist Realism and the ethos of Soviet life this new prose privileged the past, old people, village life, eccentricity, spiritual depth, the preservation of nature, and a strong Russian national identity based on a primary attachment to one's native region, the *malaia rodina*. Village Prose gave readers the impression that the real Russia consisted of many thousands of small homelands, linked by unpaved country roads. Whether directly or by implication, writers criticized the predominantly urban values of Soviet society which in their minds had led to the excesses of the collectivization drive, the subsequent neglect and mismanagement of agriculture, and the failure to appreciate the rural war effort and prevent postwar depopulation and decline.

In his 1972 article "Against Antihistoricism," Alexander Yakovlev claimed that this literature's appeal to pre-Revolutionary values and a Russian identity grounded in ethnicity could easily cross the line from non-Soviet to anti-Soviet, and from patriotic to chauvinistic.[11] He wrote that the portrayal of Soviet reality was seriously distorted by lyrical digressions on patriarchal peasant life and by a negative attitude towards the intelligentsia and urban society. The astute Yakovlev focused not on the artistic works themselves, but on critical essays by Mikhail Lobanov and a host of others—Kozhinov, Semanov, Lanshchikov, and Mikhailov—who gave this vision of contemporary life a theoretical framework with their concept of the sources (*istoki*) of national culture and moral values. Shunning words like "socialist" and "kolkhoz" and the scientific analysis of historical forces, these critics used Village Prose and other Russophile literature to advance a fundamentally non-Soviet agenda, an ideological stand (*ideinaia pozitsiia*) which Yakovlev called *neopochvennichestvo*, that is, a revival of Fedor Dostoevsky's "native soil" movement.

Yakovlev's lengthy and strongly worded defense of Soviet patriotism against peasant nationalism ought to have earned him the thanks of a grateful Party, but instead he was sent on a diplomatic mission that kept him in Canada for ten years, out of the fray. The objections Yakovlev raised to what he saw as a false idyll of rural life were to resurface, like Yakovlev himself, during the second half of the 1980s. Alexander Yakovlev was not the only official who felt uneasy about the spontaneous growth of a culturally based, backward-glancing nationalism, but the response to his broadside is one of many pieces of evidence that Village Prose was not seen as fundamentally dangerous by the Party leadership, even as writers moved further and further away from Socialist Realism and as they regularly challenged the censors. There were times when a work was too positive about religion or too negative about collectivization, but the most problematic material was generally weeded out before permission was given to publish. Throughout the "stagnant years" of Brezhnev's reign (1964–82), there is abundant evidence that a level of Russianness in rural literature was not only tolerated, but rewarded.

The nationalization of Communism that began after 1934 intensified during the war, was artificially whipped up again in 1949, and was fully in evidence under Brezhnev.[12] Perfunctory respect was still paid to the multicultural nation, but the pro-Russian faction in the Party gave substantial support to the nationalistic rural literature of Vasily Belov, Valentin Rasputin, and many others. Some theoreticians of Socialist Realism tried to accommodate this body of work under an increasingly flexible rubric of *zrelyi sotsrealizm* (mature Socialist Realism) and in that way to preserve a unified facade as long as possible.

While Village Prose was openly criticized by some as being insufficiently Soviet, it was praised by others, at least implicitly, for promoting a Russian patriotism that was not implacably anti-Communist. In an era when so much interesting writing was coming out underground (*samizdat*) or abroad (*tamizdat*), a point brought home by the publicity surrounding the Brodsky hearing of 1964 and the Sinyavsky and Daniel trial of 1966, it was important to salvage something of quality for *gosizdat* (state-approved publications).

Brudny describes the mid-1960s as the period when the government initiated a "policy of inclusion" that lasted until Brezhnev's death in 1982. To grant a "partial voice" to "the emerging group of Russian nationalist intellectuals," including writers and critics of both rural and urban backgrounds, could strengthen the regime and counteract the movement of other Soviet literature to the underground and abroad. The new ruralists frequently criticized official policy, but, unlike the writers of Youth and Urban Prose, nationalist writers were fundamentally antiwestern and pro-authoritarian so the differences did not often go beyond an acceptable level.[13] Government support and even favoritism took a number of forms: permission to found new journals, transfer of editorial control at existing journals and publishing houses, appointment to positions of authority in the Russian and Soviet writers unions, phenomenally large press runs for periodicals and books, national prizes, and some easing up of censorship. In fact, as controls tightened for many liberal urban writers beginning around 1964, they were loosened for conservative nationalists.[14] The government wished to avert the possibility of rural writers following their urban colleagues into deeply critical waters, and to buy the support of millions of readers by making lively, often moving, non–Socialist Realist texts easily available to the broad reading public.

Did the government get what it paid for? Not exactly, says Brudny. There was less frustration among readers during the Brezhnev years as nationalist journals and books offered interesting and provocative literary selections from rural writers in approximately one hundred million copies between 1971 and 1982. Periodicals with a variety of political orientations carried on spirited debates which mirrored divisions within the Central Committee itself. The radical nationalists at *Molodaia gvardiia* (Young Guard) were accused by more liberal, proreform critics at *Novyi mir* (New World) and *Literaturnaia gazeta* (Literary Gazette) of having "distorted the political message of the Village Prose writers."[15] Village Prose was not the only raw material available for nationalist commentators: they also made good use of opportunities presented in new biographies of pre-Revolutionary figures such as Faddei Bulgarin, Ivan Goncharov, and the monk Grigory Rasputin, and during the anniversary years of historical events (the medieval Battle of Kulikovo, in 1980) and great writers, such as Dostoevsky, the centenary of whose death was commemorated in 1981 following decades of relative neglect.[16]

Yakovlev's 1972 article appeared after several years of ongoing debate, with the more fervent nationalists pushing the discussion in directions that looked increasingly non-Soviet. There was some curbing of blatant challenges to Soviet ideology, but the nationalists still seemed less of a threat to the regime than the other kinds of opposition it faced at home and abroad during the last decade of Brezhnev's reign. As the years passed, these relatively privileged nationalists in the literary world became increasingly unhappy that they were not, in the end, influencing the government in any substantial way on agricultural, preservationist, and environmental issues, and that support for them was "more a golden straightjacket than a policy initiative."[17]

In 1982, Yury Andropov reestablished tighter party control and the USSR Writers Union, on orders from the Central Committee, came out firmly against discussions of collectivization that contradicted the official version; this policy of closer oversight of the ruralists was continued by Konstantin Chernenko. While the range of discussion may have been narrowed and expectations for any benefit to the government were lowered, nationalist writers still enjoyed tremendous exposure to the readers, with twenty-four million copies of books by the best-known figures appearing just between 1983 and 1985, not counting journals that also carried their work. Brudny concludes that Andropov saw the liberals failing to serve as a counterweight to the growing independence of conservative nationalists, and that one "was left with little choice but to present the party as an institution that no longer favored any particular ideological group within the Soviet intellectual elite."[18] Neither inclusion nor coercion was as effective a strategy with writers as it had been in the past.

SPEAKING FRANKLY ABOUT RURAL
LIFE (1985–1987)

Václav Havel might be expected to give primacy to the forbidden texts of the second, parallel cultures that flourished under Communist regimes in the USSR and Eastern Europe, but in fact he believed that "like it or not, it is the 'first' culture that remains the decisive sphere" and only if some of the "suppressed spiritual potential" of the people can reach this first culture does the society have a future.[19] When glasnost began in the mid-1980s, the *derevenshchiki* were praised as having been a significant factor in the preservation and transmission of just such a "moral-philosophical 'nucleus'"—and the stylistic legacy of classical Russian literature—to readers and writers for nearly three decades.[20] All past cultural resistance to Socialist Realism was seen briefly as a "single anti-world," in which Village Prose had played an important and honorable role.[21] In a society where a single text often dominated literary-political discussions until it yielded to the next "one text," the *derevenshchiki* had supplied many stimuli for debate, especially during the decade between the appearance of Belov's *An Ordinary Matter* (*Privychnoe delo*, 1966) and Rasputin's *Farewell to Matyora* (*Proshchanie s Materoi*, 1976).

It was tempting to take a retrospective look at Village Prose after 1985, because by then the movement seemed to writers and critics alike to have come to an end, no longer the vital literary genre it had been in the sixties and seventies. After more than two productive decades, its tropes were worn out and subject to parody, and, in branching out, its writers touched upon subjects like the excesses of collectivization that brought them into conflict with the censors. The group was further weakened in the first half of the 1980s by the deaths of Tendryakov, Kazakov, and Abramov, the earlier demise of Shukshin, Rubtsov, Ovechkin, and Dorosh, and by injuries Rasputin suffered in a robbery.[22] The surviving writers, however, had supporters within the Russified power structure and were still a force to be reckoned with, especially in the RSFSR Writers Union and in their role as environmental activists.

Several well-known ruralists used the window of opportunity that glasnost offered to release works that moved away from lyrical memories of childhood and a rapidly disappearing way of life into a violent present where crime and family troubles were symptomatic of deep social rifts. Rasputin's "The Fire," Astafiev's *A Sad Detective* and "Fishing for Gudgeon in Georgia," and Belov's *The Best Is Yet to Come* (*Vse vperedi*) were set, respectively, in a logging settlement, a provincial city, Georgia, and Moscow and its suburbs, far from the authors' native regions. Their bitter, hopeless tone seemed somewhat out of place when the three works first appeared in 1985–86, but eerily prescient a few years later.

Ekaterina Starikova rang the alarm bell in 1986 when she first saw a Dostoevsky-like antipathy towards "others," particularly Jews, in these stories, which she felt might add to the country's already unsettled atmosphere.[23] Dostoevsky's work, particularly *Demons* and *Diary of a Writer,* was an acknowledged influence on the erstwhile *derevenshchiki.* If anything, Dostoevsky's comments were even more negative about Jews, but Starikova reminds us that he wrote before the Holocaust and even before the wave of Russian pogroms that began in earnest in 1881; an incomparably greater artistic talent, he suffered no loss of reputation as a writer as a result of his provocative comments.[24] Rural writers, however, could not count on such a forgiving, and forgetful, attitude. Critic Natan Eidelman's troubled letter to Viktor Astafiev about the disdain for non-Russians openly displayed in the author's recent works elicited an angry response that quickly made the rounds in Russia and abroad.[25]

It is hard, and hardly necessary, to feel any sympathy for rural writers who were attacked because of the chauvinist statements issuing forth from their pens and their lips. It is equally unnecessary to abandon scholarly standards and even simple logic in evaluating the connection between their prejudice and their art. As late as the year 2000, *Partisan Review* carried critic Maxim Shrayer's essay "Anti-Semitism and the Decline of Village Prose," which re-muddied waters that had begun to clear. The author must have been aware that the audience for this journal was unlikely to have prior knowledge of the movement, and this allowed him to skip over some simple facts of Russian literary history.

The core of Shrayer's argument is that the "ethical degradation" of anti-Semitic sentiments led directly to the "aesthetic disfigurement" of Village Prose.[26] Quotations from three authors—Astafiev, Rasputin, and Belov—give an accurate sense of their clumsy, noxious remarks on the role of Jews in Russian history. Shrayer allows the reader to believe that these statements were made at a time when Village Prose was at its height, although the weight of evidence points to the opposite conclusion, that it was well past its prime and was no longer seen as a coherent movement. While similar observations from several non–Village Prose writers and earlier figures are mentioned, Shrayer's examples do not include the most obvious choice, Fedor Dostoevsky, whose essay "The Jewish Question" in the 1877 edition of *Diary of a Writer* was considered to have been vicious even at the time.[27] The term "Village Prose" is used by

Shrayer to refer to virtually any text by a rural-born writer rather than to a literary school with a well-defined aesthetic and a recognizable life span.[28] The prevailing opinion among scholars and readers is that there were only traces of anti-Jewish sentiment in published works by rural writers before the mid-1980s, but that chauvinism was at that time growing in urban circles. But for his argument to work, Shrayer has to make the most of the evidence that he has, at times resorting to the charge of prejudice-by-allegory. Such maneuvers obscure the history of Soviet Russian chauvinism, an ideological trend that arose without the help of the *derevenshchiki,* and which outlasted their active participation. It also obscures the fairly broad political spectrum along which works of Village Prose can be placed.

The open expression of prejudice against Jews in Russian society during the years after 1985 was partly a result of the freeing up of public discourse at a time when nearly everything in Soviet Russian life seemed to be falling apart. The fears aroused by the high-profile Pamyat (Memory) group in the second half of the 1980s stimulated a search for the origins of chauvinism in the literary world that soon led back to Village Prose and to a reevaluation not just of the glasnost-era work of village-born writers but of post-Stalinist rural literature as a whole. Pamyat was one manifestation of a movement that had arisen in the 1960s among urban members of the technological intelligentsia, and its sympathizers took inspiration from pre-Revolutionary tracts like the *Protocols of the Elders of Zion* and from official Soviet anti-Zionist material. A number of rural writers also began to espouse ultranationalist opinions, stepping out of the frame of artistic literature and plunging into the impassioned world of *publitsistika.* Rather than inspiring the rise of chauvinism, they seem—and this is hardly to their credit—to have been inspired and guided by it.

Brudny concentrates on the choice Russian nationalists were forced to make during these years, whether to support or oppose the process of reform. Gorbachev sought the good will and energies of the nationalist intelligentsia, and issues dear to the ruralists—like the environment and moral decline—began to be debated on a national level. But the fact that Alexander Yakovlev was back in ruling circles as the "chief ideologue of perestroika and the architect of Gorbachev's cultural policies" sent another message to the nationalists, and it is not surprising that the distance between them and the government quickly widened; many conservative and radical nationalists chose to reject glasnost and perestroika, and to "render full support to the conservative elements within the party, the army, the KGB, who were fighting to preserve a multinational empire, authoritarian form of government, and the command economy."[29]

WHERE HAS RUSSIA BEEN, WHERE IS
IT HEADED, AND WHOSE FAULT IS IT?
(1988–1996)

In the unstable atmosphere of the post-perestroika years, there was an attempt to determine the contributing factors to a host of troubles, past and present. The accusation that certain types of literature were dangerous to society came primarily from outside government and Party circles. In Writers Union meetings, in the pages of thick journals and literary newspapers, and in émigré and scholarly circles abroad, a heated debate took place over the political role that literary texts, especially Village Prose, were playing at this crucial moment in Russia's history.[30] Did *derevenskaia proza* simply advocate a return to the best of traditional Russia as the Soviet experiment reached an end? Was this literature hopelessly, impractically mired in nineteenth-century Slavophile and *pochvennik* (native-soil) philosophy? Or was its message closer to a Communist revanchism or even neo-Nazism?

Several prominent *derevenshchiki* added to the confusion by giving speeches, writing essays, and signing joint letters that sharply criticized many of the changes that had been proposed since 1985. The most widely publicized of these documents was "The Letter of the Russian Writers"—including the ruralists Rasputin, Krupin, Lichutin, Likhonosov, and Proskurin (among the original seventy-four names)—which appeared first in the March 2, 1990 issue of the newspaper *Literaturnaia Rossiia,* and then was reprinted with additional signatures, including that of Belov, elsewhere. This letter defended Pamyat, attacked those it accused of carrying out a policy of "genocide" against Russia, and went so far as imply Jewish complicity in the pogroms and the Holocaust.

The wealth of delayed and repressed works that appeared during these years included the writings of ruralists, living and dead. Tendryakov's trio of stories about collectivization, written between 1969 and 1971, were published in *Novyi mir* in March 1988; they provided a harrowing account of the excesses of the collectivization process, and further evidence of the depth of the author's talent. Soloukhin's desk drawer contained a variety of narratives, from a story about trying to bury his mother which was held back for twenty years because of its pro-Orthodox orientation, to a self-serving autobiography called *Laughter Behind My Left Shoulder* (*Smekh za levym plechom*), and an angrily ultranationalist historical novel, *The Last Stage* (*Posledniaia stupen'*).

In Belov's chronicle of collectivization *The Critical Year* (*God velikogo pereloma*), appearing in *Novyi mir* in March 1989, the primary goal seems to have been placing blame on Jews, and it provided additional examples of Belov's by then well-known opinions. Along with defending Pamyat, the most visible and widely attacked chauvinist group, some rural writers associated themselves with the emerging Red-Brown (Communist-ultranationalist) alliance all the way through the 1996 presidential election. However, at actual moments of national upheaval in August 1991 and October 1993, the *derevenshchiki* were less visible, whether from an absence of conviction or an excess of caution, somewhat like acquaintances of the Decembrists who avoided Palace Square on the fateful day. As a result of the October 1993 crisis, cultural-political groupings were disturbed, as Astafiev (and Solzhenitsyn from exile) along with many liberal members of the intelligentsia supported Yeltsin's attack on the parliament, while Andrei Sinyavsky and a number of other former dissidents wound up in opposition.

Because the situation in the disintegrating Soviet Union and the new Russian Federation was often unclear, and because the stakes were so high, the assessment of Village Prose from 1988 through 1993 was more frenzied than thoughtful. Artistic works themselves were rarely cited in extended ideological arguments, a sign that rural literature had become a *pretext* for debate and was no longer a *text* for analyis.[31] It was never clearly articulated which texts formed the basis for a given argument, and whether any distinction was being made between the sublimated politics found in a work of fiction and direct statements made by the same writer in public letters, petitions, speeches, and journalistic essays a dozen or more years later. Depending on a given critic's political stance, the rural narrative looked like a dangerously protofascist document to be condemned out of hand, or a powerful salvation text, believed implicitly and defended vehemently. Its writer could be seen as a menace or a martyr. And, as in so many political debates during those turbulent years, the health—and the very life—of the nation were said to be at risk at virtually every moment.

Viktor Erofeyev's July 1990 "obituary" for Soviet literature included *derevenskaia proza* as one of three divisions of the canon, the other two being *ofitsioznaia* (semiofficial, toadying), and *liberal'naia* (liberal).[32] Emigré poet Naum Korzhavin and critic Galina Belaya were two of the more effective voices asking that texts from the 1960s and 1970s not lose their well-deserved standing in the canon.[33] They and others began to advance the idea that a truly dangerous text is the one that does not honor historical truth. Much attention was paid to metaphors of rural literature that were ripe for misuse; Galina Belaya described the "romanticised world" of the traditional village, whose depiction in Village Prose "was fraught with hidden dangers." She identified the moment when "artistic-philosophical metaphor[s]" mutated into a "philosophy of history," and nostalgia became part of a political agenda promoting a return to the past.[34] Despite efforts to salvage the aesthetic, and to some extent moral, reputation of canonical *derevenskaia proza* for the sake of an accurate account, Village Prose during these years was given two related political readings, (1) as a Soviet literature of compromise, if not collaboration; and (2) as a protochauvinist, even protofascist Russian literature, as *natsrealizm* (nationalist Realism).[35]

In the crucial final years of the USSR's existence, Brudny notes, for all the institutional advantages the nationalists enjoyed when Gorbachev came to power they were unable to capitalize on their strong position. They did successfully lobby, along with other groups, against the planned river diversion project in 1986–87, and Rasputin, Astafiev, and Belov were appointed to the new Congress of People's Deputies in 1989, with Belov being chosen for the Supreme Soviet as well.[36] There was, of course, the very public flirtation with Pamyat and several related groups. However, while liberal backers of change organized hundreds of political groups in 1988 and 1989 and took an active part in elections for national and republic congresses, nationalists concentrated more on promoting their agenda in the cultural sphere at Writers Union meetings and in the journals they still controlled.[37] The opening up of public discourse was bringing politics out of its cultural refuge, and mass printings of journals and books could no longer be sustained by government subsidies. Cultural nationalists did not openly participate in the coup attempt in August 1991 and the uprising in October 1993, and for all practical purposes their alliance with the Communists dissolved with Zyuganov's loss in the 1996 presidential race, as Russia began to move slowly away from both the Reds and the Browns.

THE LEGACY OF VILLAGE PROSE (1997–2002)

After 1995, as the predicted apocalyptic scenarios did not materialize, the Communist-nationalist coalition disintegrated, and the more extreme political actors and parties were pushed to the periphery of Russian affairs or off the screen altogether. The spring 1999 NATO bombing campaign in the former Yugoslavia helped to speed up the ongoing movement towards a centrist national identity in Russia, as did events in Chechnya after August 1999, including the deadly explosions in Moscow and elsewhere. That autumn Alexander Yakovlev, who had warned in the past of the dangerous potential of Village Prose, upheld, knowingly or not, one of this school's basic concepts when he said that "my motherland is not Russia, but the village of Korolyovo in the Yaroslavl region."[38] No *derevenshchik* could have given a more accurate description of the "small homeland."

When asked in December 1999 to name texts that would give Americans the deepest understanding of twentieth-century Russian identity, philosopher Igor Chubais, brother of Anatoly Chubais, responded that there were cultural layers that had not been sufficiently examined for the true picture they gave of Russia. "A movement like Village Prose had great social-philosophical meaning. Why did they write about the countryside when the city was a much more comfortable, attractive place to live? Because in the village, in that small community, you couldn't lie to yourself or to others. A lie might come across the television screen but it wouldn't work in face-to-face encounters. Village Prose was a way to save ourselves in the midst of all these ideological lies, and it emphasized the Russianness and not the Sovietness of our culture."[39]

The nation was coming together around a moderate form of nationalism, with a rudimentary political process, the beginnings of a civil society, and an economy that was recovering from the August 1998 crash. At the same time, the role of contemporary literature in the life of the state and society had continued to decline, and rural writers had for the most part left the political arena. Astafiev, for example, by the early nineties had retreated to his native Krasnoyarsk, from which he criticized ongoing attempts to ethnically cleanse the Russian canon of aliens, openly abhorred any alliance between nationalists and Communists, and supported Yeltsin's attack on the parliament building in 1993. He died in 2001, and Fazil Iskander said of him that Astafiev had "stylistically conquered fate."[40] After 1996, Rasputin was often heard to voice regrets over his ten-year investment in public life. Vladimir Krupin focused on the less controversial aspects of Russian Orthodoxy, and although Vladimir Lichutin and Vasily Belov continued to sputter about the cosmopolitan menace and other threats to Russia, few outside their own circle listened anymore. All these factors taken together meant that there were fewer reasons to accuse Village Prose of having endangered Russia.

The relative calm at the end of the 1990s encouraged a new series of backward glances to sum up the twentieth century's cultural achievements, and in this retrospective view room was found for the best of Village Prose, which was said to have preserved a way of life in the national memory. If it had not improved productivity in agriculture, and had not saved the traditional village from further depopulation and decline, neither had it burned down the city, to paraphrase the accusation made against Turgenev's *Fathers and Sons* in an earlier age. Writers like Yashin, Kazakov, Shukshin, and Abramov were among those "who did not break under the weight of circumstance."[41]

In a 1999 review essay in *Novyi mir*, Olga Slavnikova, a literary figure from Ekaterinburg, explained what Village Prose had meant to her in the decades leading up to 1985. Although grounded in a detailed depiction of the annual cycles of rural life, *derevenskaia proza* had become more than a "physiological essay," adding thoughtful passages about alienation from one's surroundings and from the natural world, about the loss of a close network of family and friends, and about the economic stresses experienced in an increasingly materialistic society. Village Prose gave the Russian language, worn down by the bureaucratic style of Soviet newspapers, "a lifesaving injection" of northern Russian and Siberian dialects that were still very much in use.[42] Among the works written before the Gorbachev era there were genuine classics, not just of rural literature but of Russian literature as a whole. The texts from 1985 to 1995 were more provincial and artistically uninteresting, trying to argue one cause for a set of complex historical developments. Slavnikova saw these later works as more dangerous to the writers' own reputations than to anything else, because in violating the truth of history they had created bad, unconvincing art, but she was gratified to witness Rasputin's artistic recovery with the 1997 story "The Vision" ("Videnie") whose "radiant and sensitive" view of reality looked past "autumnal sadness" towards a light in the distance.[43]

Valentin Rasputin was the writer whose reputation had most suffered during the preceding period and his was the reputation that made the most noticeable recovery after 1996. On the occasion of his sixtieth birthday in 1997, a *Nezavisimaia gazeta* tribute saw in Rasputin a writer who had always encouraged readers to remember the past because it would give the nation the firm grounding it needed to move into the future. His most powerful works, like *Live and Remember* (*Zhivi i pomni*) had the epic quality of being "not 'against' but only 'for.'"[44] The stories Rasputin published after 1996, especially "The House in the Village" ("Izba") were well-received, stimulating what Alexander Ageev called the first "serious critical conversation" about the author since "The Fire" was published during the first year of the Gorbachev era. After that had come an avalanche of long-delayed works from a variety of writers, and Rasputin's own "incomprehensible current affairs articles which brought him neither honor nor fame."[45] Critics who had avidly read every new work of his in the 1970s could not bring themselves to discuss Rasputin as a writer during his ten-year-long political digression.

Rasputin was appointed to the government's new Council for the Russian Language early in 2000, and in the spring of that year won the lucrative Solzhenitsyn Prize.[46] In announcing the award, the *Literaturnaia gazeta* staff declared in a collective statement that while one naturally linked Rasputin with a particular sociopolitical movement, he was "unarguably one of the outstanding writers of Russian prose during the second half of the twentieth century," and that this award marked "the restoration of fairness" in the judging of literary talent.[47] At the awards ceremony writers from opposing camps were at long last willing to appear in public together after years of neither reading nor listening to one other. The words of those on the "other" side were no longer felt to be as dangerous to national well-being as they had seemed in the past.[48]

Alexander Solzhenitsyn's presentation speech, along with an enthusiastic appraisal of the laureate's career, placed Rasputin's writing in context. "In the 1970s there was a silent revolution in Soviet literature that was not immediately noticed, since it happened without upheaval, without a shadow of dissident challenge. Overturning nothing and not making an explosion just for effect, a large group of writers began to act as if no such thing as Socialist Realism had been . . . imposed. Silently neutralizing it, they began to write *simply*, without trying to please the Soviet regime, as if they had forgotten about its existence."[49] *Live and Remember* is the Rasputin work that receives most of Solzhenitsyn's attention because of its compassionate treatment of a deserter and his wife, a daring literary gesture in the seventies.

It is ironic that the year 1974, when this novel was published, was the same year that Solzhenitsyn was arrested, charged with treason, and expelled from the USSR on account of his own texts. Nine years earlier, in September 1965, Rasputin had been attending a seminar in Siberia for young writers that launched his career while back in Moscow Solzhenitsyn's archive was seized, and Sinyavsky and Daniel were arrested for sending anti-Soviet works abroad under a pseudonym. Instead of resenting the fact that Rasputin and other *derevenshchiki* were treated well in the USSR, spending no time in the Gulag or in exile, Solzhenitsyn credits them with being powerful adversaries of official Soviet literature, acting for the people and without fear of the regime. In a real sense, Solzhenitsyn reminds us that the absence of punishment does not mean that no risks were taken.

Rasputin's acceptance speech gave a thoughtful, if negative, appraisal of the post-Soviet relationship between literature and society. Describing himself as being on the losing side, he called the patriarchal character of Russia, as seen in Village Prose, "not a cemetery, but a storeroom," and added that "until quite recently our literature was an advocate for the people even in secular matters, understanding justice as truth and lawlessness as an untruth to which one must never become reconciled. . . . Literature has declined, but not completely."[50] After calling the type of literature popular in Russia in the year 2000 a "spiritual mutation," Rasputin ended with an image of himself standing with other writers on a constantly shrinking ice floe, which serves them as a kind of ark, as they gaze at the horizon in hopes of finally seeing the shore and a new Mount Ararat rising above the floodwaters.

The choice of Rasputin was not without controversy and critic Alla Latynina noted that "the political evaluation of texts still predominates over aesthetic appreciation. And 'conservative' is still a nasty word in our press." She did not like Rasputin's political journalism, but knows that "*Borrowed Time, Farewell to Matyora,* and 'French Lessons' will be part of every future textbook of twentieth-century literature. And we might just want to recall how progressive critics once wrote frenzied denunciations of Dostoevsky, Fet, and Leskov, opinions that now make only a curious footnote in these authors' collected works."[51]

The gradual passing away of the remaining leaders of this once-substantial group of writers has provided occasions for general observations on what *derevenskaia proza* meant to Russia. The deaths since 1995 of Soloukhin, Mozhaev, Zalygin, and Astafiev brought recollections of their specific contributions and of the movement as a whole. The boldness of their words and the risks they took under the Soviet regime can be overstated, as in the tribute to Soloukhin that credits him with being the first to call October 1917 not a revolution but a coup, and the first to debunk the myth of Lenin.[52] There have been attempts to show them as having truly menaced the post-Revolutionary government without ever hurting Russia itself or abandoning their homeland for warmer climes.

Although these were writers of differing talents and interests, what unified them was their deep knowledge of rural life, their attachment to the regions in which they grew up, and their concern for the future of nature and culture in rural areas. The original impact of their works and the extent to which they had been at times more honest about the past and present in the countryside than the censorship allowed became better known, and the differing responses they made to developments after 1985 were more accurately understood. It seemed fitting that Solzhenitsyn's *Gulag Archipelago,* which can be called the "last dangerous text," was published for the first time in Russia in 1989, in *Novyi mir,* whose editor, Sergei Zalygin, was a liberal nationalist writer from a Siberian village.[53]

HOW DANGEROUS WAS THE STORY OF RURAL RUSSIA? WHAT HAPPENED THAT WOULD NOT HAVE HAPPENED WITHOUT THE AGENCY OF VILLAGE PROSE?

Two arguments:

(1) Writers born in the countryside helped save Russian literature from the depths to which it had sunk by 1953. They ignored the tenets of Socialist Realism and wrote fresh, honest works using the authentic, still-living language of rural Russia. Although censorship prevented them from telling the whole truth, they still were able to convey a vivid picture of the values and rituals of traditional peasant life, and the difficulties peasants endured from collectivization, war, and postwar mismanagement. The Village Prose writers were a danger to the Party's control of literature and to the myth of a prosperous Soviet countryside.

(2) Village Prose contributed to the rise of dangerous chauvinist tendencies in Russia through its support for the nationalization of communism. It offered a falsely utopian picture of the countryside which could be put to dangerous ends since it encouraged a search for the forces guilty of destroying the idyllic places of the writers' childhood. Ruralists prospered under the Soviet regime while urban writers were suffering for their truth-telling texts. It is no surprise that the surviving Village Prose writers vigorously opposed change after 1985 and continued to support the Communist Party which had treated them so well and the urban ultranationalists who accorded them such respect.

The entire rural canon (c.1956–80) has been reexamined as a possible stimulus for the extreme nationalism that surfaced in the late 1980s. This rereading has been carried out both by those who feared the spread of chauvinism in Russia as well as by those who saw the very same phenomenon as the kind of uncompromisingly patriotic voice that was needed to save their beleaguered country. And, because much of Village Prose flourished "above ground," the movement has been examined for the political and moral implications of artistic success in a totalitarian age: What price did rural writers pay for survival and publication during the stagnant years?

An in-depth look at the life of the prominent writer Fedor Abramov (1920–83) allows us to explore key aspects of the two arguments summarized above: the potential for misuse of the utopian vision in *derevenskaia proza,* and the nature of the rural writer's relationship to the state. In 1990, Galina Belaya saw the real-life conflation of the two identities of Village Prose as "the tragic paradox of Russian culture today—the degeneration of yesterday's opponents of the regime into reactionary ideologists blocking the nation's way out of the abyss."[54] We will see how the *derevenshchiki* and their works both undermined and upheld the Soviet regime, and where they stood at the threshold of a new age.

READING FEDOR ABRAMOV

Fedor Abramov was one of the boldest, best-known, and best-connected post-Stalinist rural writers, whose works, both fiction and nonfiction, stimulated lively discussion and sometimes provoked an official rebuke. Although he died two years before Mikhail Gorbachev came to power, Abramov left behind a drawerful of delayed texts whose publication added to glasnost-era debate and gave readers a more detailed indication of what he knew and felt about rural life in the Soviet era. And yet he also left behind questions for which he himself had not found satisfactory answers.

In the 1990 article "Fedor Abramov's Path," Igor Zolotussky said that Abramov fully realized that he was one of the final chroniclers of Russian peasant life, but while he was "taking leave" of the village, "he wanted all the same to save it." Fedor Abramov's prose "is the village saved, but saved only in the imagination, in the sorrow of a grateful memory. It is the peasant Atlantis, which has already sunk to the bottom of the ocean."[55] Abramov filled the village landscape with elements that were in reality disappearing before his eyes: he put crops in the fields, fish in the rivers, berries and mushrooms in the forests, and northern-accented peasant voices in the wooden houses. While reading Abramov's stories it was possible for a moment to believe "that not everything is lost, not everything has been destroyed, that the living village hasn't been completely plundered and killed off. This is, of course, a poetic illusion. It is a moment of enchantment . . . and you don't want to part with it."[56]

In *Brothers and Sisters,* a four-novel series set in the northern village of Pekashino, Abramov describes the "forest literacy" possessed by all inhabitants of the countryside, which includes knowing the nicknames for a given village and the stories behind these nicknames; local terms for various plants, animals, and tools; and the highly specialized "cognitive map" peasants had of the village and the nature surrounding it which outsiders could never completely master. This detailed, lexically rich portrait of a vanishing way of life is a core attribute of Village Prose; and although the portrait is firmly grounded in a past reality, its distillation in literature gives it a radiant, idealistic aura and political potential.

Similarly, nothing in Vasily Belov's collection of essays on folk aesthetics called *Harmony* (*Lad*) is demonstrably false, but he presents as a simultaneous occurrence all the positive aspects of a complex folk culture that were never fully realized in any one village at any given point in time. Belov offers the best moments and the most interesting features of village life taken at a glance; in this way *Harmony* and other Village Prose narratives could easily seem to be idylls that end tragically, and not the repositories of rural life they were originally intended to be. Works of this type can be easily exploited, even by their authors, in subsequent years. As Galina Belaya has pointed out, "the romantic idealization of history is fine as long as it is an artistic philosophical metaphor," but it "does not work as a philosophy of history" or when it becomes "a programme . . . and we see that we were simply being called back in time."[57] When the lyrical is reread as the historical, it can be used to argue that a marvelous rural world was destroyed by alien forces, and that this loss is a tragedy from which Russia has never recovered.

In reading and rereading Abramov one is struck by the variety of viewpoints: he presents negative aspects of the Soviet agricultural system, but also shows how hard it was to be a chairman or brigade leader on a kolkhoz, especially during the war and postwar years, and he goes a long way towards proving how the wartime collective effort ensured the survival of the troops and city dwellers, while the village itself was irreparably weakened. Abramov began his career as a critic with an article that demolished collective farm literature; in most of the works published during his lifetime and in numerous stories that surfaced after 1985 his style and ethos placed him at some distance from Socialist Realism. Abramov championed peasants and their culture, the Russian North, and the value of studying and respecting the past, all in a political and social context that favored workers, urban life, a denationalized Soviet territory, and the absolute value of the future. Yet Abramov did not see himself as rebelling against the state in the name of any specific agenda, whether western-style democracy and capitalism or a Russian autocratic regime based on tsar, Orthodoxy, and nationality.

Given that a significant portion of Abramov's corpus was devoted to elevating the dignity of Russian peasants—even to the point of portraying a way of life as still existing that had for the most part disappeared from view—is it then fair to say that his work is to some extent "utopian"? If so, is the act of writing back into existence a harmonious, radiant village that some say never existed in the first place a conjurer's trick that has in retrospect proved to be dangerous?

"Utopian" is a problematic term as applied to Russian Village Prose in general, and to Abramov's writing in particular. If we oppose, as Auden did, visions of the past to those of the future, the Arcadian to the Utopian, and Eden to the New Jerusalem, then *derevenskaia proza* could be called Arcadian. "Eden is a past world in which the contradictions of the present world have not yet arisen; New Jerusalem is a future world in which they have at last been resolved. . . . the backward-looking Arcadian knows that his expulsion from Eden is an irrevocable fact. . . . The forward-looking Utopian . . . necessarily believes that his New Jerusalem is a dream which ought to be realized."[58] The Utopian's future vision, says Auden, "must include images . . . not only of the New Jerusalem itself but also images of the day of judgment."

"Utopia" is frequently used to mean an idealized, imaginary realm, a place that exists primarily in visionary or impractical thought. In that sense, the Russian literary view of the countryside and the peasant has been "utopian" for the past two hundred years, beginning with the Sentimental period and Karamzin's "Poor Liza." Bleakly realistic pictures of the countryside in late nineteenth- and early twentieth-century stories by Chekhov and Bunin were superseded by the peasant utopias of Esenin and Klyuev, which were themselves soon replaced by the utopias of collectivization. Few readers of Socialist Realist kolkhoz novels would deny that these are visions of the future superimposed on that peculiar form of the present known as "reality in its revolutionary development." It was this unbelievably positive picture of life in the socialized countryside that stimulated stingingly critical articles after Stalin's death, soon followed by the beginnings of what came to be known as Village Prose.

The prehistory of *derevenskaia proza* makes it clear that if one is to call it "utopian," this is to say that it corresponds to the most common approach to the rural theme during the past two centuries of Russian literature. Canonical works of Village Prose are both *ante-* (referring to a prior tradition) and *anti-* (written against) collective farm literature. The writers set themselves up in opposition to the false idyll of the kolkhoz novel, but in doing so they drew on, and added to, prior literary idealizations, especially in the pre-Revolutionary gentry novel and in certain Bunin stories.

Fedor Abramov's trajectory as a rural writer was in some sense an anomaly. He started out as a professor and critic and launched a career in fiction with the first volume of his highly acclaimed series *Brothers and Sisters* in 1958. A few years later he produced an updated version of Ovechkin in a 1963 essay "Round and About"; the controversy surrounding this work delayed by a decade the appearance of the second Pekashino volume, *Two Winters and Three Summers*.

However, Abramov's biography in many respects resembles that of other *derevenshchiki:* born and raised in the village, he left his native region for higher education and military service. After the war, he finished his studies in Leningrad, and while pursuing an academic and literary career kept in close contact with his native Arkhangelsk region and the village of Verkola, passionately defending the interests of the Russian peasant wherever possible. To say that writers like Abramov had a detailed personal knowledge of life in the countryside is not to say that there is nothing idealized or utopian about this type of writing, but it is utopian in a much different sense than in urban-driven kolkhoz literature. In Village Prose, the utopia is centered in and around the past, the native region (*malaia rodina*), the family extended through time (the *rod*), and childhood. The canonical Village Prose narrative expresses nostalgia alongside a deep concern for the present and future of the village, a concern that makes the description of the past even more radiant by comparison.

Abramov is typical in focusing not just on a generalized village, like the mostly generic locations in collective farm novels, but on a specific cluster of villages well known to the author. But even though the "village" of Village Prose is based on a specific locale, the description takes on the idealized tone we associate with the nineteenth-century gentry novel. It begins to sound a bit like "Oblomov's Dream," except that in this case the little boys are allowed to run around at will. The village, like the estate, was set off from the rest of the world, which could contribute to an idyllic or utopian reading. It is hard not to project a sense of rural harmony while recalling berry- and mushroom-picking expeditions, swimming with friends and family members, listening to a grandmother recount fairytales or recall the lives of long-dead relatives. This narrative is false only to the degree that all narratives of childhood distill both positive and negative elements into emblematic moments and images. A literature based on a writer's imaginative and often emotional reconstruction of an ever more distant rural childhood is not a dependable source of hard facts about the past; in the wrong hands it can serve a political agenda based on a willful misreading of that past.

The published works of Abramov and other rural writers were subject to intense scrutiny and often harsh criticism. The most persistent complaint was that Village Prose was overly positive about the past and indifferent or even hostile to change. The literary "nests of peasants" seemed no more acceptable to Soviet critics than "nests of gentry" had to their nineteenth-century radical counterparts. More perceptive commentators realized that in the transcript of a rural childhood it was natural to find luminous memories as well as expressions of sorrow at how much of the old life had been lost.

These discussions would have faded as Village Prose ceased to dominate the literary process were it not for the rise of extreme forms of Russian nationalism in the years after 1985. Had Rasputin, Astafiev, Belov and others not chosen to present the ultranationalist point of view, few people would have made a connection between their earlier writings and the political situation after 1985. Their new works did not qualify as idyllic or utopian, and the epic spirit was lost because they could not refrain from being more *against* than *for*.[59] I wrote in 1992 that "one sometimes feels the need to defend the legacy of Village Prose from those who used to write it"; the passage of time has supported my assertion that these writers were on the noisy periphery of chauvinism, and not at its core.[60]

Perhaps what should be asked is whether the Arcadian—that is, past-oriented—visions of canonical Village Prose can also be read as the forward-looking utopian dreams of a New Jerusalem. Did this literature prove useful in drawing up blueprints for a Russian renaissance based on the restoration of what was lost? What were the writers' political and social goals during the years when Village Prose was at its height? In commemorating what would have been Fedor Abramov's seventieth birthday in 1990, Igor Zolotussky acknowledged that Abramov had sought to save through his writing what could not be saved in reality. But for what purpose was he saving the village? Vladimir Lichutin went much further in saying that he wished the village would not die, but fall into a deep sleep which would preserve it until the day when its message could once more be heard.[61]

Through colorfully detailed scenes from the countryside, Village Prose writers sought to prove that a richly layered, traditional Russian life existed in microcosm in each village, and some implied that even in the late 1970s the roots of village Russia had not been entirely destroyed. The image of the village as a *zapovednik* (preserve) of Russianness was extended after 1985 as critics and writers presented a Russia in such danger that it needed to make a strategic retreat to a place far away from the twentieth century which had brought so little joy. Years after *derevenskaia proza* had ceased to function as a movement, its basically nostalgic, past-oriented message mutated into utopianism.[62] It would probably be fair to say that just enough of the "once and future kingdom" was written into the Arcadian village of the 1960s and 1970s to allow it to be read two decades later as the potential homeland of a New Jerusalem.

THE POLITICS OF SURVIVAL I:
WHO'S SORRY NOW?

Abramov's prose, like that of Vasily Shukshin, can only be considered a factor in the rise of extreme nationalism by those who are prepared to make a blanket judgment about all of Village Prose. There is little to support that judgment either in the texts published during Abramov's lifetime or in those that appeared posthumously, and, like Shukshin, he cannot be accused of personally stirring things up politically after 1985. Other than guilt by association, there is only the claim that any narrative that mourns the disappearance of peasant Russia was helpful to the architects of a chauvinist ideology. Extreme nationalists could make use of Abramov's stories, but these same works could serve a number of other political purposes as well.

Abramov's reputation was affected by two more post-Soviet accusations that colored the reading of his lyrical village chronicles. One area of controversy is specific to Abramov; for years it was rumored in émigré publications that during the war he worked for the Soviet counterintelligence unit Smersh (from *smert' shpionam* "death to spies"). Zolotussky recalled a conversation with Abramov during which the author freely admitted to having served in Smersh from 1943 to 1945, and confessed a fear of publishing any account of his activities, given his ambivalence about what he had been expected to do (i.e., to find every accused person guilty). Zolotussky describes the posthumously published "Who Is He?" ("Kto on?") as the author's attempt to confront his own painful memories. "Was he an investigator? He was. Did he determine the fate of innocent people. He did. Did he manage to save anybody while also saving himself? He did—but not everyone. The rest received terms of varying length in the camps, and maybe perished there."[63] What Zolotussky does not say is that Smersh is rumored to have carried out a summary kind of "justice" on some accused spies. Notes to the unfinished manuscript of "Who is He?" dated 1958–80, give evidence of the personal and artistic difficulty Abramov experienced in constructing a narrative about this stage in his life, which began after he had already served in the military for several years, had been severely wounded and evacuated across Lake Ladoga, and had just returned to active duty.[64]

It was clearly in Abramov's interest to demonstrate that he was not a heartless Soviet agent with many innocent souls on his conscience, but a frightened and confused soldier ordered to assume a crucial wartime duty. Abramov's notes bring to mind Alexander Solzhenitsyn's "Incident at Krechetovka Station" (which appeared along with "Matryona's Home" in the *Novyi mir* issue for January 1963), in which an officer wrestles with his conscience over whether his decision sent an innocent man to his doom or helped to catch a spy. Well known for his absolute moral judgments on most questions, Solzhenitsyn on this occasion treats the main character's dilemma sympathetically, if unsentimentally. If we are to assume from the notes selected and annotated by Abramov's widow Krutikova and other sources close to the author that Abramov did his best to act justly during the Stalinist years, that memories of what went on in his unit troubled him ever afterward, and that the complete truth about Smersh will never be known, then one must ask how much in the end this aspect of his life has to do with the artistic quality or moral authority of his writing.

THE POLITICS OF SURVIVAL II:
COMPETITIVE SUFFERING

The writer as a vulnerable creator of "dangerous texts" is such a powerful theme in Russian culture that it is not surprising to see the reputations of some writers who enjoyed public success during the Soviet period face greater scrutiny since new literary histories began to be written in the late 1980s. These questions were asked at a time when additional texts and new information about the behavior of certain writers had appeared in journals and in scholarly publications.

Was it better before glasnost to have published a work in Russia, albeit in censored form, or to have hidden it or sent it abroad? Was remaining silent while other writers suffered the moral equivalent of joining the attack on them? On the one side, we have urban writers whose "Old Bolshevik" parents were purged during the thirties or after the war; a number of these writers were themselves imprisoned, exiled, forced to emigrate or in other ways harassed, and their best work did not appear in Russia until after the onset of glasnost. On the other side, we have rural writers whose peasant families and villages were decimated by collectivization and the war; some joined the Party and were able to publish much of what they wrote in the USSR, although not without being subject to occasional sharp criticism and a moderate level of interference with their work. In addition, a number of the Village Prose writers held positions of authority in the RSFSR and USSR Writers Union and on the boards of literary journals.

In light of this post-totalitarian interest in the degree of success vs. the degree of suffering in a writer's life, one can easily come up with two quite different views of Fedor Abramov. In the first view he is a Socialist Realist writer who was well rewarded for cooperating with the regime at every level. Abramov was an operative in the dreaded Smersh, joined the Communist Party in 1945, followed the Party line during the anticosmopolitan campaign, made a rapid climb from graduate student to head of Leningrad University's Department of Soviet Literature, received government awards, traveled to the West, and was frequently quoted in the media. In the posthumously published correspondence of Viktor Astafiev and critic Valentin Kurbatov, Abramov is described as clever, ambitious, jealous, distant from peasant life, and a writer of academic prose (*kandidatskaia proza*).[65]

There is, however, another legitimate "reading" of Abramov's life and works. He came to Leningrad from a northern village, suffered severe wounds during the war, was one of the more outspoken opponents of the corrupted and ridiculous collective farm novel, and was an eloquent defender—both in his fiction and in public pronouncements—of the dignity of genuine rural life. And he was one of the few writers who protested Solzhenitsyn's expulsion from the Writers Union.[66] Abramov was attacked in print, prevented from publishing during the early Brezhnev years, and left behind many works that contained bolder and more artistically powerful statements than could get through the censorship during his lifetime. No one who has read "A Journey into the Past" can doubt that Abramov had a great deal more to say than was possible under Soviet strictures.

Even Astafiev, after criticizing his fellow rural writer—who had just died— said that "none of us are angels and we have all been ground down . . . by the threatening and false age in which we live."[67] Abramov's works that appeared "above ground" during the author's lifetime held great significance for many Russian readers. Fedor Abramov's prose not only saved the village "in the sorrow of a grateful memory," it also was part of the effort that freed Russian literature from the shackles of Socialist Realism.

Village Prose writers did not help rural inhabitants gain power over the land itself, but they did wrest control of the story of the countryside away from state-appointed bards. To the people who still worked the land, they gave a more dignified and accurate account of their lives, while providing the majority urban population with a colorful and poignant reminder of the country's rural origins, and the damage done to those core values and structures after the Revolution. Village Prose proved that native soil was still a meaningful concept, and that the vast, seemingly impersonal Soviet land contained many smaller Russian homelands, each of which contributed distinctive words, stories, and customs to Russian national identity.

Chapter 4 Russians and
"Others": The Text as Territory

O empire! I am your bard . . .
—*Stanislav Kunyaev*

A strong sense of territoriality has influenced the reception of literature in Russia. This is not unexpected because the Russian land, texts,
and state authority all have been marked as potentially sacred or demonic.[1] The most striking instance of this linkage involves the seventeenth-century Old Believers, who began by rejecting corrected versions of the holy texts, then denied the legitimacy of state authority,
and then finally questioned whether what had clearly become the do-
main of the Antichrist could still be Holy Russia. After the disputed
reforms were approved by a church council and confirmed by Tsar
Alexei Mikhailovich, many schismatics fled the center of what for
them had become a dangerous non-Russia.

Centuries later, Osip Mandelstam wrote as if his Russia had died,
and its former capital was now a necropolis. In the 1930 poem "Leningrad" he exclaims: "Petersburg! I still have the addresses / At which I
will find the voices of the dead," while in his poem attacking Stalin

three years later, Mandelstam says that "we live with no sense of the country under our feet."[2] Mandelstam's faded, pre-Revolutionary cognitive map did not lead him abroad but to his own inner, spectral Petersburg. Russian literature had survived the cataclysm, but for Mandelstam, only those works written without permission were worthy of entering the canon: poetry came from the land and its people and not from the powers that controlled it. In post-Revolutionary European exile philosopher Ivan Ilin struck a similar note when he spoke of the Soviet state as being "cursed non-Rus" (*okaiannaia Nerus'*), the land where he was born, but not his homeland.[3] Reading genuine artistic literature, said Ilin, would provide Russians abroad with a way to know their homeland and to find their way back when it was eventually liberated.

The spatial component of Russian national identity has been apparent almost since the beginnings of Kievan Rus, and there is ample evidence of what Mark Bassin has called "an ideological construction of geographical space."[4] The specifics of Russian geography can help explain the way that religion, ethics, culture, and politics evolved. The relationship between Russian space and Russian literature has taken a number of forms. Places on the map were prominently featured in texts: for example, the Russian North and Siberia in Village Prose, Tsarskoe Selo in Pushkin and the Acmeists, the Caucasus in Lermontov, the Crimea and Borodino in Tolstoy, and St. Petersburg in Gogol, Dostoevsky, and Bely. Both the estates of prominent writers—Pushkin's Mikhailovskoe and Boldino, and Tolstoy's Yasnaya Polyana—and the fictional estates of their characters, like the Oblomovka of Goncharov's novel, registered their presence on the nation's cognitive map.[5] These locations could become idealized to the extent that they stood for all of Russia; it is at this point that any harm or neglect they suffered was said to threaten the well-being of Russia itself. The significance of the Nazi occupation of Mikhailovskoe and Yasnaya Polyana was clear to both sides in the struggle. In the post-Soviet period, the fear that these estates would be seriously neglected for lack of funds was emblematic of the larger fear that this was a nation that could no longer afford the upkeep of its own culture.

The texts themselves came to be experienced as an internal, portable map of the country that a Russian could take into prison, exile, or emigration. Ivan Ilin wrote numerous essays on cultural subjects for his fellow exiles as a guide to the art of "reading Russia." Texts played a similar role at home in the ongoing conditions of powerlessness and secrecy, which stimulated the development of an underground cultural life. In the underground, people read, debated, wrote, copied, and hid texts. The state correctly perceived the writing of unofficial texts and the unsanctioned gatherings where they were read aloud and discussed as oppositional and subversive acts, and secret police records are replete with reports on these worrisome phenomena.

A "textual community" whose text is so closely tied to national identity and spiritual legitimacy takes great care to identify the "others" in its midst, and if these "others" do not accept their lesser status, then the integrity, the wholeness (tsel'nost') of the nation must be protected through "otherness by exclusion."[6] Those who are "NOT-LIKE-US," are an obvious danger, as we will see with the treatment of Pushkin's ancestor Abram Gannibal. Must credit for generating the premier national poet be shared with Abyssinians? Was Gannibal russified enough to render harmless his alien blood? But Russia's "Gannibals" were not a major problem. In the long run, it turned out that those who were least alien to the naked eye, who were "TOO-MUCH-LIKE-US," were actually "the most dangerous and the community's specification of their otherness thus should be a primary occupation."[7] This category has traditionally been filled by Jews in Russian cultural and political history. Andrei Sinyavsky, who concealed his Russian identity behind the name of a legendary Jewish bandit from Odessa, and who wrote an iconoclastic work about Pushkin, offers the clearest possible example of how to break all the rules with one dangerous text.

During the anticosmopolitan campaign at the end of the 1940s, Soviet critics and scholars found out that the heavily guarded Soviet border was matched by a strongly defined boundary between the Russian canon and other literatures. A reawakened Jewish identity as a result of World War II and the subsequent founding of the State of Israel put Yiddish cultural figures in the USSR in mortal danger, because Stalin saw in Israel a land and a government that might have prior claims on Soviet Jews' allegiance. While Jewish writers had long been accused of lacking a native soil, a condition that was called *bespochvennost'*, the heightened consciousness of Jewish identity that the state used to its advantage during the war, and the reestablishment of their ancestral state soon afterward, made Soviet Jews and their texts much more dangerous than in the past.

As was shown in the last chapter, from the late 1950s through the 1970s almost all that remained of the traditional Russian countryside was the reflection that it cast in Village Prose. For millions of first- and second-generation city-dwellers who experienced urban life as a kind of diaspora, this body of writing provided a way to repossess in cultural memory the land and the rural way of life they had lost control of in reality. Village Russia, whose history and culture had been primarily oral, lived on in a series of written works which tried to pre-

serve the countryside's lively voices. The contribution of this school of literature to Russian national identity was manifold: a very broad group of readers
was exposed to an attractive "Russianness" based on land and culture, while a
group of critics debated with great intensity the political implications of the destruction of rural life.

Beginning in 1985 with the rise of strong national movements in the Soviet
republics, the question was raised as to whether ethnic Russians had been "dis-
possessed" from their native land, both in the sense of the abandonment of the
village, and because of the presence of non-Russians in the country's leadership.
The general malaise was fed by other cultural and political streams and then by
the abrupt and traumatic demise of the Soviet Union, and this feeling only subsided towards the end of the nineties. The ultranationalist camp, in an inter-
mittent alliance with the Communist Party, spoke of Russia as having been invaded and dominated by alien forces, and of the Russian people as having been
marginalized in their native land; in the conflation of text and territory, Russian
literature was seen to have suffered a fate similar to that of the Russian land.
The land and the text, two pillars of Russianness, had to be defended, and the
alien forces threatening them had to be exposed.

It seemed at the time that consciously russifying the national literature
would help to protect and defend Russia by restoring the proper degree of Russianness to society. Reconstructing the thought process (*khod myshleniia*) of
the ultranationalist, ultraconservative camp from 1985–95 sheds light on the
politicization of ethnicity in the Russian literary process, and on how a Russian
writer or text could fail the test of ethnicity and be judged dangerous. This type
of russification (*russifikatsiia*) is not to be confused with the obviously beneficial process of restoring and preserving Russia's cultural past, whether in the
form of texts, buildings, religious institutions, artistic traditions, or a coherent
and complete historical narrative. Russification should also not be confused
with Dmitry Likhachev's broader notion of cultural ecology, in which Russia's
past is studied as a means of nurturing living national values.

The post-1985 search for "native soil" took many different forms; one aspect
of this search involved identifying and separating out the Russianness (*russkost'*) from the Sovietness (*sovetskost'*) in post-Revolutionary Russian literature.
The goal was to reconnect Russian literature with cultural and spiritual traditions long out of favor, and to restore the break in literary history and literary
style that came if not in 1917, then certainly by 1934. However, advocates of russification went far beyond this moderate nationalism; they foregrounded and
politicized *russkost'* in an attempt to intensify the national content of Russian

literature by artificial means, by exclusion as much as inclusion. In this sense, their intentions resembled those architects of Socialist Realism in the 1930s who sought to strengthen by decree class and Party consciousness in literature. The claim made by the nationalist Right that they were simply restoring the past and ensuring a future for Russian literature was often a mask for chauvinism as well as a power play for control of what they still felt to be the nation's voice, soul, and ultimate ideological weapon. As the epigraph from Kunyaev confidently proclaims, they hoped to be the imperial bards of a Russia that once again classified its writers as pro- or antistate and rewarded or punished them accordingly.

No sooner had long-separated strands of Russian literature begun to come together in the glasnost period than cracks began showing up in the canon. The search for an appropriate name for all the literature written in the Russian language after 1917, irrespective of place or conditions of writing or of publication, turned out to be a walk through a typological minefield. "Russian Literature of the Soviet Period" (*russkaia literatura sovetskogo perioda*) seemed to avoid the obvious pitfalls. Yet the more extreme nationalists insisted that as a single term, *russkaia literatura* failed to make the proper distinction between works of ethnically Russian writers and those who merely wrote in Russian. The use of *russkaia* to designate the entire canon was seen as an attempt to deny Russians control of their own literature, and as part of a broader process of "cultural genocide."

To combat this perceived assault, conservative nationalists came up with a set of guidelines that would have to be met by any writer who wished to merit from them the title "Russian." The requirements were ethnic (sometimes crudely genetic), spiritual, political, and artistic, all subsumed under the rubric "Russianness." It is possible to compile a list of writers and works acceptable to some or all of the nationalist right, but as Walter Laqueur pointed out, merely doing this "does not explain what *Russkost* (Russianness) really is and what kind of truly Russian culture the Russian Party wants to prevail."[8] An examination of the complicated and often inconsistent argumentation behind the right wing's division of Soviet and post-Soviet writers into "genuine" Russian (*russkii*), "Russian-language" (*russkoiazychnyi*), and "false/pseudo Russian" (*lzherusskii*), can tell us a great deal about changing concepts of ethnic and cultural identity in Russia from the mid-eighties to the mid-nineties and how this relates to texts and to state authority. The fact that writers and critics chose to make such distinctions was in part a natural reaction to the suppression of Russian nationalism during the Soviet era, although the controls were never absolute and were eased after 1934, during World II, and then again after Stalin's death. The nationalists insisted that national identity had been suppressed, with the very word *russkii* censored out of publications. Yitzak Brudny has made a strong counterargument that in the 1960s and 1970s conservative nationalists enjoyed more freedom to express their views than any other opposition group, and thus they were in a position to quickly expand their activities after 1985. Evgeny Dobrenko makes a similar case for nationalism in the period from the mid-1930s to the death of Stalin.[9]

Once the government and Party relinquished control of the literary process there was a power vacuum that quickly filled with warring groups of writers, critics, editors, and literary bureaucrats. At first this was a battle for control of well-funded branches of the Writers Union, Litfund, literary newspapers, journals, and publishing houses, but after the withdrawal of nearly all government support for such enterprises, the stakes became more openly political and abstract, while the intensity of feeling was fed by the severe economic reversals experienced by many of those involved in the literary process.[10] Brudny meticulously demonstrates that in the Brezhnev era (1964–82) nationalist writers, both individually and as a group, enjoyed the interest and respect of readers and considerable support from the state, and that both writers and the numerous critics who lived off the analysis of their works had a great deal to lose under succeeding regimes.

Beginning in the mid-1980s, the term "right-wing nationalists" covers a broad range of political-cultural beliefs, but other names used for approximately the same layer of Russian society include: radical Slavophiles, chauvinists, national Bolsheviks, neo-Stalinists, *pochvenniki* (native soil populists), and patriots. *Russkost'* was presented as a quality of writers and texts, both artistic and critical.[11] The main outlets of this more conservative national identity included the newspapers *Den'* and its successor *Zavtra, Moskovskii literator,* and *Sovetskaia Rossiia,* and the journals *Moskva, Nash sovremennik,* and *Molodaia gvardiia;* there were numerous other national and regional publications and a great deal of ephemera.

The distinctive identity of Russian literature has been a subject of interest at home and abroad for the past century and a half.[12] This chapter analyses contributions to the debate over *russkost'* as it grew in intensity after 1985. What is the core identity of Russian literature, and how can the proper distinctions be made between genuine Russian writers and mere *samozvantsy* (pretenders) to that high calling? The move to protect Russia and its culture from anyone defined as an outsider was offered as a defensive strategy, as well as a first step toward a much-needed national renaissance. Outsiders included: Russian Jews, insufficiently nationalistic ethnic Russian writers, many urban intellectuals, and most foreigners. To be a bearer and creator of cultural *russkost'* required virtually total acquiescence in articles of faith.

Although Russianness could be separated—for discussion's sake—into ethnic, spiritual, political, and artistic categories, it was perceived by those who used this term as something indivisible and instantly recognizable. Several basic assumptions underlie *russkost'*, the first being the enduring cultural importance of *dukhovnost'* (spirituality, attention to spiritual qualities) and of righteousness. Another belief is that the world is constructed around a series of oppositions, with virtually no neutral space; it is filled with *sviatye i besy* (saints and demons), *svoi i chuzhoi* (that which is one's own and that which is alien), and *drug i nedrug* (friend and enemy). Because of the inherent dangers faced in maintaining the necessary distinctions between the saintly (Russian) and the demonic (non-Russian) spheres, a high value is placed on Russian suffering for righteousness, on the righteous person, and on the glorious, self-sacrificial deed, the *podvig*. The application, by the more conservative nationalist commentators, of an ethnic test for *russkost'* from the mid-1980s through the mid-1990s was intended to cleanse the literary community and the Russian canon of the large number of Jewish writers and critics and a smaller number of other non-Russians who adopted Russian as their language of choice. This standard was applied to writers past and present, to Babel as well as Rybakov. There was a certain amount of waffling and inconsistency about accepting secular Jews and those who embraced Christianity at some level, like Mandelstam and Pasternak. As Walter Laqueur observed, any strictly applied rule would prove too costly since it would remove figures beloved to the conservatives such as: Vladimir Dal (Danish), Lermontov (possibly Scots), Gogol (Ukrainian), Herzen and Blok (part German), and even Pushkin (part African). And it would take the Ilf out of Ilf and Petrov.[13] Questions about poet Afanasy Fet's background were raised at a writers' meeting in the late 1980s in Leningrad: who was the poet's father, the ethnically Russian Shenshin or his mother's first husband, Fet, and was the elder Fet a German or a German Jew? Although Afanasy Fet himself was long dead at this point, these were not trivial questions.[14]

Even more important than emphasizing who was a *russkii pisatel'* is deciding—or revealing—who was not. The far-right nationalists did some detective work to discover not only who was Jewish, but who had been hiding that fact behind pseudonyms (which were used in earlier decades by Russian radicals as well). It was judged immoral to take advantage of such a pseudonym when criticizing basic Russian values. Such perpetrators of ethnic "fraud" were called *psevdonimniki* (people who use pseudonyms), joining the list of negative epithets that were applied to "non-Russian" literary figures: *russkoiazychnyi* (Russian-language, vs. ethnically Russian), *russofobskii* (Russophobic), *russo-fobstvuiushchi* (militantly Russophobic), *kosmopoliticheskii* (cosmopolitan), and *sionistvuiushchii* (militantly Zionist), among others. While most commentators were willing to allow these "others" to write in Russian as long as they identified themselves properly, there were a few who believed that "a poet's verse ought not to contain . . . alien genetic traits."[15] The term *russkoiazychnyi* proved to be problematic. The nationalist Right used the label "not really Russian" to great advantage in its initial house-cleaning process, but some nationalist critics and writers insisted that Jewish members of the literary community had come up with the term in order to distinguish themselves from native Russians, whom they were said to thoroughly despise. Vladimir Bondarenko called it a term "invented in Israel, but often applied to contemporary Russian life by Uncle Toms."[16] After the breakup of the Soviet Union at the end of 1991, *russkoiazychnyi* was widely used to designate the millions of ethnic Russians who suddenly found themselves living in foreign lands where the majority population did not accept them as fellow citizens. Questions about the legal status and appropriate treatment of these Russians were still being debated a decade later.

Conservative literary commentators applied ethnic standards to the entire twentieth-century canon as the far-flung branches of Russian literature were reunited and the ties binding the Soviet republics were about to be cut. They analyzed differences between the three major waves of émigré writers and within each wave. Their analysis was at times a rather predictable exercise in blood typing, with Russian-Jewish writers and critics inevitably failing the test of Russianness unless they made themselves useful by criticizing other Russian Jewish writers. Literature of the first wave was inevitably favored over the smaller and less interesting second-wave canon and the mostly "Russian-language" offerings of the third wave, whose writers were dismissed with negative epithets like *zabugorniki* (people from beyond the mound/border).[17] It was thought especially offensive that the very people who had already failed the ethnic test once, should prove their utter rootlessness by repeatedly crossing the borders to flaunt their riches and then leave for comfortable, empty lives in the West. Of the contemporary writers who had spent many years in exile, Solzhenitsyn was one of those who received high praise, and Sinyavsky, Aksenov, and Voinovich were among those most frequently and harshly criticized.

THE BIRTH OF A SAINTLY POET

It is hardly surprising that conservative nationalists would use the saint's life (*zhitie*) as a generic model for a writer's biography. In the *zhitie* of the "saintly princes"—as Cherniavsky calls them—emphasis was often placed on a death caused by *chuzhie* (others), suffered as a Russian for Russia, and on the period after death, when miracles confirmed the saintly status of the deceased, including the power to intervene for the Russian people.[18] Such a death for a writer, whether accurately reported, exaggerated, or wholly imagined, was a guarantor of his influence. When the narrative of a writer's life itself became a text in "paraliterary space," the end counted the most, but an appropriate ethnic background was also of paramount importance.[19]

The most extended discussion of a writer's origins concerned Alexander Pushkin. This was to be expected, since across the political spectrum he is revered as *nachalo vsekh nachal* (the beginning/foundation of everything), who invariably "expresses state interests," and whose own origins must be not only above suspicion but an inspiration in and of themselves.[20] The 150th anniversary of his birth in 1949 had provided appropriate material for the anticosmopolitan campaign, when "alien" scholars were accused of grafting too many foreign branches onto the poet's cultural *rodoslovie* (genealogical tree).[21] The 150th anniversary of Pushkin's demise, widely referred to not as his death but his deathlessness (*bessmertie*) was celebrated in 1987, just as radical Slavophile criticism was gathering steam, and the occasion stimulated a new wave of articles devoted to his life and works.

For the 1987 commemoration, *Nash sovremennik* sent out a critic to interview a disabled war veteran named Andrei Cherkashin, who had spent over forty years compiling the most complete Pushkin genealogy to date. Like a medieval monk whose worthiness to write a saint's life must be demonstrated, we are told that Cherkashin was an inspired and patriotic man who had sacrificed himself for Russia and was a representative of the people (*narod*) rather than an elitist academic. During the war, when he found out that he was marching through one of Russia's many *pushkinskie mesta* (places associated with Pushkin's life) Cherkashin vowed that if he survived he would learn everything there was to know about Pushkin and his origins.

The ex-soldier's injuries not only kept him from a proper job, but also made this project a difficult and at times painful one as he dragged himself from library to library often without a pencil, which forced him to commit the material to memory until he returned home. The genealogy that resulted from his labors covered a thousand years and more than five thousand names, a virtual "Who's Who" of Russian history and culture: Princess Olga, Grand Prince Vladimir, Monomakh, Yury Dolgoruky, Alexander Nevsky, and Dmitry Donskoy. The critic reassures us that there was not a single "money-grubber, rogue, careerist, traitor, coward, scoundrel, or libertine" in the lot.[22]

Not only were there no scoundrels, but the Pushkin family was related to other important families of the day: the Aksakovs, Tolstoys, Vyazemskys, Lermontovs, and Tyutchevs. Mentor (*nastavnik*) to the Russian nation, Pushkin revered his own family history and studied it closely; by analogy, the Russian people could begin to know themselves by studying every glorious detail of the poet's life. One of the only famous relatives who does not appear in Cherkashin's account is Abram Gannibal, the Abyssinian who became a Russian general and member of the nobility, was openly acknowledged by Pushkin, and was immortalized in the unfinished biographical romance "The Black Man of Peter the Great" (Arap Petra Velikogo).[23]

That Pushkin's African connection would be a sensitive subject in Russia is hardly surprising; what is surprising is that this was not always the case. In 1937, when the centenary of Pushkin's death came in the midst of the Stalinist purges, Gannibal was fully incorporated into Pushkin's birth narrative. A scholarly monograph from that year called *Pushkin's Ancestors* devoted considerable space to the general, whose family was linked to the Pushkin line in three separate places. The poet's features were said to have clearly reflected his African great-grandfather, and Pushkin's mixed heritage to have been not uncommon among the Russian gentry.[24] Judging by this book, in the second half of the 1930s Soviet literary scholars were still negotiating the space between Bolshevik internationalism and national communism, and Gannibal slipped through that gap. Ivan Ilin, in his own centenary essay, needed a wholly Russian Pushkin to inspire his fellow countrymen abroad. In an uncharacteristically muddled argument, Ilin attempted to strictly limit the physical and cultural influence of Gannibal.[25]

Celebrations of the 1949 sesquicentennial of Pushkin's birth reflected both the internal anticosmopolitan campaign and the external Cold War.[26] Pushkin's African roots were useful primarily in proving his anti-Americanism (he hated slavery), and emphasis was placed on his Russian patriotism, protosocialist views, and Lenin-like immortality. While his ethnic background could still be mixed, Pushkin's genius and his canon had been thoroughly nationalized: Soviet scholars, especially Jews, who claimed that Pushkin was influenced by French and English writers, courted danger. Pushkin locations such as

Mikhailovskoe and Tsarskoe Selo (renamed "Pushkin" in 1937) which were under German control during the war had become even more precious as their suffering merged with that of the poet.[27] There remained at this point but a few steps to the 1987 ultranationalist reading of Pushkin's birth and death, and to the claim in the early 1990s of miracle-working powers for the museum complex (*zapovednik*) at Mikhailovskoe.[28]

The Cherkashin article presented not only a model genealogy but also a model *Pushkinist:* a righteous, suffering, steadfast, frenzied (*neistovyi*), nonintellectual, ethnically pure man. In a similar way, a police investigator who spent ten years studying the mystery surrounding Esenin's death established his credentials by telling of a childhood experience during the war when he literally stumbled upon Esenin's grave, and how his father was arrested, to disappear forever, merely for humming a song written to the words of a Esenin poem.[29] The concern with literary *russkost'* touched scholarship and criticism as well as artistic writing; if the text was sacred, it mattered who held the pen. Viktor Astafiev objected to a Jewish scholar (Eidelman) studying Pushkin and Lermontov, and advocated what sounded like a nationalist monopoly on the study of Russian literature.[30]

The publication of excerpts from Sinyavsky's irreverent book *Strolls With Pushkin* (*Progulki s Pushkinym*) in the April 1989 *Oktyabr'* was greeted with the kind of rhetoric another country might reserve for reports of an enemy incursion, and in a sense it was just that. Years before, when *Progulki* was first published abroad, Solzhenitsyn called it an example of "aesthetic nihilism."[31] Igor Shafarevich, the mathematician who discovered the principle of "Russophobia," denounced the book as a Russian *Satanic Verses*.[32] A July 1989 article in the conservative nationalist weekly *Literaturnaia Rossiia* worried about the consequences of Russia losing Pushkin through neglect and disrespect. "And to be without Pushkin is the same as being without Christ, because he has already crossed all conceivable boundaries. He has stepped across them all in order to become the STANDARD BEARER OF THE RUSSIAN SOUL."[33] A conservative critic described Pushkin as "an icon equal to the icons of the church," more precious because so many icons had been lost during the Soviet period.[34] Once a writer had been identified as the embodiment of *russkost'*, everything that touched him was politicized; everything about him became an article of faith, and irony was abolished.

KILLING RUSSIAN CULTURE

The *russkost'* discussion did not stop at merely bemoaning the prospect of "aesthetic nihilism," but proceeded to focus on what it saw as a pattern of the physical annihilation of Russian literature's leaders and heroes. Interest was concentrated as much on writers' deaths as on their lives and works, and the cause of death of certain targeted writers became a highly politicized topic. This went far beyond the traditional Russian interest in the moment of a writer's demise, when those who felt themselves to be disciples of—or successors to—that writer made bold gestures of support, often in defiance of government efforts to keep a controversial or influential writer's passing a quiet affair. Consider, for example, Lermontov's Pushkin poem, the article Turgenev wrote after Gogol's death, Klyuev's "Lament for Sergei Esenin," the well-known images of Sinyavsky and Daniel carrying Pasternak's coffin, and Brodsky's high profile at Anna Akhmatova's funeral.

Considerable effort was expended on uncovering the "true" stories behind the untimely demises of Pushkin, Lermontov, Blok, Gumilev, Esenin, Mayakovsky, Nikolai Rubtsov, and other literary figures.[35] *Literaturnaia gazeta* commented on "the storm (*shkval*) of sensational publications that have stunned us with their depressing monotony: Gorky was poisoned, Mayakovsky was shot, Esenin, it seems, was hanged."[36] Various international, masonic, cosmopolitan (read "Jewish"), and other anti-Russian forces were thought to have conspired to do away with some of Russia's most talented and patriotic writers in order to weaken Russia as a whole.

If the writer died in a duel (Pushkin, Lermontov), then the task was to discover the secret identity of the opponent and the forces behind him.[37] If the cause of death was said to be illness (Blok), then poisoning was suspected. A writer's—or critic's—difficulties in publishing or editing or his being subjected to censorship or public criticism—all of this the work of sinister forces—caused so much stress that they can be blamed for the deaths of Seleznev, Vampilov, Abramov, and Shukshin.[38] Gumilev and Klyuev were the victims of Jewish-cosmopolitan Bolsheviks. If the purported cause was suicide (Esenin, Mayakovsky), then murder was a likelihood.[39] The newly expanded—with fact or fancy—"tales from the crypt" entered a rhetorical space that marked the intersection of cultural, ideological, and spiritual myths, some centuries old, others relatively new. This is an encyclopedic culture, with some pages lost and others added over the centuries, but whose national memory retains the contours and traces of ancient beliefs, if at times in distorted form. The multiplicity of sources for these paraliterary plot developments made them intense and, in narrative terms, highly overdetermined.

A primary myth, of course, was the Romantic notion that poets "die tragically and heroically" and young.[40] Svetlana Boym observed that in nineteenth-century Russia, civic Realism "preserved the Romantic structure of image making but supplanted the figure of a Romantic individualist with that of a noble sufferer for humankind."[41] Throughout the Soviet era, at both official and unofficial levels, the image of writers who prepared to sacrifice themselves for the people remained strong. The jubilee years of certain writers' deaths were marked with great fanfare, e.g. Pushkin in 1937, Gogol in 1952, and Dostoevsky in 1981.[42] This period also saw the intensification of Russia's pre-Revolutionary self-image as a righteous nation surrounded and infiltrated by alien forces, where Russian culture was one of the most important battlefields.

The unofficial underground devotion to writers has been exhaustively documented. Literature assumed additional political and spiritual roles in the Soviet era when the state turned against the population and when organized religion was denied a meaningful role in society. The glasnost years, with their almost daily revelations of past horrors, established an atmosphere in which it was assumed that everything significant had been kept secret, everything unknown was sinister, that all tragic events were caused by people whose names could now be revealed, and that no one important had died for personal reasons or simply by accident.[43]

The mythic power of the writer's death was intensified by Russian folk and religious beliefs. In folklore it was believed that the spirits of those who die violently and at too early an age remain active in the surrounding area until their natural life span has been completed. The Orthodox idea that the righteous dead are able to intercede with God for the protection of Russia also has the weight of many centuries behind it. The most powerful forces for intercession are those people who suffered a violent death, offering a blood sacrifice as *strastoterptsy* (passion-sufferers). As a new member of the family of Christian nations, Russia needed its own saints, who like the place-spirits of folklore would intervene for Russia (and against its enemies). The very first native Russians to be canonized were Boris and Gleb, two of Grand Prince Vladimir's sons, killed by agents of their brother Svyatopolk during the civil strife that followed Vladimir's death in 1015.[44] Even though Boris and Gleb had perished in a family feud, the chronicler emphasized that these new "protectors of the land of Russia" would strive in the afterlife to "subject the pagans to our princes."[45]

This event marks the onset of a "valid and recognizable historical tradition whereby martyrdom for Russia signified one's elevation to sainthood."[46] At the very beginnings of Russian Orthodoxy, there was a shift from the belief that the holy death had to be for Christ and in defense of Christianity, to the idea that the death could be kenotic—voluntary and sacrificial—in imitation of Christ and for one's own homeland and its people. In Russia, the universal and divine had in rapid order mutated into the national and patriotic. Fedotov calls these *strastoterptsy* "the most paradoxical order (*chin*) of Russian saints."[47] This category of secular saints was filled for centuries with princes whom Cherniavsky describes as "political passion-sufferers" who died because "they accepted the consequences of rulership," that is, of the powerful role they played in society. The *Lives* of these saints were "stylized" so that each repeated the original *podvig* of Boris and Gleb.[48] The people's devotional choices were not always confirmed by the church, as in the case of Paul I, who though despised by many while alive, was revered after his assassination in 1801, and represents "the last illegal offspring of this popular cult of sufferers."[49] Ivan Aksakov's eulogy for Alexander II, which uses the words "passion-sufferer" and "intercessor," shows how the rhetoric of the cult could be activated in moments of great national stress.[50] Assassinated rulers, by definition, were regarded as legitimate and righteous; the powers of intercession they were thought to have acquired by virtue of their deaths led to a posthumous rereading of their lives.

The principles behind the cult of dead rulers apply to the subsequent cult of dead writers: a beleaguered nation's need for spiritual advocacy; the sanctification of power, suffering, and the Russian land; and the belief that those who symbolize Russia are specifically targeted by the country's enemies. The protection that *strastoterptsy* provide for Russia must be periodically renewed by new national saints who speak for succeeding generations and particular regions, like the place-spirits of Russian folklore, and whose more recent martyrdom could once again unite and inspire the people.[51]

As the cult of rulers waned at the beginning of the nineteenth century it was followed by the cult of writers. It is not surprising that Silver Age poet Vyacheslav Ivanov was struck by the fact that Pushkin and Serafim of Sarov both reached the peak of their miraculous talents in 1830, representing for Ivanov a single *poryv* (upsurge) of sanctified genius.[52] Great writers, princes, and holy *startsy* (elders) all stood for Russia, as Dostoevsky made so clear in his speech on Pushkin. It followed, then, that to kill a great national writer was to attempt to kill Russian culture and to destroy Russia itself. Since leading writers were not infrequently compared to Christ, it was a crucifixion as well, an assault not merely on the nation's saints, but on one of its gods. Renewed attention to

Pushkin in his jubilee year of 1987 gave the *russkost'* movement a pattern for its necro-narrative.[53] Nikolai Zuev's 1989 *Nash sovremennik* article "Who is Guilty of the Poet's Death?" is typical of works devoted to this theme. It had long been rumored that the duel between Pushkin and D'Anthes might have been engineered by forces at court, some not of Russian origin, that were hostile to Pushkin; the emphasis was now on the *chuzhie* (others, aliens) hiding behind Russian courtiers and manipulating their every move. Zuev complained that it had become impossible to talk about a plot (*zagovor*) without being called a Stalinist or to use the word "cosmopolitan" without being labeled an anti-Semite.[54] The argument in favor of a plot was based on the belief that Pushkin saw the court being taken over by cosmopolitan forces, as reflected in his 1830 poem "Moia rodoslovnaia" ("My Genealogy") where he compared his background to that of careerists, and it was emphasized that the poet fought mightily against this development, a fight which ultimately led to his death.[55]

Poet Tatyana Glushkova picked up on this theme in her article "The Death of a Poet," where she used Lermontov's poem of the same name to structure her argument.[56] Lermontov's anguished verses, begun while Pushkin still lay on his deathbed, became in Glushkova's analysis a denunciation of the anti-Pushkin group. Because the act of writing "Death of a Poet" led to Lermontov's exile and eventual death in the Caucasus, the verse itself has a dangerous aura about it. What Glushkova distilled from "Smert' poeta," especially from the last sixteen lines which were written later on, is Lermontov's own "code of reading," providing a key to the poem and to a decoding of what she called "the crime of the century." According to Glushkova's reading of Lermontov, Pushkin saw that Russian history had taken a wrong turn under Peter the Great. The old aristocracy from which Pushkin himself descended had been replaced by newcomers, both native-born and foreign, who were united by their common *bezrodstvo* ("lack of ancestry, kin," i.e. low or unknown origin). The forefathers of these power- and money-hungry upstarts had not fought alongside Alexander Nevsky or on the Kulikovo battlefield and they had not raised up a new dynasty to end the Time of Troubles, in stark contrast to the achievements of Pushkin's own family. Pushkin expressed his anxiety and anger in works which sealed his fate at court. The references to guilty parties in Lermontov's poem seem clear to Glushkova; the words "haughty," "secretive," "masking," "greedy," "gold," "thorny crown" and the contrast of Pushkin's *pravednaia krov'* (righteous blood) to the *chernaia krov'* (black blood) of his killers could only, she felt, point to Jews.

Glushkova reminds readers of the reaction of Petr Vyazemsky, who lay prostrate and sobbing before Pushkin's coffin because he saw that "with Pushkin's demise the voice of destiny (*rok*) had entered Russian literary history, and that Pushkin's fate would weigh heavily on that of succeeding Russian poets." While we have not, she said, completely deciphered the narrative of Pushkin's death, it has become a powerful myth which cannot be tackled by narrow historians "of the fact." This could not be seen as simply a personal matter; since the poet's family was the "living embodiment of Russia." An insult to them assumed national significance and in defending his honor in this duel, Pushkin defended all of Russia.

Articles such as Glushkova's "Death of a Poet" reveal a common thread that ran through the *russkost'* debates of the late 1980s and early 1990s. This rhetoric did not simply defy logic in the conventional sense of the term. It defied the very idea of logic, fact, intellect, rationalism, learning, and objective truth. The very use of facts by the opposition seemed suspicious, unspiritual, and un-Russian.[57] In *The Russian Mind,* Stuart Ramsay Tompkins sees as two dominant features of Russian thought "a preoccupation with theory to the exclusion of facts; and . . . the acceptance as a fixed point in thought of some concept arrived at . . . intuitively."[58] He cites Alexander Herzen, historian Lev Tikhomirov, and other Russians on this subject, as well as the work of a Petersburg-based British journalist named Dillon, who wrote in 1890 of the stark contrast he saw between the Russian and British appreciation of "facts" and the unlikelihood of ever getting a Russian to "bow to a fact."[59]

The attitude towards "facts" acquired significance as part of the larger question of how different national groups arrive at the "truth," and whether an empirical or an a priori approach is preferred.[60] As discussion intensified in the late 1980s two words for "truth" were subtly redefined. *Istina* became something that had been deliberately suppressed, like the nationality of those shadowy figures who were the real powers at court in Pushkin's day. *Pravda* became the essential moral truth that everyone must accept, like the idea that Jews were primarily responsible for all negative aspects of the Revolution and post-Revolutionary Russian life, while any positive developments were due to the efforts of ethnic Russians. *Um* was opposed to *intellekt:* both words can be translated as "mind" or "intellect," but the latter is a foreign borrowing and thus can be seen as less Russian than *um.*[61] Knowledge was not acquired through the intellect or in institutions of higher education, but was the lore that was handed down through the generations. Constantly sanctified by the community, it was *narodnaia mudrost'* (folk wisdom) and *narodnye obychai* (folk customs), and of course included the teachings of the Orthodox Church, which are very conservative in nature.[62]

Nothing defied logic quite as successfully as Vladimir Soloukhin's 1992 "exposé" of people he felt were responsible for Alexander Blok's death.[63] Blok's decline and death in 1921 has always been recounted with great sadness, nowhere more eloquently than in Yevgeny Zamyatin's 1924 essay about Blok. But Zamyatin's lament that "None of us can be forgiven" for the poet's death speaks to a general sense of the age not being kind to one whose only gift was to write and then to read aloud what he had written, and who could not adapt to the demands of this new society.[64] Zamyatin witnessed Blok's refusal to petition on his own behalf for permission to travel to a sanatorium in Finland; Gorky's efforts in this same cause were ultimately successful, but the decision came too late to do Blok any good. Ignoring the testimony of people close to Blok, Soloukhin "uncovered" a plot that involved people very high up in the Kremlin leadership, who determined that Blok must not leave the country for treatment, since it would be clear to foreign doctors that he was being systematically poisoned. Soloukhin failed to explain why Blok would have been targeted for poisoning, although other articles mention Blok's negative comments about Jews in his diaries. The narrative of a careless, or callous, delay in granting permission for treatment mutated into a strategy to hide traces of poison. Soloukhin would have liked to recommend exhumation but the remains of Blok and members of his family were moved in 1944 from one cemetery to another in such a manner that it would have been difficult to separate out individuals with any certainty.[65]

In light of this admittedly ghastly chain of events, Soloukhin came up with two likely poisoners, Larisa Reisner and her husband Fedor Raskolnikov; Soloukhin was encouraged in this belief by a subtext he saw in Nadezhda Mandelstam's memoirs. In presenting these ideas to the public, Soloukhin took a few bits of accepted historical evidence—Blok's early death, the delays in granting him permission to travel, the disturbance of the family graves, the subsequent death of Larisa Reisner, and the suicide of her mother—and created what to him was the true (*po sushchestvu*) version of Blok's death, in which, to no one's surprise, all guilty parties seem to be Jewish. This was the point, of course, since what we are seeing is a politicized search for useful "truths." A writer's ethnic background became part of paraliterary space; if he was Jewish, then he was guilty of offenses against Russian culture, if he was a Russian writer, then he was the victim of an evil plot by Jews and their Russian lackeys.

Right-wing nationalists were intrigued to the point of obsession with "solving" Esenin's death. As the popular "last poet of the countryside" in an age of elite urban poets, Esenin fit the parameters of a national cultural hero for the

Right, and the year of his demise, 1925, was even said to mark the end of Russian culture.[66] The members of the Esenin study group at IMLI (the Gorky Institute) formed a commission in 1989 to investigate the circumstances surrounding the poet's violent death.[67] Esenin supporters admitted that while it would be sufficient to demonstrate that the unceasing attacks on him in the press and criminal investigations of his activities in the early twenties drove him to suicide, they would like to have proven that he was killed by others. They ignored or dismissed all available evidence of the poet's serious alcoholism, his numerous drunken anti-Semitic outbursts in public, and his frequent threats of suicide.[68] Someone who epitomized the best of Russian culture could not simply have killed himself in a drunken delirium. For the radical Slavophiles, it seemed more than likely that he was done in by those he justly and bravely criticized, especially in his verse drama "Strana negodyaev" ("The Land of Scoundrels").[69] Unfortunately for the *eseninisty* the commission, after extensive expert testimony, announced in July 1993 that there was no evidence to support the murder theory; for some this was obviously not the end of the story.[70]

It was particularly important for the conservative nationalist agenda to dismiss suicide as the cause of Esenin's death in light of the extremely negative attitude towards self-inflicted death in Russian Orthodoxy. It is virtually impossible to make a case for even unofficial secular sainthood for a literary figure who died in this way. Being killed for one's country conveniently removes that obstacle. It is significant that when the Esenin murder theory had gained some credence—before the IMLI report—a commemorative service (*panikhida*) was conducted in Moscow in 1989 and the following year in St. Petersburg.[71] Absolved by his most fervent supporters of the sin of suicide, Esenin could now enter the ranks of passion-suffering intercessors for the people, a move which was made explicit by contemporary commentators, one of whom ended an article on Esenin with the promise that "his consecrated immortality is just beginning" (*ego osviashchennoe bessmertie tol'ko nachinaetsia*) while another ended simply with "Blessed be his name!" (*Da sviatitsia imia ego!*).[72] He was, claims one of the more vehemently nationalistic Esenin scholars, the "Russian Christ" who, along with his people, would rise again.[73]

The spiritual nature of the martyred poet's role was "laid bare" not only by the pseudo-ecclesiastical language surrounding it, but also by the use of the present tense in articles devoted to solving the "mystery" of Esenin's death. This was the timeless present of sacred space, of the repeated drama of sin and expiation, ritual death and resurrection. Esenin's death marked the end of the "bard's earthly mission," but obviously not of his activities on behalf of the Russian people.[74] Similarly, it was not Pushkin's "death" which was commemorated at regular intervals, but rather his "deathlessness" (*bessmertie*). The Soviet reading of Mayakovsky's suicide also denied the reality of death; as Svetlana Boym noted, "Mayakovsky is either alive or immortal," but never merely dead.

In all this necrophilic research there was an important principle at work—that of competitive suffering. As the poet Valentin Sorokin reminded his readers, "Not all suffering is the same" (*Stradanie stradaniiu rozn'*).[75] Any number of Russian literary figures led difficult lives and a significant number died young and tragically. But only those who bore the mark of *russkost'* and could be seen to have suffered for Russia were of interest. This attitude pitted the "children of the village" against the "children of the Arbat"; the former suffered and were occasionally avenged, the latter caused suffering and sometimes got their just deserts.[76] Any unsaintly behavior by identifiably Russian writers who died young, like Nikolai Rubtsov who was murdered by his battered girlfriend, and Vasily Shukshin who suffered a heart attack, was forgotten in light of their suffering and early death. The tribulations of a writer identified as non- or anti-Russian, two categories which are frequently merged, were either dismissed or viewed with undisguised satisfaction. The deaths of Babel and Meyerhold, and Sinyavsky's years in the Gulag, were of no significance to Russian culture when seen in this light.[77]

That the myth of cultural murder was still in place, ready to be applied to contemporary events, could be seen from a 1994 issue of *Zavtra*, which gave extensive coverage to the death of Viktor Deryagin, the head of the Manuscript Division of the Russian State Library. According to *Zavtra*, Deryagin died of heart failure only in a technical sense. His zealousness in protecting Russia's literary heritage from Westerners, especially Americans, led to a campaign of persecution against him. Rather than a heart attack, this was said to be a political murder with broad repercussions for the entire nation.[78] The familiar oppositions are here: patriotic vs. traitorous Russians, and Russians vs. foreigners. In narrating Deryagin's struggles highly marked terms were employed: *podvig* (glorious deed), *bor'ba s nedrugami* (the battle with the foe), *arkhivisty-patrioty* (archivist-patriots), russophobes, *piataia kolonna "mondealizma"* (the fifth column of the new world order), with manuscript-grabbing Hassidim, and *Bol'shoi Shaitan* (Great Satan, by which they mean the United States). The article calls for Deryagin's followers, the *deriagintsy,* to carry on with his important work.[79]

While the restructuring of the Russian canon along ethnic lines was in fact a highly political enterprise, it sought to mask itself as a legitimate description and defense of national identity.[80] This process involved not just the removal of works whose authors were demonstrably "non-Russian," but also involved conferring the title of "false Russian" on certain ethnically Russian writers. "Russian writer" was not a status automatically given to those who passed their initial genetic screening; it was an honor that had to be continually merited, and a responsibility that must never be ignored.[81]

A 1991 *Molodaia gvardiia* article by Valery Khatyushin called "O lzhe-poetakh i russkoi poezii" ("On Pseudo-Poets and Russian Poetry") began with a list of the best twentieth-century Russian poets, minus both Mandelstam and Brodsky, and then proceeded to read three poets—Yevtushenko, Voznesensky, and Akhmadulina—out of Russian poetry for their betrayal of the Russian people, not only in what they had written but in how they had conducted themselves as poets.[82] Khatyushin saw Yevtushenko as a craven internationalist, a pawn of the "Zionist" press. For Akhmadulina, the critic did not make the expected ethnic argument—that she is of russified Italian and Tartar background—but said instead that she was a "bohemian hothouse poetess" (*oranzhereino-bogemnaia poetessa*) whose egotistical poetry never touched the people, and thus she could never be called a "Russian national poet" (*russkii natsional'nyi poet*).[83]

Voznesensky's problem was, according to Khatyushin, that he never really said what he meant; what was the Russian reader to understand by such lines as "Ia—Goya!"("I am Goya") or "Ia—Merlin!" ("I am Merlin") or "Ia—dvoiurodnaia zhena" ("I am his mistress")? This was an art that concealed its true intentions: "vse eto neset v sebe talmudicheskie priznaki neotkrovennogo iskusstva" ("all this bears the talmudic signs of a devious kind of art"). This was not genuine Russian art, but "plody chuzhoi nam 'kul'tury,' chuzhoi poetiki" ("the fruits of an alien culture and an alien poetics").[84] Voznesensky's cruciform poem was said to mock the image of the cross, which ought to be sufficient for removing his work from the canon of Christian as well as Russian poetry.[85] Like Shafarevich, Khatyushin spoke approvingly of Iran's condemnation of Salman Rushdie and said that Russians had been tolerant for too long. Andrei Sinyavsky preempted this sort of expulsion from the ethnic canon by giving himself the Jewish nom de plume Tertz back in the 1950s, marginalizing and criminalizing himself before anyone else could. As certain writers and works were removed from the canon, others, safely dead, were posthumously moved into the russifiers' camp. Anna Akhmatova's epigraph to "Requiem" was presented as a stern condemnation of all things "alien" to Russia: "No, not beneath a foreign sky, / Not sheltered by a foreign wing—/ I was where my people were,

/ Where, alas, they had to be."[86] In order not to lose anyone important to their cause, anti-Russian comments by an otherwise acceptable writer were dismissed as a youthful folly, anomaly, or forgery, e.g. Lermontov's poem "Nemytaia Rossiya" ("Unwashed Russia"), or similarly inconvenient works by Esenin.

For conservative nationalists, Russian art had become synonymous with Russian Orthodox art; they spoke of Christian and Orthodox prose as a very important tradition that had survived the Soviet period and which should prosper, even prevail, in post-Soviet Russia. The "liturgical resonance" of the national literature was seen as one of its key qualities; the secularization of literature and the commercialization of publishing were deplored.[87] Russian Christian prose was identified not simply as one choice in a pluralistic literary context, but as something opposed to non-Russian, non-Christian prose; these terms were not varieties, but oppositions, with no middle ground. The broad quality of *dukhovnost'* (spirituality), which could in the past have been applied to the writing of both Vassily Grossman and Vassily Belov, was given a narrower ethnic and confessional meaning.[88]

Christian prose was promoted as the literature that would save Russia from the demons of nihilism and put it on the path to spiritual renewal. Village Prose writer Vladimir Krupin emerged in the 1990s as an advocate of a literature that was based in, and provided support for, Russian Orthodoxy. "The goal of writers is to help the clergy," who had the massive task ahead of them of rebuilding a faith community, and who had been ill-treated in the works of Chekhov, Saltykov-Shchedrin, Leskov, and other Russian writers.[89] Literature, Krupin insisted, should return to its origins and use the Kievan chronicle as a model.[90]

The Russian writer was a spiritual hero (*podvizhnik*), each work was a heroic deed (*podvig*), and all genuine Russian literature showed unstinting devotion (*podvizhnichestvo*) to the self-realization of the people.[91] In the work of the eminent scholar and moderate nationalist Dmitry Likhachev these were broadly conceived, nonrestrictive cultural and spiritual concepts; he spoke of what was *russkoe* (a more abstract notion of Russianness than is conveyed by *russkost'*). Extreme nationalists precluded the participation in the literary world of anyone who was not at least ethnically Russian and thus potentially Russian Orthodox.[92] "Russian-language" writers and their Russian supporters, by way of contrast, were referred to as "betrayers of Christ" (*khristo-prodavtsy*). Once a culture was perceived in spiritual terms, the division into martyrs and demons was automatic and far-reaching.

The political beliefs required of a truly Russian writer were fairly straightforward: a strong Russia must come first, which usually meant support for authoritarian or totalitarian structures; writers were identified as being pro- or anti-*derzhavnost'*, which referred to the principle of a strong central government. Past support for the Communist regime by ethnic Russians was excused or reinterpreted as patriotism; for all others such support was condemned as russophobic opportunism and treason. A cultural figure's responsibility and loyalty to the nation took precedence over individual rights and opinions; there was to be no fundamental criticism of Russia's people, religion (meaning Orthodoxy), culture, or role in history.

The "period of stagnation" and the primarily urban and intellectual dissident movement with its relatively high percentage of Jews were both subject to major reevaluations at this point. International organizations, whether PEN or the United Nations, were suspect, as was the idea of a post-Soviet "new world order" which was demonized in *Den', Zavtra,* and other periodicals as a development that would be followed by a "Zionist-Masonic Inquisition" directed against Russian patriots.[93] In general, Russian writers were expected to feel solidarity primarily with other Russians at home and in the former republics, with other Orthodox Slavs (especially Serbs), secondarily with anti-Western regimes and groups (Iraq, Libya, Iran, radical Palestinians), and finally with right-wing nationalists in the West (in this period the examples given were Jean Le Pen, David Duke, and Patrick Buchanan). Duke went to Russia for a long stay in the year 2000 because of the affinity he felt for the Russian far right.

No foreigner was in a position to analyze or judge Russian literature, but international awards should go to genuine Russian writers.[94] Calls were made for an exposé of the "atlanto-centric" and russophobic bias of the selection committee for the Nobel Prize in literature, since it was ignoring such stars as Yury Bondarev. The literary prize was seen as recognition of the nation and not of individual talent.[95] The political characterization of a Russian writer was in some ways fairly flexible, able to accommodate such unlikely comrades as Eduard Limonov and Alexander Prokhanov. Limonov successfully transformed himself during these years from an expatriate literary bohemian to a serious right-wing nationalist writer. It helped that he was not only ethnically Russian, but from a provincial military family.

The aesthetic requirements for a Russian writer were also straightforward. Realism was a genuinely Russian artistic method, while modernism was alien and harmful to Russian culture. "Russian-language" poetry was described as a case of a "hypertrophied form in the absence of any content."[96] In contrast, Realism is not only traditional and national, it is also easy to decipher, unlike the urban, elitist products of the avant-garde. The pre-Revolutionary avant-garde's assertion that transrational (*zaumnyi*) verse like "dyr bul shchyl" contained "more of the Russian national spirit than . . . all of Pushkin" carried no weight here.[97]

Modernism, especially in art, literature, and music, was said to have been forced on Russia by the same aliens (i.e. Jews and Russian turncoats) who made the Revolution possible. In a paraphrase of "A Slap in the Face of Public Taste," a well-known avant-garde manifesto of 1913, it was claimed that "the ship of modernity had thrown overboard all Russian Orthodox culture," as a battle ensued between genuine realism and abstract art. Jews were seen as the historically "rootless" conduit through which "cosmopolitan" cultural influences had reached Russia. The Russian literary language was said to have been harmed by the style of the "Odessa school" of writing, as Orthodox art had been undermined by the influence of Judaism's ban on realistic representation.[98] Artist Sergei Kharlamov gauges the Russianness of two Jewish artists not by the fact of conversion, or by any directly expressed sentiments about ethnicity or religion, but on the basis of style. "For me, the difference between the abstract artist Vasily Kandinsky and the Realist Isaac Levitan is that the Levitan landscapes are Russian Orthodox at heart. 'Above Eternal Peace' (*Nad vechnym pokoem*) sounds like a prayer. Abstractions are anti–Russian Orthodox, so for me, Levitan is a Russian artist, and Kandinsky is not."[99]

Kharlamov makes no mention of the fact that although Levitan (1860–1900) was celebrated as the most Russian of landscape artists, he was expelled from Moscow with thousands of other Jews in 1879 and 1892 as a result of "restrictive policies rooted in the very nationalism that promoted his art."[100] He does go on to say that the word Russian (*russkii*) is "a spiritual concept" and asks why Russians, who look at nature "not just with our eyes, but with our soul," should be obliged to accept Malevich's "Black Square" as Russian, expressing as it does Madame Blavatsky's theories "about the black square of the universe, in which there is no place for the spiritual, but only for the material."[101]

The destruction of the avant-garde during the purges was hardly to be regretted; the reemergence of modernism in the post-Soviet years was a cause for great concern.

Mark Lyubomudrov complained of an attempt to replace national traditions with "ersatz subcultures in the bourgeois American style."[102] In general, he felt that the incursion of alien (*chuzherodnye*) forces into Russian culture in the twentieth century had raised the level of atheism, nihilism, and *demonfil'stvo* (demon worship). Conservative nationalists had an additional reason for demanding that the Russian writer be a Realist; they wanted literature to continue to play a political and spiritual role in Russian life and they knew that this was best accomplished by works that were accessible to a wide audience, if not always highly artistic. In the debate taking place in the diaspora over the aesthetic profile of genuine Russian literature, it was Solzhenitsyn who spoke most forcefully for Realism, while Sinyavsky defended creative freedom as the basis for all other freedoms.[103]

A smaller group on the right found that even Russian Realism was insufficiently national. Viktor Ostretsov saw nineteenth-century Russian literature as an endless succession of frivolous balls, superfluous men, and beautiful but empty words on the part of gentry writers, while the more politicized nongentry prose offered readers miserable clerks and utopian dreams. Nowhere in this "so-called" Realism could a reader find evidence of the real life of the nation, including its religious life. And it was said that when Dostoevsky brought religion into literature he misrepresented Russian Orthodox teachings in the name of a sentimental, mystical humanism of his own invention.[104]

And so we arrive at the model *russkii pisatel'*: ethnically Russian, at least nominally Orthodox, inflexibly righteous, politically conservative, and favoring a strong national state and strong military, nostalgic for the empire, loyal to his Orthodox Slavic brothers but wary of foreigners in general, a proud archaist who in his art adhered to the best traditions of Russian civic and moral realism. He must oppose pluralism in any form: political, spiritual, or cultural. He should have not merely an ancestral memory (*rodovaia pamiat'*) but a genetic memory (*geneticheskaia pamiat'*), something that mere "Russian-language" writers could not possibly possess, no matter how strong their ties to Russian culture.[105] This model *literator* was based in part on the strongly articulated self-image of the Village Prose writers who saw themselves as witnesses, chroniclers, Old Believers, pilgrims, elegists, mourners, and the righteous sons of dying mothers.[106] The difference after 1985 was that the literary shepherd had mutated into a cultural border guard and the recording angel into an avenging angel.

The checklist outlined above was followed, for example, in a 1995 article announcing that Army Captain Vladislav Shurygin had been accepted into the Union of the Writers of Russia and had also become a *Zavtra* correspondent. Everything about Shurygin, we were assured, was correct. He was Lermontov's age, looked a bit like 1812 hero Denis Davydov, was popular with women, had participated in all the recent wars (including the 1993 defense of the White House), and had a long military pedigree and a sharp and honest pen. He even attracted the right kind of reader: Orthodox, Russian, Soviet, and Slavic.[107] This gives some sense of what cultural *russkost'* meant to the nationalist Right. What they sought was control, if not official at least unofficial and moral, over every aspect of Russian literature. They wanted to determine the content of the canon and the ranking of writers past and present. Article after article demanded that Pasternak, Mandelstam, and other merely "Russian-language" writers be pushed back into the second ranks, making room for genuine Russians like Bondarev. This insistence on hierarchical control involved not only naming the saints but also expelling the demons. The nationalist Right sought to monopolize the reconstruction of literary history, to direct literary politics, censor fundamental criticism of anything Russian, guard literary style, and form public taste, especially that of the younger generation. Tatyana Glushkova, for example, thought that her verse would "strengthen the 'genetic code' of Russian readers."[108] Gaining the allegiance of young writers, critics, and readers, especially those outside of Moscow and St. Petersburg, would help to ensure control not just of the past and present of Russian literature, but of its future as well.

The right-wing's attempt to annex all cultural territory and fix its borders elicited spirited responses from those who found this cultural-ideological agenda often offensive, occasionally dangerous, and generally ludicrous. Historian Sergei Shvedov called the pronouncements of Kazintsev, Lyubomudrov, and many others self-evidently ridiculous, and believed that citing them would go a long way towards helping Russian culture develop an immunity to chauvinism.[109]

Tatyana Tolstaya answered the post-1985 genetic detective work with her own "discovery" that the best Russian writers—including Pushkin, Lermontov, Gogol, Herzen, Tolstoy, Turgenev, and Dostoevsky—were all secretly Jewish and russophobic. Her 1990 parody "I Cannot Remain Silent" revealed that Pushkin was really Pushkind, Lermontov was Lerman and wrote about "unwashed Russia," Gogol was Yanovsky and was always yearning to go to the Holy Land, Tolstoy (a critic of both church and state) was actually Leib Grossman. Turgenev's writing set fathers against children, and Dostoevsky called his Russian characters poor, insulted, and even idiotic. The contemporary team of Belov, Rasputin, and Kunyaev were in reality Weissman, Rabinovich, and Zilbermintz.[110] This parody of ultranationalist thinking was one of the most effective responses to the "exclusionary typology" that made its appearance in the literary press and at writers' meetings during the decade after 1985.

Relationships between Russian writers of differing ethnic backgrounds were the subject of a number of literary works, including Vladimir Voinovich's *The Fur Hat* (*Shapka*), in which a Russian Jewish writer, Yefim Rakhlin, is closely observed by his neighbor Vaska Tryoskin, "poet, and defender of the Russian national character against chemistry and Jews."[111] Tryoskin is so convinced that the Zionists will succeed in taking over Russia that he decides to join them, and passes a note to the uncomprehending Rakhlin which reads "Request acceptance into Yid-Masons."[112] Tryoskin even thrusts a message into Yefim's coffin, hoping for his intercession in the other world.

The responses by Tolstaya and Voinovich touched on an idea that had carried some weight with the urban creative intelligentsia from the Thaw years on: the sense of a connection between Jewishness, vulnerability, and the drive to write honestly whatever the consequences. Yevgeny Yevtushenko addressed this topic in his poem "Babii Yar," as did Sinyavsky by becoming Tertz. The conservatives put ethnic Russians hostile to their cause in the same rootless, cosmopolitan, Zionist group as Russian Jews. Following Dostoevsky's line of thought, the nationalist Right believed that Russian literature, in which Orthodox beliefs were central, had more to say to the world than other literatures, and that only a real Russian could speak for the country. One side saw all writers in Russia as "Jewish" to some degree; the other side excluded Jews and their co-conspirators from the canon. Felix Roziner addressed complex identity questions faced by Russian-Jewish writers in his *samizdat* novel *A Certain Finkelmeyer* (*Nekto Finkel'maier*); the events in the narrative take place in the 1960s, and the book was written between 1971 and 1975 when Roziner still lived in Moscow. His hero, whom he gave the unmistakably Jewish name of Aaron-Chaim Mendelevich Finkelmeyer, is a gifted poet who winds up working for the Ministry of Fisheries because anti-Semitism in the official literary world made it very hard for him to get published. When he hears that editors are looking for poetry from the indigenous Siberian population, he comes up with the idea of publishing his poems as "translations" from Tongor, the language of an obscure and rapidly dwindling tribe, and submitting it as the work of a hunter whom he heard singing a drunken, mournful song in the Arctic night. Finkelmeyer's nemesis in Moscow, who wrote the accusatory article that gives the book its name, is one Sergei Prebylov, an ultra-Russian poet who recites his verses at an evening gathering:

> He began with an autobiographical poem, informing all and sundry that he was born . . . in a haystack. . . . having made contact with Mother Earth at the moment of his birth, he had been constantly nourished by Her juices. Aggressive voice and aggressive message combined to form an *organic*, as the critics would put it, whole. . . .

nor was there a hint of ambiguity, allusion, obscure imagery, or metrical, acoustic, or linguistic sorcery. The poems were about country sandals treading asphalt streets or boots on the dusty road or bare feet in rustling grain, about out-of-the-way . . . villages that have upheld Russia's honor from time immemorial. The intelligentsia . . . appeared in the asphalt-street poems as "the rot of the Arbat mold."[113]

In his final poem of the evening, Prebylov hints about "certain elements" that prefer "things foreign to things Russian." His substandard language and bad poetic style anger Finkelmeyer and a vigorous discussion ensues about who has the right to call himself a Russian poet. Finkelmeyer is immersed heart and soul in Russian literature, with vast quantities of memorized poetry, especially Pushkin's, at his disposal, and he has an original poetic talent. Despite his gift, he is condemned at his parasitism trial for having produced "antiliterature."[114] Prebylov has one thing going for him, his genetic background, but that proves to be enough for a successful career. Finkelmeyer himself is destroyed, but his works live on in a manuscript passed down to his son.

Set in the 1960s and written in the 1970s, the novel's references to protochauvinistic literature and criticism stimulated a response both above and below the surface of official rhetoric. While the "russification" campaign could not get into full swing until after 1985, protochauvinism in literature and criticism was evident at a much earlier period. The transcript of a 1977 meeting of writers, critics, and MGU students at TsDL (Tsentral'nyi dom literatorov), which was published in Russia only fourteen years later, shows Kunyaev, Kozhinov, Lobanov, Seleznev, and Palievsky expressing chauvinist cultural views in an unsubtle way, attacking Meyerhold, Babel, and modernism and innovation in literature and the theater, and questioning the credentials of critics and directors who were not ethnic Russians.[115]

The question of where the works of Russian-Jewish writers fit into the canon could not be answered to the satisfaction of all concerned, particularly once ethnicity had been so highly politicized. From the point of view of the Russian camp, nationality was destiny: it was hard, they said, to be a Russian, but such is our proud fate (sud'ba). Russian-Jewish writers saw the question of which cultural group to ally themselves with as a personal choice, and one that did not preclude identification with both groups simultaneously. This attitude angered russifiers obsessed with the idea of an organic unity in literature, a wholeness (tsel'nost') which could be both a source of pride and a means of protection.[116]

The stylistic limitations proposed for Russian literature disturbed the creative intelligentsia as much as the underlying chauvinism did; they saw it as a "poetics of resentment." Calling this movement ivangardism emphasized its distance from the suppressed avant-garde.[117] The term *natsrealizm* (National Realism) showed its closeness to the pseudoreality and one-party spirit of *sotsrealizm* and hinted at a secondary association with National Socialist culture.[118] Alexander Ageev used the image of a "barbarian lyre" (from Blok's poem "Scythians") to describe the aesthetic weakness and ideological arrogance of the new "patriotic poetry."[119] The writer Vyacheslav Kuritsyn turned the tables on right-wing nationalists by accepting their categories at face value; from now on, he declared, we would define as "Russian" that literature which combined the pulpit, the podium, Big Ideas, and suffering, and as "Russian-language" literature that which valued aesthetics over ideology, and innovation over tradition.[120] Both sides saw culture beginning anew in the post-Soviet period, one side with an international, apolitical postmodernism, and the other with a genuine Russian literature so magnificent "that the world would tremble" (*vozniknet velichaishaia, takaia, chto mir sodrognetsia, literatura*).[121]

The liberal-democratic literary press objected to the conservative nationalist tendency to hijack "Russianness" and patriotism with the goal of russifying what the Right called an "occupied" culture. The obsession with borders and with saving the Russian writer as if he were an endangered species brought forth the accusation that the Right wished to turn Russian culture into one vast *pushkinskii zapovednik* (Pushkin preserve).[122] It was Russian literature as the village writ large, where any deviation from tradition and any alien presence was immediately noticed and dealt with severely. The image of a preserve foregrounded the idea of borders, which was crucial to the "Russian writer" argument. These are the borders of Russia or the much-missed USSR which the writer should never willingly cross. Valentin Sorokin reminded his readers that the so-called "period of stagnation" posed no real problems for those "who did not cross the Motherland's borders, but who defended them. . . . But those who dashed around international airports with suitcases full of caviar and worthless manuscripts—well, they had a bad time."[123]

There was also a strong sense of cultural borders. Glushkova insisted that there was only one Russian poetic tradition, and it was based almost solely on Pushkin's works. It was fully formed, indivisible, to be accepted without question or innovation. "To venture outside of its limits . . . is to abandon the realm of Russian poetry." But many attempts had been made to invade the hallowed cultural space; Russian-language writers were trying to "crowd out" the Russians.[124] "Why," Glushkova asked, "is so much [in Russian literature] done 'the way it was done in Odessa'?"[125] Russia and its culture were seen as "the 'shining city of Kitezh'" which was said to have descended uncorrupted to the bottom of a trans-Volga lake at the time of the first Mongol invasion."[126] The homeland (*rodina*) was a self-sufficient and self-contained place, which a foreigner's glance could not penetrate.[127]

A genuinely Russian writer should transcend neither the actual nor the cultural borders of his country. Cosmopolitan writers, at home everywhere, could never be truly Russian, even if their ethnic pedigree was otherwise acceptable. Not knowing the role planned for him by late twentieth-century ideologues, Alexander Pushkin tried unsuccessfully to cross Russia's borders, as he explained in the second chapter of *Journey to Azrum* (*Puteshestvie v Azrum vo vremia pokhoda 1829 goda*). A Cossack guide had informed him that the small Arpachai River they were about to ford was the Russian border, and Pushkin described the joyous anticipation with which he approached foreign soil for the very first time. "I rode happily into the sacred river, and my good horse carried me out onto the Turkish bank. But this bank had already been conquered: I was still in Russia."[128] Russia seemed, perversely, to expand in proportion to Pushkin's wish to cross its borders. The state and its nationalist writers and critics wanted Pushkin to be of universal significance without actually having set foot on foreign soil.

While the campaign to politicize ethnicity—as Stalin had done in the late 1940s—largely failed, the russification drive was not completely rejected outside the conservative nationalist camp. A relatively small percentage of writers and critics rushed to catch up with Western fiction and literary theory, to be part of an international literary community and not a nationally and ideologically bound literary process. Older liberals, on the whole, objected to the postmodernist literature that appeared after 1985, to the trashing of Russian classics by a few of the younger critics, and to the assumption that the ideological role of Russian literature had come to an end. Interviews in the Russian press with writers who lived abroad or were frequent travelers often contained substantial criticism of the West, especially America, and nostalgic feelings about their homeland and the role that writers and texts had played in its history. The widespread interest in the works of exiled Russian philosophers was having its effect; the essays of Ivan Ilin, for example, provided an intense and reassuring view of an enduring Russian cultural identity, and were written in such a way that they could be useful to both liberal nationalists and chauvinists.

Whether primarily the result of justified pride in a truly impressive legacy, or more the result of a search for stable values in a world that devalued all things Soviet and most things Russian, many writers and critics in the post-Soviet period saw themselves as possessing a distinctive national and cultural identity which they had no wish to lose. As a strictly defined ethnic category, *russkost'* began to lose its internal political edge by the mid-1990s, but something of its urgency remained. Russianness was a quality the intelligentsia could hold on to even as they argued vigorously over what exactly it signified and how a strong national-cultural consciousness fit into the various ideological agendas that were operative in post-Soviet Russia.

Chapter 5 Righteousness and
the Value of Suffering

The study of Russian history . . . has shown me . . . how important it is that
the country be led not by *force* and coercion but by *righteousness*.
—*Alexander Solzhenitsyn*

The willingness to suffer for truth and justice played an enduring, at
times controversial, role in Russian culture as righteous people walked
through both Russia's texts and Russia's territory. Authors and their
characters provided examples of a loyalty that could not be bought
other than with the truth—was this sufficient to make them a potential danger to the state? How did the fact of a writer's suffering at the
hands of the government itself come to be politicized? Finally, what
do the tribulations of writer or text have to do with a given work's lasting value?

RUSSIAN LITERATURE'S RIGHTEOUS
BROTHERS AND SISTERS

The *pravednik* (righteous man) and *pravednitsa* (righteous woman)
are characters with very deep roots in Russia. *Pravednik* is a "highly

charged word meaning a virtuous person just short of a saint, but well above the average run in goodness and nobility of spirit."[1] Vladimir Dal's dictionary, a key source for generations of writers, describes the righteous person as someone who lives according to God's commandments and acts justly in all matters.[2] *Pravednik* has its origins in the word *pravda*, which can best be described as a moral or just truth; it includes a whole range of commonly accepted precepts and is related to other culturally significant words like *pravdoliubets, pravdonosets,* and *pravdoiskatel'* (respectively: lover, carrier, and seeker of truth). The *pravednik* may stay at home and serve as an example for the community, or may go out in search of a just society, walking in and through the world rather than away from it. "When it is only their own persons that are involved they are meek, humble, and submissive; but where . . . the social community is concerned, they become capable of rebellion . . . rejecting and destroying overnight all that stand in the way. . . . Hence come the countless 'seekers after righteousness' . . . who so astonish the West."[3]

Unable to bear the injustice of the world, the righteous leave home to wander about Russia, fighting demons and seeking truth. This is an example of popular piety that works independently of church and state. It is important to distinguish between the Russian idea of righteousness, which is inflexible but also unselfish, and the more familiar Western notion of self-righteousness. The periodic reappearance in Russia of the *pravednik* during times of upheaval is almost a given. Nikolai Leskov resurrected the righteous hero in the late 1870s to counteract the protagonists of nihilist novels; a century later, another generation of conservative nationalists put literature through this politically charged process once again.

The humble, almost passive, type of *pravednik* is represented by Russia's first native saints, the Kievan princes Boris and Gleb, who were martyred in the cause of national unity in the eleventh century. The actively angry version is best represented by the archpriest Avvakum (1620–82), whose *Life (Zhitie)* was the first important work composed in vernacular Russian. Avvakum gives a lively account of how he led a movement—whose members came to be known as the Old Believers or Old Ritualists—that broke away from the official Russian Orthodox Church. Avvakum presented himself as an unbending figure who knew that his adherence to the old ways was the correct path, and whom no amount of persuasion could change. He was prevented from preaching, exiled, imprisoned in an underground cell, tortured, and eventually executed, but he was never broken. His written work was smuggled out of his underground cell, sometimes inside wooden crosses, and survived until it was finally published in 1861, just in time to influence the great age of Russian Realism. Tolstoy, Dostoevsky, Turgenev, and Leskov are some of the better-known writers whose characters bear a resemblance to Avvakum.

The *pravedniki* who appeared in Turgenev's "Living Relics" and Tolstoy's *War and Peace*, "Master and Man," and "Father Sergius" are primarily moral exemplars, but other literary *pravedniki* played more ideological roles. Righteousness in Russia signifies a type of behavior rather than a set of specific beliefs, and *pravda* covers different kinds of moral truth and social justice, although it is the conservative nationalist interpretation that has prevailed. Turgenev's Bazarov and Chernyshevsky's Rakhmetov were perceived as self-sacrificing heroes by members of the liberal and radical intelligentsia and as demonic nihilists by the conservatives, who responded with their own series of antinihilist *pravedniki*.

Dostoevsky vigorously attacked the rational ground on which the new radical hero stood and in *Notes from Underground* he held up for special scorn the idea that morality was a work in progress. Sixteen years later, responding to critics of his speech at the dedication of the Pushkin monument in June 1880, Dostoevsky challenged Europeanized Russians to show him their own righteous heroes, whom they "would set up in Christ's place." But, he adds, "you must know that among the People there are righteous men . . . positive characters of unimaginable beauty and strength, ones that have still not come within your purview. These righteous ones and sufferers for truth do exist, but do we really see them? . . . the People, at least, know that the righteous exist among them; they believe that such exist, they are steadfast in this thought, and they hope that when a fateful moment comes for all, such people will always save them."[4]

Worried that writers were too quick in noticing the filth in society and in people's souls, Nikolai Leskov (1831–95) wondered whether a nation that perceived itself only in negative terms could survive. Taking saints' lives as his literary model, in 1879 he began to write a cycle of narratives about righteous characters. A foreword to a collection of these stories begins with the proverb "No city can exist without three righteous people."[5] According to Leskov, *pravedniki* only seem to stand to the side of the main historical currents; in reality they "make more history than others." They are a beacon to their fellow Russians and their heroic exploits (*podvigi*) are the nation's "moral capital."[6]

Vladimir Korolenko (1853–1921), champion of the Populist cause and creator of many righteous, progressive heroes, found the Revolution of 1917 morally unacceptable; he engaged in an epistolary debate with Anatoly Lunacharsky, Commissar of Culture, a debate ended by Korolenko's death in 1921.

"A Righteous Man," Lunacharsky's eulogy for the writer, acknowledged that a *pravednik* would have difficulty condoning the violence and bloodshed of the day, but then added that this was an age that demanded not just self-sacrifice, but also "the sacrifice of others." There was an ominous tone in the remark that "righteousness and the most unsullied appearance undoubtedly include something that is deeply unacceptable for revolutionary epochs."[7]

While a righteousness based on Russian Orthodox traditions and values was insupportable in the new Soviet state, the basic structure and appearance of righteousness fit in quite well, since it could be spiritual without being religious. Agitprop pamphlets during the Civil War made use of personified figures of *pravda* and *krivda* (falsehood) borrowed from Christian-influenced Russian folklore. In these newly minted fables, the supporters of *krivda* were the "tsars, princes, landlords and the bourgeoisie."[8] The Red Army, not surprisingly, was the champion of truth and justice. The use of religious categories in the Lenin cult is well documented; from the assassination attempt in 1918 until decades after his death, Lenin was called a savior, prophet, apostle, ascetic, and passion-sufferer, and his written works were seen as a modern equivalent of the Ten Commandments and the Gospel.[9]

In the early 1930s, the architects of Socialist Realism co-opted saintly and activist models for their own Communist heroes as Katerina Clark demonstrated in her landmark study of the Soviet novel.[10] A host of exemplary, self-sacrificing, and, most importantly, unbending characters graced the pages of Soviet literature. This time the righteous ones were agronomists, kolkhoz brigade leaders, engineers, soldiers, and, of course, Party zealots. While borrowing certain aspects of the familiar and culturally acceptable *pravednik*, Socialist Realism made some profound changes to fit the requirements of a very different political agenda and code of ethics.

The old and new variants of the self-sacrificing, stubborn hero differed on the crucial point of righteousness vs. consciousness. Righteousness is oriented towards an already-existing faith—Orthodoxy, Holy Rus, and the Russian God. The goal of the righteous person is to stand up for the ancestral faith and for truth in a society which may have lost sight of its origins and its values. In traditional Russian culture a person cannot learn to be righteous; it is a state of being. Someone well versed in sacred texts might also be living a righteous life, but the educated person has no advantage over—and some disadvantages against—an illiterate, even uneducable, Russian, as in the case of the *iurodivy* (holy fool).

Although serving a cause larger than himself or herself, the righteous person still retains the privilege of spontaneity, something that Katerina Clark has shown to be anathema to progressive literature from Chernyshevsky to Fadeev. The *pravednik* or *pravednitsa* may wake up one morning and decide to wander about Russia bearing witness to the truth, or may search, as the Old Believers did, for the Rus that was thought to have been lost in the seventeenth century. The righteous ones do not seek to glorify or advance themselves. They have complete confidence in their beliefs, and they are given substantial freedom of movement by those who believe in this special, divinely granted role.

In the "master plot"—as Clark called it—of progressive literature, on the other hand, the hero sets off not on his own initiative but usually at a time and for a purpose decided on by those superior to him in the hierarchy.[11] He is sent to perform the same function that others were performing elsewhere. There is a uniform command structure, a uniform process, and a goal that can be conveyed by a single word—communism—but which in practice is the subject of detailed directives. The progressive hero learns to master his spontaneity in order to reach the level of consciousness required of him. Katerina Clark describes the spontaneity/consciousness dialectic as one that must be mastered in order for the potential heroic state to be realized.[12]

In this cultural paradigm, the behavior of the conscious hero was fairly predictable; he was a danger to the tsarist regime, but a servant of the Soviet state, and since the agenda was determined from above, when it changed, the conscious hero unquestioningly accepted new directives. The righteous hero, on the other hand, is unpredictable, self-motivated, and feels free to choose how, when, and where to be righteous, staying within the letter of the law and then deliberately violating it. No regime can own such a person because the righteous ones retain control over their own souls to the end, as they act for the good of the community. The members of the intelligentsia deported in 1922 and Father Pavel Florensky who was sent to Solovki made it very clear that they could not be intimidated by the new regime.

A text by or about a righteous person could be a dangerous affirmation of elemental spiritual freedom (*volia*). After Stalin's death, traditional Russian *pravedniki* reappeared as characters in stories about the Russian countryside. Nikolai Zhdanov's "A Trip Home" (1956) features an urban bureaucrat who travels back to the village for his mother's funeral. His complacent attitude is disturbed not only by the example of his mother's simple, unselfish life, but also by the question she asks him in a dream: "Are the peasants being treated fairly by the government?" Yury Kazakov's 1957 story "The Old Woman by the Sea" focuses on ninety-year-old Marfa, who spends her days taking care of a large peasant home filled with reminders of the past, and her nights praying to Old Believer icons. She represents and helps to preserve the old order, and her face is "ancient and dark" like the saintly images that adorn the walls of her house. She is a figure frozen in time, exemplary, but not overtly or actively righteous. Kazakov's restraint is a combination of his naturally laconic style, heavily influenced by Ivan Bunin, and the subtlety necessary for literary survival; it was written, after all, only four years after Stalin's demise.

The Kazakov story marked the beginning of Village Prose, a literary movement which featured numerous upright peasant characters. What hard-line Party spokesmen saw as the undesired resurgence of pre-Revolutionary cultural and ethical values other Soviet critics defended as examples of traditional, patriotic Russianness. Since Youth Prose and later Urban Prose foregrounded characters even less exemplary from a socialist point of view—Western-oriented, alienated, feckless—the defense of these *pravedniki* was to a large extent successful. The writers, mostly of rural origin, justified their stories as artistically reworked memoirs of childhood and as an appropriate gesture of gratitude for the heroic but largely unrewarded wartime achievements of Russian peasants.

The delicate balance achieved by the Village Prose writers was upset when "Matryona's Home" was published in *Novyi mir* in January 1963. While Solzhenitsyn's 1962 story *One Day in the Life of Ivan Denisovich* was fundamentally in harmony with Khrushchev's de-Stalinization campaign, "Matryona's Home" pressed up against the boundaries of the permissible. Its final passage on the importance of righteous people to the nation's well-being made moral, almost ideological, claims for its traditional peasant heroine. The rhetoric of conservative nationalism had entered post-Stalinist rural literature, but it was silenced by the censors almost immediately and was not heard again for over twenty years.

The folk-religious roots of Solzhenitsyn's *pravednitsa* are easily recognized, as are Matryona's ties to nineteenth-century Russian literary heroines. The author had planned to use the Russian proverb "Without a righteous person no village can stand" (*Ne stoit selo bez pravednika*) as the story's title; this was changed to the more neutral "Matryona's Home" to allow its publication. The ultimate effect is that the proverb's appearance at the very end is unexpected and powerful. Solzhenitsyn's narrator begins to fully appreciate his landlady's worth only after her untimely death. He is most impressed by her lifelong refusal to accumulate material goods and her habit of helping anyone who asked. Matryona's fellow villagers took her for granted and even despised her generosity of spirit.

> We had all lived side by side with her and never understood that she was that righteous one without whom, as the proverb says, no village can stand.
>
> Nor any city.
>
> Nor our whole land.[13]

What was a dramatic but somewhat conventional story of rural decline and of a generous gesture that ended in tragedy was transformed into a stern warning about what happens to a nation whose righteous ones perish.

In light of the pre-Revolutionary roots of Matryona's character, it is interesting to note how closely Solzhenitsyn's description of her matches the characterization of a canonical Socialist Realist heroine, albeit with all the signs reversed. Galina Nikolaeva's 1950 story "The Manager of the Machine-Tractor Station and the Chief Agronomist" featured a female agronomist who seems to one of her co-workers miraculously energetic, humble, and smart. He wonders whether she is just a lively girl or a person of great strength, "who could support heaven knows what weight on those slender shoulders of hers. Then the thought occurred to me that she might be that Russian woman . . . of [whom] I had read and heard: courageous and selfless, daring and reliable in work, simple and quiet in appearance, fearless and noble in deed. . . . Perhaps hers was this very same character and I had not recognized it in her? It happens, you know, that sometimes you work side by side with a person . . . and yet you do not know or understand him."[14]

The comparison of Village Prose and Socialist Realist texts simply shows that righteousness is a powerful behavioral model in Russian culture, and that the model can be used for quite different, even antithetical, ideological purposes. The Socialist Realists chose to preserve those aspects of the pre-Revolutionary literary heritage that suited their needs, but after 1953 other writers began reclaiming these cultural-literary models in a way that undermined Socialist Realism, and ultimately socialism itself. Solzhenitsyn made an overly stark contrast in 1963 between "the current spiritual impoverishment of the enslaved village" and "that sought-for, lofty *righteousness*."[15] One *Oktiabr'* critic complained that key principles of Soviet life were portrayed as "a hostile oppressive force but the Russian righteousness to which Solzhenitsyn alludes appears positive."[16]

The reaction to "Matryona's Home" was compounded by the general tightening of controls on literature that began the following year when Khrushchev was deposed. But even during the ensuing period of "stagnation" the parade of righteous peasants continued although the narrative surrounding them was less openly didactic. Rural authors were criticized and their stories parodied by

Communist hard-liners but a great deal made its way through the censorship. A reading of Village Prose of the 1960s and 1970s yields numerous examples of *pravedniki,* some of them even identified as persecuted Old Believers. These characters commented unfavorably on the present and waxed nostalgic about the past; they tried to carry on as many traditional practices and ignore as much of Soviet reality as they could get away with. Authors made it clear that their heroes were in every way superior to most younger villagers and to the agricultural experts and Party operatives sent from the city. The crowning achievement of this period was the magnificent portrayal of Darya Pinigina in Valentin Rasputin's *Farewell to Matyora* (1976). This story of a three-hundred-year-old island community that must give way to the floodwaters of progress from the Angara River hydroelectric project was elegiac and apocalyptic, patriarchal and environmentalist.

Darya is acknowledged to be the moral center of the island village of Matyora, its memory and its conscience, and her simple home is the place to which villagers come for tea, conversation, and refuge from Soviet progress. In general she goes calmly about her business but she can be roused to a righteous fury by those who would dishonor the village dead, like the men who are sent from the mainland to clear the cemetery in preparation for the floodwaters. We are led to believe that she will die if the waters are released before she leaves, but it is her own choice to remain on Matyora with her living friends and her dead relatives. She knows that "truth is in memory," and in order to learn the whole truth of past generations, she has to see Matyora to its end. Rasputin clearly admires her ability to "stand up for more than herself," but unlike Solzhenitsyn he does not see his righteous heroine as belonging to an endangered species. "In every village of ours there always was and is one, or sometimes, two, old women with a temper to whom the weak and suffering come for protection; and it is inevitable that if one such old woman lives out her days and dies, her place will immediately be taken by another woman who has grown old, strengthening her position among the others with her firm and just temperament."[17]

Farewell to Matyora marked the high point of Village Prose, which had added so many characters to the pantheon of the righteous. To both author and critics this story seemed to "logically complete the village theme."[18] The movement wound down by the early 1980s for a number of reasons, including the natural evolution of literary styles; the deaths of leading writers and the injuries that prevented Rasputin from writing for several years; the sense that Village Prose had ceased to be original; parodies of this literature; and tightened censorship on the subject of collectivization.

It is difficult to say what readers and scholars in the West expected of Russian literature after 1985, and it is even more difficult to characterize what appeared. For those who looked for signs of a cultural renaissance, it was surprising to discover that there was a partial resurgence of the dark ages as well. Some of the best-known new works of the early Gorbachev years (1985–87)—Valentin Rasputin's "The Fire," Viktor Astafiev's *A Sad Detective,* and Vasily Belov's *The Best is Yet to Come*—feature "righteous" heroes, and angry ones at that. These works were controversial at home and abroad, and cast a pall over the otherwise euphoric beginning of glasnost.

Valentin Rasputin's "The Fire" has been called an "emblem" of the period of change that began after Gorbachev came to power.[19] Rasputin was well regarded in the Soviet Union for the four short novels that he published between 1967 and 1976: *Money for Maria, Borrowed Time, Live and Remember,* and *Farewell to Matyora.* All of these focused on a moment of crisis in a peasant family or community in Siberia. Eschewing the flat, homogeneous style of much of Soviet literature, Rasputin had enriched his works with the voices of contemporary Russian peasants and with traditional folk expressions. Rasputin was also known for his short stories, including "Vasily and Vasilisa," "Downstream," and "You Live and Love," and for essays on ethnographic subjects.

"The Fire," which appeared in the journal *Nash sovremennik* in July 1985, fulfilled the promise Rasputin made after *Matyora* to "follow" his island characters to new settlements in order to see what their lives would be like there. The story is set in Sosnovka, which was constructed around a logging camp that attracts a rowdy group of temporary workers and which took in the uprooted inhabitants of six flooded villages. After twenty years in the new settlement, it is painfully clear that the old villages "died" twice; first they disappeared physically, and then the transplanted inhabitants forgot the old ways that had helped them cope with trials much worse than a fire that sweeps through the Sosnovka warehouses. Unable to work the fields that were submerged with their old villages, they have lost the whole way of life that accompanied agricultural work. Their new occupation encourages an indifference towards nature and, eventually, towards the common good.

The absence of the old ways is experienced not as a luminous memory, as it had been in canonical Village Prose (1956–80), but as dark, angry pain. Such supportive structures as home, a sense of a native region, fulfilling work, a reverence for nature, and village solidarity have all but disappeared; harmony has given way to disharmony. The evil atmosphere in Sosnovka is as thick as the acrid smoke that pours forth from the burning warehouses. There is no special satisfaction in saving most of the settlement from fire because in a few years, when the surrounding forests have been depleted, many residents will be leaving anyway. "The village is burning, our dear, native village," words from a Russian folk song that serve as an epigraph to the story, have an ironic resonance; the settlement will never be native to anyone.

Against this dark background, two righteous figures emerge. Uncle Misha Khampo is an old man with a lame arm and limited powers of speech. He serves as a watchman and self-appointed guardian of traditional values which do not allow him to steal anything that belongs to the whole community. He is killed by hooligans because of his failure to adapt to their code of behavior which permits, even encourages, looting during the fire. The old man manages to kill his attacker, vanquishing at least one of the "demons" who have invaded Sosnovka. The narrator reminds us, though, that upon receiving these two people, it is for the earth to make the final judgment about who is righteous and who is guilty.

The other *pravednik* is the hero, Ivan Petrovich Egorov. He submitted to the inevitable when his village of Egorovka was abandoned, moving his *izba* (peasant home) to the new location. In moving, he lost the historical significance of his last name, which derived from the name of his former village. Instead of being "Egorov of Egorovka," he is now "Egorov without Egorovka."[20] Egorov now means as little as did Sosnovka (from *sosna* "pine") in a settlement whose sole reason for existence is to cut down trees. He thinks of leaving to join a son who lives far away, but feels that this would be an abdication of his responsibility to preserve the memory of Egorovka. His departure would also leave a moral vacuum in Sosnovka, where he works as a truck driver and speaks out on every possible occasion about carelessness, waste, and theft. Newcomers call him a "fuzzy truth-seeker" (*pravdoiskatel' pliushevyi*) and they sabotage his truck. For Ivan Petrovich, *pravda* is a natural force, a river whose waters cannot be reversed or diverted into other channels, and it is with him wherever he goes. At the story's end, Egorov walks through the spring forest, seeking to recapture his inner sense of a homeland, of something native and dear. He cannot fight single-handedly against the disorder that surrounds him, he can only try to restore his own feelings of harmony, his "inner village." Critics called this story a parable, confession, and lament, both a warning of what was to come and an appeal for Russians to change before it was too late.[21]

Six months after Rasputin's "Fire," Viktor Astafiev's *A Sad Detective* appeared in the January 1986 issue of *Oktiabr'*. Astafiev brought together two popular and seemingly disparate literary forms, the detective story and Village Prose, to create one of the most original works of the 1980s. Even though the detective,

Soshnin, has retired because of injuries, and the narrative is set on the outskirts of a provincial city, this novel still encompasses the thematics of the detective story, crime and criminals, along with many of the characteristics and values of Village Prose.[22] Astafiev chose the detective story format to interest the mass readership of traditional *detektivy,* but he hoped that fans of this genre would realize that crime was the manifestation of an evil that was corroding Russia's soul. And he wanted the readers, and perhaps writers, of Village Prose to understand that idyllic conditions no longer prevailed in the countryside, if they ever had.

The hero, now a full-time writer, models himself on Dostoevsky, who he feels reached almost through to the center of man where the "self-devouring" beast lurks. Soshnin's first stories were about police work, but, like Dostoevsky, he wants to go beyond the topicality of the crime question, telling his editor that the broader theme is "all mankind." Soshnin tries to understand the Russian soul, the part that does evil and the part that all too easily forgives the evildoer. His years on the police force have drained all such sympathy from Soshnin and what he feels now is a weary agitation.

The hero's righteousness is reflected in his feelings about crime, the decline of peasant life and family values, and his vocation as a writer. A second-generation townsman, Soshnin has lived all his life on the edge of the city in an old wooden house left standing by mistake that represents for him "the memory of childhood and a place of refuge." He has maintained strong ties with the nearby countryside through visits to his wife's family. Astafiev lovingly describes genuine peasants, juxtaposing them to peasant bureaucrats and peasant criminals. He also contrasts authentic folk culture with the decorative arrangements of folk objects found in the apartments of urban pseudo-intellectuals.

The "village soul" of *A Sad Detective* is further illustrated by two episodes near the end of the story. The first is the funeral of his neighbor, Granny Tutyshika, which Soshnin willingly attends even though the old woman led a far from exemplary life. The occasion of this funeral brings Soshnin to the snow-covered cemetery, where he thinks of his own dead, of the earth that gave them life and received them when they died, of the cycle of the generations, and of the growing lack of respect for the dead. At the graves of his mother and aunt, he takes off his hat and bows low to the earth, making what Russians call a *zemnoi poklon,* feeling physical pain but spiritual relief. As he leaves the cemetery he encounters his estranged wife and his daughter, who on the pretext of attending the funeral feast follow him home. Reverence for the dead has unexpectedly saved his family.

When he awakens in the middle of the night and sees his daughter asleep on an old peasant trunk that belonged to his Aunt Lina, Soshnin has more than a conventionally sentimental response. He sees the evidence of what has been lost, since his daughter knows nothing of her rural forebears, and a sign of restoration, because his immediate family is with him once again. With village roots and family ties on his mind, he consults a well-worn edition of Dal's folk sayings on the subject of family values and faces a blank sheet of paper, ready to go on with his writing. As a detective, he lost the battle against crime, but as a writer he launches another vigorous assault on historical and generational amnesia against the "demons" threatening to take over the country. For him, *pravda* is a force of nature that cannot be ignored, both the highest goal in life and the pathway to it.

Critics saw *A Sad Detective* as a family novel, a writer's diary on the Dostoevsky model, a bitter satire, a civic sermon, a confessional cri de coeur, a series of physiological sketches, an anti-intellectual diatribe, an anti-alcoholism tract, and a *detektiv* overloaded with serious material even by Soviet standards. While the regular readers of detective stories were unsatisfied, the book was a big hit among professional criminologists.[23] Most reviewers noted that it was an angry and divisive work; just a few of them questioning the specific objects of the author's anger, which included (along with criminals) women, mass culture, intellectuals, the literary establishment, and Jews.[24] Unlike Rasputin's Egorov, the narrator and hero of *A Sad Detective* are not resigned to change.

A third neo-*pravednik* appeared in Vasily Belov's ironically titled novel *The Best Is Yet to Come* (*Vse vperedi*) of 1986.[25] Belov was known for his novels *That's How Things Are* and *The Eve*, the story cycles *Carpenter Tales* and *Vologda Whimsies*, and *Harmony*, a collection of lyrical ethnographic essays. His works, like those of Rasputin and Astafiev, were enthusiastically received by readers during the years of stagnation (roughly 1964–84), and although he was nationalistic and conservative there was little indication of the righteous anger that lay ahead.

The Best Is Yet to Come has been called an "antiurban" novel. "Everything in the city is 'anti.' Anticoncord. Antiharmony. Antiattachment. Antifriendship. Antilove."[26] Even though the setting is the city and the surrounding suburbs, the patriarchal village and peasant "Rus" loom large in this book as emblems of an idealized past in which proper values were upheld: men did manual labor, women had babies, and nobody went to France to sample the pornography, as several of the book's characters are rumored to have done.

The debilitated but righteous Dmitry Medvedev (*medved'* means "bear") is the rather modest source of hope for Belov. Formerly a successful urban *intelligent* who spent six years in prison after an accident at his institute, Medvedev, bearded and looking like a peasant, refuses to return to Moscow, preferring to live on the outskirts of the city. He declares to his friend Ivanov, himself a righteous crusader against alcoholism, that he is proud to call himself not just a conservative but a reactionary, because "it is the peasant's hut that has always been the salvation of Russia."

Belov's novel rejected the illusion shared by several of its negative characters that "everything lies ahead." The danger in idealizing the past, we are told, cannot be compared with the danger of idealizing the future. "According to Belov, the past is not only a sacred object. . . . It is part of the chain of 'continuity' that extends from centuries past. Only 'demons' can fail to respect the past. Only 'demons,' Belov says, are capable of looking at the present as an 'experiment.'"[27] It is by looking to the past that these future-oriented demons can be thwarted. Belov had written in earlier Village Prose works of the need, in broad cultural and ethnographic terms, to preserve the traditional peasant life of the Russian North, but his use of the past in *The Best Is Yet to Come* is narrowly ideological.

Critics of the novel called it an artistic failure, in which the author's anger and prejudice distorted the portrayal of characters like Lyuba and Brish who are, respectively, Medvedev's wife and the Russian Jewish man for whom she left him.[28] Supporters rejected any aesthetic appraisal of a work whose "truths" were so relevant to contemporary life. Several of them, forgetting that Misha Brish was Belov's own creation, went much further than the author in their attacks on Brish and the "evil forces" he represented.[29] *The Best Is Yet to Come* ends with Medvedev on the verge of losing his children, since their mother and stepfather may take them to far-off Arkansas, a somewhat fanciful destination for Russian émigrés. He and his friend Ivanov stand in the middle of a Moscow bridge, arguing about the best way to combat this and other evils. Ivanov urges a more aggressive approach, and the novel's final pages seethe with resentment, frustration, and the potential for violence.

That these three works were published within the space of a year was seen as more than a coincidence. The most important living rural writers, who had done so much in the past to weaken the grip of Socialist Realism, had moved their works out of the village, taking on an expanded role that the critic Lavlinsky called "nation-preserving."[30] In these new settings they were actively "defending the village from the city and protecting it from being infected by urban culture."[31] And the village stood for all of Russia, as these writers attempted to revive pre-Revolutionary values in a world in which both rural traditions and post-Revolutionary structures were rapidly disintegrating.

These were just the most important of a series of truth-seeking works that appeared during the second half of the 1980s. Some others in this group were Yuri Bondarev's *The Game* (1985), Vladimir Lichutin's *Lyubostai: The Devil of Passion* (1987), Astafiev's "Lyudochka" (1989), and Belov's *The Critical Year* (1989). Delayed works that were published during this period—for example, Fedor Abramov's "A Journey to the Past" (written 1963–76, published in 1989)—also featured *pravedniki*, who were generally less angry than the protagonists of the more recently written stories. A number of the writers themselves assumed roles as spokesmen for a rapidly evolving conservative nationalist agenda. While the vehemence of these works and their authors was unexpected, their righteous heroes were recognized as the cyclical reappearance of an enduring Russian type. Few readers missed the obvious parallels with "Matryona's Home," one of only a handful of Solzhenitsyn works published in the USSR prior to glasnost. But critics also noted the far deeper cultural roots of this character type, going back a thousand years to the beginning of Christianity in Russia.

It is interesting to see that while canonical Village Prose followed an established cultural model in its depictions of the righteous, in post–Village Prose there is an angry Soviet righteousness, a determination to impose one's beliefs on society as a whole, even if it meant, to paraphrase Lunacharsky, "the sacrifice of others."[32] As the Soviet Union lumbered towards its end, Soviet and conservative nationalist streams came together in a Red-Brown alliance that lasted from the late 1980s through the mid-1990s. Rasputin, Astafiev, and Belov's Gorbachev-era works remind us of Zamyatin's observation in the 1923 essay "On Literature, Revolution, Entropy, and Other Matters" that literature signals changes that are already in process, but which are not yet fully and publicly visible.

When controls on literature started loosening up in 1985, there were new opportunities for all writers, from liberal democrats to ultranationalists, as well as for those with more purely artistic goals. Rasputin, Astafiev, Belov, and others took advantage of this change to publish works that were much more overtly critical of what had happened in Russia than anything they had done previously. And, although their righteous heroes were a familiar cultural type, the anger and despair of these newest *pravedniki* was disconcerting on both aesthetic and political grounds. The radiant old women of previous decades had been replaced by angry men prone to violence. And while it was still acknowledged that Village Prose writers had helped rid Russian fiction of its *partiinost'* (Communist Party spirit), it looked to some as if they did so in order to fill the empty space with their own political agenda.

Writers could not only speak out in their fiction, they could speak out in public on matters of national importance. Conservative writers and critics were bitter about the past, mistrustful about the present, and anxious about the future. If Old Believers had feared losing the Russian God, these writers feared losing Russia itself as a distinctive ethnic and cultural identity; phrases like "spiritual genocide" and "russophobia" became commonplaces of their journalism. They refused to accept that truth or righteousness could come from those in other political or ethnic camps, rejecting outright Vassily Grossman's heroes and Rybakov's *Children of the Arbat.* Like writers before them, they looked for *pravedniki* to lead them out of the present morass and they found inspiration in figures like Avvakum, Gogol, and Dostoevsky, and in contemporaries like Alexander Solzhenitsyn and Valentin Rasputin.

Astafiev was most active in 1986, when his correspondence with the respected critic Natan Eidelman became virtually a matter of public record. Eidelman had written to Astafiev, objecting to the Russian chauvinism of *A Sad Detective* and other recent stories. In Astafiev's venomous reply, he raised the question of the appropriateness of Eidelman, a Russian Jew, being allowed to write about the nation's greatest cultural treasure, Alexander Pushkin.[33] This same demand for righteous and ethnically pure authors and critics had appeared in a 1909 essay by Andrei Bely that was, not surprisingly, republished in 1990.[34] That Astafiev did not invent this argument from ethnicity does not make the exchange with Eidelman any less painful to read.

Valentin Rasputin was active in public life before the era of glasnost as an impassioned spokesman for the growing environmentalist movement. While he continued to be a tireless advocate for Lake Baikal and for Siberia as a whole, in 1985 he began to add new topics to his publicistic portfolio: the growing Western intrusion into Russian life; the dangers that nature, culture, and the Russian people faced; and Russia's long history of suffering. "We don't need mighty upheavals, we need a mighty Russia!" was a favorite slogan he borrowed from Stolypin.

Vasily Belov concentrated for a while on the internal politics of the Writers Union, transforming himself into the unlikely figure of a righteous literary bureaucrat. The late 1980s saw a veritable civil war in the various branches of the disintegrating writers' organizations; as subsidies for literary activities evaporated, squabbles increased over the spoils—journals, buildings, funds—and over the right to speak for Russian literature. The liberal democrats, especially Yevtushenko, were themselves righteously angry and venal at times, but they presented no particular threat to Russia's stability.

The philosopher Nikolai Berdyaev (1873–1948) saw that among Russians "everything takes on a religious character; they have little understanding of what is relative . . . everything was appraised and assessed according to categories of orthodoxy and heresy." The national striving, well represented by Russia's writers, has not been directed towards freedom-as-such or material well-being, but towards "a more righteous life."[35] Compromise was a poorly developed national strategy; in Russian folk belief, a contract is an agreement made with the devil.[36]

Righteousness was a behavioral model not just for literary characters, but for authors and critics as well. The writer-*pravednik* was hardly an invention of the glasnost years; one need only think of Avvakum and of nineteenth-century writers thundering out their messages to the world, led by the furious (*neistovyi*) Vissarion Belinsky. The year 1991 saw the publication in Russia of Alexander Solzhenitsyn's *The Oak and the Calf,* a manual for the righteous cultural activist. These literary memoirs had long been available in the West and had circulated unofficially in Russia, but their appearance at home codified this distinctively Russian literary-spiritual profile, as did other memoirs and archival material on the lives of Russian writers which followed.

Solzhenitsyn, like Avvakum, composed a "saint's life" for himself, full of suffering and achievement: there was childhood deprivation, coming to adulthood during the purge years, dangerous wartime service, arrest, prison camp, cancer, internal exile, and, after many precarious years as a mostly underground writer, expulsion from the Soviet Union. Throughout this long narrative, the author emphasized that in his texts he spoke not for himself, but for all the *zeks* (prisoners), especially those who did not survive the labor camps. He believed that by keeping their memory alive he could transform the nation through a call to remembrance and repentance. His encounters with literary and government officials were welcome opportunities for him to display his inflexibility (*nepreklonnost'*), the most salient aspect of his righteousness, because he knew that the authorities feared "strength and steadfastness" most of all. Like a saint, his activities would continue after death.[37]

Russian saints' lives emphasized the *podvig* (heroic deed); for Solzhenitsyn, each of his texts was yet another heroic achievement. From his prison years until he was forced to leave the USSR in 1974 he had to find the time and energy to research, write, memorize, copy, recopy, hide, and distribute his works, and then send them safely out to the West.[38] He presents himself as the creator and protector of endangered texts, and yet at the same time he presents the texts as both invulnerable and impersonal: "It was not I who did it—mine was merely the hand that moved across the page!"[39] The writer was a holy man, called by God to save Russia.

Solzhenitsyn was not alone in seeing his role as the bearer and preserver of historical truth. When "Matryona's Home" was first published, letters from readers identified Solzhenitsyn himself as the person "without whom our country cannot stand."[40] Years later, he was still being identified as a lover of truth and justice (*velikii pravoliubets*), martyr (*muchenik*), and prophet (*prorok*); in the late 1980s, this same constellation of terms was applied in the conservative nationalist press to writers like Rasputin, Belov, Astafiev, Yuri Bondarev, and Vladimir Soloukhin.

There are many varieties of Russian spirituality that are reduplicated in literature and in literary life: martyrs, prophets, miracle-workers, wise elders, ascetics, hermits, pilgrims, *iurodivye* (fools-for-Christ), *ugodniki* (those who are pleasing, especially to God), intercessors, and *molchal'niki* (those who take a vow of silence). But one of the most enduring and socially influential types was not the one who retreats from an imperfect earthly existence, but the one who bears witness to the truth at home or who takes truth boldly into the world. The central role assigned to literature in Russian society encouraged writers to see themselves and their characters as these so-necessary *pravdonostsy* "bearers of truth and justice.'

The latter part of the 1980s brought a debate about the traditional role of literature as the nation's primary spiritual and political "space" and the writer as the nation's conscience. Many younger writers and critics saw "truth bearing" as a burden; they sought a "normal" literary life like the one they imagined prevailed in the West. Writers who accepted literature's ideological role struggled over how to read the past (asking which writers and works were harmful or helpful to Russia), the present (asking who now spoke for Russian literature), and the future (asking what could or should literature do for a Russia in distress). In this context, it is easy to understand why readers and critics in Russia and the West were dismayed to see that in a time of inevitable change one of the most prominent heroic types was the *pravednik*, the righteous one whose defining characteristic was precisely the refusal to change. Andrei Sinyavsky had warned in the mid-1970s that "our age has taught us that there are times when we should beware the righteous man more than the known informer."[41] However rich a cultural treasure, Avvakum and his descendants may not have been the best guides for building a new Russia. For the readers of post-totalitarian literature, another Russian folk expression may have provided a more appropriate response: "We don't need righteous people, we need people who can get along with each other."[42]

THE SUFFERING OF RUSSIA'S LITERATURE

Suffering! Why it's the sole cause of consciousness!
—*Fedor Dostoevsky*

Whatever else we may or may not know, we know how to suffer.
—*Yevgeny Zamyatin*

A popular folk song tells of a righteous hero who had "suffered long and hard for justice" (Za pravdu on dolgo stradal), a situation which characterizes the fate of many writers and texts in Russia.[43] Of the various forms that suffering has taken in Russian literary history, the best-known aspect is suffering within the text, as hosts of beaten-down characters drag themselves across the narrative stage: suicides, madmen, hysterical women, betrayed and betraying spouses, nihilists, child molesters, orphans, and insulted and injured peasants and even their dogs, as we know from Turgenev's memorably lachrymose story "Mumu." There were also neurotic clerks, repentant noblemen, victims of national battles and personal duels, dissidents, prisoners, and, in the late Soviet period, miserably postmodernist men and women. Tolstoy once complained to Maxim Gorky that in Dostoevsky's writing "it is all painful and useless, because all those Idiots, Adolescents, Raskolnikovs, and the rest of them . . . are not real; it is all much simpler, more understandable."[44] It was not that Tolstoy sought to reduce the amount of suffering in fiction, but that he preferred a less intellectually complex, more universal, more Tolstoyan kind of pain. Success was not presented as an attractive option in fiction, as we see from the truly wooden Stolz of *Oblomov* and his generally lifeless literary cousins.

Given the strong metaliterary impulse in Russian culture, it is not surprising that there are scores of suffering writer-heroes in the canon, particularly after the Revolution; Zamyatin's *We,* Bulgakov's *The Master and Margarita,* and Pasternak's *Doctor Zhivago* provide just the best-known fictional portrayals of the beleaguered creators of dangerous texts. This familiar character type is treated satirically in such works as Dostoevsky's *Demons,* Tertz's "Graphomaniacs" (1960), and Voinovich's "Skurlatsky, Man of Letters" (1972) and *The Fur Hat* (1989). In *The Fur Hat,* Yefim Rakhlin, a writer of politically acceptable adventure tales, is obsessed with his professional standing. When a variety of fur hats are distributed to members of the Writers Union, Rakhlin, a Jew, receives medium-fluffy cat fur (*kot srednei pushisosti*); his sense of humiliation sets in motion events that end with his untimely death. Feliks Roziner's novel *A Certain Finkelmeyer* (*Nekto Finkel'maier,* written 1971–75) satirizes the politicization of ethnicity in the literary process, but the satire does not encroach upon the suffering of the hero, Finkelmeyer, or the almost sacred aura surrounding his poems.

The pages of Russian history far outdo fiction in providing narratives about writers who sacrifice themselves for their texts. The text as *podvig* (heroic achievement) and the writer as *podvizhnik* (hero, champion) are powerful Russian cultural myths. The last fifteen years of the twentieth century brought new and fuller information on this subject in such forms as memoirs from Russia and abroad, and secret police archives, but by itself, more information brought neither clarity nor closure. Attention to the past mistreatment of writers and the delay or destruction of their work stimulated a range of responses and more than a little controversy. The analysis of competitive suffering in the previous chapter showed how an inflated ethnicity influenced the telling of literary history: *our* writers suffered more, but were also more widely read and more deeply revered than *theirs*.[45] The expression *stradanie stradaniiu rozn'* (there's suffering, and then there's suffering) reminds us that the division of the cultural pantheon into *one's own* (*svoi*) and *others* (*chuzhie*) skewed the interpretation of lives and texts.

With a well-grounded expectation that the best writers suffered for the best texts, past success can become problematic and controversial. Along with the binary contrast of my struggle vs. your struggle, there was the opposition of my noble struggle vs. your shameful success. Such mutually exclusive measures of literary achievement complicated the process of reading writers' lives. Prior to 1985, it was virtually impossible to get past the censors and reach readers without making at least some concessions, but these could range from a talented writer agreeing to some cuts in a work all the way to a literary bureaucrat being rewarded for loyalty with publication of his works; there is even a special derogatory term for this latter type of literature, *sekretarskaia,* in reference to the powerful secretaries in the hierarchy of the Writers Union. If at one end of the spectrum lay struggle and silence, at the opposite end lay a world of attractive possibilities: massive print runs, generous royalties, awards, appointments to the Writers Union leadership or the editorial boards of important journals (positions that brought with them significant amenities), and for some, permission to travel abroad. The higher a writer climbed, the less it mattered whether his works genuinely interested readers or wound up being pulped; his success was an official, documented fact.[46]

In a posthumously published addition to his novel *Memory* (*Pamiat'*), Vladimir Chivilikhin described a 1965 encounter on a Moscow street with a weary-looking Leonid Sobolev, a fellow Siberian writer who headed the Russian Federation Writers Union. With sympathy and admiration Chivilikhin lists the activities in which Sobolev must participate because of the high office he occupies: "assemblies, meetings, governing bodies, councils, conferences, commissions, juries, committees, congresses, collegiums, conventions, sessions, seminars, plenums, symposiums and so forth, literary and supraliterary emergency meetings, brief discussions, executive and planning sessions . . . and solemn occasions of all sorts, anniversary celebrations, collective remembrances of the deceased, awards, the delivering of speeches of one sort or another, receptions, send-offs, formal parties, dinners and so on."[47] This stunning list, Gogolian in all but its lack of humor, gives a clear sense of how the Writers Union bureaucracy created, and carefully controlled, a simulation of literary life which brought rich rewards and some degree of protection, albeit often temporary, to those who chose to follow the rules.

A number of Soviet *literatory* who were seen not as a danger but as a source of pride to the state, received the most coveted reward of all, permission to go abroad. The destinations ranged from the socialist world to *kapstrany* (capitalist countries), that much-desired, if officially despised, realm. The literary figure on an international *komandirovka* (business trip) was not just a casual observer, but was expected to interpret the outside world for readers back home. While still in Russia in the 1960s, Solzhenitsyn complained about writers "who flood our literature with lightweight sketches about life abroad."[48] Aleksandr Korneichuk, one of the literary world's "frequent travelers," replied that going abroad was in fact very hard work, but was necessary in order to carry on the struggle for communism. "We return home worn out and exhausted, but with a feeling of having done our duty."[49]

In contrast to the writers who traveled, there was a group of conspicuous nontravelers, well-known writers obsessed with the idea of a journey abroad, but who never received the necessary permission. In *No Day without a Line*, Yuri Olesha dreamed of sojourns in Europe "that never took place." "Is it fame that I want? No, not fame, but a trip around the world. It's even hard to imagine that there is another world."[50] Mikhail Bulgakov got up with this desire every morning and went to sleep with it every night. He sent petitions to the government and while he waited for an answer he sketched out plans for travel books with which he would justify his trip, all to no avail. He finally realized, as he wrote to a friend in 1931, that "there will simply be no reply."[51] And, as the terror of the thirties grew around him, his travel-mania alternated—even coexisted—with agoraphobia. The writer who wanted to see the world was frequently afraid to leave his apartment unaccompanied. The literary history of the Soviet era is full of such bitter ironies.[52]

The "pursuit of success" was no more acceptable for the creators of Russian literature than it was for their characters.[53] In the discussions that began in the Gorbachev era a lot of hard, and ultimately unanswerable, questions were posed about the ethics of success versus suffering. Was it better before glasnost to have published a work at home, albeit in censored form, to have hidden it, or to have sent it abroad? Was remaining silent, while other writers suffered, the moral equivalent of joining the attack? By one set of values, not to have taken part in official literary life before 1985 was the better choice. Zamyatin laid out this kind of schema in his 1918 essay "Scythians?" where his writing takes on the strongly religious overtones that remind us of Saints Boris and Gleb and the profoundly Christocentric nature of Russian Orthodoxy, with its emphasis on luminous suffering. "Defeat, martyrdom on the earthly plane—and victory on a higher plane, the plane of ideas. Victory on earth—and inevitable defeat on the other, higher plane. No third alternative exists for the true Scythian, for the spiritual revolutionary, for the romantic. . . . Free Scythians will not bow to anything."[54]

In the writing of Russian literary history and the shaping of the canon from the mid-1980s through the mid-1990s, literary value was frequently calibrated to suffering, and there was a temptation on the part of writers and critics who promoted their works to retrospectively add this experience to their biographies. One should at least have done something politically risky (riskovanno) and have produced a text judged to be dangerous. Vladimir Soloukhin insisted that he had suffered more in the course of attacking Pasternak—an act which he deftly excused with the phrase "something came over me" (tut bylo kakoe-to pomrachenie)—than Pasternak suffered by being attacked. Pasternak, he adds, did not even know how to suffer correctly, unlike Solzhenitsyn, who stood firm and did not renounce his Nobel Prize in Literature.[55]

Writers who took a principled stand against interference by the censors, or who otherwise incurred the negative attention of the authorities, faced nonpublication of their prose and poetry, nonperformance of their plays, economic hardship, the temptation to use samizdat and tamizdat to reach an audience, and, if caught, the possibility of exile, imprisonment, or expulsion. In judging published vs. suppressed texts, the work not officially permitted to appear was thought by many intelligentsia readers to have greater moral and artistic worth, greater truth, than the one that earned the official censor's stamp of approval for publication. Václav Havel cautioned against such a "sectarian view . . . that whatever does not circulate only in typescript . . . is necessarily bad."[56]

One measure of value in Russian literature depended on the degree to which the text suffered as it struggled to reach the surface or tried to remain hidden; the more perilous the journey or precarious the hiding place, the more significant the work of literature. A story that was published more or less intact in the Brezhnev era, like Rasputin's *Farewell to Matyora,* lost weight on this scale, while an interesting but artistically limited work like Anatoly Rybakov's *Children of the Arbat* gained, at least in the short run. Sergei Zalygin and Naum Korzhavin, joined by Viktor Astafiev in the early 1990s, were among the relatively few voices calling for a more consistently aesthetic, nonpoliticized judgment of fiction, but the stories of suffering texts were numerous and colorful.

From Avvakum's *Life* to Grossman's *Life and Fate,* the censorship, suppression, confiscation and even arrest of manuscripts were part of Russian literary history. Publication did not preserve a text from future suffering through mandated changes, or, in the case of the author's subsequent disgrace, of banishment from circulation and from critical discourse. Solzhenitsyn, for whom the most extensive paper trail exists, complained in 1967 that stories of his that were printed in *Novyi mir* were never reissued in book form, restricting readers' access to them. In 1970 he demanded that the Soviet government "eliminate the ban against library use of the surviving editions of my previously published short stories."[57] Withdrawal of already published texts from the general public, the decision not to reprint popular works or to keep them out of the school curriculum, were some of the damage control strategies used against the dangerous texts of writers living and dead.

Texts that lay quietly in a desk drawer could be seized and kept from distribution at home (and abroad) or they could be circulated against the author's wishes, as in the case of Solzhenitsyn's verse play *A Feast of Victors* (*Pir pobediteli*). Texts lived a precarious physical existence because of the materials used to record them and the places in which they were stored. Anatoly Kuznetsov was denounced in the Soviet press for admitting that he sealed his manuscripts in preserving jars and, under cover of darkness, dug holes in which to hide them.[58] Sinyavsky was excited and encouraged by the secret life of manuscripts as they snuck across borders to an uncertain fate in the West; it meant that after a long dry spell of *gosizdat* there was once more literature in Russia of great value, as confirmed by the dangerous life it led.

The prisoner Sinyavsky embedded new texts in letters to his wife, saying that "A sheet of paper is for me what a forest is to a man on the run."[59] Sometimes lines lived inside a person's head, one memory away from extinction. Irina Ratushinskaya and Alexander Solzhenitsyn both came up with imaginative ways to preserve their new works until it was safe to write them down. Akhmatova preserved the poem "Requiem" in her memory for more than twenty years, while many of Mandelstam's poems went from his to his wife's memory, with only a fleeting existence on paper until well after his death. Saving unofficial texts was an achievement of heroic proportions, a true *podvig,* especially when the writer was out of favor or even imprisoned.

There is great pathos in the story of Bulgakov's works, but also great irony, since he was forever chucking manuscripts into the stove. "The stove long ago became my favorite editor. I like it for the fact that, without rejecting anything, it is equally willing to swallow laundry bills, the beginnings of letters and even, oh shame, verses!"[60] He endured many disappointments and terrors but there were interesting moments along the way; the best of Russia's writers would drop by his apartment, and for a while he and his wife were regular guests at lively American Embassy parties. And no amount of rejection or potential danger could stem the creative flow; each rejected text stimulated a new project. With memoirs of the Soviet era more available than ever before, we can witness—at a distance—not only the lives of literary texts, but also the texture of literary lives.

There are any number of compelling examples from Russian literary history of writers accepting their own vulnerability but struggling to protect their written legacies from destruction. Few stories are more dramatic than that of Nikolai Bukharin, writing to Stalin in 1937 to plead that four prison manuscripts, including the novel *How It All Began,* not be destroyed along with their author. "Don't let this work perish. . . . *Have pity!* Not on me, *on the work!*"[61] For whatever reasons, his plea was heard. The manuscripts were preserved in Stalin's own archive, unearthed at the prodding of Bukharin scholar Stephen Cohen in 1992, and published in Russia over the next four years.[62]

Not every work had so fortunate a fate, and Vitaly Shentalinsky, who in 1988 began to press for the release of the KGB's archival material relating to writers confesses at the end of his first book that the impossibility of locating the twenty-four folders confiscated from Isaac Babel, and the death of the one agent who might have known their location, reminded him of the other things that have been lost, or are still hidden away in the deep recesses of the Party and presidential archives. "For years," Shentalinsky tells us, "a soot-stained chimney released a steam of smoke over the Lubyanka and for decades sprinkled Moscow with the ash of incinerated manuscripts. How many books were consumed by that chimney, never to be read again."[63]

FROM INDIVIDUAL SUFFERING
TO COLLECTIVE SURVIVAL

In reading the "life" of Russian literature, emphasis has been placed on the struggles of the individual Russian writer, since we tend to think in terms of the actions of individuals in history, and on loss, since the Soviet period was a time of deprivation and destruction in every sphere, among them culture. But much of what was going on may be invisible to us if these are the only lenses we use. Looking at a collectivity of writers and readers and at the indestructibility of texts is one way to gain a more comprehensive understanding of how literature functioned in the Soviet period, and of whether the nation's identity and spirit was more nurtured by what was available than starved by what was not.

The third of the ten maxims outlined in the first chapter of this book claims that one text would be on everyone's mind at a given time until the next work replaced it in a chain of intensely experienced words and works.[64] A close reading of the literary process during the Soviet era, especially in the years after Stalin's death, makes it clear that in many ways the role of the text outweighed that of the individual writer. Literary texts were, as Pushkin said, "a monument not made by human hands" (*nerukotvornyi*); they were in some sense impersonal or suprapersonal, with more resonance than a single author's voice. Socialist Realism was, by definition, the work of "engineers of human souls," who represented the whole Soviet people, but non–Socialist Realist and underground authors also stood for much more than just themselves. Solzhenitsyn reiterated throughout his memoirs and in his Nobel lecture that he spoke for all the prisoners, and especially for all the fallen writers.

> To reach this chair from which the Nobel Lecture is delivered . . . I have mounted not three or four temporary steps but hundreds or even thousands, fixed, steep, covered with ice, out of the dark and the cold, where I was fated to survive, but others, perhaps more talented and stronger than I, perished. . . . And today how am I, accompanied by the shades of the fallen, my head bowed to let pass forward to this platform others worthy long before me, today how am I to guess and express what *they* would have wished me to say?[65]

In the poem "Requiem," Anna Akhmatova served as the voice of all the women who waited outside prison walls to hand in packages for their loved ones and to try to learn their sentences; she called herself a witness to their common fate. An inhabitant of the world inside those walls, Andrei Sinyavsky named one of the books he wrote in prison *A Voice from the Chorus.*

Official literature, *gosizdat,* had its own collective life: a text that went through official channels was poked, probed, pruned and rewritten through a dozen levels of censorship before final permission was received. According to the poet Viktor Sosnora, writing in 1967, the twelve censors were: the author, the editor who first received the book, the editor assigned to work on the manuscript, the first reviewer, the second reviewer, the senior editor, the editorial board, the editor in chief of the division for artistic literature (*belletristika*), the publishers' council, the editor in chief of the publishing house, the director, and the local "office of ideological control."[66] With this many levels of oversight, the unexpected publication of a daring work was a surprising story in itself.

The reproduction and preservation of unofficial texts also often turned into a collective enterprise. *Samizdat* required lots of energy and lots of connections: tireless spouses, trustworthy friends, armies of volunteer workers, intrepid foreign co-conspirators, and hard-to-obtain supplies. It was an illegal, continually risky business. Russia even has the grotesque distinction of having produced a typist-martyr, a woman who committed suicide after being interrogated by the KGB because of her connection to Solzhenitsyn. As Solzhenitsyn explained, weak links in this chain could endanger the entire enterprise, whose goal was to send the work out into the world to prevent its being destroyed and its message lost.

After a text was written, it had to be reproduced—recopied, retyped, sometimes photographed—and then distributed both domestically and abroad (to ensure preservation and an international audience, and for broadcast back into the Soviet Union). Any serious reader who lived in Russia during the sixties and seventies can tell of receiving a text for one evening only and having to pass it on to the next reader in a chain that only ended when the ragged copy fell apart. Readers knew that they were sharing in this experience with many other people throughout the country. While faded carbon copies were the norm, Solzhenitsyn received letters from Russians who said that they had read his books on cigarette paper. An edition of Akhmatova's poetry from the early 1990s includes a photograph of a minuscule birch-bark notebook in which one of her poems had been copied by a prisoner for whom it had served as a prayer and a charm.[67]

Despite the risk inherent in simply possessing unofficial texts or Russian books printed outside the country, let alone being part of a reproduction and distribution network, these were all widespread practices. In an almost humorous passage, Solzhenitsyn relates how after the arrest of Sinyavsky and Daniel, "all Moscow . . . had been running around in a panic, transferring *samizdat* and illegal émigré books from one hiding place to another, carrying bundles of them from house to house and hoping that they were doing the right thing."[68] Texts could be—and often were—confiscated. Solzhenitsyn's archive, including *The Gulag Archipelago,* was carted off to the Lubyanka in 1965 and a number of his texts were soon circulating in a limited secret edition produced by the government.[69]

The travails of literature in the Soviet period included everything from the three-year-long incarceration of Bulgakov's *Heart of a Dog* and his diary of 1926 to an astounding two-hundred-year prison sentence intended for the text of Grossman's *Life and Fate* in 1961. When Bulgakov's diary was returned to him he burned it, and it was thought to have been lost forever. But in a strange fulfillment of the claim made in *The Master and Margarita* about the invulnerability of the written word, the secret police had made a copy, which was released and eventually published.[70] Some texts were genuinely lost, but less of the canon than one might fear; in the end, the more significant losses to Russian literature lay in those works that never got written.

Throughout the entire post-Stalinist period, and especially after Gorbachev's ascendancy, texts began to resurface, as Solzhenitsyn had predicted. "We, the host in gleaming casques, would rise from the sea only posthumously and figuratively. Our books, preserved by faithful and ingenious friends, would rise and not our bodies: we ourselves should be long dead."[71] Sinyavsky spoke in 1974 of the voices that were only just then reaching the reader: "Only thirty years afterward, like some underwater specter, some man drowned in that epoch, did Bulgakov's novel *The Master and Margarita* float to the literary surface."[72] Decades earlier, Marina Tsvetaeva had similarly imagined the fate of her texts; what she wrote came to apply mostly to the émigré writers' lack of a readership abroad and the unavailability of their texts to readers back home.

> Scattered in bookstores, grayed by dust and time,
> Unseen, unsought, unopened and unsold,
> My poems will be savored as are rarest wines—
> When they are old.[73]

In the postwar period, even the arrest and imprisonment of authors failed to stem the flow of texts. In fact, the more coercion, the more texts. Sinyavsky tells us to remember Avvakum, whose texts thundered forth from his seventeenth-century prison; this charismatic priest's style and his stance have continued to exert an influence in his homeland.[74] Prison did not always remove voices from the chorus; it gave at least some of these imprisoned voices the authority to speak for more than themselves.

AN END TO THE CULT OF SUFFERING

> . . . the myth of the Great Russian Writer, martyr and saint, is as much a part of the Soviet past as the Five-Year Plan.
> —*David Remnick*

What could be called a cult of suffering in Russian literature was beginning to lose its currency and its appeal by the early 1990s.[75] Sergei Chuprinin complained that during the years of Thaw and stagnation there appeared "a halo of sacrifice and heroism" around certain works and movements, and Village Prose writers positively wallowed in a "persecution complex" (*sindrom gonimosti*).[76] The memory of suffering, a kind of corporate experience, remained with the writers, despite having achieved public success: "Even among those who had made it, old wounds ached. . . . even decades after their ordeal was over and awards and large print runs (*tirazhi*) had made their situation secure."[77]

Chuprinin's openly expressed wish to bring the politicized literary process to an end involved weakening the links between literature and suffering. State power no longer endangered writers or their texts, except through a lack of material support, and suffering ceased to be a political category. Vyacheslav Kuritsyn also reacted to the cant of the ultranationalists, saying that he was prepared to accept a canon split in two: "Russian Literature" (*russkaia literatura*) would combine the pulpit, the podium, Big Ideas, and suffering; and "Russian-Language Literature" (*russkoiazychnaia literatura*) would emphasize aesthetics over ideology, and innovation over tradition.[78]

And yet even those seeking to demythologize and desanctify suffering fell under the power of old paradigms. Dmitry Prigov spoke of the years when "the status of the unofficial writer was taken over by Solzhenitsyn, Vladimov, Sinyavsky—all the names you know, the political and the social writers," while Prigov belonged to a group of aesthetic dissidents who had had to do nonintellectual work, like making playground equipment, to earn a living.[79] Looking back, he claims that his group opposed not only state power but the dissidents as well. In the deconstruction of myths and the reconstructing of literary history even those who were tempted to undermine the authority of past suffering in general still wanted their own risks and their own struggles to be acknowledged and valued. The suffering of the creative writer has, thankfully, ceased to be an ongoing political reality and attention can be directed to writing an account of the past. But it has proved difficult to reach consensus on a literary martyrology that adequately remembers and honors those who suffered and helps the nation know more fully its cultural, political, and moral history.

Chapter 6 The End of Soviet Literature and the Last Dangerous Text . . .

The keys to those days are still lying around.
—*Andrei Voznesensky*

The last fifteen years of the twentieth century marked a profound shift in how the government read writers' lives and works, as the Gorbachev era brought promise and possibility, along with upheaval and uncertainty, to the literary world. In 1985, Socialist Realism was moribund, Village Prose had ceased to function as a powerful movement, and a number of talented writers had recently left the country, or had died, further reducing ranks seriously thinned by emigration and expulsions in the 1970s. But as the old prohibitions evaporated, the country was treated to new works, to a wealth of formerly "dangerous texts," and to information on writers' lives at home and abroad during the Soviet period. Critics in Russia finally had access to virtually all significant twentieth-century literature written in Russian and the right to discuss everything they read. The intense textual community that was torn asunder after 1917 had, at first glance, been made whole again, and could begin to compose an objective and comprehensive analysis of Russian literature in the Soviet period.

It was naive to think that when all the strands of post-Revolutionary Russian literature—from Soviet, émigré, and *samizdat* canons, and from previously unopened desk drawers—began to come together, a unified conception of national literature would be the result. What Belinsky had once worked so hard to divide, and what political and historical forces had forcibly separated, resisted easy reunification. Even within published Soviet literature, internal fault lines were evident during the critical debates of the Brezhnev era, and after 1985 fissures in the literary community turned out to run even deeper than expected. From being a nation where "one text" could dominate society at a given time, Russia became a place where groups with clearly marked political identities read their own texts, past and present, and wrote their own versions of literary history, either ignoring, downplaying, or denouncing works associated with other groups. Literary reviews and essays, transcripts of Writers Union meetings, new fiction, and other texts from these years frequently revealed more irritation than relief.

It was a time of tremendous disruption, with too many variables and too few constants. From 1985 through 1991, the Russian people experienced the end of: totalitarianism, Communist Party dominance, a viable economy, most cultural subsidies, the once-powerful Writers Union, and the Soviet state itself. These foundational changes caused anxiety in the nation as a whole and in every Russian reader, writer, and critic. Like onlookers at the funeral feast for Marmeladov in *Crime and Punishment,* we could observe how *agape* quickly degenerated into *skandal.* There was the familiar sound of "who is to blame?" and "what is to be done?" as the search for closure became an occasion for assigning guilt and settling scores. A survey of critical articles from the years 1985–93 makes it clear that despite the freeing up of political discussion, literature and criticism were still functioning as a surrogate politics. The old paradigm was, for the moment, intact, and it was only in the mid-1990s that these cultural debates, which resonated far beyond the literary realm, gave way to a new and more distant relationship between literature and politics.

The project of compiling a comprehensive literary-historical record was marred from the start by a protracted and divisive struggle over ownership of the national literature. One of the first and most contentious issues raised was over the right of the dominant ethnic group to shape cultural identity. Was "Russian Literature of the Soviet Period" Russian enough? An existing school of nationalist literary criticism emerged more forcefully after 1985 with analysis of artistic works in pseudoreligious terms as pure or impure, as a path to salvation or the work of satanic forces. Writers and critics were judged to be either righteous and prophetic or heretical and demonic.[1] Focusing their energies on calculating the degree of Russianness in Russian culture, the nationalists spoke of cleansing the canon of authors who were not ethnically and spiritually correct, and whose works violated nationalist standards for style, characterization, and ethos.

According to these criteria, the Revolutionary-era modernist writers had brought great harm to Russian culture and to the nation, and even the ethnic Russians among them were spiritually cosmopolitan (i.e., Jewish). The adjective "Russian" was a badge of honor to this group and critics did not award it lightly. The ultranationalists would place a cordon sanitaire around the authentic canon in order to protect it from harmful influences and help it evolve in an acceptable way. Advocates claimed that this process would unify and strengthen Russia, whose texts would henceforth speak with an undiluted native voice.

Along with a move to define and control Russianness, the imminent end of the Soviet era stimulated a reexamination of the Sovietness of artistic literature. In 1934 it was clear what was in theory supposed to happen when writers became "engineers of human souls" and Socialist Realism replaced all other styles; by the beginning of the 1990s the cumulative results were not so easy to characterize. In his July 1990 "obituary" for Soviet literature, instead of talking about what had unified the canon, Viktor Erofeyev suggested that the dead or dying Soviet literary heritage could be divided three ways: "semi-official" (*ofitsioznaia*), "rural" (*derevenskaia*), and "liberal" (*liberal'naia*). Rather than bringing any kind of closure, this article opened up a lively and protracted debate.[2]

What is, in fact, the Soviet character of Soviet literature? If this was a chronological term, then can we use it in talking about literature written from October 1917 on? Or should we wait until the formation of the USSR in 1922 or the first Writers Congress in 1934? Do we stop using it for works written from the moment Gorbachev came to power, or after the Soviet Union ceased to exist at the end of 1991? And what about literature written soon after the Revolution by people born and raised in Russia but forced into exile? First-wave émigré literature had already begun to take shape in Russia days after the Bolshevik takeover with verse written by Zinaida Gippius.[3]

What kind of devil, what hound, found this to its liking?
And in the grip of what kind of nightmarish dream
Did the people kill their own freedom in a fit of madness?
And not even kill it—but lash it with a whip?[4]

Some writers and critics "headed for the Smolny" to support the Revolution with militant exuberance; among those alienated from the new government, one group fled soon afterward, but a significant number remained in the country as "spiritual" and "internal" émigrés. Vasily Rozanov, who did not leave (but who lived only two more years) began in November 1917 to publish *An Apocalypse of Our Time*. One exceptionally poignant passage expresses the feelings of those who stayed behind: in an imaginary play, an "iron curtain" descends noisily over Russian history as a voice announces that the performance is over. The audience rises, and someone says that the time has come to get their coats and go home. "They looked around. But there were no coats, and no homes to return to."[5] Only in the act of juxtaposing those who embraced the Revolution and those who rejected it could Russia begin to write its history.

Alexander Zholkovsky saw how Olesha's *Envy* (1927) and Mandelstam's *Egyptian Stamp* (1928), both bearing the imprint of Soviet life but not of Socialist Realism, engaged in a lively, "intertextual" dialogue on the new Soviet Man, the precipitous decline of the intelligentsia, and the reorientation of Russian society in the first post-Revolutionary decade.[6] Perhaps this literary history must be approached indirectly, looking between the texts, behind the lines, and on the margins in order to hear all the voices—loud, soft, and unspoken—that made up literature and the literary process in this period. In essays written in Russia after 1985 we can see an effort to recover not just texts, but also texture, not just single voices but the often discordant polyphony of literary life.

If "Soviet" is a geographical designation, then to what extent did it refer to a body of works not just from Russia, but from the many republics and autonomous regions that made up the USSR? A few non–native speakers—Aitmatov, Iskander, Bykov—wrote in Russian, and some translations from the more than seventy other USSR languages gained popularity with readers, but Russian literature dominated the canon and discussions of Russian works dominated critical discourse. Critic Evgeny Dobrenko used "Soviet" to characterize the tradition that evolved after the destruction of literary groups and the weakening of the creative intelligentsia in the 1930s; it also meant the linking of literature to socialist production, the myth of one big, happy, Soviet family, and the leveling of the Russian literary language to the point where there was very little to be lost in translation. In the end, Dobrenko felt that there was no unified "Soviet" literature as such, but that each national literature in the USSR went through a "Soviet" period. Writers expressed "Sovietness" (*sovetskost'*) in their works to the degree to which they wanted to write themselves into this larger enterprise. Fadeev made himself a Soviet writer, while Bulgakov retained his Russian literary identity.[7] Zamyatin's *We* "was written in Soviet Russia, but obviously could not become part of Soviet literature."[8]

The broadest understanding of "Soviet literature" included everything that was officially published in the USSR, all *gosliteratura*. This approach generally conflated Soviet literature with Socialist Realism, so that "Soviet" carried both an ideological and an aesthetic value. By the end of the 1980s, the qualifier "Soviet" in some circles had also gained a behavioral connotation as rigid, intolerant, and hierarchical. This certainly fits Kochetov's pro-Stalinist, xenophobic novel *What Do You Really Want?* But when it first appeared in the journal *Oktiabr'* in 1969, over two dozen prominent members of the intelligentsia signed a collective letter to Leonid Brezhnev, arguing that such a divisive and "malicious caricature of reality" could "hardly be called a Soviet work." By that point "Soviet" implied no particular ethos or style, and was basically a way to designate anything publishable within the USSR.[9]

The sheer variety of published texts complicated any attempt to portray the Soviet canon as a monolith because the number of "permitted anomalies"[10] had increased until variety within the constraints became a feature of the system. In a 1971 review of translated selections from *Novyi Mir,* Robert Conquest was struck by "the richness and variety of Soviet work—and of *published* work at that," although he goes on to note that to be permitted did not mean to have escaped persecution.[11] By 1984, when a declining Konstantin Chernenko presided over the fiftieth anniversary of the First Writers Congress, Socialist Realism was only one of a number of options from which Soviet writers could choose. Distinctive types of prose had evolved in the years since Stalin's death: Youth, Urban, Village, War, confessional, and lyrical-philosophical prose, the works of the "forty-year-olds," and numerous other thematic and stylistic categories, many expressing some level of ideological variation as well.

Literary criticism from this period is frank about the proliferation of subliteratures that did not fit the 1934 parameters, but which were permitted by Glavlit albeit with frequent cuts. While newly written Socialist Realist novels appeared well into the 1980s, there were many other new works after 1953 that served to undermine Socialist Realism, sometimes through satire or parody, more often by simply ignoring the rules. Some Party stalwarts attacked the alien organisms; others tried gamely to include such works as Aksenov's "Halfway to the Moon," Solzhenitsyn's "Matryona's Home," and Rasputin's *Farewell to Matyora* under the rubric of "mature Socialist Realism."

In literary analyses that were written after 1985, having adhered to Soviet aesthetics was not as controversial as a given writer's past relationship to the Party and the government. One of the ten common beliefs about the literary process is that writers should avoid unnecessary contact with state power. Questions began to be raised about the nature and the consequences of a given writer's cooperation with the Soviet state. Osip Mandelstam's straightforward distinction between writing done with or without permission has the effect of delegitimizing some very interesting works; if used consistently, it brings into question almost all pre-Revolutionary literature as well. Zamyatin, like Mandelstam, but with the opposite intent, observed in 1923 that the critics of his day divided works into two categories: progovernment, and everything else. Strict binary formulae were applied to the past and present at various stress points, including the late 1980s.[12]

The glasnost-era discussion of the post-Revolutionary canon encompassed a number of related themes, including that of competitive suffering. Soviet authorities had been comparatively lenient with rural writers after 1956, and they had eased up from time to time on other groups and individuals as well. This ought to have made it difficult during glasnost for any one camp to have issued categorical condemnations or justifications, but critics of different political persuasions, shielded from the whole truth by selective amnesia, forged ahead. It was mostly the older writers and critics who called for a less judgmental and more realistic view of literary survival before glasnost.

In the course of this discussion, the Communist and Russian camps came together around the idea that literature was a state-building and state-preserving entity, and that ethnic Russian literature deserved to dominate the Soviet canon. Writers should identify with the ruling power, and the term "non-aligned" (*netendentsioznaia*) was used negatively, to criticize works that had taken no clear stand on the issues of the day.[13] One body of progovernment literature and art they did not approve of was from the period 1917–34, which they saw as dominated by a mainly Jewish, pro-Bolshevik avant-garde.[14]

This same avant-garde was revered by supporters of glasnost, who for the most part also respected works that had somehow managed to get through the censorship after 1934 while remaining liberal, honest, and anti-Soviet, a literature of resistance like Alexander Solzhenitsyn's *One Day in the Life of Ivan Denisovich* and Mikhail Bulgakov's *Master and Margarita*. But the liberals did make negative evaluations based on connections they saw between certain types of Soviet literature and worrisome political developments after 1985. While there was residual affection and respect for the classic works of rural literature written between the mid-1950s and the mid-1970s, the Belov and Rasputin of 1989 were seen as having a harmful effect on society, and their works, past as well as present, were labeled in ways that made little distinction between Rasputin's lyrical *Borrowed Time* and the unambiguous writings of Vladimir Chivilikhin or Sergey Semanov. Some critics drew lines leading from the narratives of village *starukhi* (old women) to glasnost-era fictional diatribes and protofascist tracts and trends.

With some justification, the liberal-democratic community said that conservative nationalist writers had prospered more and suffered less than other cultural figures in post-Stalinist Russia. A variety of terms were used to designate works by those who had kept to the Party line and had risen high in the Writers Union: some referred to the writer's rank (*sekretarskaia, apparatnaia*), or to a general compatibility with the authorities (*ofitsioznaia*). Literature that flourished during the Brezhnev years and contributed to the general atmosphere was called *zastoinaia* (stagnant) or *seraia* (gray). *Siusiurealizm* was a sarcastic reference to Socialist Realism, emphasizing the subservient manner of those who wished to succeed in the official literary world (from *siusiukat'*, to lisp or talk in a fawning manner).[15] The work of writers with the "thoroughly Soviet" demeanor of a "homo Sovieticus" was called *sovkovaia*.[16]

There were critics for whom it became important, some forty years after the fact, to ferret out who had written poems lauding Stalin in the early 1950s (among others, Yevtushenko on the left and Soloukhin on the right), and to remind readers which literary figures had gone to the trouble of joining the Party (the Old Bolshevik parents of the urban writers Gorenshtein, Sinyavsky, Aksenov, and Trifonov, plus many rural writers, and critics of all persuasions).[17] The quality of *partiinost'* (party spirit, political correctness), rather than disappearing from literary discussion, reached a new intensity by 1990. Literary censorship was for all practical purposes gone, and there were nascent political alternatives to communism, but the intolerant Party mentality remained.[18]

In the midst of these skirmishes, "Russian literature of the Soviet period" did not receive the analytical attention as a concept or as a system that might have been expected. Although key issues had been raised in conferences organized abroad at the beginning of the 1980s, it was clearly too soon for most Russian critics and writers to calmly contemplate the century's writing in toto, and many interesting questions were left unasked, or if asked, were not adequately answered. For instance, how do Russians gauge the impact of works that appeared out of their time, like Bulgakov's *Master and Margarita,* written between 1928 and 1940, first published in censored form in the USSR in 1967–68, then in a more complete version in 1973, but not fully available until glasnost? Or his *Heart of a Dog*, which had to wait until 1987 to appear, over six decades after it was confiscated from the author's apartment? How are the histories of creation and reception to be coordinated? How much access was there for writers and critics in Soviet Russia to literature available only in *samizdat* or *tamizdat*? Is it possible to write a chronologically coherent, aesthetically comprehensive, and politically accurate analysis of twentieth-century Russian literature?

At a conference held in Moscow in September 1993 on the cultural heritage of the first emigration, it was said that the idea of writing a single, integrated history of Russian literature in the twentieth century, an idea that had been advanced at a Lausanne symposium in 1978, was no longer controversial, but was still a complex undertaking.[19] If the literatures of Soviet Russia and Russia abroad could be brought into one history, could the same be done for the politically charged literary process in each context?[20] The dramatic and divisive events in Moscow during the weeks that followed the 1993 conference highlighted both the necessity and the difficulty of calm reflection in the new Russian Federation. Street battles are hardly conducive to the writing of a complex literary history.

Russian critics and scholars hoped to bring the culture of the diaspora home and achieve a longed-for sense of wholeness (*tsel'nost'*). Studying and incorporating the legacy of the first-wave writers could provide an understanding of which cultural directions were lost in 1917 and what kind of Russian cultural identity was preserved abroad. But any sense of a unified tradition proved elusive through most of the 1990s. Somewhat like Rozanov's Revolutionary-era theatergoers, people were still in shock from the dissolution of the social, economic, and political order, and then of the Soviet Union itself. Culturally, and in most other spheres, this was still a dysfunctional and traumatized national family.

By the beginning of the 1990s, when so many politically suppressed texts had appeared in print, questions were advanced about the future of the "literary process" now that artistic words no longer had to substitute for political thoughts. "The process of 'raising sunken ships,' in Marietta Chudakova's phrase—that is, of publishing previous suppressed writers, works, themes, and styles—seems now to be nearing completion, and to be yielding to another process, that of 'normalization' of the literary situation (for better or for worse) as we understand that word."[21]

Writers for *Ogonek* thought in the late 1980s that a more pluralistic and tolerant way of thinking and writing could evolve. A few years later, though, it seemed that in all its history, Russian literature had rarely been so rigidly partitioned.[22] Turkov complained of the absence in Russia of "the habit of civilized discussion" (*kul'tura diskussii*). Critics wrote about writers and about each other as if they were describing neighbors in a communal apartment—the *anan'evy* and *pristavkiny* (the Ananev and Pristavkin families)—and their reprehensible behavior. Any weapon at hand was permissible against enemies in paraliterary space (*v okololiteraturnom prostranstve*).[23] It was reminiscent of Roman Jakobson's description of the literary atmosphere of the 1920s with its vicious rhetoric, but this time, while talent may have been squandered and reputations diminished, lives were not destroyed.[24]

A number of images were offered to characterize this boisterous post-1985 literary process. Some saw it as a series of horseraces (*ippodromnye skachki*), or a marketplace with goods competing for the buyers' attention.[25] At times it seemed more like a "dogfight" where "he hits you in the face and you bash him in the ear" (*On vas v rylo, a vy ego v ukho*), or like kitchen gossip that led to denunciations.[26] Russian literature was described as a "map" on which the country's borders were being reconfigured, where previous errors were being corrected and blank spots filled in, as was in fact the case with maps of the USSR which had in the past been deliberately erroneous.[27] A related image for these years was of an archeological dig, with layers upon layers of the past revealed. For Erofeyev, the process was a "wake" for the body and concept of Soviet literature; holding this wake was essential for the future of literature and criticism in Russia and hardly a sad occasion since Erofeyev did not much care for the deceased. In 1990, a correspondent for the émigré newspaper *Russkaia mysl'* working out of Leningrad said that observing the artistic intelligentsia's struggles was like watching a dying psychopath compose a last will and testament.[28]

For critic Yury Kashuk, Soviet literature and commentary by the mid-1980s was undergoing "biocenosis," i.e. the struggle for existence between competing organisms, all to one degree or another "Soviet."[29] He identified four main literary "organisms." (1) "Soviet Literature" was literature of and for the system. (2) "Anti-Soviet Soviet literature" included writers who from time to time would fall afoul of the system and then send their works abroad, enter them into the *samizdat* network, or put them back in the desk drawer (a phenomenon which Kashuk cleverly labeled *nigdeneizdat* "nowhere-publishing"). (3) "Foreign Soviet literature," in which writers living abroad continued to write the same kind of works as they had under the Soviet system. And (4) an "Alternative Soviet literature" that began to set itself apart in the 1980s from the prevailing ideology, aesthetics, and literary process, and yet was still influenced by what it claimed to reject.[30]

Discussions of the Russianness and Sovietness of post-Revolutionary litera- ture were intensified by reactions to the "delayed" and newly written works that began to appear after 1985. Viktor Erofeyev hoped that once Soviet Literature had passed away, the stage would be clear for new developments.[31] The *sotsart* that used the detritus of Sovietness to comic effect did not really meet that re- quirement. "Alternative" (*drugaia*) prose was said by the nationalist Right to be at heart "neo-Bolshevik" in its advocacy of an international modernism at the expense of traditional Russian realism.[32] The far right exposed the trace ele- ments of the cosmopolitan Bolshevism they found in some works, while their liberal counterparts were discovering harmful Communist and chauvinist in- fluences which they labeled "anti-urban" and "Elderly Guard" in literary works emerging from their opponents' camp.[33] A 1988 article by the literary depart- ment of *Ogonek* complained that its archenemy *Molodaia gvardiia* was dredg- ing up categories from the past like "Trotskyites" and "cosmopolitans"; and even when a less provocative lexicon was substituted, "the grammar remained the same."[34] Tempers ran very high in these years.

The nationalist right, unhappy with most of the changes that had taken place since 1985, seemed much more interested than the left in preserving the literary-political status quo. Critics frequently reacted to new works of litera- ture depending on how much of an investment they had in the continuation of the literary process and whether they saw the work in question as strengthening or weakening it. Younger liberal critics and writers questioned the traditional role of literature and literary criticism as the nation's central spiritual and polit- ical "space." Their goal was for paraliterary space to become just literary space, and for artists to be freed of the burden of serving as national conscience, mem- ory, moral compass, witness, and virtual "second government." These critics sought a separation of literary and political agendas, whether pro- or antistate, in order to hasten the "normalization," "secularization" and "privatization" of Russian culture. To a great extent, they got their wish, and while there is a his- tory to be written of post-Soviet artistic literature, it is not a history of "danger- ous texts."

How can we best approach the now historical subject of Russian literature in the Soviet era? Where should we focus in post-Soviet scholarship—on reorder- ing the canon to arrive at a more complete narrative of literary history, or on de- vising codes of reading for formerly unexamined or previously incomplete works with the expectation that this will give us a clearer view and a bigger picture? So much in the reexamination of literature of the Soviet period concerns the fragmentary and the marginal, and the attempt to place pieces side by side to make a whole. Sometimes we are chemists, precipitating the subversive essence out of a superficially harmless Soviet work. On other occasions we resemble archeologists, struggling to turn a box full of shards into something identifiable and meaningful. J. A. E. Curtis's book *Manuscripts Don't Burn* takes this process a daring step further. Curtis gathered together letters to and from Mikhail Bulgakov, as well as his and his third wife's diaries, to create a powerful "memoir" that existed only potentially before Curtis began her project. As scholars, we have the power not only to interpret but to re-create or re-form segments of literary history, to make the silences resonate with words rescued from the past.

Socialist Realism, the brittle heart of official Soviet literature, was, in Yeatsian terms, a "center that could not hold." While all those official meetings were in session, "powerfully underground / Roots twist and thrust like a gnarled hand."[35] The most powerful literature of this period defined itself against the hollow official core; it is at the borders of the visible literary world that we will find what we need to fill in the blank pages. And this vast amount of anomalous material must be incorporated into the canon, first chronologically, and then generically, stylistically, thematically, spiritually, and along several other lines. The various spheres of literature were kept separate for so long that it will take time to get used to thinking in terms of one "Russian literature of the Soviet period" when questions of the evolution of literary style, influence, and parallel development arise. It is important to accept as a first premise the fact that virtually everyone who wrote in Russian, whatever the location or conditions might be, was reacting in some way to the Revolution and the country it brought into being. Everyone was to one degree or another "border conscious."[36]

Mark Kharitonov's prizewinning novel *Lines of Fate, or Milashevich's Trunk* (*Linii sud'by, ili sunduchok Milashevicha*), completed in 1985 but not published until 1992, is emblematic of the transitional period between late Soviet literature and what followed. *Lines of Fate* tells of the discovery of a literary archive preserved on the back of paper meant to be cut up for candy wrappers (*fantiki*). The trunk full of literary fragments both excites and torments Lizavin, the researcher who finds it while working on his dissertation. Lizavin nearly loses his health and his sanity, juxtaposing one candy wrapper's message to another as he attempts to piece together a coherent narrative. It is only when he accepts the *fantiki* as a genre in themselves, reflective of the disjointed time in which they were inscribed, that he has truly deciphered these "lines of fate." The revised literary histories that can finally be written will involve this kind of encounter with the tantalizing fragments of Russia's literary past. As a bridge between the Soviet society in which it was written and the post-Soviet world in which it appeared, *Lines of Fate* celebrated the survival, at all levels, of Russian literature in the twentieth century.

Rather than seeing the Soviet period primarily as a time when authors were effectively silenced, one can just as easily see it as a time of widespread graphomania. Authors who enjoyed the regime's favor were widely published and a print run of over 200,000 was not uncommon; their collected works filled many volumes, as did the accompanying critical analyses. The intense world of underground writing received its own measure of commentary, including Sinyavsky's brilliantly satirical story "Graphomania." If the official silence about unofficial works tormented writers, it was not a silence of production, but of reception. Bulgakov saw himself deprived of any audience beyond a very small circle, and according to a letter he wrote to Pavel Popov in March 1937, he was not comforted by the prediction that everything he had written would be published posthumously. "Some of my well-wishers have adopted a rather strange way of consoling me. More than once have I heard their suspiciously unctuous voices: 'Never mind, it will get printed after your death!' I am very grateful to them, of course!"[37]

Judging by his letters and his wife's diary from the 1930s, Bulgakov increasingly felt that he was condemned to be buried alive in his apartment with his manuscripts. In July 1931, he wrote to a friend about his severe disappointment over never having had the promised conversation with Stalin, and at not being allowed to travel abroad. Bulgakov said that there were two theories about him circulating in Moscow: according to the first, Bulgakov was "under the closest, most unremitting surveillance, and therefore my every line, thought, phrase and step is being weighed up." The second theory had few advocates, but among them was Bulgakov himself. "According to this theory, there's nothing there at all! No enemies, no crucible, no surveillance, no desire for praise . . . nothing. No one is interested, no one needs it. . . . There will simply be no reply."[38] To be traumatized into not writing or into writing differently, or deprived of an audience for one's creations, was all too common an experience. Vladimir Mayakovsky wrote wrenchingly beautiful lines about "stepping on the throat of his own song." The persona of Pasternak's "Hamlet" listened in the quiet theater for a hint as to what his fate would be, having forgotten for a moment which character he was playing.

In Andrei Voznesensky's 1971 poem "Phone Booth" (*Avtomat*), the poetic persona goes through a number of possible scenarios as to why someone keeps trying to call him from a public phone (is it his lost conscience or his forgotten voice?) with the obvious implication that the calls could be meant to harass him, or as part of some ongoing surveillance. The final stanzas give the feeling of a writer suspended in a too quiet universe:

> The planet's communications are broken.
> I'm tired of saying *hello.*
> My questions might as well be unspoken.
> Into the void my answers go.
>
> Thrown together, together
> With you, with you unknown.
> Hello. Hello. Hello there.
> Dial tone. Dial tone. Dial tone.[39]

Andrei Sinyavsky described the communication gap between writers and regime in the early 1970s as a monologue before a television set with the sound turned off. As figures on the screen listen and applaud speeches soundlessly he sees a parallel to the relationship between literature and society. "Perhaps, just as we in front of the screen hear nothing, *they* can neither hear nor understand anything of what is going on here, among those of us involved in the literary process—we who are constantly trying to explain something to our government and offering for its attention book after book, which seem to us remarkable, absolutely irrefutable, and constructive, but which simply never come within earshot of those shadowy figures on the screen. Books to them are inaudible, unnecessary."[40]

There were works that received more exposure than they deserved and others that were buried alive. The full canon of Russian literature in the Soviet period is an amalgam of a diverse group of officially published works, a fully developed counterliterature, an extensive body of diaspora writing, intertextual parodies within and between all these levels, and a massive amount of criticism and memoirs. For those who had been present at the 1934 Writers Congress, the course of cultural life in the decades that followed would present more than a few surprises. The confidently constructed Socialist Realist system did not prevail in the way that Zhdanov had expected, but neither did the creative vacuum that Babel had feared. And while the official proclamations had in the end only a hollow ring, many unofficial voices, labeled "dangerous" in their own time, have thundered down to our age.

THE PARADIGM REVISITED

They have read your novel," began Woland, turning to the master.[41]

Do the common beliefs about the literary-political nexus that were sketched out at the beginning of this book hold up under closer examination? There can be no doubt as to the existence of a danger zone for Russian texts and their authors, a "paraliterary space." Whatever pre- and post-Revolutionary leaders actually believed, they behaved as if certain texts were potential sources of danger to the state, and everyone involved in the publishing process acted accordingly. By its very nature, artistic literature invites multiple interpretations of plot developments, character portrayal, and dialogue, of what has been said and what has been left unsaid. The author might insert a politically daring message in hopes of getting it past the censors, but that space between the lines was also filled in by intelligentsia readers and by the government. All sides took literature seriously. The state censored provocative sections of texts or suppressed them altogether, critics suggested the political implications of published works, and, for works that could not be published, unofficial reproduction and distribution networks provided artistic variety and a forum for ideological debate to a smaller group of intelligentsia readers. The politically sensitive Russian literary process that functioned both above and below ground is widely considered to be among the factors that undermined both the tsarist and the Soviet regimes.

It was said that the text virtually disappeared when it entered paraliterary space; the work in question was widely referred to but infrequently quoted in most legal proceedings, and was not read completely or carefully by those who most vigorously judged it to be harmful. While this is generally true, especially where popular frenzy was deliberately whipped up over works that the public would not see until glasnost, texts might be inspected closely, because reading them could provide the authorities with more precise ammunition. Literary texts were confiscated, read, and "preserved forever" as material that might prove useful for future criminal cases. And although people were sent to prison for their contact with dangerous texts, prison was also a place where daring literature might be read or written. Vladimir Bukovsky, imprisoned for political dissidence that began with a youthful literary journal, found that Lefortovo prison had a wonderful library, full of books unavailable outside the gulag.[42] Bukovsky studied the criminal codes so he could use them against the system, while his investigator, frustrated by the fact that he himself only got to read what turned up in searches, grilled the prisoner on other works. Bukovsky knew that this information would be spread further to the official's friends, and was not surprised that the man left the KGB not long after Bukovsky had met with him.[43]

At times rulers themselves examined texts closely: Catherine II did not just read her copy of Radishchev's *Journey;* she made copious notes in the margins. Nicholas I took time out from his coronation trip to Moscow to personally examine a verse parody written by a student at Moscow University. The unlucky fellow later told Alexander Herzen that he had never seen his poem "so carefully copied and on such splendid paper."[44] Nicholas was deeply disturbed by the Marquis de Custine's book *Letters from Russia,* and wanted no mention of it made in Russia or even in negative reviews by Russians abroad (although the imperial government was not above sponsoring negative French responses to de Custine) but the tsar could not ignore it himself. "The Emperor Nicholas I is said to have flung the volume to the floor in anger after perusing the first few pages, moaning . . . that 'I am alone to blame; I encouraged and patronized the visit of this scoundrel.' Later, though, it seems that curiosity got the better of him and that he read considerable parts of it aloud to his family in the long dull evenings of palace life."[45]

In the late 1850s, Herzen's periodicals were published in Europe and smuggled into Russia, and among their many readers were not just the intelligentsia, but also Alexander II and other members of the imperial family and high government officials.[46] A nineteenth-century German source reported that "it is taken for granted that the emperor at that time always read *The Bell (Kolokol)* to inform himself of matters which were kept secret from him."[47] Censors, editors, and the secret police on the whole took a good look at the texts, published or unpublished, that came their way, hoping to avoid the later removal of a work already in production or in circulation. The government's familiarity with what was being written helped authorities to determine the currents of opinion that were flowing just beneath the surface.

The Soviet period saw a number of pre-Revolutionary patterns replicated. Supplementing many other sources, Vitaly Shentalinsky's examination of secret police files on Soviet-era writers details the attention paid to texts in the decades after the Revolution. When Osip Mandelstam was first arrested in May 1934, the investigator Shivarov showed him a copy of the Stalin poem obtained from an informant and asked the poet to recite it, carefully noting any differences between the oral recitation and the police copy. Mandelstam, who had never before committed the poem to paper, was then asked to write out his revised version and sign it. That signed version survived in the files sixty years later, long after the gulag had consumed its author.[48]

The dossier on Mikhail Bulgakov began with a copy of a notice the young writer placed in a Berlin newspaper in 1922, asking for help in compiling a guide to contemporary Russian writers at home and abroad.[49] Over the years, the file came to include letters, texts, and informants' reports on unofficial literary gatherings which summarized what Bulgakov had read aloud, with an indication of anti-Soviet nuances and audience reaction. There were newspaper articles, the author's letters to Stalin and other officials, and accounts of official visits to play rehearsals, after which a decision would be made to permit the opening or not. There is a record of Stalin's comments about Bulgakov plays he had seen or read, and a report about the May 7, 1926 raid on the writer's apartment, which yielded, in addition to *Heart of a Dog* and a diary, a manuscript called "Reading My Thoughts" ("Chtenie myslei"), and works by several contemporary poets in *samizdat* copies. When it was being considered for publication by the Nedra publishing house, *Heart of a Dog* was read by Lev Kamenev at the request of one of the editors.[50] After it was confiscated, "rumors circulated among contemporaries that members of the Politburo themselves took it in turns to read its contents," perhaps, Shentalinsky speculates, because they were afraid the author could read their hearts and would reveal his findings to others.[51]

Bulgakov spent years trying to get these manuscripts returned; as a result of his first two letters to the OGPU on this subject, he was invited to stop by headquarters for a talk, after which the questionnaire he filled out and a transcript of the discussion were added to his file. Bulgakov gave detailed answers about the political implications of his work, refusing only to name others who belonged to the "Green Lamp" literary group. In a delusional state during his final days, Bulgakov feared that "they" would come and also take away the manuscript of *The Master and Margarita*.[52] If that had actually occurred, there is a strong possibility that "they" would have read it and preserved it with care.

The extensive Solzhenitsyn files that became available in 1992 reveal a serious and sustained acquaintance with his writings in certain official circles.[53] In 1966, after a raid on the apartment of his friend Teush, the Central Committee's Culture Department prepared twenty-four copies of the unpublished play *A Feast of Victors* and handed them out to prominent writers prior to a meeting of the Secretariat of the USSR Writers Union at which the author would be present (Docs. 5, 6). Copies distributed to high officials with some democratic sympathies made their way to a wider circle through the officials' children.[54]

In 1967, the Secretariat of the Writers Union reported that extra time was needed to get ready for the September 22 meeting because the unpublished works they had to familiarize themselves with ran to more than fourteen hundred pages (Docs. 17, 34). The Solzhenitsyn "task force" had to become more efficient over the years in response to the author's tremendous output: a 1973 report refers to a twenty-six-page KGB summary of the 1,014-page *Gulag* manuscript that had been confiscated from Voronyanskaya, the Solzhenitsyn typist who subsequently committed suicide (Docs. 84, 88). On January 2, 1974 the KGB sent the USSR Council of Ministers three copies of *Gulag Archipelago*, part of which had already been published in the West (Doc. 97). Just before he was deported, Solzhenitsyn complained through a foreign reporter that a January 14, 1974 article in *Literaturnaya gazeta* cited sections of *Gulag* that had not yet appeared in print abroad, and which could only have come from a stolen copy of the manuscript (Doc. 114). Keeping a close watch on the prolific and indefatigable Alexander Solzhenitsyn turned out to be a labor-intensive enterprise.

In taking a second look at the paradigm, it is clear that the artistic texts that fell into paraliterary space were deprived of the immunity from prosecution that imaginative literature not violating moral standards was generally allowed to claim. Cases brought against their authors did not depend on a close reading, and yet there are many instances in which texts were examined at some length by the authorities, whether out of the need to identify suspicious material between the lines or out of a genuine curiosity about the thoughts of those who would speak truth to power.

THE TEN MAXIMS IN RETROSPECT

1. The Russians read more than any other people
2. Literature is where the formation of politics, prophecy, and national identity took place in Russia
3. One text would be on everyone's mind at a given time

Russians Reading

> The Russian people do not read.
> —*Alexander Herzen*[55]

First of all, were Russians really the enormously engaged reading public of legend? Many members of the intelligentsia were obsessed with literature and criticism, but this is certainly not the case for the vast majority of the population before 1917, who, if they were literate, were reading a quite different set of texts, as Jeffrey Brooks has shown.[56] Take for example the 1860s, when major works of literature and commentary appeared in the leading journals and stimulated widespread discussion not only in Moscow and St. Petersburg but in the provincial capitals as well. A partial list of thought-provoking works from this period includes Ostrovsky's *The Storm,* Turgenev's *On the Eve* and *Fathers and Sons,* Chernyshevsky's *What Is to Be Done?,* Dostoevsky's *Notes from Underground, Crime and Punishment,* and *The Idiot,* Tolstoy's *War and Peace,* and important essays by Dobrolyubov, Chernyshevsky, and Pisarev.

A fuller transcript of life in Moscow during this period gives the impression that there were other words in the air that cut across class lines and attracted the interest of a far greater number of people, as shown in Ewa Thompson's study of the cult of the *iurodivyi* (holy fool). Russia's overwhelmingly illiterate peasants, in addition to an acquaintance with the exemplary lives of saints (*zhitiia*), knew of "apocryphal literature which had accumulated around the *yurodivye* over the centuries," and both respected and revered these righteous visionaries. Despite government and church attempts to delegitimize this behavior and conflate it with mental illness, holy fools still wandered around the country. Later on, a number of *iurodivye* wound up in the newly opened mental hospitals, which rapidly became places of pilgrimage for the faithful, and "an embarrassment for the administration . . . [but which] had to be permitted for the sake of public tranquillity."[57] It was dangerous to have holy fools on the loose, but even more dangerous to forcibly cut them off from their followers.

One *iurodivyi,* Ivan Koreisha, lived in Moscow's Transfiguration Hospital for over forty years, and every day large numbers of people came to seek his advice. He had originally been committed in 1822 as an act of revenge by a nobleman whose marriage Koreisha had prevented. When he died in 1861, Koreisha was considered a saint and his body acclaimed as a sacred relic, and "several hundred thousand people attended his funeral, and in the course of five days over two hundred requiem masses were celebrated for him in Moscow alone." Despite this massive reaction to his death, the press was silent, and "neither Koreisha's existence nor his famous funeral were granted recognition either in the Slavophile or Westerner press. It was as if he never existed. And yet, his influence on the Russian people of his generation was incomparably greater than that of the many members of the intelligentsia who wrote for the 'thick journals.'"[58] Thompson reasons that the government did not want the image of a still primitive Russia widely publicized at the same time it was trying to demonstrate to European states that the Russian Empire was bringing civilization to the lands it had conquered. Progressive journalists, for their part, saw in the popularity of the holy fool, whose power was based on nonrational utterances, an inconvenient atavism.

Nikolai Leskov believed that such righteous ones did not stand apart from historical currents, but "make more history than others," which gives some context to his decision in the late 1870s to devote a cycle of stories to religious characters. Leskov was not simply showing respect for spiritual heroes and disdain for nihilists; he was countering both radical politics and official religion with the true spiritual values of the majority. In the 1909 anthology *Vekhi* (*Landmarks*), philosopher Sergei Bulgakov was concerned by the fact that the progressive intelligentsia rejected popular religion while simultaneously usurping religious categories and constructing an abstract notion of the people.[59] In 2001, writer Viktor Erofeyev sounded a similar note when he complained about Russian literature's baneful influence on the intelligentsia, who were led to believe that "the Russian people are wiser than the government and everyone else put together."[60]

The suppressed Koreisha story expands the notion of dangerous texts. As was the case with most holy fools, Koreisha's statements were often incoherent mumblings unrelated to the questions posed, and were not accompanied by charitable acts or even by kindly treatment of his visitors, who included peasants, clergy, and nobles. But the belief that prophetic words have magic power was so strong that Koreisha's utterances were "'translated' into comprehensible language by experienced *iurodivyi* watchers."[61] To publish an account of this babbling, which reached more Russians than any contemporary novelist, playwright, or poet, would not have been to the benefit of either the tsarist government or those working to undermine it. And Koreisha was just one of the more popular of these fools: by the late nineteenth century "every mental hospital in Russia had its Koreishas of both sexes and served as a place of pilgrimage. . . . self-censorship or state censorship, or both, prevented Russian scholars from writing about this. . . . Only the devil-may-care radicals like [Ivan] Pryzhov dared to investigate this layer of Russian subculture. Pryzhov did not manage to change the terms of discourse, however."[62] The holy fools were seen as a potential threat to social order because, even more than the great writers, telling the truth as they saw it was the only thing they knew how to do.

In Vladimir Voinovich's priceless parody "Skurlatsky, Man of Letters" (1972), set just after the assassination of Alexander II in 1881, the asylum to which the hero is sent is filled to the brim with visionaries. "Skurlatsky . . . made such a powerful impression on the patients that two of the six resident Napoleons began to call themselves Skurlatsky, while another adopted the dual last name Zhelyabov-Perovskaya, after the famous Nihilists. It is also said that subsequently a new form of mental illness was discovered in that hospital, a collective delusion of grandeur—an entire group of patients declared themselves to be the Executive Committee."[63]

The Old Believers, a group that ran afoul of both church and state, were perceived to be backward and politically unreliable, but they actually had a higher rate of literacy than their Orthodox brothers and sisters, because schismatics had to be able to "distinguish between true and false texts."[64] As literacy rates increased across the population, a mass market developed, but not for Tolstoy's morality tales, despite the fact that he wrote them expressly for this audience. Jeffrey Brooks' list of the most popular works of the period between 1861 and 1917 includes adventure stories, detective serials, and melodrama. While members of the intelligentsia were arguing at great length over the politically-charged contents of the thick journals, "the thin magazine . . . provided a source of light reading, serious fiction, and news for a diverse group of readers, including provincial gentry as well as village schoolteachers and parish clergy."[65]

A century later, in a "Letter to Soviet Leaders" (1973), Alexander Solzhenitsyn worried about what Russians of his day were and were not reading. The official ideology was dead, there was no articulated moral code, the educational system was underfunded, military conscription was dehumanizing, family structure was weak, and leisure time consisted of "television, cards, dominoes and . . . vodka; and if anybody *reads*, it is either sport or spy stories, or else that same old ideology in newspaper form."[66] Censorship forbade the publication of figures on illiteracy in the Soviet Union, but the existence of a vast readership for serious works cannot be questioned.[67] As readership grew under Brezhnev, tastes changed. On the one hand, more people wanted to have their own libraries where they could read privately, instead of having to rely on state-run libraries. On the other hand, there was tremendous interest in lighter reading.[68] The leisuretime material that Solzhenitsyn treated dismissively is precisely what interested the critic Kardin, who called popular literature—detective stories, spy novels, science and adventure fiction, and historical novels—the most unexamined genre of all.[69] He stressed the need to consider the category of popularity when analyzing the reading public; even without a genuine book market, readers expressed preferences, something to which literary critics paid only minimal attention.

The post-Soviet years brought concerns over every aspect of text life, including the choices being made by a public with less time to read and more interesting television programs to choose from. How would Russia evolve as a nation without the traditional attention to worthy texts? According to Valentin Rasputin, in the course of just a few years Russia had stopped being the *chitaiushchaia strana* (well-read country) it once was, and had become a nation interested in neither literature nor politics.[70] Author Boris Strugatsky did not join the chorus of those in the 1990s who lamented the decline in the quantity and quality of works being read. During the communist period, readers looked to *nauchnaia fantastika* (science fiction) for both veiled political commentary and a welcome escape, and that genre was still popular in post-Soviet Russia, so from Strugatsky's point of view, tastes had not undergone a radical change.[71] And, well into the 1990s, exposure to Solzhenitsyn, Grossman, Venedikt Erofeyev, Brodsky, and Nabokov had not managed to diminish interest in Pikul, a popular writer of conservative pot-boilers.[72]

The phrase "the people who read the most in the world" was used during this period ironically, even poignantly, as in the case of the headline above a 1998 *Literaturnaia gazeta* photo of Muscovites picking books up off the ground.[73] The books were the leftover stock of a store on Kuznetsky Most. When it was time for the store to be renovated and the recycling people failed to show up, hundreds of unsold volumes were left lying on the ground and the public was allowed to sort through volumes by Abramov, Bitov, Klyuchevsky, and many others and take home as much as they could carry. The photograph shows mostly older people who perhaps hoped to find titles they could sell to supplement an insufficient income. Or perhaps these really were the same serious readers who in the past regularly stood in line, scoured the book stalls and used book stores, and even tapped into black-market sources for texts they simply had to have.

By the late Soviet period, Russians were called "the people who read more Pikul than any one else" (*samyi chitaiushchii Pikulia*) and it was said that there had been a *pikulizatsiia* (Pikulization) of literary taste. Stephen Lovell confirms that "the Soviet people may have been the *samyi chitaiushchii v mire*, but it also read a high proportion of what was, in the eyes of the intelligentsia, bilge."[74] The low level of spoken Russian caused a Moscow journalist to complain that Russians had tired the world "with boasts of how well-read and literate we are" while following mid-nineteenth-century language norms set by a russified

Dane, Vladimir Dal.[75] Rassadin argued in 1990 that the much-publicized large press runs for artistic prose did not signal a rise in the cultural level of the masses; he saw the myth of the "best-read people" originating in the government's wholesale takeover of publishing in the early Stalinist period.[76]

In *The Russian Reading Revolution* Lovell identified the two most important aspects of what he calls the Soviet reading "myth": (1) in the USSR, people used to read a lot; and (2) the people were united and imbued with a Soviet value system by what they read. The virtual removal of reading material from the world of commerce meant that "it was possible to believe (and to make-believe) that the Soviet *narod*, by virtue of being the best-read, was also the most *dukhovnyi* (spiritually profound)."[77] The first maxim, that the Russians read more than other people needs to be reformulated in order to have greater explanatory power. It has always implied not only a quantity of readers and texts, but also that this reading was consequential, serving either to build up or tear down the government. Has the number of avid readers of significant texts between the 1820s and the 1990s been overestimated?

When attempting to gauge the effect of texts on politics how much should numbers count? Václav Havel believes that even if an unpublished novel were known to only twenty people "the fact of its existence would still be important."[78] Did the proportion of people reading serious as against popular works change in the post-Soviet period? In casting off literature's traditional responsibility for "coordinating values," to use Solzhenitsyn's term, had post-Soviet writers lost the readers' interest along the way? Kardin lamented that "literature did not acquire even a modest role of its own in the society that was being revived, and some people tried to make the case that there was nothing more for it to do."[79] And yet even without a well-defined role or close connection to political discourse, by the end of the year 2000 serious works represented an increasingly significant share of the publishing boom in Russia.[80]

Russia's Second Government

The belief that writers from Pushkin through Solzhenitsyn constituted a virtual second government is not so much incorrect as not fully articulated. George Steiner believed that "all of Russian literature is essentially political," and Donald Fanger's response was: "political *to whom,* and *how?*"[81] We are reminded that some observations about the canon are so widely accepted that they rarely get a second look or fuller argumentation. If writers accepted the role of being a "second government" in nineteenth-century Russia, it was not as a government in any modern sense, but as a second *Russian* government, in which rulers exercised a sanctified power and were seen not just to represent the nation, but actually to be the nation. Russian literature was Russia, and to read Russian literature was to read Russia. The strongly spatial nature and cultural base of Russian identity were fused. As a second government, writers did not develop a specific politics between the lines of literary works to counteract the policies of the first government. They witnessed, remembered, and recorded the life of the people in the most powerful language of which they were capable. Their concerns were truth, conscience, righteousness, justice, and Russia's special identity and destiny, and not anything as limiting, and unlikely to be published, as a political program.

From Pushkin through Solzhenitsyn, writers saw an aura of holiness surrounding their texts, which were felt to be of almost divine origin—in the sense of the "Russian God"—and indestructible. The system of censorship for all printed matter was applied to them with great care because of worries over the potential impact of their words. Standing outside this civilization, it may seem odd that tsars and the Communist leaders who succeeded them should have looked into literary matters so closely and should have, from time to time, addressed writers directly. Writers seemed to have unique access to power above, as manifested in the ruler, and power below, as manifested in the Russian people. They and their texts symbolically bound the nation together, even when it seemed to be flying apart. When we try to explain why Russia did not disintegrate, literary culture must be figured into the equation as one of the links in the chain of national identity that did not give way.

Writers were seen by the authorities as potential rivals for the allegiance of the population, and it came to matter greatly whether they communicated the same principles and practices as the tsarist and later the Soviet state. A stand against official Russia could only be intimated, but even that was enough to stimulate readers who were as attuned to Russia's muted political life as the authors. Andrei Amalrik, Vladimir Bukovsky, Václav Havel and others veterans of dissident movements under communism all relate how post-Stalinist literary life, including official and unofficial public readings of new and old poetry, raised interest and hope in many Soviet and Eastern European citizens, especially those from the younger generation. It was the government's harsh reactions to any kind of unsanctioned activity or new thinking that pushed an informal movement from a primarily cultural sphere towards broader questions of civil and human rights. Havel calls this transitional stage "pre-political," not starting off as a program, but capable of developing into one. In the case of

Czechoslovakia, one of the defining moments came with the trial of a rock group called "The Plastic People of the Universe."[82]

By the end of 1963, Bukovsky had been sent to a mental hospital for the first time, where he found that quite a few of the other "patients" were in there for anti-Soviet propaganda, espionage, and "contacts with foreigners." It seemed clear that the time for confining dissidence to poetry and clandestine conversations had passed, but "until the majority of us had freed ourselves of the psychology of the underground, of the rage for justice, our descendants were doomed to go on arguing in their kitchen."[83] While Bukovsky did move out of the underground, it was not with the goal of getting involved in politics and programs. His weapon was "not propaganda, but publicity. . . . The rest depended on each individual's conscience. Neither did we expect victory—there wasn't the slightest hope of achieving it."[84]

Because writers could not be explicit and turn their restless characters into true political actors, their texts did not think things through. Critics found ways to further develop the potential of texts, but faced limitations as well. To look to Russian literature for a coherent political program is to be disappointed; where it existed it was generally to the detriment of artistic quality. Virtually everything about literature was politicized, yet for all the sense of proximity to the state or to the people, even underground literature did not often directly contemplate either acquiring or exercising power (*vlast'*). Writers did, however, bring the state and people closer to an understanding of the true life of society.

In the mid-nineteenth century, as Russia moved towards emancipation, Turgenev's stories made it harder to look down on—or away from—the peasant masses, but as Pavel Annenkov points out, "the ground for *Notes of a Hunter* had already been prepared, and Turgenev gave clear and artistic expression to the essence of an attitude of mind which was already . . . in the air."[85] Dostoevsky's *Demons* brilliantly described psychological power plays and petty intrigues in the absence of belief in a loving God; his *Crime and Punishment* had earlier revealed the consequences of choosing the wrong historical role models and testing the wrong limits. *Notes from Underground* was a reminder that human beings are drawn towards irrational and self-destructive behavior, rendering a noncoercive utopia unrealizable. Even with the reconciliation-in-Christ endings favored by Dostoevsky, none of this can be reduced to a workable plan for a complex society.

While we do not see an ideology or a plan for action, what we do see is the preservation of historical truth and national memory, and belief in the power exercised by a single conscience, a single soul tormented by injustice. Literature did not—could not—make policy; it supported or opposed the status quo, or gazed in another direction, towards the past, nature, family life, rural Russia, or to the spiritual world, that is, towards all the places where power was *not* located and politics was *not* done. The philosopher Ivan Ilin (1883–1954), whose profound attachment to Russian literature is obvious from his essays, never mistook the spiritual depths of his favorite works for political waters. While praising the identity-sustaining power of Pushkin and other writers, Ilin stressed the need for members of the intelligentsia in exile to lay aside imponderable and unanswerable questions and devote their energies to sketching out plans for the inevitable end of the Soviet regime. His two sets of essays on this subject are appropriately called "The Russia-to-be" (*O griadushchei Rossii*, 1940–41) and "The Tasks at Hand" (*Nashi zadachi*, 1948–54). Ilin asks what kind of government would work best for Russia. Will a temporary nationalist dictatorship be necessary to prevent chaos? How will non-Russian citizens be peaceably incorporated into what must and will be a Russian Orthodox state? What is the best way to bring the rule of law to Russia? Ilin issued a call for serious strategies to be in place when the day eventually came, as he knew it would, that Russia was no longer Soviet. Ilin was a rarity, but his politics did not come from reading between the lines of literary works, which were his anchor but not, in the end, his compass.

How could one realistically expect concrete plans for a future Russia from a society that generally privileged the nonrational, and elevated the spontaneous gesture—what Chaadaev called a "lazy boldness"—over "depth and perseverance"?[86] For well over a century writers had offered primarily negative views of reality and vague utopian directions for the future. Russian autocracy did not suffer rivals gladly, and any plan to change Russia as a whole implied that the status quo was less than perfect. So hints were made indirectly: Turgenev's Insarov (*On the Eve*) goes off to fight a tyrant in Bulgaria, his Rudin abandons schemes for improving provincial life and leaves for France and the 1848 uprising, while Goncharov's Oblomov allows his written plans for reform to gather dust while he is still young.

A quick survey of the canon shows that characters who do carry a plan through to completion are at best dull and naive, and at worst are criminal to the point of being demonic. In *Demons,* it is to Stavrogin more than anyone else that people look for leadership, but his path leads to self-destruction. The capable and progressive lawyer whom Odintsova marries in *Fathers and Sons* suf-

fers from even the author's indifference. There is Goncharov's commendable—
and, literally, "wooden"—Stolz, but for every one of him there are several
Oblomovs who are described in far more interesting terms. What we are left
with is a tradition in which idea-bearing characters observe their troubled
country, but can offer few coherent solutions—only bits and pieces that adhere
poorly to each other and to the nation, like Gogol's Kovalyov, whose nose at
first refused to stick to its owner's face.

In the Soviet period, Socialist Realism made the Plan a blueprint for the Radiant Future, but after Stalin's death the power and integrity of the Plan was
challenged in both official and unofficial literature and criticism. Ilin's call to
"plan for the future" could have found little support among Russian writers,
who inherited negative attitudes about planning from both the superfluous
men of the pre-Revolutionary canon and the Soviet plan-obsessed state. Instead of planning, there would be the very Russian expectation that when the
time came, good people would lend a hand (*dobrye liudi pomogut*). In their
powerless state, to be *anti-* was sufficiently dangerous to quiet one's conscience,
but as Sinyavsky asked, "How can you define yourself in relation to a negative?"[87]

Writing Russian Identity

The contribution of Russian writers to national consciousness is undeniable,
although it resists measurement. There were writers who spoke to and for a
broader segment of the population during their lifetimes, such as Tolstoy,
Chekhov, Esenin, Shukshin, and Rasputin, but in the Soviet period, writers
made contact with the people as part of a closely controlled school curriculum
emphasizing the Russian and Soviet classics. There is no way of knowing, let
alone calculating, the power of individual teachers and family members to subtly inculcate more than what the prescribed curriculum intended, or of individual readers to have their own powerful encounters with the classic texts, either during their school years or afterward. Russian literature may have been
short on concrete answers, but it was long on thought-provoking questions.
Historian Robert Conquest emphasizes the power of literature to supply "an alternative set of principles" in an autocratic state. "If any single factor can be
given credit for preventing the total and irrevocable atomization and Staliniza-
tion of Russia, it is the voices of . . . Turgenev and Chekhov, of Dostoevsky and
Tolstoy, which were never totally suppressed."[88]

A series of colloquia on post-Soviet identity held in Russia in 1998 and 1999
reinforced this point in an unexpected way.[89] None of the questions addressed

to the participants, who ranged from Grigory Yavlinsky and Alexander Yakovlev to professors of history at Tomsk University, asked how the classics shaped their identity or that of the country as a whole, but in the discussion that ensued it was striking to see how the Russian literary heritage provided a lingua franca for people of fundamentally different professions and ideological camps. A participant had only to mention an author's name, the first lines of a song or poem, or the beginning of an anecdote for it to be clear which people, texts, ideas, and attitudes were being brought to the table. Russian literature, and Russian culture in its entirety, had brought the nation this far, not unscathed, but without irreparable damage to its soul or its conscience. As we try to measure the effect of Russia's officially "dangerous" texts, it is important to realize as well the power of those texts which remained available because the state thought it had sufficiently controlled their interpretation in the schoolroom to render them harmless.

One Text, One Nation

Sometimes the attention of a fairly broad swath of the reading public focused on a single, provocative text that had somehow made it through the censorship, but usually it was the intelligentsia that occupied itself with "one text," certainly in the case of *samizdat*, while the majority of the reading public chose the kind of works Kardin had in mind when he wrote about popular literature, which was easier to obtain, more entertaining, less risky, and required less decoding. An astute analyst of the intelligentsia in the late Soviet period spoke of the drawbacks of assuming a world of meaning between the lines.

> Because of the tendency towards embedding secret messages, many literary and artistic works have become virtually inaccessible to those lacking either the intellectual sophistication or the knowledge of history and politics necessary to decode them. In fact, as a result of censorship, a special symbolic language has emerged within the intellectual community, knowledge of which is needed to understand much of contemporary Soviet culture. It has thus become nearly impossible for those outside the Soviet intellectual scene to understand films like Tarkovski's *Mirror*, or novels like Trifonov's *The Old Man*.[90]

At the December 1999 Moscow colloquium on national identity, the question was still being asked: "Did anyone really understand *The Mirror?*"[91]

There was a marked change in the one-text paradigm by 1990, when *The Gulag Archipelago*—generally acknowledged to be the last dangerous text from the past—was published to great fanfare, but what appeared to be relatively little effect, competing for attention with the many new and returned works that were released in the midst of tremendous political, economic, and social upheaval as the Soviet Union lived out its final year. We see at this point the opposite of the "one text" paradigm, as even the smallish core of serious readers and critics split up into groups that ignored—or defined themselves against—each other. One critic identified at least ten "literary subcultures, each with its own aesthetics, morality, readership, and relationship to the authorities, whose representatives were in conflict with one another."[92]

The introduction of annual Booker Prizes was meant to strengthen the newly liberated literary world but it became common and acceptable to not have read all the entries, and an "anti-Booker" prize was introduced.[93] One of the editors of *Novy mir* said without any embarrassment in 1996 that he had not bothered to read Georgii Vladimov's most recent novel *The General and His Army* (*General i ego armiia*), an admission which he says would not have been possible five years earlier.[94] That claim would have disappointed the late *Novy mir* editor Alexander Tvardovsky, whose late-night reading of Solzhenitsyn's *One Day in the Life of Ivan Denisovich* had energized the one-text paradigm thirty years earlier. The serious reader (*bol'shoi chitatel'*) was constructing a reading list according to political and stylistic criteria, switching to detective stories, or becoming a serious television viewer (*bol'shoi telezritel'*) along with less-educated Russians.[95] There was, in the second half of the 1990s, one text that still brought together a diverse public—the script for the weekly televised political satire *Kukly* (*Puppets*).

4. In Russia, poets get shot
5. But manuscripts don't burn
6. Although they can cause fires
7. Writers must avoid all contact with *vlast'* (power)
8. The burden of a political function weakened art
9. Censorship stimulated the imagination of Russian writers more than freedom

Before the Revolution, Russia's writers were well aware that every text, whether read aloud to a circle of acquaintances or published with official permission, had a potential political impact and was never out of sight of a vigilant state. In 1888, Plekhanov proposed a "martyrology of Russian literature" that would begin in the late eighteenth century with Nikolai Novikov and end in the present, when "almost all the talented writers . . . have been or still remain in exile."[96] However dramatic the pre-Revolutionary story of the censorship of texts and the harassment of writers, the genuine writer-martyrs and lost texts of the nineteenth century were relatively few, especially when compared to personal and textual casualties in the Soviet period, both in Russia and in the emigration. The increased access in the 1990s to secret police materials on writers, and the heroic work done by Vitaly Shentalinsky and others to prepare these materials for publication, has given us a much more detailed picture of what had already been known in part. The history of lost or silenced writers and delayed, distorted, and disappeared texts would take many volumes to tell, and the story can never be known in its entirety, nor can we judge with any certainty how many "fires" were caused by texts above and below ground, and by works spirited in from abroad.

Avoiding the State

Russian writers could hardly avoid contact with an intrusive state, but there was an expectation that they should never seek such contact for their own benefit; after 1917 this expectation begins to resemble a loyalty test. Faddei Bulgarin had a gift for cooperating with the authorities, and in that he was a true precursor of Writers Union secretaries of the Soviet era. As an author and an editor, Alexander Pushkin submitted to the attentions of the censor, addressing his concerns to Count Benckendorff and at times even to the tsar. Nikolai Gogol grumbled at censorship requirements that were occasionally more bizarre than his own creations, but towards the end of his life he warmly praised the authoritarian regime in *Selected Passages from a Correspondence with Friends,* to which Belinsky responded in what became a famous and dangerous letter. The final absurdity was that after Gogol's death in 1852, all discussion of him in the press was forbidden, and trying to circumvent this prohibition put Turgenev briefly in a prison cell.

Poets and Censors

In *A Fence around the Empire,* Marianna Tax Choldin examined the censorship of foreign ideas under the tsars, and identified what she calls the "poet-censors"—among them Fedor Tyutchev, Yakov Polonsky, Apollon Maikov, Vladimir Odoevsky, and Prince Vyazemsky's son Pavel—who served for many years on the Foreign Censorship Committee.[97] When the wealthy Turgenev attacked Ivan Goncharov for taking a job with the censorship, Goncharov responded that his role was "protecting literature against the invasion of stupidity"; the artist Serov felt that being a censor was no worse than any other disagreeable job; and the bibliophile Nikolai Egorov said that it was a position that enabled him to spend his days reading foreign-language books and magazines.[98]

The experiences of the poet-censors support this benign view of their activity. Tyutchev and Goncharov both refused to take part in the Council on Press Affairs, which they saw as a bureaucratic attempt to stifle thought, and when a proposal was made to publish a journal that would counter the effect of Herzen's *Kolokol,* Tyutchev said that it would only attract participants if it were seen not "as a work of the police, but . . . a work of conscience; and that is why they would believe themselves in the right to demand the full measure of liberty a really serious and effective discussion implies and necessitates." He went on to analyze the long-term effects of repression on the "social organism," urging the government to co-opt its opponents by having confidence in its own ideas, and to accept the reality that "wherever there is not a sufficient measure of freedom of discussion nothing is possible, but absolutely nothing, morally and intellectually speaking." Choldin believes that Tyutchev was appointed chair of the Foreign Censorship Committee not in spite of this letter, but rather as a result of it. His colleagues saw how he was able to "always stand above his era" and make a genuine difference within an apparently rigid structure. Of his own decisions Tyutchev said that they were based "not on a literal interpretation of censorship principles, but, rather, on an organic view of society."[99]

The record shows that Tyutchev, and later Maikov, were able to moderate the application of the 1828 censorship laws on foreign publications to allow more works through not only in the original languages but also with permission for translation into Russian. In a poem written for a colleague's album in 1870, Tyutchev referred to his fellow censors as serving as "a *guard of honor*" over ideas. Choldin suggests that in his annual reports Tyutchev's forceful statements about the dangers posed by the Russian press abroad were a strategy "to divert his superiors' attention from the true situation," in which the censorship was actually letting in more foreign literature than ever before.[100]

This is not to say that Tyutchev ever represented a fifth column; he applied censorship laws while criticizing censorship policy and the utter mediocrity of career bureaucrats who were eager to stem all dangerous texts and provocative ideas, people who inhabited a world "which will collapse under the weight of their own stupidity." He reacted strongly to such absurdities as the proposed banning of a book by the writer August Theodor Grimm, who at that very time served as tutor to the future Alexander III.[101] And, despite extensive controls placed on the printed word, virtually every banned text was available for a price, and the censorship office itself was empowered to loan forbidden texts to people who applied to read them.

When Mikhail Zlatovsky first joined this group in 1862, he was overwhelmed by the presence of Tyutchev, Polonsky, and Maikov. Contemporaries remembered with great fondness the weekly meetings of the Foreign Censorship Committee: "our Wednesdays were our academy, where we enhanced our knowledge and broadened our intellectual horizons." Choldin comments that "the notion of 'our academy' surfaces repeatedly in accounts of the censorship careers of the three poets; they supported and protected one another and formed a sort of literary seminar centered at the committee."[102] In Russia, a literary circle could form almost anywhere.

The Writer at the Imperial Court

A paradigm constructed around the principle that a writer should have no unnecessary contact with *vlast'* (power) ignores two possibilities. The first is that there are writers who are sincere *gosudarstvenniki,* people who on the whole identify with and support the state and who wish to protect it from internal and external enemies. They may at the same time think that many highly placed bureaucrats are fools—or worse—and that the tsar is at best ill-advised. In the nineteenth-century it was not unusual for writers from the gentry and aristocracy to have connections at court; Tyutchev's daughter was a lady-in-waiting to the empress, and Maikov was a favorite of Alexander III.

Fedor Dostoevsky openly supported the tsarist regime as being Russia's only choice for a secure and worthy future; he admired Alexander II for bringing about the emancipation of the serfs and other reforms, and was also personally thankful that soon after assuming the throne the emperor had restored his hereditary nobility and allowed him to return from Siberia.[103] In his last notebook, Dostoevsky stated that he, like Pushkin before him, was the tsar's servant, but he was not hesitant to offer criticism where it was warranted.[104] "Not being in the opposition, the writer was ready for an open and frank dialogue with the rulers about the ulcers on the social body, and the flaws in government administration, and about essential reforms."[105]

Richard Wortman, the gifted chronicler of the Russian court, traced Dostoevsky's close acquaintance with the royal tutor and advisor Konstantin Pobedonostsev. When the writer was introduced the heir, he marked the occasion with a gift of *The Brothers Karamazov,* a novel which was read in the imperial family circle along with others of his works.[106] Even before this meeting, in

November 1876, Pobedonostsev had advised Dostoevsky to send the heir a copy of *Diary of a Writer,* so that he could familiarize himself with certain key articles.[107] Dostoevsky's proposal for an Assembly of the Land appealed to the "national authoritarian views" of Alexander Alexandrovich, especially in its opposition to the noisy democratic practices favored in Europe.[108] Dostoevsky was introduced to the tsar's other sons in 1878; their tutor Arsenev said that the tsar saw Dostoevsky as a potentially "beneficial influence" on his children. Arsenev asked in April 1878 that the writer speak to Grand Dukes Sergei and Paul about "the role they might play in the light of the present situation of society, of the usefulness they must manifest."[109] Anna Dostoevsky says that these contacts continued until the writer's death.

There appear to have been several meetings between Dostoevsky and members of the Romanov family, including at a reception held in the Winter Palace in March 1878, and even more extensive contact with the Grand Duke Konstantin Konstantinovich, at whose residence Dostoevsky would read aloud from his latest works.[110] An argument has been made that although Dostoevsky was brought into the imperial circle from time to time, this is not to say that they considered him *svoi chelovek* (one of their own). "The Romanovs did not hear, did not want to hear, either his advice or his warnings."[111] The Romanov (by marriage) most deeply affected by his work was Sergei Alexandrovich's wife Elizaveta Fedorovna, who never met the writer, only arriving in Russia after his death.[112]

Dostoevsky did not seek to profit from royal attention in his lifetime, but benefited from it posthumously nonetheless. When he died in January 1881, the disdainful metropolitan refused permission for burial at the Alexander Nevsky Monastery, calling Dostoevsky a novelist "who had never written anything serious," and seeking to avoid any disorder that might accompany the funeral. Pobedonostsev, by then head of the Synod, successfully pressed the church to allow the burial. Dostoevsky's widow turned down official help with funeral expenses, saying that her husband had wanted them paid for from his earnings as a writer and editor, but she did accept the emperor's offer of a pension appropriate to a general's widow to support the family.[113] Other Romanovs sent condolences from abroad and Konstantin Konstantinovich invited Anna Grigorevna and the children to visit him not long after the emperor's own tragic death less than two months later.[114]

In the following decade, the Symbolists accepted financial support from the tsar for their sumptuous journal *The World of Art,* which appeared between 1898 and 1904; this imperial generosity is not surprising, given that a number of articles in *Mir iskusstva* "were decidedly opposed to everything the Russian intelligentsia had stood for since the 1860s."[115] The poet-censors were not ostracized by the intelligentsia but had close ties of family and friendship with them. Personal connections between the establishment and its critics prevailed into the early twentieth century. Vladimir Nabokov's father, an active and highly-cultured member of the intelligentsia, spent most of his days criticizing the tsarist government in print and some of his evenings at court functions as a Gentleman of the Chamber; in 1904 he refused to drink the health of Nicholas II and "is said to have coolly advertised in the papers his court uniform for sale."[116] The following year, in the fateful month of January 1905, his court title was revoked. Nabokov senior was imprisoned by the tsar, pursued by the Bolsheviks, and assassinated by a Russian fascist who later served Hitler. Nabokov junior learned to avoid all political force fields, while making no secret of his disdain for the communist regime he had fled with his parents and siblings, and the Nazi regime from which he later escaped with his wife and son.

Standing between the State and the People

The fourth chapter explored the writer's role as a passion-sufferer (*strastoterpets*) for the nation, a function that had earlier been the exclusive property of Orthodox saints beginning with Grand Prince Vladimir's sons Boris and Gleb, and looked at the way in which the cult of dead writers paralleled but did not totally supplant the cult of dead rulers. A related role that writers assumed is that of a *zastupnik* (protector) offering *pokrov* (intercession), visualized most dramatically in icons of the Mother of God in which she holds out her veil to shield Russia from the righteous anger of the Almighty. This visual pledge of advocacy is one of the most powerful images in Russian Orthodoxy.

The church hierarchy had long counseled the state on important matters, including asking mercy for those whom the ruler intended to punish. But the integrity of this latter function was compromised in 1566 after Ivan the Terrible, angry over betrayals, conspiracies, and criticism of his rule, abandoned the throne and left Moscow. Novgorod archbishop Pimen was dispatched to the temporary camp at Alexandrova Sloboda to entreat the tsar to return, saying that Ivan could identify his enemies and "punish them as he likes" in the future. "This momentous concession struck at the very heart of the Orthodox Church, for it abolished what was most precious in its advisory role to the tsar: the voice of mercy."[117]

The agreement was implemented with the division of the kingdom into two parts and the organization of the infamous band of marauders called *oprichniki* to carry out state terror, impervious to pleas from any source. The sheer blasphemy of the period that followed, with its elaborate mockery of religion, demonstrated the extent to which the image of the church had been affected. In the following century, Alexei Mikhailovich curtailed a reassertion of church authority, and in the eighteenth century Peter the Great moved to bring the church into the state bureaucracy; a gradual whittling away of church properties in succeeding reigns compounded the damage. By the early nineteenth century, the official church was a resource to be called upon when necessary, such as during the Napoleonic invasion in 1812, but was not a serious influence on Alexander I, whose spiritual interests lay elsewhere. In contrast to the more limited function of the church, by the end of Alexander's reign Russian literature was beginning to find its voice and its role in national life.

In 1836, Pushkin proclaimed his role as a living writer-intercessor in the poem that begins "I built myself a monument" (*Ia pamiatnik sebe vozdvig*). This significantly expands on Derzhavin's 1795 poem "The Monument," in which the poetic persona claims to lighten the atmosphere at court while making sure that the sovereign hears the truth.[118] The sacred connection in Pushkin's verse is made obvious when the monument that he builds for himself is described as *nerukotvornyi*, a reference to one of the most revered of icons, *Spas nerukotvornyi* the "Savior not made by human hands." In the next to last stanza, the poet, having claimed a universal appeal for his art, says that "In my cruel age, I sang hymns to Freedom / And begged for compassion for those who had fallen" (*Chto v moi zhestokii vek vosslavil ia Svobodu / I milost' k padshim prizyval*).[119]

After Pushkin, writers, especially poets, could see themselves as living intercessors between *vlast'* and *narod*, the power and the people. On the one hand, this role was a potential threat to the writer's integrity, while on the other hand, it endangered his continued well-being. If the church no longer interceded, then writers must try to speak Derzhavin's truth and make Pushkin's plea for mercy. The goal of improving the atmosphere at court got lost along the way; Nicholas I was more likely to amuse himself at a writer's expense than be amused by liberal comments, however witty, and laughter had died with Decembrists to be reborn as bitter irony in subsequent decades.

Pavel Annenkov saw in Belinsky's article "A View of Russian Literature in 1847" an appeal to writers to "undertake, as the final goal of their labors, service to social interests, intercession on behalf of the lowest, deprived classes of society."[120] In the essay, Belinsky describes how critics and gentrified readers are disturbed by realistic pictures of the lives of the poor, and he goes on to praise those writers who have brought such characters to the public's attention.[121] Literary intercession on behalf of the serfs, which both stimulated and reflected a wider discussion in Russian society, was halted by the government's panicky reaction to the European uprisings of 1848, and it was not resumed in earnest until after the accession of Alexander II in the middle of the following decade. Alexander II saw Turgenev's *Sportsman's Sketches* as a kind of intercession on the peasant's behalf and the sketches are commonly believed to have strengthened the tsar's resolve to act on this question before the serfs acted on their own.

The writer and editor Nikolai Nekrasov urged Tolstoy in 1856, at the very beginning of his career, to remember that "in our country the role of the writer is above all the role of a teacher and, as far as possible, an intercessor for the mute and oppressed."[122] A quarter-century later, in the wake of the assassination of Alexander II, Tolstoy asked the new emperor to deport the assassins as a sign of the country's moral outrage rather than to make martyrs of them. He asked that mercy be extended not for the sake of the killers, but to "break the chain of violence" that threatened the nation.[123] This was not the first time Tolstoy had interceded with the authorities, and in later years he addressed himself to Nicholas II in a similar tone, and with a similar lack of results.

Asked by the St. Petersburg Jewish community to objectively report on the role of the empire's Jews in the wake of the 1881 pogroms, Nikolai Leskov wound up speaking as their strong advocate. Chekhov, in protesting to a Russian newspaper that had criticized Zola over the Dreyfus case, said that even if Dreyfus were guilty "Zola would still be right, because it is the business of writers not to accuse or prosecute, but to intercede even for the guilty, once they have been condemned and are undergoing punishment. . . . There are enough accusers and prosecutors as it is."[124] Lidiya Chukovskaya observed that in tsarist Russia Dostoevsky's *Notes from the House of the Dead*, Tolstoy's *Resurrection*, and Chekhov's *Sakhalin Island* all spoke on behalf of prisoners of the state.

After the Revolution, it was Maxim Gorky who took up the mantle for writers in distress. Yevgeny Zamyatin recalled that even when Alexander Blok refused to ask for help for himself, "Gorky went from office to office with papers and appeals. . . . Blok tossed in agony. Gorky went from official to official."[125] Chukovskaya spoke of Gorky as having used "all his authority to save writers not only from cold and hunger but also from prison and deportation. He wrote dozens of letters of intercession and, thanks to him, many writers were able to resume their work."[126] Others spoke of the risks Gorky took when he "frequently interceded with authorities on behalf of writers who found themselves in political trouble."[127] His independent voice and his habit of advocacy led Lenin to insist in 1922 on the writer's going to Europe for an open-ended stay. On a return trip to the Soviet Union in 1928–29, Gorky was given a tour of the prison complex in Solovki, and in the *Gulag Archipelago* Solzhenitsyn speaks of "the hope placed in Gorky's arrival" as "an ancient example of native *trustfulness.*"[128] In the following decade, Boris Pasternak, whom Stalin called to inquire about his opinion of Osip Mandelstam as an artistic master, was scorned for having failed to intercede successfully for a fellow poet in trouble.

Joseph Brodsky's conviction and exile as a parasite began to stir the forces of compassion in the community of writers and literary scholars, as evidenced by the tireless support of such figures as Lidiya Chukovskaya and Efim Etkind. The arrest and prosecution of Andrei Sinyavsky and Yuly Daniel in 1965–66 brought many advocates from the literary world and other branches of the intelligentsia to plead their cause. The "Letter of 63 Moscow Writers" to the Presidium of the Twenty-third Party Congress included such names as Kornei Chukovsky, Ilya Ehrenburg, Bella Akhmadulina, Vladimir Voinovich, Samuil Markish, Bulat Okudzhava, and Mikhail Shatrov, and requested that Sinyavsky and Daniel be released "on our surety."[129] This was in fact the moment at which the nascent democratic movement received its greatest stimulus. Russians may have been influenced by civil and human rights ideas from the West, but the important role of the intercessor was organic to their own civilization. Vladimir Voinovich's short novel *The Fur Hat* provides another example of parody reinforcing the paradigm as a writer thrusts a piece of paper in the dead Rakhlin's hand, hoping for intercession. What, muses this chauvinist, if the Jews really were favored? Better to join them and receive the protection of their God.

In the post-Soviet period, attention is being paid to the history of relations between Russian writers and state power, and to the issue of advocacy. And, although many aspects of the political role of writers and texts have ceased to function, there was for several years a vestige of the spiritual role of writers as the last hope of the fallen and a moral voice to which the government was inclined to listen. Writers and critics, including Anatoly Pristavkin, Marietta Chudakova, and the late Bulat Okudzhava, served on a presidential pardons commission set up in 1992 to examine prison sentences. Pristavkin, in terms that would have sounded familiar to Pushkin, Tolstoy, and Gorky, said that he did not address the politics of a case, but acted "on the laws of charity and humanity." Another commission member, playwright Mark Rosovsky, stressed the changed historical context since the end of the Cold War that allowed, for example, the pardon of the alleged American spy Edmond Pope at the end of 2000; literary scholar Marietta Chudakova, went far beyond that stand in her criticism of the judicial process that had led to a conviction in the first place.[130] President Putin had sufficient reason to pardon Pope without the commission's unanimous vote, but its writers served not only as a buffer between Putin and Edmond Pope, but between Putin and Russian hard-liners.

It has been said that the Russian intelligentsia as a whole "always occupies an intermediate position" between the state and the people, receiving privileges from the former because of its "significant cultural mission" to the latter.[131] The intelligentsia, especially its literary branch, "acts as a mediator between state and society. . . . it implements and interprets commands from the top downward . . . [and] articulates values from below and represents embryonic interest groups." The changes in power structures that culminated in the dissolution of the Soviet Union ended the two pillars of this relationship: "strong state power, and a high degree of tension between state and society."[132] This may be true, but it presents the idea of mediation as involving writers, in their capacity as members of the intelligentsia, functioning as communicators of policy from above and a nascent politics from below. As intermediary, or intercessor, the writer plays a fundamentally different role.

As with most spiritual categories in Russian civilization, there is a binary opposite to the writer-advocate, the anti-intercessor, who helps or at least encourages the state to punish literary figures. Mostly this involved behind-the-scenes work by members of the Writers Union in Stalin's time, which is better known now because of the opening of secret police archives, but there were also ritually abusive newspaper articles by literary critics about the state's victims or victims-to-be from the 1920s on. There are examples from the post-Stalinist period of writers joining in organized criticism of wayward members of their union, one of the best-known episodes being the attack on Pasternak after the publication abroad of *Doctor Zhivago* and the awarding of the Nobel Prize.

Yevgeny Yevtushenko avoided signing letters of support for writers in trouble at home and criticized them during his frequent trips abroad, while still trying to market his own reputation as a risk-taking liberal figure.[133] In 1966, Mikhail Sholokhov stood out from the crowd of those supporting Sinyavsky and Daniel by advocating a harsher sentence for the men he referred to as traitors. Decades later, Sinyavsky was deeply anguished when liberal members of the intelligentsia, including fellow writers and critics, gave their approval to Yeltsin's shelling of the parliament and then insisted that Communist-nationalist periodicals be suppressed. In Russia, to petition the state to take harsher measures than it had already planned is not a culturally legitimate gesture. If one engages with the state, with the force field known as *vlast'*, it must be to ask for mercy for those cast down.

The Writer-State Relationship After 1917

In the pre-Revolutionary period, the government confiscated foreign works, censored domestic texts, conducted surveillance on authors at home and abroad, and was generally suspicious of writers, critics, and readers, but serious casualties were relatively few. Ryleev, after all, was executed as a Decembrist conspirator, not as a poet. But Novikov, Radishchev, Griboyedov, Pushkin, Lermontov, Herzen, Dostoevsky, Turgenev, Chernyshevsky, and a number of other literary figures all felt the power of the state to crush them if it so wished. After 1917, the hardening government attitude towards literature and its creators, and the more efficient means developed to control the written word, made cooperation/noncooperation with state power a more significant ethical and professional decision, one that was judged at home and in the diaspora. As Osip Mandelstam wrote out the Stalin poem for his jailers, writer Petr Pavlenko lurked in the shadows. Between these two extremes, there were writers who could be called "permitted anomalies" and "licensed critics."[134]

"Permitted anomalies" wrote about topics like nature and childhood that did not often bring them near to paraliterary space. Their treatment of these topics did not honor the spirit of Socialist Realism as it was first conceived, but that became less of a requirement as time went on; the state needed to provide the public with works of high aesthetic quality but low subversive potential, which goes far in explaining the support for Village Prose, whose nationalist leanings were seen as a steadying force. "Licensed critics" were allowed, at times encouraged, to press issues that were not inherently political, or were being debated within the Party, and whose public airing would not weaken the pillars of the state. Both before and after the Revolution this could be a delicate balance for any writer, but particularly for a satirist, to maintain. When Mikhail Zoshchenko's monkey left the cage to see the world for himself, he went too far afield for cultural commissar Andrei Zhdanov, although, as Edward Brown observed, "Adventures of a Monkey" attacks nothing specifically Soviet, and gives no evidence of either a pro- or anti-Soviet value system.[135] Zoshchenko learned in his day what Novikov had discovered during Catherine the Great's reign: licenses can be revoked.

The ethics of having written with or without the censor's permission is a topic whose urgency fades as distance from the age of persecution increases. A history that awaits the telling is the story of talented, honest writers in personal or professional jeopardy who addressed themselves directly to the state, either by letter, or with a flattering or useful work of art. Mandelstam's anti-Stalin poem is widely known; what of his pro-Stalin verse, or that of Akhmatova when her son was in the gulag? Babel and Bulgakov both worked at some point on projects that came close to lending legitimacy to the myths of the Soviet state. These were terrible years, whose chronicle makes for painful reading.

Zamyatin and Bulgakov asked to leave the Soviet Union when they could neither publish their stories nor see their plays performed. Zamyatin received permission to go; Bulgakov got a call from Stalin and was given a job, but was never allowed to take the trip abroad of which he constantly dreamed. In a moment of despair he asked Stalin to be his "first reader" and dreamed of a face-to-face meeting. Pasternak also hoped for a chance to continue the conversation that Stalin had begun with him by phone. In the decade before he was deported, Solzhenitsyn directly engaged the state through numerous letters to top officials. For someone who had already experienced prison and exile, this was a courageous act. While it is easy to understand the bitter passion of Mandelstam's comments about writing with permission, even he wavered for an instant on the brink of the abyss.

Political Functions, Political Pressure, and Artistic Value

If the burden of political responsibilities, whether pro- or antigovernment, weakens art, then the absence of such a function ought to have the opposite effect for a given writer and for literature as a whole. But for those who developed as writers in a totalitarian state—when they tried to get the most powerful message possible to readers above ground or to find readers through unofficial channels—the years after 1985 were frequently disorienting. The high cost of daring words was replaced by the high cost of publishing, and of obtaining the basics of everyday life. Under an oppressive state, the role of writers was clear; in a more democratic and market-oriented context, no matter how corrupt or inefficient, their role has been less clear, and the ability of many writers to earn a living much diminished.

In *The Master and Margarita,* the hero's novel is not only saved from the flames and memorized by the Master: we are told that it was also read. And yet, despite the sacrifices and risks taken by him and his beloved for the book, the Master is not given the ultimate reward, a place in the light. The Yershalayim text has the power to strengthen Margarita's love and bring about Pilate's longed-for conversation with Yeshua, but there is little trace of these events in Moscow, where the Master's rescue and the punishment of various miscreants are due to the intervention of demonic rather than divine forces. So, while the manuscript does not burn, it does fail to act in the world. When permission finally came to publish a censored version of Bulgakov's novel in the Soviet Union in 1966, the decision had to do with such factors as the acceptance of Jesus as a historical figure and the need to counteract bad publicity resulting from the 1966 trial of Sinyavsky and Daniel. The appearance of one work no longer seen as dangerous could help undo the negative effect of other texts, not so much Sinyavsky and Daniel's stories as the transcript of their trial that had been smuggled into *samizdat* and out to the West.

The fate of another canonically "dangerous text," *Doctor Zhivago*, challenges the paradigm as well. In 1958, Pasternak's novel was vilified as traitorous at home while being praised in the West as a mighty weapon in the Cold War, and yet when it finally appeared in print in Russia in 1987, it fell curiously flat. What kind of hero was Yury Zhivago for the turbulent second half of the 1980s? Zhivago in 1905 was exhilarated by the movement of history out on the street, but by the late 1920s, he had been pushed back and forth across Russia by forces with which he no longer sympathized, his health broken in the process; he dies on the eve of the violent period that stretched from collectivization in the early 1930s to Stalin's death in 1953. Zhivago understood what was going on around him but lost his ability to act in history; in the most famous of the Zhivago poems he is simultaneously Hamlet and a Christ-like passion-sufferer, whose passive acceptance of death may protect the nation.

Zhivago reflected the dilemma faced by Russian writers on whose shoulders so much political and historical burdens were thrust for a century and a half. *Doctor Zhivago* went on the booksellers' tables just as the sharpest period of ideological and cultural wrangling and economic upheaval was beginning and as a result the novel never had a chance to flourish in a reunified literary community. During that stressful, angry time Zhivago's world and Pasternak's values were rather beside the point. But Zhivago was emblematic nonetheless: a writer-hero unable to function successfully in a rapidly changing historical context that violated all the principles by which he lived and wrote. Bulgakov's Master and Pasternak's Zhivago displayed artistic genius but weak nerves, and their loss of moral energy, their retreat from the historical stage and from the roles of hero (*podvizhnik*), righteous man (*pravednik*), and intercessor (*zastupnik*), earned them eternal peace, but not eternal light.

10. Writers undermined the authoritarian state until it collapsed. In the end, the most dangerous Russian writer/ text of them all was —— [fill in the blank]

At the beginning of his book *Forbidden Best-Sellers of Pre-Revolutionary France*, Robert Darnton remarks on the "unmanageable" nature of history's big questions: "What causes revolutions? Why do value systems change?"[136] To ask about the connection between the Enlightenment and the French Revolution "begins to look like a *question mal posée*," separating out one area of culture as the way of explaining the Revolution "as if it could be traced through the events of 1789–1800 like a substance being monitored in the bloodstream." Darnton asks many provocative questions on this subject. Generations later, how do scholars describe the path from texts to changes in public opinion, and then to actions in history? How does "a climate of public opinion" become public opinion, "or background connect with foreground?" Was the destructive action of one branch of publishing "a necessary condition for the general collapse?" Darnton allows for the possibility that "perhaps forbidden books did not affect public opinion at all; perhaps they merely reflected it."[137] This observation can be juxtaposed to the statement about Russian writers attributed to Herzen: "we are not the doctors, we are the pain."[138]

The Russian experience of the links between texts, the state, and political change suggests several models. There are texts that reflected public opinion or the atmosphere of the age: Turgenev's *Fathers and Sons*, and Chekhov's *Cherry Orchard*. There are texts that moved the people who moved history: Turgenev's *Sportsmen's Sketches*, Chernyshevsky's *What Is to Be Done?* Solzhenitsyn's *Gulag Archipelago*. And there are texts whose authors, like the sailors climbing aloft in Zamyatin's essay "On Literature, Revolution, Entropy, and Other Matters" (1923), peered from the present into the future, and saw the warning signs of "catastrophes" that lay ahead: Dostoevsky's *Demons*, Zamyatin's *We*, and Mayakovsky's *The Bedbug*. Valentin Rasputin resigned himself to the fact that "no writer can save Russia. In this regard we were deluding ourselves."[139] Perhaps that is true, but it was a powerful illusion, and one to which Rasputin's best writing had made a substantial contribution.

If one were to pick a single figure as most dangerous to the Soviet government it would be difficult to argue for anyone other than Alexander Solzhenitsyn. No writer fought longer or harder to bring down the Communist regime; in *The Oak and the Calf* he expressed complete confidence in his ability, and that of other writers, to make a difference in history, to redirect their country's path. There is no room for doubt or ambiguity between the lines of this memoir: the regime had to go. "Solzhenitsyn did not so much create something new as destroy every Soviet lie."[140] He saw his texts as powerful weapons against the Soviet colossus, and the story of his life gives us both the paradigm and the ways in which that paradigm began to change in the second half of the 1980s.

Solzhenitsyn was an active Komsomol member, a loyal Soviet military man, clearly a supporter of state power. The "dangerous" literary phase of Solzhenitsyn's life began with a letter critical of the conduct of the war, written by the war-weary officer to a friend. This letter led to prison and exile. There, Solzhenitsyn wrote and hid texts, first in his memory and then in various clandestine places until he began to be published in 1961. Within three years he was again concealing his activities, as he did research, wrote, and headed an informal production company that guarded his growing archive while copying and distributing texts at home and abroad. By this point he could already see that the regime was living on borrowed time, to judge by a telephone conversation recorded in 1965 by the KGB. "This is a government without prospects. They have no conveyor belts connecting them to ideology, or the masses, or the economy, or foreign policy, or to the world communist movement—nothing. . . . Honestly, I have that impression. They're paralyzed."[141]

He never hid his beliefs, demands, or suggestions from the authorities, as evidenced by his 1967 letter to fellow writers demanding an end to state control of literature. Solzhenitsyn sent copies to all three hundred delegates to a forthcoming Writers Union Congress. Poet Viktor Sosnora assured the union's leadership that suppressing this letter was beside the point, because thousands of additional copies had already been made and circulated.[142] The attention by state organs to the activities of the author and his supporters was massive and sustained, and provides excellent examples of how expansive paraliterary space could be.

From the First Circle to the End of the Line?

> My books have not been read.
> —Solzhenitsyn[143]

In his Nobel lecture Solzhenitsyn spoke eloquently of his books—"unpublished, alas, in my own country."[144] For decades Solzhenitsyn worked and waited for the day when his writings would no longer be banned in Russia. That dream was realized, but the accompanying wish, even expectation, of transforming the nation and its leaders proved elusive. Literary columnists asked aloud what it meant that Solzhenitsyn's work had so little impact when it was finally published in his homeland. A correspondent interviewing the author on Russian television said that there was as yet no Russian reader for *The Red Wheel,* a cycle that took twenty-three years to complete.[145] While there was still a Soviet monolith to demolish Solzhenitsyn was an acknowledged power to be reckoned with, but he seemed a spent force soon after his return to a post-Soviet society in 1994. The new challenge for Solzhenitsyn and other writers was how to "go to the people," that classic intelligentsia gesture of *khozhdenie v narod,* and find an audience once more.[146]

The influential theater director Lev Dodin was worried that the appearance of these long-delayed texts had not stimulated a soul-searching analysis of twentieth-century Russian history. "There was a time when I thought that if everyone read Solzhenitsyn's *Gulag Archipelago,* everything would change. But 10 years have passed and *Gulag Archipelago* remains unread. It is not only as if the book and everything that has happened to Solzhenitsyn did not exist, but it was as if the gulag itself did not exist either.'[147] An exhausted nation and a precarious new publishing world could not support the printing of a multivolume set of Solzhenitsyn's works in the mid-1990s.

In the nontransparent economy and virtual politics of postcommunist Russia, Voinovich's parody of the Great Russian Writer legend in *Moscow 2042* seemed a vastly more fitting text for the new age. But ironies abound here as well and Voinovich had his own share of disappointments: he found that with the rise of the internet, his works could be downloaded for free, which diminished his ability to make a living as a writer and undermined his sense of the reader. His answer, in part, was to take up painting. And after 1993 the ironic Sinyavsky/Tertz, as we have seen, was stranded in the paradigm of opposition, supporting Gorbachev's hopeless 1996 presidential campaign and taking an interest in the nationalist-Communist alliance.

Solzhenitsyn, Full Circle

The circle of writer-power relations made several further revolutions. Although Solzhenitsyn supported government actions during the October 1993 upheaval and in Chechnya, he generally distanced himself from the Russian leadership, bewailing the impoverished, corrupt, and demoralized society that reform had created, and refusing a government award from the hands of Boris Yeltsin. But on September 20, 2000, state power paid a friendly, respectful visit to Alexander Isaevich in the person of President Vladimir Putin, who, it turns out, had contacted the author on more than one occasion prior to that day. Was this an example of Putin's acknowledgment of authoritative voices, his adept maneuvering between rival camps, his desire and need for mentors, or his wish to give a sign "of the normality of our leaders"?[148]

The visit, which took place at Solzhenitsyn's home at Troitsa-Lykovo outside of Moscow, made an unexpectedly positive impression on the author. Interviewed on television the following day, Solzhenitsyn praised Putin for being "quick to catch on," having "no thirst for power," being "genuinely and wholly involved in the interest of public affairs," and understanding "all the colossal domestic and foreign problems that he inherited and must put right."[149] The writer seemed genuinely surprised to be in agreement with a Russian leader on a number of important issues and to be able to have a lively discussion of the areas where they differed.

The possibility that Solzhenitsyn's words might once again be in a position to alter the course of Russian history brought strongly negative reactions from several quarters. A dissident from the Brezhnev period, Alexander Podrabinek, said that he respected Solzhenitsyn, but thought very little of Putin and found it difficult to understand the author's enthusiastic appraisal of the new president.[150] How could a former political prisoner, a man followed by an entire division of the KGB and even targeted for possible assassination, trust an ex-agent in a position of power? The fact that contact between Putin and Solzhenitsyn had been established by former prime minister Yevgeny Primakov, himself a veteran of the intelligence community, only added to the incongruity of the situation.

Anatoly Chubais, the best-known and least-popular member of Yeltsin's economic team and an architect of the 1996 election victory, seemed even more unnerved than former dissidents by this visit and what it might portend for Russia. Would the forward-looking Putin begin to plot Russia's future according to the out-of-date coordinates in Solzhenitsyn's fiery sermons? If Solzhenitsyn's writings filled the empty space of state ideology, then they might once again become dangerous texts. Some feared that Solzhenitsyn's blessing would empower the government to continue its present course; others feared that a government seeking that blessing might be contemplating a move to realize some of Solzhenitsyn's ideas. One newspaper joked that this prospect might lead Chubais to flee abroad.[151]

What would the ever judgmental Solzhenitsyn have found to praise in Putin? It could have been the appearance of a quiet religiosity—a simple cross given him by his mother, a private chapel in the Kremlin—the president's attempts to root out corruption, to bring closer together, without force, some of the former Soviet republics, the admission that he makes mistakes, and in general the impression that he had spoken more honestly to the public than any leader before him. And, after all, he did not come from the KGB generation that followed Solzhenitsyn's every move and persecuted so many Soviet citizens; he was, rather, a leader of KGB background and Orthodox faith who came to Solzhenitsyn in a respectful way to explain himself and to hope for some level of support. In a sense, Putin was presenting his credentials to a person whose good opinion, in a society plagued by corruption, could not possibly be bought. Putin's subsequent visit to the graves of Ivan Bunin and other émigrés outside of Paris had—in some ways—the same goal as the literary prize Solzhenitsyn had instituted a few years earlier—to encourage the divided literary community and the nation to come closer together.[152]

Nabokov's Relatives, Sharikov's Children, and the Heirs of Solzhenitsyn

> Who is his father, then?
> —*Knyazhnin*[153]

During the late 1980s, ultranationalists claimed that Russian honor was being blackened by daily negative revelations about the Soviet era, as if there were no Soviet identity other than that of the vividly drawn protagonist of Bulgakov's *Heart of a Dog*, as if all Russians were *deti Sharikova* (Sharikov's children). Ten years later, in the midst of preparations for the Nabokov centenary, it was suggested that the writer—for whom time had frozen when his golden youth abruptly ended in 1917—was in fact "what we did not become because of the Bolsheviks."[154] In a mock contest conducted by the journal *Ogonek* in the late 1990s the drowned dog in Turgenev's story "Mumu" was said to be emblematic of the Russian people and the Russian idea, and designs were sought for a Moscow River memorial to the immortal canine. By 2001, the dean of Moscow University's Journalism School—lamenting the latest batch of literature textbooks—seriously questioned whether one could be a fully developed Russian without having read "Mumu" in school.[155] Angrily, wistfully, ironically, the search for Russian identity and for a path to the future was sought in the literary context more than any other place.

There has not been, and cannot be, any final estimate of the influence of one figure or one work. The primary experience of the text above or below ground comes down to one person reading silently, and, for that reason, experiences of dangerous texts in the Soviet period are mostly hidden from the researcher. All literary works from that period counted at some level, whether in building up the Soviet state, or in giving Russians the strength to endure, the resolve to sacrifice themselves for the state, or the determination to undermine what they saw as an evil empire. But it is difficult to avoid singling out Solzhenitsyn as the seminal figure, not for the beauty of his prose but for the sheer tenacity with which the life of the engaged writer has been lived.

It has been said that the long-delayed publication of *The Gulag Archipelago* did not transform the nation. But work on newly released archival materials by members of *Memorial*—and others who read *Gulag*—continues in freedom the labors Solzhenitsyn began under quite different conditions.[156] The memory remains of the first reading of the *samizdat* manuscript, and of the network of trust which made possible *Gulag*'s journey abroad and its preservation and distribution at home. Solzhenitsyn's legacy is to have helped demolish state lies, and to have resisted considerable government efforts to stop his truth-bearing texts from seeing the light of day by his organization of so many "invisible allies." He leaves a body of writing and a vivid example of moral fortitude and practical energy. That, more than the specifics of his political theories, is something that can help Russia move forward.

Afterword Dangerous Texts
in the New Russia

The old paradigm survived the demise of the Soviet Union primarily in the pages of the ultranationalist and Communist press, where artistic and critical prose was still seen as a political weapon. The newspaper *Den* and its successor *Zavtra*, and the journals *Nash sovremennik* and *Molodaia gvardiia*, among others, marked literary texts, writers, and critics as either patriotic and Russian, or cosmopolitan and a danger to the nation. Attempting to adapt to the reality of political choice in the mid-1990s, the values of the Red-Browns were transformed into campaign rhetoric.

During the December 1995 Duma elections and the two rounds of the 1996 presidential contest, Communist Party leader Gennady Zyuganov seemed at times to come close to taking control of the government; if he had, he would likely have assigned literature a far greater political role than did Yeltsin. In interviews with *Zavtra* from this period, Zyuganov divided writers not into Communists and democrats, but into loyal nationalists and others, and insisted that with Russia on the edge of the abyss, there was too much at stake for writers and their texts to be written or read apolitically. Leaving the finer points of economics and foreign policy to his advisors, he displayed a serious interest in literary questions, and the influential *Zavtra* championed his cause and supplied him with a ready-made cultural-political platform. In April 1996 *Zavtra's* chief critic, Vladimir Bondarenko, conducted a lengthy interview with Zyuganov called "Russia—the Land of the Word" in which we get a clear indication of one of the key sources of Zyuganov's ideology.[1]

Along with the classics of Russian prose, the candidate revealed a profound knowledge of Russian verse, reciting from his favorite poems. These included the lines from Nikolai Gumilev, "like bees in an emptied hive, / Dead words have a nasty smell"—an ironic choice, since Gumilev was killed by the Bolsheviks in 1921. From rural poet Nikolai Rubtsov, Zyuganov chose the following: "Russia, Rus! Save yourself! / Be careful—once again from every direction they approach your forests and valleys, / The Tatars and Mongols from another age." There was praise for Boris Primerov's prayer-like: "Oh God, who allowed the Soviet state / To flourish in miraculous power and glory, / Oh God, who saved the Soviets from misfortune, / Oh God, who crowned them with the thunder of victory, / Oh God, have mercy on us in these terrible days, / Oh God, return Soviet rule to us!"

This campaign theme involved more than the candidate's comments about novels he had read and verse he had memorized. In his travels around Russia, Zyuganov visited the hometowns of famous writers, places he described as "sacred to every Russian." He went to Vasily Shukshin's Altai, Sergei Esenin's Ryazan, Alexander Tvardovsky's village near Smolensk, and the northern Caucasus region where Mikhail Lermontov perished in a duel. The interviewer pointed out that Zyuganov himself came from the Orel-Tula-Kursk region, Russia's "third literary capital" after Moscow and St. Petersburg, the homeland of Tolstoy, Turgenev, Bunin, Andreev, Leskov, Prishvin, and the poets Fet and Tyutchev. It was an impressive national base from which to court voters proud of Russia's rich culture.

The contemporary writers on Zyuganov's list—Rasputin, Belov, and Lichutin—were known for passionate and often angry ultranationalist views. They and others whose names graced the pages of *Zavtra* had raised issues on which nationalists and Communists could agree: that Russia should once more be a large, invincible state (the former USSR is blithely called "Greater Russia"), that it was imperative to revive a strong military, and that ethnic Russians should dominate the nation's cultural life. Zyuganov and his allies borrowed the rhetoric of racism, colonialism, and the Holocaust, and applied it to Russia's present troubles, which they insisted were worse than those of any other country at any time in history. They claimed that occupation forces controlled the nation's media while genocide reduced its population. In the game of competitive suffering, these were skilled players.

Zyuganov said that Russia fell apart when it ceased to believe in the power of "the Word" and allowed non-Russian "others" to tear the people away from their cultural roots, and from Russian and Soviet classics. He upheld the political and spiritual role of literature that had been a distinctive feature of Russian civilization from Pushkin's day until the demise of the Soviet Union. Through this lens, everything in the literary world acquired ideological resonance. If Zyuganov's favorite works were not being translated in the West, he said it was because the West did not want to understand the real Russia. If writers retreated from political involvement while Russia was on the brink of destruction, it was a sign of their Russophobia. "Everyone must choose: either you're for Russia or you're against it." He added that without the support of writers, composers, and artists it would be impossible to formulate a new national ideology to fill the present vacuum.

The Party leader realized that the election had to involve more than a choice between Yeltsin and an anti-Yeltsin Communist, because fears about a return to the negative aspects of the Soviet period could easily turn the tide against the challenger. To prove the legitimacy of his presidential aspirations Zyuganov attached himself to literature, the single most important source of Russian identity for two hundred years. He chose to do this through an alliance with a newspaper that represented a motley crew of mutant Communists and nationalists, whose beliefs were not all that distant from those of the much less polished Vladimir Zhirinovsky. Between 1992 and 1996, *Zavtra* editor Alexander Prokhanov had patiently constructed a culturally based political philosophy, and even with the usual inflammatory rhetoric toned down for the campaign, it was not necessary to read very deeply to find an agenda that reflected antagonism towards Jews, people from the Caucasus, Americans, and a host of related demons.

Other political candidates had comparatively little contact with the literary world, sensing the widening gap between serious contemporary writing and the concerns of the voting public. The shelling of the parliament building in October 1993 had led to a new split between many writers and the government as well as within the literary community, and even those writers who had supported Yeltsin's actions hardly rejoiced at the prospect of a second term. These fissures worked to the advantage of antidemocratic forces which enjoyed the unqualified support of a substantial number of authors, many of them still deeply involved in the events of the day.

The candidate who posed the only serious challenge in Russia's second presidential election was indeed a literary man. Unlike Yeltsin and other presidential hopefuls, he realized, with help from Prokhanov, that a clever strategy for reaching the voting public was to use one of the least tarnished sources of national pride. Zyuganov's literary rhetoric, however, framed a political vision that—if realized—would surely have brought more upheaval rather than less, based as it was in the politics of anger and exclusion. Gennady Zyuganov may have been a man of letters, but he was no Václav Havel, and therein lay the danger. In any case, thoughts of reviving the literary-political process as a campaign strategy ended with Zyuganov's presidential prospects.

CULTURAL NETWORKING
AND NATION BUILDING

Zyuganov was mistaken in thinking that in 1996 he could use Russian literature to revive the Communist Party's fading prospects, but the legacy of genuine communal activity was far from dead, despite a new emphasis on individualism. One of the most widely held beliefs about Russian identity involves the importance of the collective spirit. The peasants lived in villages and were organized into *obshchiny* before the Soviet government brought them into the *kolkhozi*, which were artificial and forced but still linked to previous traditions of rural life. The Russian Orthodox church, at the level of the hierarchy and the congregation, was infused with the principle of spiritual collectivity, *sobornost'*. After the Revolution, virtually all institutions—schools, the military, the workplace—treated citizens as members of groups more than as individuals, but lifelong bonds also formed in a more natural way, for instance, between people who attended university together, especially during the post-Stalin years.[2] Vladimir Shlapentokh said in 1989 that "the majority of the Soviet people make up their own informal groups within collectives, which play significant roles in their lives and which have nothing to do with the collective as it is presented ideologically."[3] While it may be argued that these examples of traditional behaviors served for the most part as drags on the development of personal initiative, they generally represent positive networking in an environment that was always challenging and often threatening.

A negative kind of networking existed as well in the system of police informers, in the ineradicable webs of corruption—so colorfully portrayed by Nikolai Gogol, Vladimir Voinovich, and other Russian writers—that have existed as long as there has been a state bureaucracy, in the extensive criminal operations that developed with particular ferocity in the USSR, as well as in the wide-spread "institution" of *blat*. A post-Soviet study of *blat* defines it as "the system of informal contacts and personal networks which was used to obtain goods and services under the rationing which characterized Soviet Russia."[4] The numerous legal, semilegal, and illegal groups "turned the whole of Soviet society into closely interwoven networks," one of whose functions was to help serious readers get hard-to-find *gosizdat* and foreign publications.[5] During the post-Stalin period there was a decline in state authority and at the same time "the creation of a civil society based on the private activity of the Soviet people."[6]

The types of networking mentioned above are not adequate to the task of characterizing the impact of the literary-political process on national identity. As the imperial state and modern secular literature evolved, with control mechanisms firmly in place to mute the political power of the written word, networks developed for the exchange of literary opinions and artistic texts and to help writers targeted by the state for punishment. This is true of above-ground culture as well as that which grew underground. The "one text" model introduced at the beginning of this book describes the reception of texts which, before and after the Revolution, survived the gauntlet of censorship with enough provocative materials intact to excite virtually all serious readers and link them in the experience of the "text of the moment." When in the summer of 1836 Alexander Herzen received a copy of the journal *Telescope* while exiled in the provinces, he was astounded to find Petr Chaadayev's ominous "Philosophical Letter." He read it to several acquaintances, and believed that "exactly the same thing was happening in various provincial and district capitals, in Moscow and Petersburg and in country gentlemen's houses."[7] With Chaadayev's silencing on order of the tsar—clear evidence of the "recognition that thought had become power"—"the authority of the 'insane' Captain Chaadayev was recognized" and "the 'insane' power of Nicholas Pavlovich was diminished."[8] Circles multiplied, and while "there were no secret societies . . . the secret agreement of those who understood was extensive."[9]

Belinsky was unable to be as blunt in print at home as Herzen was when composing his memoirs in English exile, but in 1846 he did write about the way literature was contributing to the Russians' growing consciousness of social conditions, and to their willingness to sacrifice personal interests for the common good. In the people of various classes who gathered together to talk about new works he saw "the true beginning of an educated society which literature has established. . . . a multitude of people linked *internally* together."[10] In analyzing the government's treatment of the Petrashevtsy circle three years later, a Dostoevsky scholar explains that the government was not trying to crush just one secret society, but to limit the "secret fraternization" (*tainuiu obshchnost'*) of people with inappropriate thoughts.[11]

In the "period of stagnation" between 1964 and 1984, films and theatrical performances with a critical edge stimulated widespread discussion and the sense of a shared experience, and in the continual pushing of the envelope by Soviet filmmakers John Lloyd saw "the development of something like an artistic civil society."[12] Art exhibits and amateur theatrical groups encouraged an active response with comment books (*knigi otzyvov*) in which visitors and audience recorded their impressions. Amateur theater, a permitted but unfunded anomaly—to expand on Lotman and Uspensky's category—drew spectators into the creative process through "audience clubs that included participants in a variety of theatrical activities" ranging from functioning as "nascent lobbying groups" with local authorities (to obtain improved facilities), to sewing costumes and donating money (which was technically illegal).[13]

The most talented writers of permitted literature, *gosizdat,* ignored or denigrated official collective life, while elevating friendship and family ties.[14] Underground literature linked far fewer people than *gosizdat,* but it bound them in highly significant ways. The phenomenon of *samizdat* could not have existed without organizational skills, energy, and trust between people who knew firsthand or through their families how such bonds had been deliberately and severely damaged during the purge years. Alexander Solzhenitsyn's book *Invisible Allies* (*Nevidimki*), written in 1974–75 in Zurich as a supplement to *The Oak and the Calf,* charts the activities of his personal network and evaluates the key figures, including both his first and second wives.[15] The list of helpers is a long one, and the author did not know everyone in his support system. Some of these "invisible" helpers devoted years of their lives to this work, while others performed a single task at a crucial moment. There were researchers, planners who set up elaborate schemes and coding systems for storage, retrieval, reproduction, and dissemination, and implementers who carried out these tasks.

The invisible brigade included former *zeks,* well-known literary figures, foreign correspondents, émigré publishers, Solzhenitsyn's second wife's ex-husband, and grandmothers with large shopping bags who moved manuscripts and microfilms from one location to another. Some locations held libraries of forbidden materials; one dissident turned out, when arrested, to have 250 *samizdat* publications in his apartment.[16] Despite occasionally successful secret police raids, multiple copies of works were preserved and the archive reached the author after his expulsion from the country in 1974. Solzhenitsyn's memoirs paint a colorful picture of a solitary, driven writer and the busy and courageous collective that helped his work to survive. It gives us a rare glimpse at the kind of people who volunteered for this work, how much they were able to accomplish, and what, if anything, happened to them as a result of their clandestine efforts. At the end of the book Solzhenitsyn contrasts his allies with another undercover group, the KGB agents assigned to monitor his movements and to thwart his efforts to be heard.

This is the best-organized and best-documented network, but we can infer a much broader phenomenon from the simple fact of decades of *samizdat* on a variety of subjects from many sources, some known and others anonymous. Soviet Russian citizens wrote, copied, hid, distributed, and read unauthorized literature. "Informal groups . . . refugees from the big, official collective" allowed people who trusted each other "to make some contribution to the common cause."[17] No individual knew the identities of more than a segment of this network, but there was the sense that many others were taking part in reading and passing on provocative works, both literary and nonliterary, that the government would never have agreed to publish. Vladimir Bukovsky asked whether it was "possible to speak of an absence of freedom of information in a country where tens of millions of people listen to Western radio, where *samizdat* exists and is regularly sent abroad, and everything said today will be public knowledge tomorrow."[18] The state's control of culture and information was challenged, and discourse was kept alive. While this involved a minority of the population, the total would not have been a trivial figure.

Some of this comes under the heading of "kitchen table" politics, and Bukovsky was one of the most outspoken members of a generation that realized that "until the majority of us had freed ourselves of the psychology of the underground, of the rage for justice, our descendants were doomed to go on arguing in their kitchen." He traces the paths by which some of the young Muscovites who gathered around Mayakovsky's newly dedicated statue in 1958 to read "the poems of forgotten or repressed writers, and also their own work" then moved on to other activities like copying and distributing the work of banned authors, stimulating "real discussions" at official lectures, and eventually rallying in support of writers and others arrested and prosecuted for political crimes. Bukovsky was surprised at how well coordinated these efforts were, as "each of us, like a nerve cell, participated in this amazing conductorless orchestra" which took advantage of the "channels of trust " that had begun to develop in the mid-1950s. What had been a source of terror in the 1930s—the secret police search of someone's apartment—now brought out a group of the suspect's friends to party while spiriting away as many incriminating texts as possible. [19]

Václav Havel has described as thoughtfully and eloquently as any veteran dissident of the communist system the "power of the powerless," the title of one of his most famous essays. Out of sight of even the most vigilant secret police there was a "hidden sphere."[20] It did not represent a "unit of real power," but had great "potential," which could spread quietly throughout society, "including official power structures." In this "semidarkness," forms of independent political discussion went on and "everyone who shares this independent culture helps to spread it." Havel valued those honest works that managed to reach the surface. When we look at Russia, the combined force of people who glimpsed the truth behind the official lies and began to act like citizens and not subjects was enough to make a difference in the complex transition to a postcommunist society. A handful of writer-dissidents rose to positions of power—fewer in Russia than elsewhere, but the painstaking building of a civil society, however difficult a process it has turned out to be, owes some portion of its success to the traditions of independent thought and action kept alive through the collective efforts of many people under the previous authoritarian regime. Their work took many forms and was "decentralized," but in the end its influence may turn out to have been quite significant.[21] The more the state educated the people to take the written word seriously while it simultaneously enforced a strict censorship, the more the educated grew "a whole army of thankful readers," which included some of the enforcers themselves.[22]

DANGEROUS TEXTS IN THE CIVIL
SOCIETY ARCHIPELAGO

At the beginning of the new century, the phrase "dangerous texts" could no longer be applied to contemporary Russian literature and its criticism, which disengaged itself—or was cut loose—from contemporary political battles and posed little threat to the state, despite some occasional publicity surrounding an author or a work. When the progovernment youth group "Walking Together" demonstrated against the works of Sorokin and called for action, the Minister of Culture rejected their demands. When the writer Limonov was prosecuted, it was for the real weapons and not the lethal words in his possession. In the new economy, a little political noise was even good for sales. *Two Hundred Years Together*, Solzhenitsyn's history of Russian-Jewish relations (published in 2001 and 2002), followed the established paradigm in that it was often discussed without having been read, but the only "power" that was involved was the power of public opinion. One critic described the project as an attempt to "defuse" the topic, although the second volume appears to have had the opposite effect.[23]

Enriched by newly released archival material, the history of powerful texts and embattled authors entered the structure of broader histories and martyrologies, while artistically and spiritually significant works from the past functioned as components of national identity rather than as factors in national politics. The reintroduction of the national anthem written by Alexandrov during World War II was controversial not because of its text, which was revised for a second time by Sergei Mikhalkov and made maximally vague, but because the music itself was deeply evocative of Soviet life. There were some who felt that the original text with its praise of Stalin would continue to "shine through" between the lines and pose a danger to a society still trying to define itself and its relationship to the past. The wordless "Patriotic Song" by Glinka posed no such threat.[24]

If there were dangerous documents in Russia after the mid-1990s, the majority of them were no longer literary texts. As the Gorbachev era was replete with *chernukha* (negative revelations in print, generally about the Soviet past), the Yeltsin era was rich in *kompromat* (compromising material) about public figures which was distributed—and sometimes generated—in an effort to shift the balance in power struggles by bringing down opponents. The Putin era has added "black PR" and deceptive e-mails to the political sphere. Investigative journalism could also pose considerable dangers for its practitioners from the forces that were exposed in bold stories about corruption and related crimes. Those who challenged key figures on Russia's political and economic "power grid" (the presidential administration, regional leaders, the military, the oligarchs, organized crime) frequently faced reprisals.

The Russian government's already uneven relationship with the media appeared to worsen after Putin's rise to power. The Security Council drafted a lengthy new doctrine on information security, which pledged to protect the right to disseminate material while voicing concerns about the spread of "'misinformation' about state policy," a situation which could weaken the nation.[25] Freedom of speech issues achieved a high profile both at home and abroad, and fears were expressed about the ability of radio, television, newspapers, and even texts in cyberspace to resist government control and report the truth fully and openly. While most official forms of censorship ended during the Gorbachev years, texts linked to national security matters—the conflict in Chechnya, military-induced environmental damage, Russian weapons systems, and anything labeled an antiterrorist operation—could cause those who wrote, published, or broadcast them great difficulty and could even be equated with treason. Regional leaders often treated their administrations as off-limits to criticism and Moscow tended not to interfere when the exercise of free speech was hindered at the local level.

The government's tolerance of dissent, mockery, and what it called knowingly false reports was markedly greater during the Yeltsin era, and one of the murkier episodes at the beginning of the new millennium concerned media owned by Russian oligarchs. As one analyst asked: "Whose war was this?" Was it an attack on political freedom, the triumph of capitalism, or a complex settling of accounts? Those trying to decide between political and economic explanations were advised that in Russia, at that point at least, there was "no economics not dependent on politics."[26] Official attention focused on the oligarchs, who openly tried to influence state politics with the help of fortunes initially acquired at the expense of the Russian people. A 1993 article about the New Russians accurately captured the behavior of this group by contrasting them to athletes who play on one side of the net, for the white or for the black. Unlike these athletes, New Russians were not on one side of the net, but "on the side of the ball."[27] For those who feared the worst, there was no immediate cessation of criticism, but perhaps the government was not going to attempt anything so dramatic and self-defeating, intending instead "to set up controlled 'opposition' media"—those same "licensed critics" we saw in the Soviet period, except with greater license.[28]

A former dissident, Viacheslav Bakhmin, who joined the human rights movement in 1968 and spent four years as a political prisoner, summed up the situation after 1991 in the following way: "You can express your own opinion, and calmly criticize any decision the government makes. There's just one problem—no one listens or reacts to these opinions, although they won't put you in prison for them either."[29]

LITERATURE'S ROLE IN POST-SOVIET NATIONAL IDENTITY

The more mainstream type of nationalism that evolved in the second half of the 1990s was in fact anchored firmly in the nation's cultural heritage, seen more broadly and less politically. Russia's literature was a common source of pride and a common frame of reference, and its teaching was still taken very seriously. How could the schools cut back on the classics, when "you can't be a real Russian without having read a lot of Pushkin, Dostoevsky, Chekhov, and Gogol. . . . these aren't simply artistic texts, they're part of our worldview . . . our Russianness."[30] Discussions about post-Soviet national identity with prominent Russians that took place in Moscow and Siberia in 1998 and 1999 demonstrate a reliance on images, characters, and observations from well-known literary works of the past. Zhirinovsky's Liberal Democrats and Zyuganov's Communists were described by one participant as being "the same Manilovs and Sobakeviches"—familiar to Russians from Nikolai Gogol's novel *Dead Souls*—when what the country needed was the entrepreneurial type favored by Gorky. Yabloko party leader Grigory Yavlinsky used a Russian fairytale to focus on the civilization-shaping choices the nation faced. He went on to say that Russia has "Pushkin, Dostoevsky, and Tolstoy, and they're all different, but they are all part of Russian identity" which includes "the territory, and the government, and culture."[31] The literary canon was the acknowledged primary influence on national identity, but it was also the source of the language and the mode of thinking which participants brought to any important topic. How to explain the binary contrasts of Russian history? Through Kornei Chukovsky's two-headed camel who looks simultaneously in different directions, and by examining the behavior of Gorky who was at home both in Europe and as the bard of the White Sea Canal.[32]

Because of its central role in national identity and national memory, literature fed other cultural streams as well: film, television, and advertisements, for example. Yury Mamin's 1990 film *Sideburns* (*Bankenbardy*), reflected the tensions of the late 1980s with a combination of kitsch and political commentary, featured gangs whose members dressed like Pushkin, Lermontov's Heroes of our Time, and yellow-shirted Mayakovskys. The television show *Kukly* (Puppets) used familiar plots and characters from folklore and literature.[33] Petr Vail wrote of this as a transitional age in which images and sounds were crowding out pages and words, with the remnants of the literary nation showing up in unexpected places. "In the city of Yuzhno-Sakhalinsk alone you can dine in the 'Master and Margarita' restaurant, stop in at the 'Doctor Zhivago' snack bar, and be rendered speechless by the 'Ivanhoe' kiosk, whose walls are covered with packages of condoms."[34] In order to survive, the Writers' Bookshop on Moscow's Kuznetsky Most shared space with a jewelry store, yet another example of "our unique national character."[35] But there was a limit to how much tampering with the classics serious readers would tolerate. A move to create a Bulgakov theme park—with a cluster of monuments that included a forty-foot-high stove and a statue of Christ walking on water—in the much-loved Moscow neighborhood known as Patriarch's Ponds brought out demonstrators in 2003 who generated enough negative publicity to cause the project to be scaled back to one statue of the author.[36]

Bizarre developments at the intersection of politics and the media did not go completely unnoticed in literature. Contemporary writers were no longer actively guiding politics, but they still made ironic reflections on current trends, for example, in Viktor Pelevin's 1999 novel *Generation "P".*[37] Pelevin's amusing but ultimately bleak world offers no real politics, just the advertising of virtual candidates that uses culture to sell the product. The novel was widely read, but even to some of its admirers it seemed strangely unsatisfying. One critic insisted that "If you are going to fight, then fight to the end, until you've won something, or else it makes no sense for a writer to get involved."[38] Another critic called it an "antiliterary" attack, the strongest in recent years.[39]

If Russia's writers seemed to be adrift in a society that was still in its formative stages, the critics had not entirely given up on literature's power to be a significant factor in national life. Along with the authors of essays and memoirs and those who worked in newly available archives on a more complete history of Soviet Russia's dangerous texts, critics professed a fervent belief in culture's traditional work of "describing the world in order to save it."[40] For the past two centuries, they said, Russia had known itself—and in part had become what it was—through its writers and their sensitivity to political currents. Sometimes the most commonly held beliefs about a civilization need not be abandoned, but simply reargued. For example, in studying rabbinic Judaism, "the book-religion model fails because it works too well . . . and takes us back to the beginning so fast, that we meet no one new along the way."[41] In a similar fashion, the literary-political model may work "too well" for Russia. This book has attempted to go back and see the relationship anew while still accepting, and in the end celebrating, its enduring validity.

Notes

PREFACE

1. Princeton: Princeton University Press, 1992.
2. Jacob Neusner, *Studying Classical Judaism: a Primer* (Louisville: Westminster/ John Knox Press, 1991), 60–62.
3. Ibid., 60.
4. Daniel Rondeau, "L'homme qui chuchotait," *L'Express International,* March 23, 2000.
5. Marianna Tax Choldin, *A Fence Around the Empire: Russian Censorship of Western Ideas under the Tsars* (Durham: Duke University Press, 1985), 38–39.
6. Ibid., 39–40, 63.
7. This point is made by Terry Godlove in *Religion, Interpretation, and Diversity of Belief: The Framework Model from Kant to Durkheim to Davidson* (Cambridge: Cambridge University Press, 1989), 117–18, 146. Godlove looks at sets of religious precepts that allow researchers to distinguish between religions and moral philosophies.
8. ". . . rozovoshchekii amerikanskii slavist, dlia kotorogo vsiakoe soedinenie russkikh bukv i est' russkaia literatura." Pavel Basinskii, "Chego zhe ty khochesh'?" *Literaturnaia gazeta* 43 (1999).
9. Evgeny Dobrenko, *The Making of the State Reader: Social and Aesthetic Contexts of the Reception of Soviet Literature,* trans. by Jesse Savage (Stanford: Stanford University Press, 1997), 201.

10. Anna Dostoevsky, *Dostoevsky: Reminiscences,* trans. and ed. by Beatrice Stillman, introd. by Helen Muchnic (New York: Liveright: 1975), 249–51.

11. Vladimir Bukovsky, *To Build a Castle—My Life as a Dissenter,* trans. by Michael Scammell (New York: Viking, 1979), 258.

12. Mikhail Bulgakov, *The Master and Margarita,* trans. by Diana Burgin and Katherine O'Connor (New York: Vintage, 1996), 305. Abraham Joshua Heschel describes in *The Sabbath* (New York: Farrar, Straus and Giroux, 1997) how the weekly Sabbath removes us from worldly concerns to a peaceful realm, while in the eternal Sabbath we not only achieve peace, but are also privileged to glimpse the light of the Shechinah, the Divine Presence. Bulgakov's distinction between the Master's two possible rewards comes very close to this concept.

13. Michael Cherniavsky, *Tsar and People: Studies in Russian Myths,* rev. ed. (New York: Random House, 1969), 126–27.

CHAPTER 1. LITERATURE AND POLITICS IN RUSSIA

1. Marianna Tax Choldin, *A Fence Around the Empire: Russian Censorship of Western Ideas Under the Tsars* (Durham: Duke University Press, 1985), 42.

2. "Nexus" has been defined as "an archway through which crucial ideas and people passed," in Matthew L. Wald, "Jam Sessions," a review of Robert Buderi, *The Invention that Changed the World,* in the *New York Times Book Review,* June 22, 1997: 31. In *Russian Village Prose: the Radiant Past* (Princeton: Princeton University Press, 1992), I used this term to mean "the complicated interactions among writers, their works, critics, and ideologues" (xiii).

3. Stephen Lovell, *The Russian Reading Revolution: Print Culture in the Soviet and Post-Soviet Eras* (London: Macmillan, 2000), 47. Lovell's book provides a detailed discussion of relations between consumers and producers of print culture from the Revolution through the end of the twentieth century.

4. "Russkie—eto samyi chitaiushchii v mire narod." Aleksandr Ageev, in "Pisateli gazet," *Znamia* 3 (1999): 197–98.

5. Yitzak Brudny lists the impressive 1971–85 print runs for nationalist writers, who the government hoped would support the status quo and lead the rest of Russia along with them. See *Reinventing Russia: Russian Nationalism and the Soviet State, 1953–1991* (Cambridge: Harvard University Press, 1998), especially 105–7, and 127–28.

6. In one of his final interviews, Bulat Okudhzava described his songs as being 'a dialogue with people who understood each other with half a hint—a quiet dialogue. I did not have to explain anything to them, they knew exactly what I wanted to say without me saying it.' As cited in: Arkady Ostrovsky, "Quiet Symbol of the Soviet Thaw," *Financial Times,* June 21–22, 1997: viii.

7. James C. Scott, *Domination and the Arts of Resistance: Hidden Transcripts* (New Haven: Yale University Press, 1990).

8. Vladimir Korobov, "Knig mnogo—knig net, ili Novye izdatel'stva," in *Literaturnaia gazeta,* Aug. 3, 1994: 5. "So Many Books, Yet So Few, or the New Publishing Crisis," trans. Marian Schwartz, in *Russian Studies in Literature* 32, no. 3 (Summer 1996): 52.

9. "Da, my vsegda byli literaturotsentrichny, a seichas takovymi ne iavliaemsia." Lev Anninskii, "Nikuda drug ot druga ne denemsia," part of the roundtable "Dialog posle pauzy. Vstrecha v Peredelkine," *Druzhba narodov* 3 (1999): 186.

10. Igor' Zolotusskii, "Pervyi russkii vopros," *Literaturnaia gazeta* 52 (Dec. 27, 1995): 4. Emphasis in the original.

11. "Krome literatury, idti bylo nekuda." This is from Part II of *Notes from Underground*, as the narrator remembers being a young man in the 1840s. At the February 17, 1999 Seminar on Russian National Identity at the Library of Congress, Sergei Komaritsyn, the editor of the newspaper *Evening Krasnoyarsk*, said that the intelligentsia "was formed around literature," but that younger people were no longer reading serious American or Russian literature, and this constituted a profound change.

12. "Literatura vypolniala nekuiu vysokuiu missiiu, i kritik, govoria o literature, byl etoi missii prichasten." Ageev, "Pisateli gazet," 201.

13. Franco Moretti, *Atlas of the European Novel 1800–1900* (New York: Verso, 1998), 29–32.

14. The rest of this paragraph summarizes remarks and citations by Donald Fanger from "Russian Writing in America," in *Intellectuals and Social Change in Central and Eastern Europe*, a special issue of *Partisan Review* 4 (1992): 657–58. This is the transcript of a conference held at Rutgers University, April 9–11, 1992.

15. Brudny, *Reinventing Russia*, 135. Although said of the Soviet period, this is equally true of much of nineteenth-century Russia.

16. Michael Cherniavsky, *Tsar and People: Studies in Russian Myths* (New York: Random House, rev. ed., 1969), 36.

17. Excerpted in *The Literature of Eighteenth-Century Russia*, ed. and trans. by Harold B. Segel, vol. 1 (New York: E. P. Dutton, 1967), 384–85, 389.

18. Alexander Pushkin, *The Captain's Daughter*, trans. by Natalie Duddington (New York: Vintage/Random, 1936), 139.

19. Fedor Dostoevskii, "Pushkin (A Sketch): Delivered on June 8 at a Meeting of the Society of Lovers of Russian Literature," in *A Writer's Diary*, vol. 2: *1877–1881*, trans. and annotated by Kenneth Lantz (Evanston: Northwestern University Press, 1994), 1293–94.

20. Yevgeny Zamyatin, *A Soviet Heretic*, ed. and trans. by Mirra Ginsburg (Chicago: University of Chicago Press, 1970), 109.

21. Alexander Herzen, *My Past and Thoughts*, trans. by Constance Garnett, abridged by Dwight Macdonald (Berkeley: University of California Press, 1991), 247.

22. James Billington, *The Icon and the Axe: An Interpretive History of Russian Culture* (New York: Vintage, 1966), 329–30.

23. "Prazdnik sotsialisticheskoi kul'tury" [no author listed], introduction to *A. S. Pushkin 1799–1949: Materialy iubileinykh torzhestv*, ed. S. I. Vavilov et al. (Moscow-Leningrad: ANSSSR, 1951), 15.

24. Aleksandr Solzhenitsyn, *The First Circle*, trans. by Thomas P. Whitney (New York: Bantam, 1969), 415 (Chap. 57).

25. Donald Fanger, "'A Sort of Second Government': Solzhenitsyn's Authority Is Moral as Well as Literary," *Boston Globe*, June 5, 1994: 67–68; as cited in Amy Singleton, *No Place Like Home: The Literary Artist and Russia's Search for Cultural Identity* (Albany, N.Y.: State University of New York Press, 1997), 143–47. Gogol's infamous collection of essays

from 1846–47 includes many observations about the high calling of the Russian writer, which brings with it many important duties: see Nikolai Gogol, *Selected Passages from Correspondence With Friends*, trans. by Jesse Zeldin (Nashville: Vanderbilt University Press, 1969), esp. Letters 4 ("A Question of Words"), 10 ("On the Lyricism of Our Poets"), 13 ("Karamzin"), and 31 ("On the Essence of Russian Poetry and Its Originality").

26. Leo Tolstoy, *War and Peace*, The Maude Translation, ed. by George Gibian, 2d ed. (New York: Norton, 1996), 453–54. This scene provides the central image for Orlando Figes in *Natasha's Dance: A Cultural History of Russia* (New York: Metropolitan Books, 2002). Figes asks (xxvi) whether we are to assume "as Tolstoy asks us to in this romantic scene, that a nation such as Russia may be held together by the unseen threads of a native sensibility?"

27. Steven Cassedy, *To the Other Shore: the Russian Jewish Intellectuals Who Came to America* (Princeton: Princeton University Press, 1997), 26.

28. S. Ansky, "The Destruction of Galicia: Excerpts from a Diary, 1914–1917," in *The Dybbuk and Other Writings*, trans. by Golda Werman, ed. and intro. by David Roskies (New York: Schocken, 1992), 180.

29. Geoffrey Hosking, *Russia: People and Empire, 1552–1917* (Cambridge, Mass.: Harvard University Press, 1997), 293.

30. Ibid., 308.

31. Jeffrey Brooks, *When Russia Learned to Read. Literacy and Popular Literature, 1861–1917* (Princeton: Princeton University Press, 1985), 298–99.

32. Kathleen Parthé, "Russia's 'Unreal Estate': Cognitive Mapping and National Identity," an *Occasional Paper* of the Kennan Institute for Advanced Russian Studies (1997).

33. William Scott Green, "Writing With Scripture: The Rabbinic Uses of the Hebrew Bible," in *Writing with Scripture: The Authority and Uses of the Hebrew Bible in the Torah of Formative Judaism*, ed. by Jacob Neusner and William Scott Green (Minneapolis: Fortress Press, 1989), 14, 16.

34. As cited in notes to *The Pentateuch and Haftorahs*, ed. by J. H. Hertz (London: Soncino Press, 1992), 42.

35. Peretz Smolenskin, "It Is Time to Plant," in *The Zionist Idea: a Historical Analysis and Reader*, ed., introd., and afterword by Arthur Hertzberg (Philadelphia: The Jewish Publication Society, 1997), 147. The Smolenskin essays were translated by the editor. This essay makes a striking contrast to Fedor Dostoevsky's infamous comments on the Jewish question in Russia which appeared in the March 1877 issue of his journal *Diary of a Writer*.

36. Cassedy, *To the Other Shore*, 28–29.

37. Ibid., 28–29. A *kheyder* is a Jewish religious school for children.

38. David Remnick, "Letter from Jerusalem: The Afterlife," *New Yorker*, Aug. 11, 1997: 62. See also Dina Siegel, *The Great Immigration: Russian Jews in Israel* (New York: Berghahn Books, 1998).

39. Ivan Il'in, "Rodina i genii," *Molodaia gvardiia* 3 (1994): 182–89.

40. Ivan Il'in, "Tvorchestvo I. S. Shemeleva," in *O t'me i prosvetlenii: Kniga khudozhestvennoi kritiki* (Moscow: Skifi, 1991), 144.

41. Vladimir Novikov, "Siniavskii i Terts," preface to vol. 1 of Abram Terts/Andrei Sini-avskii, *Sobranie sochinenii v dvukh tomakh* (Moscow: SP "Start," 1992), 12.

42. Lev Aizerman, "Russkie klassiki v strane 'novykh russkikh.'" *Novyi mir* 7 (1999): 169.

43. Ibid., 161.

44. "Gliantsevitye zhurnaly—to iskomoe edinoe prostranstvo . . . zdes' s utra do nochi proiskhodit obretenie iskomogo natsional'nogo soglasiia." Ageev, "Pisateli gazet," 201. Ageev refers several times to "a single literary expanse" (edinoe literaturnoe prostranstvo, 197) and "a certain unified supertext" (nekii edinyi supertekst, 201).

45. Boris Kuz'minskii, as cited by Iurii Miloslavskii, "Estetika stilisticheskogo razocha-rovaniia," *Literaturnaia gazeta* 29 (July 15, 1992): 4.

46. Igor' Zolotusskii mentions seeing this in a newspaper not long before he wrote his own article, "Pervyi russkii vopros," 4. Zolotusskii believes that a more important and more specifically Russian question comes from the title of one of Tolstoy's pamphlets: "V chem moia vera?" (What do I believe in?).

47. David Remnick, *Resurrection: The Struggle for a New Russia* (New York: Vintage/Random, 1998), 222.

48. William Scott Green, "Diversity and Tolerance: Religion and American Pluralism," conclusion of *The Religion Factor: An Introduction to How Religion Matters,* ed. by William Scott Green and Jacob Neusner (Louisville: Westminster John Knox Press, 1996), 263. In Green's article, the reference is to the Jews' return from exile at the invitation of the Persian king Cyrus in 538 B.C.E.

49. As cited in Joseph Frank, *Dostoevsky: The Stir of Liberation, 1860–1865* (Princeton: Princeton University Press, 1986), 45.

50. Kathryn Feuer, *Tolstoy and the Genesis of "War and Peace,"* ed. by Robin Feuer Miller and Donna Tussing Orwin (Ithaca: Cornell University Press, 1996), xii. Tolstoy's movement away from a political novel is examined and charted at length by Feuer in her well-argued monograph.

51. Tolstoy, *War and Peace,* 1087.

52. Joseph Frank, *Dostoevsky: The Miraculous Years, 1865–1871* (Princeton: Princeton University Press, 1995), 350.

53. Ibid., 453. The remark is attributed to Apollon Maikov, and was endorsed by Dostoevsky himself.

54. Gary Saul Morson, "Dostoevsky's Anti-Semitism and the Critics: A Review Article," *Slavic and East European Journal* 27, no. 3 (Fall 1983): 311.

55. Aleksandr Kazintsev in "Tvorit' svoiu tsivilizatsiiu," a roundtable discussion involving Kazintsev, Vladimir Lichutin, Vladimir Bondarenko and others, in *Den'* 18 (May 9, 1993): 7.

56. Sergei Chuprinin, "Normal'nyi khod," *Znamia* 10 (1991): 223.

57. Valentin Kurbatov, "Predchuvstvie," *Nash sovremennik* 1 (1992): 186.

58. Sergei Chuprinin, "Nedoskazannoe: K itogam literaturnogo goda," *Znamia* 10 (1993): 203.

59. William Scott Green, "Otherness Within: Towards a Theory of Difference in Rabbinic Judaism," in *"To See Ourselves as Others See Us": Christians, Jews, "Others" in Late Antiq-*

uity, ed. by Jacob Neusner and Ernest S. Frerichs (Chico, Calif.: Scholars Press, 1985), 54–55.

60. As cited in Vitaly Shentalinsky, *Arrested Voices: Resurrecting the Disappeared Writers of the Soviet Regime,* trans. by John Crowfoot (New York: The Free Press/Martin Kessler Books, 1996), 172. Shentalinsky's research appeared in Russian periodicals, and in book form as *Raby svobody v literaturnykh arkhivakh KGB* (Moscow: Parus, 1995), 227. This statement originally appeared in Nadezhda Mandelstam, *Hope Abandoned: A Memoir,* trans. by Max Hayward (London: Collins and Harvill, 1989), 11.

61. Shentalinsky, *Arrested Voices,* 6. Robert Tucker quotes a figure of one thousand writers killed and approximately another thousand who survived imprisonment, in "The Scripted Culture," in *Stalin in Power,* 578.

62. Alexander Solzhenitsyn, *Nobel Lecture,* trans. by F. D. Reeve (New York: Farrar, Straus and Giroux, 1972), 9.

63. As quoted by Avrahm Yarmolinsky in *Turgenev: The Man, His Art and His Age* (New York: Orion, 1959), 204.

64. James Billington, *Fire in the Minds of Men: Origins of the Revolutionary Faith* (1980; rpt., New Brunswick: Transaction, 1999), 413.

65. William Mills Todd III, *The Familiar Letter as a Literary Genre in the Age of Pushkin* (Princeton: Princeton University Press, 1976), 27, 39–40.

66. Ibid., 75.

67. As cited in Abbott Gleason, *European and Muscovite: Ivan Kireevsky and the Origins of Slavophilism* (Cambridge: Harvard University Press, 1972), 45–47.

68. Vladimir Bukovsky, *To Build a Castle—My Life as a Dissenter,* trans. by Michael Scammell (New York: Viking, 1979).

69. Osip Mandelstam, "The Fourth Prose," in *The Noise of Time,* trans. by Clarence Brown (San Francisco: North Point Press, 1986), 181. This piece was written between 1928 and 1930.

70. Yevgeny Zamyatin, "The New Russian Prose," in *A Soviet Heretic,* trans. and ed. by Mirra Ginsburg (Chicago: University of Chicago Press, 1975), 92.

71. The first term is from David Joravsky, "Glasnost Theater," *New York Review of Books* (Nov. 10, 1988): 34. The second term comes from a discussion of the premodern canon in Iurii Lotman and Boris Uspenskii, "New Aspects in the Study of Early Russian Culture," trans. by N. F. C. Owen, in *The Semiotics of Russian Culture,* ed. by Ann Shukman, Michigan Slavic Contributions No. 11 (Ann Arbor: University of Michigan, 1984), 38.

72. Maxim Gorky, *Reminiscences of Tolstoy, Chekhov, and Andreyev,* trans. by S. S. Koteliansky and Leonard Woolf (New York: Viking Press, 1959), 41–42.

73. Ibid., 15.

74. Feuer, *Tolstoy,* 18.

75. The three drafts of a preface and "Some Words about *War and Peace*" can be found in *War and Peace,* 1087–96. The quotation is on 1090.

76. Lev Tolstoy, letters of Dec. 6 and 8, 1867, trans. by George Gibian, in the background materials section of *War and Peace,* 1086.

77. See Feuer, *Tolstoy,* 51, where she explains how Tolstoy deflected his political impulses while composing *War and Peace* by writing this play, "with its fierce attack on liberal in-

tellectuals and bureaucrats and its violent defense of the morality of the cultured landowner."

78. Miklos Haraszti, *The Velvet Prison: Artists Under State Socialism*, trans. by Katalin and Stephen Landesmann, and Steve Wasserman (New York: Basic Books, 1987), 9.

79. "Ochen' mnogim, ia dumaiu, mereshchilos', chto bol'shoi russkii pisatel' sposoben napisat' i rastolkovat' vse, chto tol'ko mozhet kasat'sia strany i liudei. . . . klassik v silu genial'nosti pochti vsemogushch i liuboe delo sdelaet luchshe liubogo drugogo." Ol'ga Slavnikova, "Derevenskaia proza lednikogo perioda," *Novyi mir* 2 (1999):201.

80. "Russkaia literatura XX veka sostoialas' v protivostoianii diktature." Vitalii Shentalin-skii, "Okhota v revzapovednike (Izbrannye stranitsy i stseny sovetskoi literatury)," ibid., 12 (1998): 196.

81. As cited in Nikita Eliseev, "Kritika: poslednii prizyv," *Znamia* 12 (1999): 149.

82. As cited in Tat'iana Kasatkina, "Kritika: poslednii prizyv," *Znamia* 12 (1999): 151.

83. Joseph Frank, "N. G. Chernyshevsky: A Russian Utopia," *Southern Review* 3 (1967): 68. Cited in Michael Katz and William Wagner, "Chernyshevsky, *What Is to Be Done?* and the Russian Intelligentsia," introduction to Nikolai Chernyshevsky, *What Is to Be Done?*, trans. by Michael Katz, annotated by William Wagner (Ithaca: Cornell University Press, 1989), 1.

84. Frank Ellis, *Vasiliy Grossman: The Genesis and Evolution of a Russian Heretic* (Oxford: Berg, 1994), 1.

85. Yevgeny Yevtushenko, "The Cradle of Glasnost," trans. by Antonina Bouis, in *Early Poems*, trans. and ed. by George Reavey (London: Marion Boyars, 1991), iv.

86. Ibid., v.

87. Charles Radin, "Passion, Daring Stir Russian poet," *Boston Globe*, Nov. 24, 2000.

88. From Michael Scammell's introduction to *The Solzhenitsyn Files: Secret Soviet Documents Reveal One Man's Fight against the Monolith*, ed. and introd. by Michael Scammell, trans. under the supervision of Catherine Fitzpatrick (Chicago: edition q, 1995), xxvi.

89. Remnick, *Resurrection*, 155.

90. Ibid., 154.

91. Haraszti, *The Velvet Prison*, 156.

92. Ostrovsky, "Quiet Symbol of the Soviet Thaw," viii.

93. Nadezhda Mandelstam, *Hope Abandoned*, 88.

94. On the Irish case, see: Alan Ward, *The Easter Rising: Revolution and Irish Nationalism* (Arlington Heights, Ill.: Harlan Davidson: 1980), especially Chap. 1, "The Easter Rising," 3–15. One of the seven, Sean MacDiarmada, wrote on the eve of his execution, in terms familiar from Russian hagiography, that 'our blood will rebaptise and reinvigorate the land' (10). The rebellion had a worthy poet in William Butler Yeats, whose "Easter 1916" ends with the refrain "A terrible beauty is born."

95. *The Russian Primary Chronicle: Laurentian Text*, trans. and ed. by Samuel Hazard Cross and Olgerd P. Sherbowitz-Wetzor (Cambridge, Mass.: The Medieval Academy of America), 117. I am indebted to Simon Franklin and John Shepherd in *The Emergence of Rus 750–1200* (London: Longman, 1996), for their remarks about the high value placed on books by the Kievan princes after 988, as described in the Chronicle (237).

96. *The Russian Primary Chronicle*, 137.

97. Ibid., 137.

98. Ibid., 237–38.

99. Ibid., 114–16.

100. James Scott, in *Domination and the Arts of Resistance,* brings materials from a number of cultures, including Russian, to his penetrating assessment of forms of dissimulation. Scott is one of many essayists who have quoted Shakespeare on the absence of slander in an "allowed fool" (177).

101. Giles Fletcher, "Of the Russe Commonwealth," in *Rude and Barbarous Kingdom: Russia in the Accounts of Sixteenth-Century English Voyagers,* ed. by Lloyd Berry and Robert Crummey (Madison: University of Wisconsin Press, 1968), 218–20.

102. Elena Eleonskaia, *K izucheniiu zagovora i koldovstva v Rossii* (Moscow: Shamordinskaia pustynia, 1917), 15; as cited by Linda Ivanits, *Russian Folk Belief* (Armonk, N.Y.: M. E. Sharpe, 1989), 89.

103. Ivanits, *Russian Folk Belief,* 89; she refers to A. N. Afanas'ev, *Poeticheskie vozzreniia slavian na prirodu,* v. 3 (Moscow: 1865–69), 429–34.

104. Ivanits, *Russian Folk Belief,* 157. The demonic baby appeared after a monk drew water from a well without having first uttered a prayer; dark, deep, watery places were one of many locations where evil spirits lay in wait for those who failed to utter the correct protective words.

105. Richard Chancellor, "The First Voyage to Russia," in *Rude and Barberous Kingdom,* 39.

106. Lloyd Berry and Robert Crummey, Introduction to Giles Fletcher, "Of the Russe Commonwealth," in *Rude and Barberous Kingdom,* 107.

107. Fletcher, "Of the Russe Commonwealth," 213–14, 218.

108. Berry and Crummey use the example of a Russian government complaint in the 1580s that English traders "had carried on treasonous correspondence with enemies of Muscovy and . . . were planning to intercept the ships of other nations which should approach Russian ports." In *Rude and Barbarous Kingdom,* 89–90.

109. Gary Marker, *Publishing, Printing, and the Origins of Intellectual Life in Russia, 1700–1800* (Princeton: Princeton University Press, 1985), 17–20. See also Fletcher, "Of the Russe Commonwealth," 214.

110. Jeffrey Brooks mentions changing government regulations concerning the printing and selling of *lubki* in the nineteenth century. Restricting the activities of *lubok* sellers during the relatively liberal period in 1865, the government eased up on these restrictions during the markedly tighter postassassination period in July 1881, having more faith in popular devotion to tsar, church, and country than in the elite. Brooks, *When Russia Learned to Read,* 300–301.

111. Marker, *Publishing, Printing. and the Origins of Intellectual Life in Russia,* 19–20.

112. Ibid., 20.

113. Michael Cherniavsky, "The Old Believers and the New Religion," *Slavic Review* 25, no. 1 (March 1966): 12.

114. *Medieval Russia: A Source Book, 850–1700,* 3d ed., ed. by Basil Dmytryshyn (Fort Worth: Holt, Rinehart and Winston, 1991), 439–41.

115. From an 1875 book on Solovki by Vasily Nemirovich-Danchenko; as cited in: Natalia

Kuziakina, *Theatre in the Solovki Prison Camp*, trans. by Boris Meerovich (Luxembourg: Harwood, 1995), 8–10.

116. Billington, *The Icon and the Axe*, 160.

117. Choldin, *A Fence Around the Empire*, 41. She is citing Sidney Monas, "Shishkov, Bulgarin, and the Russian Censorship," in *Russian Thought and Politics*, Harvard Slavic Studies, 4 (Cambridge: Harvard University Press, 1957), 139.

118. Herzen, *My Past and Thoughts*, 272.

119. This influence was still evident in the twentieth century; Nadezhda Mandelstam, for example, said that her husband was "always reading" Avvakum; *Hope Abandoned*, 110.

120. On Peter's reforms in printing and writing, see Marker, *Publishing, Printing, and the Origins of Intellectual Life in Russia*, 20–40.

121. Cherniavsky, "The Old Believers," 35.

122. David Warnes, *Chronicle of the Russian Tsars* (London: Thames and Hudson, 1999), 126.

123. See: Marc Raeff, *Origins of the Russian Intelligentsia: The Eighteenth-Century Nobility* (New York: Harcourt Brace Jovanovich, 1966).

124. Choldin, *A Fence Around the Empire*, 43–44.

125. Isabel DeMadariaga, *Politics and Culture in Eighteenth-Century Russia* (London: Longman, 1998), 292.

126. Choldin, *A Fence Around the Empire*, 22–23.

127. Todd, *The Familiar Letter*, 33, 41, 82–83.

128. As quoted by Glenn Barratt, in *Voices in Exile: The Decembrist Memoirs* (Montreal: McGill-Queen's University Press, 1974), 142. The full text can be found in *Vosstanie dekabristov: materialy po istorii vosstaniia dekabristov*, vol. 1: *Dela verkhovnogo suda i sledstvennoi komissii*, ed. by M. N. Pokrovskii (Moscow: Gosizdat, 1925), 7–9, 156, 226, 294–95, 343, 400, 429–31.

129. *Vosstanie dekabristov*, 430. In the course of the investigation, Bestuzhev implicated a number of people in what proved to be a successful attempt to save his own life.

130. Nabokov's comments comprise the second volume of his two-volume set, the first of which is the translation. Vladimir Nabokov, *Eugene Onegin* (Princeton: Princeton University Press, 1964; rev. ed. 1975), vol. 2, 245–49.

131. Biographical information about Aleksandr Griboedov is taken from the *Handbook of Russian Literature*, ed. by Victor Terras (New Haven: Yale University Press, 1985): 184–85.

132. Herzen, *My Past and Thoughts*, 635–36.

133. Ibid., 117–20. See also the entry for Polezhaev by Nina Perlina in the *Handbook of Russian Literature*, 348.

134. Ibid., 549–52.

135. Choldin, *A Fence Around the Empire*, 174.

136. Herzen, *My Past and Thoughts*, 627.

137. Jeffrey Brooks, *When Russia Learned to Read*, 64–65. Brooks makes the point that *lubki* were still produced after this ruling; they used traditional images with some updating to reflect the changing interests of the buyers (65).

138. Herzen, *My Past and Thoughts*, 640.

139. This characterization of Herzen's view comes from Salo Baron, *The Russian Jew Under Tsars and Soviets*, rev. ed. (New York: Macmillan, 1976), 148. Baron mentions this in the context of a discussion of Russian Zionists, who viewed Western Jews as experiencing the opposite—'slavery within freedom.'

140. Herzen, *My Past and Thoughts*, 640. The memoirist is identified in a note as D. K. Schedro-Ferrotti (Baron F. I. Firks), whose *Etudes sur l'avenir de la Russie: Nihilisme en Russie* was published in 1867. Herzen makes a similar observation in the 1851 essay "The Russian People and Socialism, an Open Letter to Jules Michelet," in *From the Other Shore and The Russian People and Socialism,* introd. Isaiah Berlin, no trans. listed (New York: Meridian Books, 1963), 198.

141. Ibid., 640.

142. Ibid., 223.

143. Ibid., 535. Some information on the movement of radical material from Europe to Russia is provided in: Michael Futrell, *Northern Underground: Episodes of Russian Revolutionary Transport and Communications through Scandinavia and Finland 1863–1917* (New York: Praeger, 1963).

144. Fyodor Dostoevsky, *Demons,* trans. by Richard Pevear and Larissa Volokhonsky (New York: Random, 1994), especially Part 1, Chapter 1.

145. Dostoevsky, *Demons,* 364, 424–25, 447.

146. Fyodor Sologub, *The Petty Demon,* trans. by S. D. Cioran (Ann Arbor: Ardis: 1983), 71; see also 101. The novel was published in 1907.

147. Choldin, *A Fence Around the Empire,* 60.

148. Brooks, *When Russian Learned to Read,* 110–11.

149. Frank, *Dostoevsky: The Miraculous Years,* 451–52.

150. Frank, *The Stir of Liberation,* 145–59.

151. In a letter to Turgenev of September 26 (October 9), 1861, as cited in the critical appendix to Ivan Turgenev, *Fathers and Sons,* ed., and rev. trans. by Ralph Matlaw, 2d ed. (New York: Norton, 1989), 178–79.

152. Joseph Frank, *The Miraculous Years,* 45.

153. Ibid., 495.

154. Ibid., 438.

155. Herzen, *My Past and Thoughts,* 536–38.

156. Ibid., 552–54.

157. Frank, *Dostoevsky: The Stir of Liberation,* 284–86; also Katz and Wagner, "Chernyshevsky," 21–23, who both summarize and quote Frank, while expanding on the presentation of this incident.

158. Frank, *The Stir of Liberation,* 285.

159. The Central Censorship Authority approved the same passages several months later. For a discussion of this incident, see Frank, *The Stir of Liberation,* 28–30.

160. From a letter to Apollon Maikov, cited in Frank, *The Miraculous Years,* 299.

161. Ibid., 429.

162. Fyodor Dostoevsky, *A Writer's Diary,* vol. 1, trans. and annotated by Kenneth Lantz, intro. by Gary Saul Morson (Evanston: Northwestern University Press, 1993), 359–60, 776n.

163. Choldin, *A Fence Around the Empire*, 125, 130–31, 183–84, 198.

164. S. Ansky, "The Sins of Youth," trans. by Lucy Dawidowicz, in *The Dybbuk and Other Writings*, 70–76.

165. Arthur Hertzberg, introduction to *The Zionist Idea*, ed. and with notes by A. Hertzberg (Philadelphia: The Jewish Publication Society, 1997), 54.

166. Cassedy, *To the Other Shore*, xxi.

167. Billington, *The Icon and the Axe*, 36.

168. Ibid., 147.

169. Ibid., 33, 50–1.

170. Ibid., 163–64.

171. Brooks, *When Russia Learned to Read*, 111, 211.

172. M. O. Menshikov, as cited ibid., 331.

173. A. N. Nikoliukin, "'Ne v izgnanii, a v poslanii': Missiia literatury," *Kul'turnoe nasledie rossiiskoi emigratsii 1917–1940*, ed. by E. Chelyshev and D. Skakhovskoi, book 2 (Moscow: "Nasledie," 1994), 6–16.

174. Zamyatin, "Autobiography," in *A Soviet Heretic*, 6.

175. Zamyatin, "Letter to Stalin," in *A Soviet Heretic*, 306.

176. Ibid., 308.

177. Evgeny Dobrenko, *The Making of a State Reader: Social and Aesthetic Contexts of the Reception of Soviet Literature*, trans. by Jesse Savage (Stanford: Stanford University Press, 1997). The Nazi plan to destroy the Jewish people, religion, and culture in their midst and then establish a museum takes this line of thinking several deadly steps further.

178. Dmitrii Likhachev, *Stat'i rannikh let* (Tver': Tverskoe oblastnoe otdelenie Rossiiskogo fonda kul'tury, 1993), 5–8.

179. Ibid., 8–14.

180. Likhachev, "Solovetskie zapisi: 1928–1930," and "Solovki: Zapiski," in *Stat'i rannikh let*, 15–30 and 31–44, respectively.

181. Michael Meerson-Aksenov, "The Dissident Movement and *Samizdat*," in *The Political, Social and Religious Thought of Russian "Samizdat"—An Anthology*, ed. by M. Meerson-Aksenov, trans. by Nicholas Lupin (Belmont, Mass.: Nordland, 1977), 25.

182. One of the sources on "White Tass" is a partial transcript of a Writers' Union meeting held in March 1956 to discuss Khrushchev's Twentieth Party Congress speech, reprinted in *An End to Silence. Uncensored Opinion in the Soviet Union, from Roy Medvedev's Underground Political Diary*, ed. and introd. by Stephen Cohen, trans. by George Saunders (New York: Norton, 1982), 110. Others are: Robert Kaiser, *Russia: The People and the Power* (New York: Pocket Books, 1976), 252–53; and Hedrick Smith, *The Russians* (New York: Ballantine, 1976), 474–76. Smith goes most deeply into the various levels of Tass.

183. Smith, *The Russians*, 477–78. Smith also describes the careful distribution of foreign newspapers and journals, and censorship of mail to and from abroad, using as a source Zhores Medvedev, *The Medvedev Papers* (1971).

184. Bukovsky, *To Build a Castle*, 163.

185. "Final Plea by Andrei Sinyavsky," from *On Trial: The Soviet State versus "Abram Tertz" and "Nikolai Arzhak*," trans., ed. and introd. by Max Hayward, rev. ed. (New York: Harper and Row, 1967), 174–75.

186. Sinyavsky, *On Trial*, 182.

187. C. T. Nepomnyashchy, "An Interview with Andrei Sinyavsky," *Formations*, 6, no. 1, 21.

188. Bukovsky, *To Build a Castle*, 139–45.

189. See the foreword by Kevin Close and the editors' note in *Metropol*, ed. by Vasily Aksyonov et al., trans. by George Saunders et al. (New York: Norton, 1982). A Russian edition appeared at the end of the nineties: *Metropol'* (Moscow: "Podkova" "Dekont+": 1999).

190. Igor' Dedkov, "The Road to Truth, or Those Who Seek a New Jerusalem," trans. by Nancy Condee and Vladimir Padunov, *Soviet Studies in Literature* 25, no. 1 (Winter 1988–89): 33. The original article, "Khozhdenie za pravdoi, ili vzyskaiushchie novogo grada," appeared in *Znamia* 2 (1988): 199–214.

191. Dedkov, "The Road to Truth," 34.

192. This was followed in January 1963 by "Matryona's Home" and "Incident at Krechetovka Station."

193. Francis Fukuyama, "The End of History?" *The National Interest* 16 (Summer 1989): 3–18; and his subsequent book *The End of History and the Last Man* (New York: The Free Press, 1992).

CHAPTER 2. THE DISAPPEARING TEXT

1. The first epigraph is from the draft of a letter to Count Benckendorff, written in February 1832, in *Letters of Alexander Pushkin*, trans. and introd. by J. Thomas Shaw (Madison: University of Wisconsin Press, 1967), 548–49. The second epigraph is from Alexander Herzen, *My Past and Thoughts*, trans. by Constance Garnett, rev. by H. Higgins, abridged by Dwight Macdonald (Berkeley: University of California Press, 1973), 641.

   Rosalind E. Krauss, "Poststructuralism and the Paraliterary," in *The Originality of the Avant-Garde and Other Modernist Myths* (Cambridge: The MIT Press, 1986), 292. Russian essayists use a similar phrase, *okololiteraturnoe prostranstvo* (the space surrounding literature) for writing related to artistic texts, but not itself *khudozhestvennaia literatura* (artistic literature). I have employed Krauss's term somewhat differently, to more accurately reflect the situation in Russia. The collection of essays is available in Russian: *Podlinnost' avangarda i drugie modernistskie mify*, trans. by A. Matveeva et al. (Moscow: Khud. Zhurnal, 2003).

2. From an 1876 diary entry, as cited in Anna Dostoevsky, *Dostoevsky: Reminiscences*, trans. and ed. by Beatrice Stillman, introd. by Helen Muchnic (New York: Liveright, 1975), 399–400.

3. C. T. Nepomnyashchy, "An Interview with Andrei Sinyavsky," *Formations* 6, no. 1 (Spring 1991): 21.

4. Nikolai Aleksandrov, in "Kritika: poslednii prizyv" (statements by a dozen critics) *Znamia* 12 (1999): 144.

5. "From the Minutes of a Politburo Meeting," January 7, 1974, doc. 99 in *The Solzhenitsyn Files: Secret Documents Reveal One Man's Fight against the Monolith*, ed. and introd. by Michael Scammell, trans. by Catherine Fitzpatrick et al. (Chicago: edition q, inc., 1995), 283.

6. Abram Tertz (Andrei Sinyavsky), "The Literary Process in Russia," trans. by Michael Glenny, in *Kontinent* (Garden City, N.Y.: Anchor/Doubleday, 1976), 107.

7. ". . . migom obletala stranu, chasto operezhaia, a inogda i zameniaia soboiu neposredstvennoe znakomstvo s tekstom"; Sergei Chuprinin, "Normal'nyi khod," *Znamia* 10 (1991). Trans. by Deming Brown, *Russian Studies in Literature* 29, no. 1 (Winter 1992–93): 221.

8. Efim Etkind, *Notes of a Non-Conspirator,* trans. by Peter France (Oxford: Oxford University Press, 1978), 256, 261.

9. Linda Ivanits, *Russian Folk Belief* (Armonk, N.Y.: M. E .Sharpe, 1989), 103–24.

10. NEP refers to the New Economic Policy, a strategic reintroduction of some elements of a market economy that began in 1921 so as to allow a more rapid recovery from the wartime years since 1914. Yevgeny Zamyatin, *A Soviet Heretic,* ed. and trans. by Mirra Ginsburg (Chicago: University of Chicago Press, 1970), 306.

11. William Scott Green, "Writing with Scripture: the Rabbinic Uses of the Hebrew Bible," in Jacob Neusner and William Scott Green, *Writing with Scripture: the Authority and Uses of the Hebrew Bible in the Torah of Formative Judaism* (Minneapolis: Fortress Press, 1989), 14.

12. Vitaly Shentalinsky, *Arrested Voices: Resurrection of the Disappeared Writers of the Soviet Regime,* trans. by John Crowfoot, introd. by Robert Conquest (New York: Free Press, 1993), 171–73.

13. Krauss, "Poststructuralism," 293. She stresses the inaccessibility of such criticism to any but a relatively small group, because in its obsession with theory, both the actual text and the expected hermeneutic function of criticism—to tease out a text's meanings for the reader—get lost.

14. Varlam Shalamov, "The Used-Book Dealer," trans. by John Glad, in *Kolyma Tales* (New York: Norton, 1982), 214.

15. Osip Mandelstam, "The Egyptian Stamp," trans. by Clarence Brown, *The Noise of Time* (San Francisco: North Point Press, 1986), 161.

16. Marianna Tax Choldin, *A Fence Around the Empire: Russian Censorship of Western Ideas* (Durham: Duke University Press, 1985), 23, 26.

17. Vladimir Bukovsky, *To Build a Castle—My Life as a Dissenter,* trans. by Michael Scammell (New York: Viking, 1979), 125, 132.

18. Stanislav Rassadin, "Legenda o velikom chitatele," *Strana i mir* 6 (Nov.–Dec. 1990): 134.

19. Petr Vail', Aleksandr Genis, *60-ye: Mir sovetskogo cheloveka* (Ann Arbor: Ardis, 1989). This paragraph paraphrases and quotes material from 146–51.

20. This is a summary of material presented throughout Choldin's *A Fence Around the Empire.* The treatment of Russian royalty is from 148–61.

21. W. Gareth Jones, "Politics," in *The Cambridge Companion to the Classic Russian Novel,* ed. by Malcolm Jones and Robin Feuer Miller (Cambridge: Cambridge University Press, 1998), 67.

22. Vissarion Belinsky, "Letter to N. V. Gogol, July 3, 1847," no trans. listed, in V. G. Belinsky, *Selected Philosophical Works* (Moscow: Foreign Languages Publishing House, 1956), 543.

23. Alexander Herzen, *My Past and Thoughts,* trans. by Constance Garnett, abridged by Dwight Macdonald (Berkeley: University of California Press, 1991), 239.

24. Evgeny Dobrenko, *The Making of the State Reader: Social and Aesthetic Contexts of the Reception of Soviet Literature*, trans. by Jesse Savage (Stanford: Stanford University Press, 1997), 208.

25. Vissarion Belinsky, "A View of the Principal Aspects of Russian Literature in 1843," in *Selected Philosophical Works*, 200.

26. Ibid., 200–207.

27. The discussion of linkages appears in "Thoughts and Notes on Russian Literature" (1846) and the discussion of progress in Belinsky's essay "A Survey of Russian Literature in 1847" (1848); see. Belinsky, *Selected Philosophical Works*, 355–69, and 420–519, respectively.

28. Mikhail Bulgakov, *The Master and Margarita*, trans. by Diana Burgin and Katherine T. O'Connor (New York: Vintage/Random House, 1996), 121.

29. V. G. Belinsky, "A Survey of Russian Literature in 1846," in *Selected Philosophical Works*, 372.

30. From a letter of April 6/18, 1869 to Nikolai Strakhov; as cited in Joseph Frank, *The Miraculous Years: 1865–1871* (Princeton: Princeton University Press, 1995), 355–56.

31. Jones, "Politics," 72.

32. Yitzak Brudny, *Reinventing Russia: Russian Nationalism and the Soviet State, 1953–1991* (Cambridge: Harvard University Press, 1998), 175–76.

33. Leon Trotsky, *Literature and Revolution*, trans. by Rose Strunsky (Ann Arbor: University of Michigan Press, 1971), 194.

34. Ibid., 195.

35. Ibid., 209.

36. Stephen Lovell, *The Russian Reading Revolution: Print Culture in the Soviet and Post-Soviet Eras* (London: Macmillan, 2000), 30–31.

37. Zamyatin, "Letter to Stalin," in *A Soviet Heretic*, 306–7.

38. Ibid., 307.

39. "From talmudic times the term referred to the Jewish people in relation to God owing to the allegorical interpretation of the Song of Songs." Dan Cohn-Sherbok, *The Blackwell Dictionary of Judaica* (Blackwell: Oxford, 1992), 503.

40. Nataliia Vovsi-Mikhoels, *Moi otets Solomon Mikhoels* (Moscow: "Vozvrashchenie," 1997), 107–8.

41. Ibid., 128.

42. Ibid., 128.

43. Etkind, *Notes of a Non-Conspirator*, 254–55.

44. Ibid., 259.

45. "Delo Brodskogo po dnevniku Lidii Chukovskoi," compiled by Elena Chukovskaia, 160, entry for January 9, 1964. The selection of letters was in the same issue as "Okololiteraturnyi truten'" an article by A. Ionin, Ia. Lerner, and M. Medvedev, *Vechernyi Leningrad*, Nov. 29, 1963. Chukovskaia called this article the beginning of the attack which culminated in the court case.

46. Rassadin, "Legenda," 139.

47. Bukovsky, *To Build a Castle*, 257.

48. Aleksandr Solzhenitsyn, interview with correspondents of the *New York Times* and the *Washington Post* on March 30, 1972, in the Appendix to *The Oak and the Calf: Sketches of Literary Life in the Soviet Union*, trans. by Harry Willetts (New York: Harper and Row, 1980), 505–6.

49. *The Solzhenitsyn Files;* see docs. 102, 104, 107, 110, 111, 112, 130, 132, and from previous years, docs. 31, 63. This collection does not include all government records on Solzhenitsyn, only those which were released from the Politburo files. The Russian texts are available in *Kremlevskii samosud: Sekretnye dokumenty Politburo o pisatele A. Solzhenitsyna*, compiled by A. Kurotkov, S. Mel'chin, and A. Stepanov (Moscow: "Rodina" / edition q, 1994).

50. *The Solzhenitsyn Files,* doc. 130.

51. Vasily Aksenov, "The Steel Bird," trans. by Rae Slonek, in *Contemporary Russian Prose*, ed. by C. and E. Proffer (Ann Arbor: Ardis, 1982), 43–46.

52. V. [Emil' Vladimirovich] Kardin, "Sekret uspekha," in *Gde zaryta sobaka?* (Moscow: Sovetskii pisatel', 1991), 254.

53. Abram Tertz (Andrei Sinyavsky), "Graphomaniacs (A Story from My Life)," trans. by Ronald Hingley, in *Fantastic Stories by Abram Tertz* (New York: Grosset and Dunlap, 1967), 208–9.

54. Vladimir Voinovich, *Moscow 2042*, trans. by Richard Lourie (New York: Harcourt Brace Jovanovich, 1990), the chapter entitled "Checkpoint Two," 146–54.

55. See, for example: Evgenii Dobrenko, "Gosudarstvo kak avtor," *Literaturnaia gazeta* 16 (April 15, 1992): 3.

56. Voinovich, *Moscow 2042*, especially the chapters "Paplesslit" (229–37), "A Secret Is Revealed" (242–49), and "Paplit" (258–62).

57. Ibid., especially the chapter "A New Leonardo Da Vinci," 43–49.

58. Svetlana Boym, *Common Places: Mythologies of Everyday Life in Russia* (Cambridge: Harvard University Press, 1994), especially Chap. 3, "Writing Common Places: Graphomania," 168–214. The quoted phrases are from 170 and 171, respectively.

59. Naum Korzhavin, "My ne raskhodilis' s russkoi literaturoi," *Literaturnoe obozrenie* 5 (1993): 17.

60. Nabokov comments on this in his 1962 foreword to *The Gift*, trans. by Michael Scammell with the collaboration of the author (New York: Vintage, 1963). The complete text of *The Gift* was published in 1952 by the Chekhov Publishing House in New York.

61. Richard Borden, *The Art of Writing Badly: Valentin Kataev's Mauvism and the Rebirth of Russian Modernism* (Evanston: Northwestern University Press, 1999). The rest of this paragraph is a summary of 121–36 of the Borden book. The ironic choice of a title is discussed on 131–32.

62. Ibid., 124.

63. See Voinovich, "Skurlatsky, Man of Letters"; also his historical novel, *Stepen' doveriia: Povest' o Vere Figner* (in the *Plamennye revoliutsionery* series) (Moscow: Politicheskaia literatura, 1973), Chap. 20, 314–29.

64. Abram Tertz (Andrei Sinyavsky), *Strolls with Pushkin*, trans. by Catherine Theimer Nepomnyashchy and S. Yastremski (New Haven: Yale University Press, 1993), 55.

65. When asked about being a pallbearer at Pasternak's funeral, Sinyavsky said "Yes, there's even a picture, and there's an epigram about it, that Sinyavsky and Daniel are carrying their prisoner's dock." See: Nepomnyashchy, "An Interview with Andrei Sinyavsky," 15.

66. Andrei Sinyavsky, "Dissent as Personal Experience," trans. by Maria-Regina Kecht, *Yearbook of Comparative and General Literature* 31 (1982): 29.

67. Ibid., 29.

68. At a conference in Los Angeles in 1981, Sinyavsky mentioned this attitude among émigrés: "They doubted whether I had been in the camp at all. Because, you see, since I wrote about Pushkin, maybe the KGB had made some sort of library available. . . . especially for me to write such a lampoon [*paskvil'*], and then go to the West and cause divisions in the Russian emigration." "Sinjavskij o sebe," in *The Third Wave: Russian Literature in Emigration,* ed. by Olga Matich with Michael Heim (Ann Arbor: Ardis, 1984), 108. In this short presentation Sinyavsky expressed surprise at the response to the Pushkin text among émigrés who put him "on trial" as a writer once again (108).

69. "Competitive suffering" is a term I began to use after examining Russian ultranationalist rhetoric for the years 1985 to 1995. This concept is analyzed at greater length in subsequent chapters.

70. This was said in answer to a 1989 questionnaire from the Russian journal *Foreign Literature.* "Rezonans: Na anketu "IL" otvechaiut pisateli russkogo zarubezh'ia," *Inostrannaia literatura* 2 (1989): 241–43. Sinyavsky made similar comments in other articles and talks, including: Nepomnyashchy, "An Interview with Andrei Sinyavsky," 6.

71. Aleksandr Solzhenitsyn, "Koleblet tvoi trenozhnik," *Vestnik Russkogo Khristianskogo Dvizheniia* 142 (1984): 151. This article was reprinted in *Novyi mir* 5 (1991): 148–59. In the 1930s, the émigré philosopher Ivan Il'in spoke of the "aesthetic Bolshevism" of the Russian modernists.

72. See: Donald Fanger, "On the Russianness of the Russian Nineteenth-Century Novel," in *Art and Culture in Nineteenth-Century Russia,* ed. by Theofanis Stavrou (Bloomington: Indiana University Press, 1983), 40–56; and Fanger, "Conflicting Imperatives in the Model of the Russian Writer: The Case of Tertz/Sinyavsky," in *Literature and History: Theoretical Problems and Russian Case Studies,* ed. by Gary Saul Morson (Stanford: Stanford University Press, 1986), 111–24; and Fanger's contribution to "Intellectuals and Social Change in Central and Eastern Europe," a special issue of *Partisan Review* 4 (1992): 656–65.

73. Nepomnyashchy, "An Interview with Andrei Sinyavsky," 9–10; as quoted in Nepomnyashchy, "Introduction," *Strolls With Pushkin,* 5, 7.

74. Igor' Shafarevich, "Fenomen emigratsii," *Literaturnaia Rossiia* 36 (Sept. 1989): 4–5; "The Emigration Phenomenon," trans. by Dobrochna Dyrcz-Freeman, *Russian Studies in Literature* 28, no. 1 (Winter 1991–92): 45–55.

75. Catherine Nepomnyashchy broaches the subject in the first chapter of her book on Tertz. In the introduction to the translation of *Progulki s Pushkinym,* Nepomnyashchy discusses the question of Pushkin and national identity/Russianness.

76. Catherine Nepomnyashchy, *The Poetics of Crime* (New Haven: Yale University Press, 1995), Chap. 1, "The Trials of Abram Tertz," n. 20.

77. V. Khatiushin, "O lzhepoetakh i russkoi poezii," *Molodaia gvardiia* 1 (1991): 264, 266.

Tertz satirized the use of *lzhe-* ("pseudo-") and the role of pretenders in the Russian historical narrative in his novel *Spokoinoi nochi* (*Goodnight!*) which features a False Stalin, False Lenin, and False Kirov.

78. Andrei Sinyavsky, Mariia Rozanova, "Mesto intelligentsii vsegda v oppozitsii: Vstrecha v Literaturnom Institute" (An interview conducted by Sergei Esin), *Zavtra* 43 (1994): 6. Sinyavsky has said that the pseudonym "contains two stylistic nuances: Abram Tertz is a criminal and he's a Jew." This seemed to be one nuance too many for critics. See Nepomnyashchy, "An Interview with Andrei Sinyavsky," 7.

79. Sinyavsky's father was an aristocrat who became a Left Socialist Revolutionary and then a defender of the Revolution. "Dissent as a Personal Experience," 22.

80. Remnick, "Letter From Moscow: Exit the Saints," *New Yorker* 70, no. 21 (July 18, 1994): 57. See also Galina Belaia, "'Sryv kul'tury': Neraspoznannoe porazhenie," *Voprosy literatury*, Jan.–Feb. 2003. Belaia discusses the gradual erasing of differences between "Soviet and noncanonical art" (3).

81. Remnick, "Letter From Moscow," 57.

82. This stage in the evolution of Soviet dissent is analyzed, among numerous other places, in Bukovsky, *To Build a Castle,* in particular 145–64.

83. Sinyavsky, "Mesto intelligentsii," 6.

84. Andrei Sinyavsky, "Chtenie v serdtsakh," *Novyi mir* 4 (1992): 210; originally published in *Sintaksis* 17 (1984).

85. The presentation of the volumes took place in October 1992, during a conference at the New State Humanities University (RGGU); I was present at this event.

86. Andrei Sinyavsky, "'Do sikh por eto vse u menia bolit . . . '," as retold by Grigorii Tsitriniak, *Literaturnaia gazeta* 12 (March 26, 1997).

87. This is a term used in the post-Soviet period to refer to political groups that are created ex post facto, basically to support a sitting government, such as "Our Home is Russia" and "Unity" in the second half of the 1990s, later to join together as "United Russia." Vladimir Voinovich returned to this theme in the days after Vladimir Putin's election. See Voinovich, "Russia's Blank Slate," *New York Times,* March 30, 2000.

88. Sinyavsky, "Mesto intelligentsii," 6.

89. Andrei Sinyavsky, *The Russian Intelligentsia,* trans. by Lynn Visson (New York: Columbia University Press, 1997). I summarize an argument that runs throughout the book, which is based on a series of lectures that Sinyavsky gave at Columbia University in 1996.

90. Abram Tertz [Andrei Sinyavsky], *The Trial Begins and On Socialist Realism.,* introd. by Czeslaw Milosz, trans. by Max Hayward and George Dennis (Berkeley: University of California Press, 1982), 199.

91. Tertz, "The Literary Process in Russia," 195–201.

92. Sinyavsky, *The Russian Intelligentsia,* 1.

93. The contributions to this idea by Emile Durkheim and Donald Davidson are discussed by Terry F. Godlove Jr. in *Religion, Interpretation, and Diversity of Belief: The Framework Model from Kant to Durkheim to Davidson* (Macon, Ga.: Mercer University Press, 1997).

94. *On Trial: the Soviet State versus "Abram Tertz" and "Nikolai Arzhak,"* rev ed., trans., ed., and introd. by Max Hayward (New York: Harper and Row, 1967), 182.

95. The discussion was introduced by Sergei Esin and recorded by Vladimir Bondarenko.

IMLI (Institut mirovoi literatury imeni Gor'kogo) is where Siniavskii worked at the time of his arrest in 1965.

96. "Pochemu narod bezmolvstvuet?" *Zavtra* 49 (1994), a discussion recorded by A. Fefelov. The title refers to a line in Pushkin's *Boris Godunov*, especially resonant with Russian readers since the early nineties was often referred to as a new "Time of Troubles" (*smutnoe vremia*) with a leader conveniently named Boris.

97. "Pochemu narod bezmolvstvuet?"

98. Vladimir Bondarenko, "Pravo na istinu Andreia Siniavskogo," *Zavtra* 9 (1997).

99. Viktoriia Shokhina, "Eres' i kharizma Andreia Siniavskogo," *Nezavisimaia gazeta,* literary supplement *Ex Libris NG* 3 (1997).

100. Yevgeny Zamyatin, "On Literature, Revolution, Entropy and Other Matters," in *A Soviet Heretic,* 109.

101. Ibid., 109.

CHAPTER 3. THE DANGEROUS NARRATIVE OF THE RUSSIAN VILLAGE

1. Lilia Vil'chek used the term *kod prochteniia* in her article "Derevenskaia proza," in *Sovremennaia russkaia sovetskaia literatura,* ed. by A. Bocharov and G. Belaia (Moscow: Prosveshchenie, 1987), 52–53. That the codes evolve is clear; when my book *Russian Village Prose: The Radiant Past* (Princeton: Princeton University Press, 1992) was published, the fourth code was still dominant and the fifth not yet in sight.

2. The first three stages were covered in *Russian Village Prose;* I give them less attention here, and concentrate on the period after 1989.

3. In an attempt to write a revisionist history of Village Prose, Soloukhin stated in 1990 that the Ovechkin-style *ocherk* had been harmful to literature, because its writers accepted collectivization, and merely wished that the kolkhozes were run more efficiently. Vladimir Soloukhin, "Eto byl boets, voin, rytsar' . . . K 70-letiiu so dnia rozhdeniia Fedora Abramova," *Moskva* 2 (1990): 167–68.

4. Petr Vail', Aleksandr Genis, *60-ye: Mir sovetskogo cheloveka* (Ann Arbor: Ardis, 1989), 145.

5. Yitzak Brudny, *Reinventing Russia: Russian Nationalism and the Soviet State, 1953–1991* (Cambridge: Harvard University Press, 1998). This excellent book, based on Brudny's dissertation, does contain fundamental gaps in that it takes little advantage of research appearing after 1991, although it was published seven years later.

6. Ibid., 23, 38.

7. Ibid., 13.

8. Ibid., 41.

9. The Solzhenitsyn and Tendriakov stories appeared in *Novyi mir,* and the Abramov story in *Neva.*

10. A. P. Petrik, "'Derevenskaia proza': Itogi i perspektivy izucheniia," *Filologicheskie nauki* 1 (1981): 66.

11. Aleksandr Yakovlev, "Protiv antiistorizma," *Literaturnaia gazeta,* Nov. 15, 1972.

12. In the following chapter I discuss a 1977 meeting at the Central House of Writers (TsDL), the transcript of which gives ample evidence of chauvinism in semiofficial cultural quarters.

13. Brudny, *Reinventing Russia*, 15, 16.

14. Ibid., 59.

15. Ibid., 85, 97, 83.

16. Ibid., 117, 176, 181–83.

17. Ibid., 132.

18. Ibid., 122–27.

19. Václav Havel, *Open Letters: Selected Writings 1965–1990*, ed. by Paul Wilson, trans. by Paul Wilson, A. G. Brainy (New York: Vintage, 1992), 283–84.

20. Iurii Davydov and Nikolai Anastas'ev, "Chto takoe russkaia literatura?" *Literaturnaia gazeta*, March 1, 1989: 2 (the quote is from Davydov). See also: Anastas'ev and Davydov, "Liubov' k blizhnemu cheloveku," *Literaturnaia gazeta*, Feb. 22, 1989: 2.

21. Galina Belaia, "The Crisis of Soviet Artistic Mentality in the 1960s and 1970s," trans. by Lesley Milne, in *New Directions in Soviet Literature: Selected Papers from the Fourth World Congress for Soviet and East European Studies, Harrogate, 1990*, ed. by Sheelagh Duffin Graham (New York: St. Martin's Press, 1992), 4.

22. Two other talented rural writers, the poet Nikolai Rubtsov and the writer-actor-director Vasilii Shukshin, died in the 1970s.

23. E. Starikova, "Kolokol trevogi," *Voprosy literatury* 11 (1986): 80–99; trans. as "The Alarm-Bell," *Soviet Studies in Literature* 24, no. 4 (1988): 13–30. The passages referred to is on 87 (Russian) and 18–19 (English).

24. I discuss this at greater length in *Russian Village Prose*.

25. N. Eidel'man and V. Astaf'ev, "Perepiska iz dvukh uglov," *Sintaksis* 17 (1987): 80–87.

26. Maxim D. Shrayer, "Anti-Semitism and the Decline of Russian Village Prose," *Partisan Review* 3 (2000): 474–85. The format of this journal does not include scholarly citation and Shrayer does not provide evidence in the text of other opinions on the subject, except for a fleeting reference to Iurii Karabchevskii.

27. Gary Saul Morson, introduction to *A Writer's Diary*, trans. and annotated by Kenneth Lantz, vol. 1 (Evanston: Northwestern University Press, 1993), 37–38.

28. I go into these subjects in detail in *Russian Village Prose*.

29. Brudny, *Reinventing Russia*, 192–93, 197.

30. See, for example: A. Iu. Bolshakova, "Teoriia avtora u M. Bakhtina i V. Vinogradova," from Book 1 of the Seventh International Bakhtin Conference, June 26–30, 1995 (Moscow: Moscow State Pedagogical University, 1995), 151–57.

31. Brudny has made a tremendous effort to track down the political maneuvering behind the government's treatment of nationalist writers from 1953 to 1991, and yet the texts themselves are for all practical purposes absent from the book, and the millions of readers not in the *nomenklatura* are invisible.

32. Viktor Erofeev, "Pominki po sovetskoi literature," *Literaturnaia gazeta*, July 4, 1990.

33. Naum Korzhavin, in "Rezonans. Na anketu *IL* otvechaiut pisateli russkogo zarubezh'ia," *Inostrannaia literatura* 2 (1989): 249. Belaia, "The Crisis of Soviet Artistic Mentality," 1–17. For a further discussion of this question, see *Russian Village Prose*, especially chap. 8. Naturally, I hope that my book and articles contributed to a more rational assessment of these works.

34. Belaia, "The Crisis of Soviet Artistic Mentality," 5, 8, 16.

35. Vladimir Zviniatskovskii, "Partiinaia literatura bez partiinoi organizatsii," *Znamia* 2 (1992): 233–37.

36. Brudny, *Reinventing Russia*, 226–29. See also Peter Duncan, "The Rebirth of Politics in Russia," in Geoffrey Hosking, Jonathan Aves, and Peter Duncan, *The Road to Post-Communism: Independent Political Movements in the Soviet Union 1985–1991* (London: Pinter, 1992), 75.

37. Brudny, *Reinventing Russia*, 221–36.

38. The interview, "No Such Thing as a National Idea," was published in "The Russia Journal" (www.russiajournal.com) for September 20, 1999 and was reposted on *Johnson's Russia List* 3542 (October 3, 1999).

39. "The Search for a New Russian National Identity—Russian Perspectives," compiled and edited by James. H. Billington and Kathleen Parthé, available on-line at www.loc .gov/about/welcome/speeches/russianperspectives/index.html. In the pdf version, 88–89.

40. From an obituary in *Kul'tura* 46–47 (Dec. 6–19, 2001).

41. Aleksandr Rubashkin, "Syn Verkoly, syn Rossii. K 80-letiiu so dnia rozhdeniia Fedora Abramova," *Literaturnaia gazeta* 9 (Feb. 23, 2000).

42. Ol'ga Slavnikova, "Derevenskaia proza lednikogo perioda," *Novyi mir* 2 (1999): 198–207.

43. Ibid., 207. "Videnie" was published along with several other Rasputin stories in *Moskva* 3 (1997). A new biography of Rasputin was written by a Siberian literary scholar, Nadezhda Tenditnik, *Valentin Rasputin: Kolokol trevogi* (Moscow: Golos, 1999), and was reviewed by Irina Strelkova, "Zhertvovat' soboi radi pravdy," *Moskva* 4 (2000): 200–202.

44. Sergei Fediakin, "Materoi pod vodoi: Valentinu Rasputinu—60 let," *Nezavisimaia gazeta* 46 (March 14, 1997).

45. Aleksandr Ageev, "Rasputin novyi i staryi." *Znamia* 6 (1999): 218.

46. Information on the Council from a number of sources was reposted on *Johnson's Russia List* 4232 (April 7, 2000).

47. "Premiia Aleksandra Solzhenitsyna prisuzhdena Valentinu Rasputinu," *Literaturnaia gazeta* 9 (March 1, 2000).

48. "Na vruchenii premii Solzhenitsyna Valentinu Rasputinu vstretilis' dva vrazhdebnykh pisatel'skikh lageria," *Literaturnaia gazeta* 19–20 (May 17, 2000).

49. Aleksandr Solzhenitsyn, "Slovo pri vruchenii premii Solzhenitsyna Valentinu Rasputinu 4 maia 2000," *Novyi mir* 5 (2000): 186.

50. Valentin Rasputin, "V poiskakh berega: Rech' na vruchenii Solzhenitsynskoi premii," *Literaturnaia gazeta* 19–20 (May 17, 2000).

51. Alla Latynina, "Vakantsii kak raz otkryty," *Literaturnaia gazeta* 10 (March 8, 2000).

52. Inna Simonova, "Posledniaia stupen' Vladimira Soloukhina," *Nezavisimaia gazeta* 86 (May 14, 1997).

53. "Pamiati S. P. Zalygina," and A. I. Solzhenitsyn, "Sergei Pavlovich, Rossiia vas ne zabudet," *Literaturnaia gazeta* 17 (April 26, 2000).

54. Belaia, "The Crisis of Soviet Artistic Mentality," 3.

55. Igor' Zolotusskii, "Tropa Fedora Abramova: K 70-letiiu so dnia rozhdeniia," *Literaturnaia gazeta* 9 (Feb. 28,1990): 5.

56. Ibid., 5.
57. Belaia, "The Crisis of Soviet Artistic Mentality," 8, 16.
58. W. H. Auden, "Dingley Dell and the Fleet," *The Dyer's Hand and Other Essays* (New York: Vintage, 1968), 409–10. My thanks to Robin Feuer Miller for bringing this passage to my attention.
59. Fediakin, "Matera pod vodoi."
60. Parthé, *Russian Village Prose,* 125.
61. Vladimir Lichutin, "Tsep' nezrimaia," *Druzhba narodov* 8 (1989): 231–47.
62. Aleksandr Genis, "Vzgliad iz tupika," *Ogonek* 52 (1990): 17–19.
63. Igor' Zolotusskii, "Orientir," *Literaturnaia gazeta* 14 (April 7, 1993): 4. Zolotusskii also mentions SMERSH in "Tropa Fedora Abramova."
64. Fedor Abramov, "Kto on? Fragmenty iz nezavershennoi povesti," ed. by L. Krutikova-Abramova, *Znamia* 3 (1993): 140–60.
65. Viktor Astaf'ev, Valentin Kurbatov, *Krest beskonechnyi: V. Astaf'ev—V. Kurbatov; Pis'ma iz glubiny Rossii,* ed. and introd. by G. Sapranov, afterword by L. Anninskii (Irkutsk: Izd. Sapranov, 2002), 117–19, 183–86.
66. Rubashkin, "Syn Verkoly."
67. Astaf'ev and Kurbatov, *Krest beskonechnyi,* 186.

CHAPTER 4. RUSSIANS AND "OTHERS"

1. The epigraph is from a Kuniaev poem published in *Den'* 20 (March 23, 1993): 7. See Kathleen Parthé, "Russia's 'Unreal Estate': Cognitive Mapping and National Identity," *Kennan Institute Occasional Paper* 265 (1997): 1–30.
2. Ibid., 14.
3. Ivan Il'in, "'Sviataia Rus': 'Bogomol'e' Shmeleva," in *Odinokii khudozhnik* (Moscow: "Iskusstvo," 1993), 130. Il'in sketches out a cosmic battle in which *Sviataia Rus'* (Holy Rus) and *Okaiannaia Nerus'* struggle for the soul of *nesviataia Rus'* (unholy, i.e. pagan Rus). In "Russia's 'Unreal Estate'," I explain the distinction Il'in makes between *rodnaia zemlia* and *rodina,* and the concept of an "internal Holy Rus" that can be carried into exile.
4. Mark Bassin, "Russia Between Europe and Asia: the Ideological Construction of Geographical Space," *Slavic Review* 50, no. 1 (Spring 1991): 1–17.
5. "Cognitive mapping" is a term I borrowed from psychology and have applied—metaphorically more than technically—to Russian cultural history in order to more precisely articulate the spatial component of national identity. For an early discussion of cognitive mapping in the sense of spatial orientation and spatial schemata, see E. C. Tolman's 1948 article "Cognitive Maps in Rats and Men," *Psychological Review* 55: 189–208.
6. William Scott Green, "The Difference Religion Makes," *Journal of the American Academy of Religion* 62, no. 4 (1994), 1191–1207.
7. Jonathan Z. Smith, as cited by William Scott Green in "Diversity and Tolerance," in *The Religion Factor: An Introduction to How Religion Matters,* ed. by William Scott Green and Jacob Neusner (Louisville: Westminster John Knox Press, 1996), 266.
8. Walter Laqueur, *Black Hundred: The Rise of the Extreme Right in Russia* (New York: Harper Collins, 1993), 130.

9. Yitzhak Brudny, "The Heralds of Opposition to *Perestroyka*," *Soviet Economy* 5, no. 2 (April–June 1989): 162–200, and in his monograph *Reinventing Russia: Russian Nationalism and the Soviet State, 1953–1991* (Cambridge: Harvard University Press, 1998). Evgeny Dobrenko, "Stoi! Kto idet?! U istokov sovetskogo manikheistva," *Znamia* 3 (1993): 180–89; and, *Metafora vlasti: Literatura stalinskoi epokhi v istoricheskom osveshchenii* (Munich: Otto Sagner, 1993).

10. See, for example: Vladimir Lichutin, "Zagovor diletantov: Strikhi k portretu antigeroia," *Den'* 52 (Dec. 27, 1992): 7. This is the third part of the article; the first and second parts appeared in *Den'* 50 and 51 (1992). Lichutin's attack on Sakharov, playwright Mikhail Shatrov, Korotich, and others is interspersed with anguished comments on his suddenly impoverished circumstances.

11. On the range of Russian cultural nationalisms, see: John Dunlop, *The Faces of Contemporary Russian Nationalism* (Princeton: Princeton University Press, 1983), and *The New Russian Nationalism* (Armonk, N.Y.: Praeger, 1985).

12. The rest of this paragraph paraphrases and summarizes three articles by Donald Fanger in which he examines the evolution of this concept. See: "On the Russianness of the Russian Nineteenth-Century Novel," in *Art and Culture in Nineteenth-Century Russia,* ed. by Theofanis G. Stavrou (Bloomington: Indiana University Press, 1983), 40–56; "Conflicting Imperatives in the Model of the Russian Writer: The Case of Tertz/Sinyavsky," in *Literature and History: Theoretical Problems and Russian Case Studies,* ed. by Gary Saul Morson (Stanford: Stanford University Press, 1986), 111–24; and his contribution to "Intellectuals and Social Change in Central and Eastern Europe," a special issue of the *Partisan Review* 4 (1992): 656–65. There is also a very interesting discussion of this topic in G. S. Morson, "Introductory Study: Dostoevsky's Great Experiment," in Fyodor Dostoevsky, *A Writer's Diary,* vol. 1: *1873–1876,* trans. and annotated by Kenneth Lantz (Evanston: Northwestern University Press, 1993), 1–4.

13. This dilemma is discussed by Walter Laqueur in "From Russia With Hate," *New Republic,* Feb. 5, 1990: 24. See also his book *Black Hundred,* 127–32. Ilf and Petrov's *The Twelve Chairs* was criticized by some as being amusing but Russophobic. See: Iurii Arkhipov, "Ovtsy i kozlishcha (Iz dnevnika kritika)," *Moskva* 7–8 (July–August 1992): 143.

14. This anecdote is courtesy of Vladimir Krutikov.

15. Valentin Sorokin, "Nas oni doprashivaiut, a sami svoi khvosty priachut," *Moskovskii literator* 25 (July 1992): 3. See also Viktor Astaf'ev, "Perepiska iz dvukh uglov" (the Astafiev-Eidelman correspondence of August–September 1986), *Sintaksis* 17 (1987): 85.

16. Bondarenko, "Literaturnye rasisty," *Den'* 6 (April 19, 1992): 7. Bondarenko complained elsewhere that Jews in the first wave of emigration felt themselves to be part of a unified Russian cultural diaspora, but later behaved like a separate group. "It was they who introduced the term 'Russian-language literature,' in order to distinguish it from that which was simply Russian"; "Sredi druzei i vragov," *Den'* 40 (Oct. 4, 1992): 7. Mark Liubomudrov attributes the distinction between "sobstvennaia russkaia literatura" (true Russian literature) and "literatura na russkom iazyke" (literature in Russian) to the conservative nationalist critic Iurii Seleznev, who died in 1984. Mark Liubomudrov, "Izvlechem li uroki? (O russkom teatre i ne tol'ko o nem)," *Nash sovremennik* 2 (1989): 172.

17. Arkhipov, "Ovtsy i kozlishcha," 144.

18. Mikhail Cherniavsky, *Tsar and People: Studies in Russian Myths,* 2d ed. (New York: Random House, 1969), Chap. 1.

19. This term comes from Rosalind Krauss, "Postructuralism and the Paraliterary," in *The Originality of the Avant-Garde and Other Modernist Myths* (Cambridge: MIT Press, 1985), 292–93.

20. On Pushkin and state interests, see Georgii Vasilevich, director of the Pushkin museum complex at Mikhailovskoe, in "Ikona 'Pushkin'," an interview conducted by Vladimir Bondarenko, *Zavtra* 22 (1997): 8.

21. See, for example, A. Dokusov, "Protiv klevety na velikikh russkikh pisatelei," *Zvezda* 8 (1949): 181–89.

22. Vladimir Shikin, "Skol'ko predkov u Aleksandra Pushkina," *Nash sovremennik* 6 (1989): 136. By the 1999 bicentenary of Pushkin's birth, databases and web sites devoted to Pushkin's genealogy were available.

23. Similar commentary has been published since 1985, some of it written in earlier decades. See, for example, Il'in's essays from the 1930s, where he goes to great lengths to argue against any influence of Gannibal on Pushkin's appearance or personality. Il'in, *Odinokii khudozhnik,* 70–71. Il'in states elsewhere that he is happy to count as Russian poets those of Jewish, German, and other backgrounds (192). See also: N. N. Granovskaia, *Rod Pushkinykh miatezhnyi: Iz istorii roda Aleksandra Sergeevicha Pushkina* (St.Petersburg: "Iliad," 1992), which complains that Gannibal has unjustly overshadowed the poet's Russian ancestors.

24. M. Vegner, *Predki Pushkina* (Moscow: Sovetskii pisatel', 1937), 11.

25. Ivan Il'in, "Pushkin v zhizni. 1799–1837," *Odinokii khudozhnik,* 70.

26. V. Desnitskii, "Pushkin i ego vremia," *Zvezda* 46 (1949): 137. Also: Dokusov, "Protiv klevety," 182; "Prazdnik sotsialisticheskoi kul'tury," introduction to *A. S. Pushkin 1799–1949: Materialy iubileinykh torzhestv* (Moscow-Leningrad: ANSSSR, 1951), 15; B. Meilakh, "Genii russkoi kul'tury," *Zvezda* 6 (1949): 148.

27. A. Gordin, "V sele Mikhailovskom," *Zvezda* 6 (1949): 113; M. Ivin and M. Medvedev, "Gorod poeta," ibid., 119.

28. Bondarenko, "Ikona 'Pushkin'," 8.

29. Eduard Khlystalov, "Taina gostinitsy 'Angleter'," *Moskva* 7 (1989): 179.

30. See Astaf'ev, "Perepiska iz dvukh uglov," 85. For a discussion of comments in a similar vein made by Andrei Bely (in an essay written in 1909, which was republished in 1990), see: Vadim Rossman, *Russian Intellectual Antisemitism in the Post-Communist Era* (Lincoln: University of Nebraska Press, 2002), 174–76.

31. Aleksandr Solzhenitsyn, "Koleblet tvoi trenozhnik," *Vestnik Russkogo Khristianskogo Dvizheniia* 142 (1984): 151.

32. Igor' Shafarevich, "Fenomen emigratsii," *Literaturnaia Rossiia* 36 (Sept. 8, 1989): 5. For a discussion of the reception of *Strolls With Pushkin,* see C. Nepomnyashchy, "Andrei Sinyavsky's 'Return' to the Soviet Union," *Formations* 6, no. 1 (Spring 1991): 24–44.

33. Taras Kudritskii, "Bez pamiati? Neveselye zametki molodogo literatora," *Literaturnaia Rossiia* 28 (July 14, 1989): 7. Emphasis in the original.

34. Ernst Safonov at a Columbia University meeting in 1990, as cited in Catharine Nepom-

nyashchy's "Introduction" to Abram Tertz (Andrei Sinyavsky), *Strolls with Pushkin*, trans. by C. Nepomnyashchy and Slava Yastremski (New Haven: Yale University Press, 1993), 44.

35. The murder of poet–rock singer Igor' Talkov in August 1991 fit very neatly into this paradigm.

36. V. Radzishevskii, "Esenin: Samoubiistvo ili ubiistvo?," *Literaturnaia gazeta* 27 (July 7, 1993): 3.

37. Laqueur cites a 1991 article about a film produced by actor Nikolai Burliaev that blamed Lermontov's death on a Judeo-Masonic conspiracy. See: Mikhail Buianov, "Masonophobia," *Novoe vremia* 42 (1991), as quoted in Laqueur, *Black Hundred*, 44.

38. "In 1981 *Nash sovremennik* was severely attacked; Iurii Seleznev, the young leader of the Russian patriots, was deprived of work, and in essence, condemned to death." Aleksandr Kazinstev, "Pridvornye dissidenty i 'Pogibshee pokolenie'," *Nash sovremennik* 3 (1991): 173. John Dunlop discusses the *Nash sovremennik* affair in *The New Russian Nationalism*, 19–25. Mark Liubomudrov hints as much about Vampilov in "Izvlechem li uroki?," 173. This theory is applied to the present as well. An attack on Valentin Rasputin or Vasily Belov or the delayed return of Solzhenitsyn's work to Russia was seen as a way to keep Russian culture and the people weak. See, for example, "Obrashchenie k chitateliu," a letter signed by the editorial board of *Literaturnyi Irkutsk*, which includes A. Baiborodin and N. Tenditnik, *Literaturnyi Irkutsk*, Dec. 1989.

39. "Esenina udavila okkupatsionnaia staia khishchnikov. Bloka okkupatsionnaia staia umorila golodom. Maiakovskogo zastrelila. Naivnyi, chut' prozrevshii Tal'kov—ubran negodaem, nyrnuvshim v Izrail'." ("Esenin was strangled by a pack of predatory invaders. The same occupying hordes killed Blok by starvation. They shot Mayakovsky. And naive Talkov, who had just begun to see things clearly, was done away with by a scoundrel who then fled to Israel.") V. Sorokin, "Nas oni doprashivaiut," 3.

40. Svetlana Boym, *Death in Quotation Marks: Cultural Myths of the Modern Poet* (Cambridge: Harvard University Press, 1991), 4. The author restricts her investigation to poets because "since Romanticism, the *poet* has been the primary example of the intersection of work and life and its poetic mythification" (11). It is certainly true that the necromyths that figure so prominently on the *russkost'* agenda virtually all concern poets. See also *Ogonek* 29 (1993) featuring a previously unknown description of Mayakovsky's death and funeral; the cover, designed by Andrei Voznesenskii, reads "*Poet + Pulia—populiarnost'*" ("A Poet + A Bullet = Popularity").

41. Boym, *Death in Quotation Marks*, 6.

42. As observed by Igor' Zolotusskii, "Nashi nigilisty," *Literaturnaia gazeta* 25 (June 17, 1992): 4.

43. In attempting to make sense of the deaths of Mayakovsky and other poets in the post-Revolutionary years (the essay dates from 1931), Roman Jakobson saw something ominous in the subtitle of the poem "Ob etom" ("About That"): "From personal motives, but about the general way of life." See Jakobson, "On a Generation that Squandered its Poets," trans. by E. J. Brown, in *Major Soviet Writers: Essays in Criticism*, ed. by Edward J. Brown (New York: Oxford University Press, 1973), 27. In a different context, John Dunlop quotes Ivan Aksakov, who attributed Fedor Dostoevsky's death, a great loss for

Russian nationalists, to "divine punishment" See Dunlop, *The Faces of Contemporary Russian Nationalism,* 210.

44. "Russian society took advantage of the first opportunity to gain a particular and effective advocacy for itself with the new and all-powerful Lord of the Russian people." Michael Cherniavsky, *Tsar and People,* 9.

45. This is taken from the Samuel H. Cross translation of the Primary Chronicle, partially reprinted in *Medieval Russia's Epics, Chronicles and Tales,* ed. by Serge Zenkovsky, rev. ed. (New York: E. P. Dutton, 1974), 105.

46. Cherniavsky, *Tsar and People,* 6.

47. G. P. Fedotov, *Sviatye drevnei Rusi (X–XVII st.)* (Paris: YMCA Press, 1931), 32.

48. Cherniavsky, *Tsar and People,* 11, 13.

49. G. P. Fedotov, *The Russian Religious Mind: Kievan Christianity, the Tenth to the Thirteenth Centuries* (New York: Harper and Row, 1960), 110. Nicholas II and his family subsequently received official ecclesiastical attention, first in the church abroad and then in Russia, as well as a great upsurge of popular interest after 1985. They were included in the group of new martyrs (*novomuchenniki, novoslavlennye sviatye*) of the Revolution and Russian Civil War period, and the newspaper *Den'* called for Nicholas's canonization. The remains of Nicholas, Alexandra, and three daughters were identified by a British-Russian forensic team in July 1993. In July 1998, on the seventieth anniversary of the executions, the remains were reburied in the Peter-Paul Cathedral in St. Petersburg, with President Yeltsin, Academician Likhachev, and members of European royal families in attendance. The patriarch and some Romanov descendants, disputing the authenticity of the remains, attended an alternative ceremony at Sergiev Posad.

50. Ivan Aksakov, *Polnoe sobranie sochinenii* (Moscow, 1886), 21–22; as quoted by Cherniavsky, *Tsar and People,* 187.

51. There is a study of pre-eighteenth-century saints, both *sviatye* and *podvizhniki blagochestiia* ("zealots of piety"), which divides up the subject by the region with which the holy person was most closely associated. See Arkhimandrit Leonid, ed., *Sviataia Rus', ili svedeniia o vsekh sviatikh i podvizhnikakh blagochestiia na Rusi (do XVIII veka) obshche i mestno chtimikh* (St. Petersburg, 1891).

52. Vitalii Shentalinskii, "Oskolki serebrianogo veka," *Novyi mir* 6 (1998): 187.

53. In contrast, during the two-hundredth anniversary of Pushkin's birth in 1999, attention was mostly focused on his life and legacy as a measure of the greatness of Russia. The political atmosphere had changed and the dire voices from 1987 had been marginalized.

54. Nikolai Zuev, "Kto vinoven v gibeli poeta?" *Nash sovremennik* 6 (1989): 138–39.

55. The literature on Pushkin is vast and the poet's attitude to those at court is referred to in many places, for instance in Victor Terras, *A History of Russian Literature* (New Haven: Yale University Press), 1991, 204.

56. Tat'iana Glushkova, "Smert' poeta," *Den'* 20 (May 23, 1993): 6. The following two paragraphs summarize Glushkova's analysis of the Lermontov poem.

57. In this context, see Soloukhin's remarks on the examination of the remains of the tsar and his family: "they are dead, they are martyrs, they are saints. Do not disturb their memory with 'versions,' 'expertise,' and various conjectures. That is a petty and unworthy activity." Liana Polukhina, "Sobesednik na pominkakh" (interview with Soloukhin),

Literaturnaia gazeta 48 (Nov. 25, 1992): 5. The language of anticosmopolitan articles of the late 1940s resurfaced in articles from the nationalist right, e.g. Dokusov, "Protiv klevety," which called offending critics *bukvoedy* ("pedants"—literally"letter-eaters") and derided the scholarly dissection of Russia's great literature.

58. Stuart Ramsay Tompkins, *The Russian Mind, from Peter the Great Through the Enlightenment* (Norman: University of Oklahoma Press, 1953), 237.

59. Cited ibid., 236.

60. Ibid.

61. "For poetry it is the *mind* (*um*) in the old-fashioned meaning of that word, that is required and not the 'dramatically' intense 'intellect' (*intellekt*), which safeguards so-called 'intellectual poetry'—that stillborn child of our criticism. To defend this child, one has to place the supposedly universally triumphant 'intellect' above the old-fashioned concept of 'heart' and the provincial idea of 'emotion.'" Tat'iana Glushkova, "Traditsiia—sovest' poezii," Part 2, *Literaturnoe obozrenie* 2 (1978): 41. The first part of this article is ibid., 1 (1978): 28–35.

62. Russian peasants displayed a wariness towards those who possessed exceptional knowledge or skill; such people were thought to be linked to the occult and apt to use their knowledge as much for evil as for good. Sorcerers were often referred to as "znaiushchie liudi" (learned people). See Linda Ivanits, *Russian Folk Belief* (Armonk, N.Y.: M. E. Sharpe, 1989), 85, 111–12.

63. Vladimir Soloukhin, "Pokhoroniat, zaroiut gluboko . . . Nekotorye soobrazheniia v sviazi s neob"iasnennoi smert'iu Aleksandra Bloka," *Literaturnaia Rossiia* 4 (Jan. 24, 1992): 15. This article was cited by critic Andrei Turkov as one of the most depressing literary events of 1992 in "Zdes' nuzhen golos: Kritiki o literature v godu minuvshem i v godu nastupivshim," *Nezavisimaia gazeta* 3 (Jan. 11, 1993): 7.

64. Yevgeny Zamyatin, "Alexander Blok," in *A Soviet Heretic: Essays by Yevgeny Zamyatin*, ed. and trans. by Mirra Ginsburg (Chicago: University of Chicago Press, 1970), 215. The vulnerability of poets in the new age is also discussed in Jakobson's essay "On a Generation that Squandered its Poets."

65. D. Maksimov, "Memoria. O perenesenii prakha Al. Bloka," *Literaturnoe obozrenie* 5 (1987): 65–66. The original grave was in Smolenskoe Cemetery, scheduled for destruction as part of a construction project. The remains were transferred to Volkovskoe Cemetery on September 26, 1944, to save them from disappearing completely, a fact which Soloukhin failed to mention when quoting from this memoir. In the end, the Smolenskoe and Blok's original gravesite were left intact.

66. Natal'ia Egorova in a roundtable discussion led by Vladimir Bondarenko, "Posle pogorel'shchiny," *Den'* 8 (Feb. 26, 1993): 7.

67. Historian Sergei Shvedov speaks of the "carefully cultivated version of Esenin's murder" which received support from some literary scholars and representatives of the Orthodox Church. Myths about the "ritual" murder of important cultural and historical figures by outsiders, Shvedov reminds the reader, can garner significant support in times of upheaval. See S. Shvedov, "'Oglobli vzletiat', ili logika pravykh," *Ogonek* 35 (Aug. 24, 1991)): 9–11.

68. David Shepherd paraphrases a 1978 interview, in which Leonid Leonov revealed that in

researching Moscow's criminal underworld during the NEP period for *The Thief* "he was often accompanied by the poet Sergei Esenin, who served as a prototype for the character of Don'ka, the highly sexed criminal poet." David Shepherd, *Beyond Metafiction: Self-Consciousness in Soviet Literature* (Oxford: Clarendon Press, 1992), 41–42 n. 39.

69. Iurii Chekhonadskii and Iurii Prokushev, "Esenin segodnia, zavtra i vsegda," *Literaturnaia Rossiia* 39 (Sept. 25, 1992): 10–11. See also Sergei Kuniaev, "Zolotaia sorvi-golova," *Sovetskaia Rossiia* 3 (Oct. 3, 1992). Kuniaev offers a list of acceptable deaths for the poet. "Esenin might have gotten a bullet in the brain or a knife in his back. He might have perished under the wheels of a train, or he might have drunk a glass of wine, poisoned by a 'well-wisher.' He might have been consumed by Spanish flu, or have fallen into an abyss. There is only one thing he could not have done—and that is to kill himself." Esenin's Jewish wife Zinaida Raikh, whom he left for Isadora Duncan, later married Vsevolod Meyerhold, who was arrested in June 1939 and executed the following year. Raikh was murdered in July 1939, a crime which was never seriously investigated. Mark Liubomudrov called Meyerhold's death a fitting retribution for having destroyed the traditional Russian theater. See "Agoniia nigilizma (Puti rossiiskogo avangarda)," *Molodaia gvardiia* 11 (1990): 261–82. One of Esenin's sons (not by his marriage to Raikh) was executed in the late 1930s, and his sister and her husband were arrested.

70. Radzishevskii, "Esenin," 3.

71. Khlystalov, "Taina gostinitsy 'Angleter'," 97.

72. Ivan Lystsov, "Ubiistvo Esenina," *Molodaia gvardiia* 10 (1990): 274; and Khlystalov, "Taina gostinitsy 'Angleter'," 98.

73. Valentin Sorokin, "Poet, narod, Rossiia," *Moskovskii literator* 40 (Oct. 26, 1990): 3–4. See also Sorokin, "Nas oni doprashivaiut," 3–4.

74. Lystsov, "Ubiistvo Esenina," 254.

75. Valentin Sorokin, "Svoi chuzhie," *Nash Sovremennik* 9 (1989): 170.

76. A similar contrast is made in Boris Lapin and Nadezhda Tenditnik, "Deti Arbata i Deti Rossii," *Sibir'* 3 (1989): 113–25; the article focuses on the vast differences between two groups of writers, the "children of the Arbat" and the "children of Russia."

77. The suffering of living conservative writers is elevated to the level of martyrdom (Rasputin, Solzhenitsyn). Soloukhin complained bitterly about censorship of his texts and reprimands he received from above, and claimed that an order (unfulfilled) went out to severely punish him in 1985. As to his own part in condemning Pasternak at a Writers' Union meeting, he blamed those who allowed to him to go astray and Pasternak himself for not having the courage to stand firm. See Polukhina's interview with Soloukhin, "Sobesednik na pominkakh," 5.

78. Igor' Viktorov, "Ubiistvo," *Zavtra* 31 (Aug. 1994): 6. In 1995 there was a follow-up interview with Deriagin's widow conducted by I. Viktorov; see "S nim voiuiut, budto on zhivoi," ibid., 16 (April 1995): 8.

79. The final illness of émigré writer Vladimir Maksimov was said to have been worsened by anxiety over his homeland. "In essence, [his] death . . . is on the conscience of the current leaders of Russia." Vladimir Bondarenko, "Pamiati pisatelia-patriota," ibid., 14 (April 1995): 6.

80. "The nineteenth-century romantic stereotypes still pertain not only in belles-lettres but

among ethnographers as well. 'Ethnic' is passed off as 'national,' and 'political' merges with 'genetic.'" Vladimir Zviniatskovskii, "Partiinaia literatura bez partiinoi organizatsii," *Znamia* 2 (1992): 235.

81. In an article on émigré writers, Galina Litvinova quotes poet Igor' Severianin: "Rodit'sia russkim slishkom malo, / Im nado byt', im nado stat'" (It is not enough to be born Russian, / It's something you have to be, something you have to become.). See: G. Litvinova, "Russkie amerikantsy," *Nash sovremennik* 12 (1992): 123.

82. *Lzhe-* is a highly charged prefix, implying illegitimacy, the status of pretender to a powerful position, or usurpation of such a position. In Russian cultural memory, *lzhe-* is inevitably associated with *Lzhe-Dmitrii* (the False Dimitrii), the name applied to three pretenders to the throne during the Time of Troubles, each of whom claimed to be the son of Ivan the Terrible, rumored to have been murdered by order of Boris Godunov in 1591. Even the canonization of Prince Dmitrii of Uglich in 1606 and the bringing of his remains to Moscow did not stop the proliferation of False Dmitriis. Vladimir Voinovich and Sinyavsky/Tertz both satirized the role of pretenders at times of national upheaval, the former in the 1972 story "Skurlatsky, Man of Letters," and the latter in the fourth chapter of the 1983 novel *Goodnight!*.

83. V. Khatiushin, "O lzhepoetakh i russkoi poezii," *Molodaia gvardiia* 1 (1991): 264, 266.

84. Ibid., 267.

85. Andrei Voznesenskii, "Iz zhizni krestikov," *Literaturnaia gazeta* 39 (1989).

86. "Net, i ne pod chuzhdym nebosvodom, / I ne pod zashchitoi chuzhdykh kryl—/ Ia byla togda s moim narodom, / Tam, gde moi narod, k neschast'iu, byl." Translated by Amanda Haight and Peter Norman, quoted from: Amanda Haight, *Akhmatova: A Poetic Pilgrimage* (Oxford: Oxford University Press, 1990), 100. See Tat'iana Glushkova, "Kuda vedet 'Ariadnina nit'?" *Literaturnaia gazeta* 12 (March 23, 1988): 4.

87. "Vozvrashchenie Rossii (Beseda Anatoliia Baiborodina s Valentinom Grigor'evichem Rasputinym)," *Sibir'* 1 (1991): 31. Rasputin said that a strong case was being made for canonizing Dostoevsky. Another article declared that "Russian literature is a liturgical process" and decried the "Petrine western avant-garde" that weakened the "invisible spiritual dome" of traditional Russian writing. Grigorii Iunin, "Ten' ruki s gusinym perom," *Den'* 50 (Dec. 13, 1992): 6.

88. The quality of "spirituality" in Russian literature was devalued by the indiscriminate use of this term by official champions of Socialist Realism.

89. Vladimir Krupin, "Ne sogreshi slovom," *Zavtra* 3 (March 1998): 9.

90. See: Elena Gradova, "Knigi vse tolshche, smysla vse men'she" (an interview with Vladimir Krupin), *Literaturnaia gazeta* 42 (Oct. 14, 1992): 3.

91. In *The Oak and the Calf* Solzhenitsyn composed a "saint's life" for himself, in which each text, written and preserved with difficulty, is a *podvig*, not achieved for personal glory but in memory of all Russians who suffered for Russia in the twentieth-century, especially those who perished in the Gulag. See: Alexander Solzhenitsyn, *The Oak and the Calf*, trans. by H. T. Willetts (New York: Harper and Row, 1981).

92. See Iurii Seleznev, *Glazami naroda* (Moscow: Sovremennik, 1986), 109.

93. Sorokin, "Nas oni doprashivaiut," 3.

94. The uproar over the award of the English-funded Booker Prize to Mark Kharitonov in

December 1992 illustrates this line of thought. Vladimir Bondarenko could not imagine how Eurocentric atheists and Protestants, along with their Russian partners, could hope to judge what was best in Russian literature. "Neither Viktor Astafiev nor Vladimir Sokolov will ever get a Nobel Prize, no matter how fine their works are, and despite the fact that they represent the very summit of Russian literature." Bondarenko, "Literaturnye rasisty," 7. For similar sentiments see Tat'iana Glushkova's remarks in "Posle pogorel'shchiny," 7: "And it is not for the learned rationalist to approach our mysteries!" This was a rejection not simply of "alien" judgments of Russian literature, but of academic, rationalist discourse in general.

95. Iurii Baranov and Lev Bobrov, "Diskriminatsiia velikoi literatury," *Molodaia gvardiia* 7 (1992): 184–92.

96. Gennadii Stupin, in "Posle pogorel'shchiny," 6.

97. A. Kruchenykh and V. Khlebnikov, "The Word as Such," first published in 1913 in Moscow; the first section has been translated by Anna Lawton and Herbert Eagle in *Russian Futurism through Its Manifestoes, 1912–1928*, ed. by A. Lawton (Ithaca: Cornell University Press, 1988), 60.

98. Arkhipov, "Ovtsy i kozlishcha," 143. See also: Rossman, *Russian Intellectual Antisemitism*, 177.

99. "'Byt' russkim ochen' trudno'" (Natal'ia Iartseva's interview with artist Sergei Kharlamov), *Moskva*, April 2000, 188. Levitan's landscapes have been described as "silent, timeless, undisturbed by human presence. . . . simultaneously lyrical and melancholy." Evgeniia Kirichenko, *Russian Design and the Fine Arts, 1750–1917*, compiled by Mikhail Anikst, trans. by Arch Tait (New York: Abrams, 1991), 95.

100. *Russian Jewish Artists in a Century of Change*, ed. by Susan Tumarkin Goodman (New York: The Jewish Museum, 1995), 192.

101. Iartseva, "Byt' russkim," 188.

102. "Erzatsami subkul'tury na burzhuazno-amerikanskii lad"; Liubomudrov, "Izvlechem li uroki?" 173–74. It was argued that Western Slavists were not helping by being "duped" into championing the *mastery andergraunda*. See Vladimir Bondarenko, "Fekal'naia proza Sorokina Vovy," *Den'* 16 (April 19, 1992): 7.

103. See Aleksandr Solzhenitsyn, "The Relentless Cult of Novelty and How It Wrecked the Century," trans. by Ignat and Stephan Solzhenitsyn, *New York Times Book Review*, Feb. 7, 1993: 3, 17. One of Sinyavsky's most important statements on Russian Realism and modernism is the essay *On Socialist Realism*. The two authors debated these questions in émigré and (after 1985) Russian periodicals. See also: Liubomudrov, "Agoniia nigilizma"; Arkhipov, "Ovtsy i kozlishcha"; and Dale Peterson, "Solzhenitsyn Back in the USSR: Anti-Modernism in Contemporary Soviet Prose," *Berkshire Review* 1981: 64–84.

104. Viktor Ostretsov, "Velikaia lozh' romantizma," *Slovo* (*v mire knig*) 6 (1991): 9–14.

105. For a discussion of "genetic memory," see: Vladimir Bondarenko, "Obretenie rodstva," *V mire knig* 7 (1989): 11–17. Vadim Rossman describes this belief system in which the writer's origins carry great weight; see *Russian Intellectual Antisemitism*, 177.

106. For a discussion of the self-image of the *derevenshchiki*, see Kathleen Parthé, *Russian Village Prose: The Radiant Past* (Princeton, Princeton University Press, 1992), 18.

107. Evgenii Nefedov, "Nashego polku pribylo," *Zavtra* 21 (May 1995): 7.

108. "Ukrepiat 'geneticheskii kod' russkikh chitatelei"; "Vtoraia tragediia" (an interview with Tat'iana Glushkova by Sergei Kuniaev), *Moskovskii literator* 4 (March 1993): 6.

109. Shvedov, " 'Oglobli vzletiat', ili logika pravykh," 11.

110. Tatiana Tolstaia, "Ne mogu molchat'," *Ogonek* 14 (March 31, 1990).

111. Vladimir Voinovich, *The Fur Hat,* trans. by Susan Brownsberger (New York: Harcourt Brace Jovanovich, 1989), 32. In the play *Tribunal,* Voinovich parodied, among other things, the deliberately archaic language and hypocritical behavior of an ultranationalist rural writer. See Vladimir Voinovich, *Tribunal* (London: Overseas Publications Interchange, 1985).

112. Voinovich, *The Fur Hat,* 99.

113. Feliks Roziner, *Nekto Finkel'maier* (London: Overseas Publication Interchange, 1981), 254–56. The translation condenses a passage that refers to Prebylov's regional accent and ungrammatical Russian. See Felix Roziner, *A Certain Finkelmeyer,* trans. by Michael Heim (New York: W. W. Norton, 1991), 164. The novel was published in Russia shortly before the English translation came out. In 1984, Joseph Brodsky used the same image to criticize the nationalistic fervor that had entered Russian literature in the previous decade: "I am talking here obviously of the 'peasant prose,' which, in its Antaeus-like desire to touch the ground, went a bit too far and took root." See Brodsky, "Catastrophes in the Air," in *Less Than One: Selected Essays* (New York: Farrar Straus and Giroux, 1986), 294–95.

114. Roziner, *A Certain Finkelmeyer,* 321. Roziner's novel, under its *samizdat* name of *Pyl' na vetru* (Dust/Ashes in the Wind) received the Vladimir Dal Literary Prize in Paris in 1980, an irony, considering the nationalist right's high regard for Dal's work on Russian language and folklore.

115. "Klassika i my," *Moskva* 1–3 (1990).

116. On Jewish writers in Russia, see: Alice Nakhimovsky, *Russian-Jewish Literature and Identity* (Baltimore: Johns Hopkins University Press, 1992).

117. Proposed by M. Zolotusskii and quoted by Natal'ia Ivanova in "Russkii vopros," *Znamia* 1 (1992): 198. Ivanova blamed this development on the anticosmopolitan campaign of the late forties, the Village Prose movement of the sixties and seventies, and those poets and critics who allied themselves with the rural writers. In another article, Ivanova called the cultural chauvinists *pozhilaia gvardiia* (the middle-aged/elderly guard) a play on *Molodaia gvardiia* (*Young Guard*) the journal most closely linked with national Bolshevism and neo-Stalinism. See: Ivanova, "Pozhilaia gvardiia," *Sintaksis* 26 (1989): 203–9.

118. Zviniatskovskii, "Partiinaia literatura bez partiinoi organizatsii," 233–37.

119. Aleksandr Ageev, "Varvarskaia lira: Ocherki 'patrioticheskoi' poezii," *Znamia* 2 (1991): 221–31.

120. Viacheslav Kuritsyn, "Postmodernizm: Novaia pervobytnaia kul'tura," *Novyi mir* 2 (1992): 226.

121. The Kuritsyn article discusses the importance of postmodernism. The conservative future vision of Russian literature is taken from writer Iurii Kozlov's remarks at the round-table "Vek zolotoi eshche vernetsia, *Den'* 50 (Dec. 13, 1992): 6.

122. Sergei Chuprinin objected to the exclusivity advocated on the right, which he saw as a

move towards self-isolation. "The furthest extension of this is a 'reservation' for patriotic literature (*rezervatsiia patrioticheskoi slovesnosti*), voluntarily fenced off before our very eyes by those who want the exclusive right to love their Homeland, and the exclusive duty of feeling themselves to be Russian and at one with the people." See his contribution to an article called "Nedoskazannoe: K itogam literaturnogo goda," *Znamia* 1 (1993): 202–4.

123. Valentin Sorokin, "Svoi chuzhie," *Nash sovremennik* 9 (1989): 176. On the image of "borders" in Village Prose, see: Parthé, *Russian Village Prose*, 5–7, 68–72.

124. Gennadii Stupin, "Posle pogorel'shchiny," 6.

125. The reference is not merely to Odessa as a city with a large Jewish population, but to a story by Isaac Babel. See: Glushkova, "Vtoraia tragediia," 6.

126. James Billington, *The Icon and the Axe: An Interpretive History of Russian Culture* (New York: Vintage, 1970), 368, 540.

127. Ageev, "Varvarskaia lira," 225. Ageev quotes a poem by Iurii Kuznetsov which expressed this view very strongly.

128. A. S. Pushkin, *A Journey to Arzrum*, trans. by Birgitta Ingemanson (Ann Arbor: Ardis, 1974), 50–51.

CHAPTER 5. RIGHTEOUSNESS AND THE VALUE OF SUFFERING

1. Michael Scammell, *Solzhenitsyn* (New York: W. W. Norton, 1984), 386n. The epigraph is from *The Oak and the Calf*, trans. by H. Willetts (New York: Harper and Row, 1981), 513.

2. Vladimir Dal' (1801–72) studied and recorded folklore and dialect forms; he is best known for his dictionary, the *Tolkovyi slovar'*, first published in 1863–66, and for his published collections of folk sayings. See also T. Lopukhina-Rodzianko, *Dukhovnye osnovy tvorchestva Solzhenitsyna* (Frankfurt: Possev, 1974), 21.

3. Pierre Pascal, *The Religion of the Russian People*, trans. by R. Williams (Crestwood, N.Y.: St. Vladimir's Seminary Press, 1976), 34.

4. Fyodor Dostoevsky, *A Writer's Diary*, vol. 2: *1877–1881*, trans. by Kenneth Lanz (Evanston: Northwestern University Press, 1994), 1301.

5. The centrality of righteousness in the Russian tradition is one of several points of contact with Judaism which can be traced through the teachings of the Desert Fathers, who borrowed heavily from Judaism even as they defined themselves against it; cf. Genesis 18, where Abraham asks the Lord to spare the righteous of Sodom.

6. As quoted in A. Gorelov, "Pravedniki i 'Pravednicheskii' tsikl v tvorcheskoi evoliutsii N. S. Leskova," in *Leskov i russkaia literatura*, ed. by K. Lomunov and V. Trotskii (Moscow: Nauka, 1988), 58.

7. The material on Korolenko and Lunacharsky is from: Andrei Sinyavsky, *Soviet Civilization: A Cultural History*, trans. by Joanne Turnbull (New York: Little, Brown, 1990), 124–25.

8. Nina Tumarkin, *Lenin Lives! The Lenin Cult in Soviet Russia* (Cambridge: Harvard University Press, 1983), 70–72. A more positive view of the tsars and princes was decreed after the mid-1930s, as communism in Russia began to undergo a process of nationalization.

9. On the use of religious symbolism in this context, see ibid., esp. Chap. 3.

10. Clark, *The Soviet Novel: History as Ritual.* 2d ed. (Chicago: University of Chicago, 1985), 159–76.

11. Ibid., 162.

12. Ibid., 173.

13. Alexander Solzhenitsyn, "Matryona's Home," trans. by H. T. Willetts, in *The Portable Twentieth-Century Russian Reader*, ed. by Clarence Brown (New York: Penguin, 1985), 464.

14. Galina Nikolaeva, *The Newcomer (The Manager of the MTS and the Chief Agronomist)* [no trans. listed], (Moscow: Foreign Languages Publishing House, 1950), 121.

15. Leonid Rzhevsky, *Solzhenitsyn: Creator and Heroic Deed*, trans. by Sonja Miller (Alabama: University of Alabama Press, 1978), 47; emphasis in original.

16. As quoted in Rzhevsky, *Solzhenitsyn*, 47.

17. Valentin Rasputin, *Farewell to Matyora*, trans. by Antonina Bouis, with a foreword by Kathleen Parthé (1979; rev. ed., Evanston: Northwestern University Press, 1991), 70.

18. Liliia Vil'chek, "Vniz po techeniiu derevenskoi prozy," *Voprosy literatury* 6 (1985): 72.

19. Gerald Mikkelson and Margaret Winchell, "Valentin Rasputin and His Siberia," introduction to *Siberia on Fire: Stories and Essays by Valentin Rasputin* (DeKalb: Northern Illinois University Press, 1989), xvii.

20. Anatolii Lanshchikov, *Ishchu sobesednika (O proze 70–80kh godov)* (Moscow: Sovetksii pisatel', 1988), 6.

21. David Gillespie, "Valentin Rasputin's 'Pozhar'," *Quinquereme: New Studies in Modern Languages* 9, no. 2 (July 1986). See also F. Chapchakov, "Dom ili pribezhishche? (Zametki o povesti Valentina Rasputina 'Pozhar')," *Literaturnaia gazeta*, Aug. 7, 1985: 4.

22. For a description of Village Prose, see Kathleen Parthé, *Russian Village Prose: The Radiant Past* (Princeton: Princeton University Press, 1992). Chapter 7 analyzes the use of the detective story format for rural themes. A version of this chapter was translated into Russian by I. Gurova and appeared as "Dva syschika v poiskakh derevenskoi prozy," in *Russkaia literatura XX veka, issledovaniia amerikanskikh uchenykh*, ed. by B. Averin and E. Neatrour (St. Petersburg: Petro-Rif, 1993).

23. Iurii Kariakin et al., "Khudozhnik ili publitsist-kto prav? (Nekruglyi stol)," *Literaturnaia gazeta*, Aug. 27, 1986: 2; L. Lavlinskii, "Zakon miloserdii (Po stranitsam novykh proizvedenii Viktora Astaf'eva)," *Literaturnoe obozrenie* 8 (1986): 19. Several reviewers noted that the novel was heavy going for a detective story, but was obviously good for the soul: Oleg Shevchenko, "Neizbezhnost' Dostoevskogo," *Pod"em* 11 (1986): 131; Evgenii Prigozhin, "Bol' i nadezhda," *Neva* 4 (1987): 162.

24. For a fuller discussion of the chauvinist aspects of this work and critical reaction to it, see Parthé, *Russian Village Prose*, 180 n. 35. See also her "Viktor Astafiev's *A Sad Detective Story*: A Reader's Opinion and Two Critics' Replies," in *Soviet Studies in Literature* 24, no. 4 (Fall 1988): 4–43.

25. It appeared in the July and August issues of *Nash sovremennik*. The novel also appeared in English: Vassily Belov, *The Best is Yet to Come*, trans. P. O. Gromm (Moscow: Raduga, 1989).

26. Natal'ia Ivanova, "Ispytanie pravdoi," *Znamia* 1 (1987): 202–3; this article was translated as "Trial by Truth," *Soviet Studies in Literature* 24, no. 3 (Summer 1988): 5–57.

27. Igor' Zolotusskii, "Otchet o puti," *Znamia* 1 (1987): 22. This article was translated as "A Progress Report," *Soviet Studies in Literature* 24, no. 3 (Summer 1988).

28. V. Lakshin, "Po pravdu govoria: Romany o kotorykh sporiat," *Izvestiia,* Dec. 3, 1986: 3, continued on Dec. 4, 1986: 3; trans. as "To Tell the Truth: Novels That Are Being Debated," *Current Digest of the Soviet Press* 38, no. 51 (Jan. 21, 1987): 9. See also D. Ivanov, "Chto vperedi?," *Ogonek* 2 (1987): 12; and "Chitateli o romane V. Belova 'Vse vperedi'," *Nash sovremennik* 8 (1987): 176–81.

29. V. Gorbachev, "Chto vperedi? (O romane Vasiliia Belova *Vse vperedi*)," *Molodaia gvardiia* 3 (1987): 250–77; I. Spiridonova, "Bezoblachnoe sirotstvo (o romane V. Belova *Vse vperedi*)," *Sever* 4 (1987): 110–17. Spiridonova does fault Belov on his female characters, who are presented only from a male point of view, and have no voice of their own.

30. Lavlinskii, "Zakon miloserdii," 18.

31. Zolotusskii, "Otchet," 224.

32. See note 7.

33. N. Eidelman and V. Astafiev, "Perepiska iz dvukh uglov," *Sintaksis* 17 (1987): 80–87.

34. Vadim Rossman, *Russian Intellectual Antisemitism in the Post-Communist Era* (Lincoln: University of Nebraska Press, 2002), 174–75.

35. Nicolas Berdyaev, *The Russian Idea,* trans. by R. M. French (Boston: Beacon Press, 1962), 27.

36. Iu. M. Lotman, "'Agreement' and 'Self-Giving' as Archetypal Models of Culture," trans. by N. F. C. Owen, in *The Semiotics of Russian Culture,* ed. by Ann Shukman (Ann Arbor: University of Michigan Press, 1984), 125–40.

37. Alexander Solzhenitsyn, *The Oak and the Calf,* trans. by Harry Willetts (New York: Harper Colophon, 1981) 181, 197, 8.

38. For the author's tribute to some of those who helped him, see Aleksandr Solzhenitsyn, *Invisible Allies,* trans. by Alexis Klimoff and Michael Nicholson (Washington: A Cornelia and Michael Bessie Book/Counterpoint, 1995).

39. Solzhenitsyn, *The Oak and the Calf,* 146.

40. Rzhevsky, *Solzhenitsyn,* 48.

41. Abram Tertz (Andrei Sinyavsky), "The Literary Process in Russia," trans. by Michael Glenny, in *Kontinent* (Garden City, N.Y.: Anchor/Doubleday, 1976), 105.

42. "Ne nuzhny nam pravedniki, a nuzhny ugodniki."

43. "Za dikim step'iam zabaikal'ia" (Beyond the wild Baikal steppes).The first epigraph is from Part 1, Chap. 9 of *Notes from Underground* in the David Magarshack translation. The second epigraph comes from Evgenii Zamiatin's 1914 essay "Sirin," trans. by Mirra Ginsburg for *A Soviet Heretic: Essays by Yevgeny Zamyatin* (Chicago: University of Chicago Press, 1970), 19. Mikhail Bulgakov dedicated his 1922 work *Notes on the Cuff (Zapiski na manzhetakh)* "To the floating, traveling, and suffering writers of Russia" ("plavaiushchim, puteshestvuiushchim i strazhdushchim pisateliam russkim"). For a study of the importance of suffering in Russian civilization, see Daniel Rancour-Laferriere, *The Slave Soul of Russia: Moral Masochism and the Cult of Suffering* (New York: New York University Press, 1995).

44. Tolstoy's remarks are quoted in Maxim Gorky, *Reminiscences of Tolstoy, Chekhov, and An-*

dreyev, trans. by S. Koteliarsky and Leonard Woolf, introd. by Mark Van Doren (New York: Viking Press, 1966), 42.

45. In an essay written in the late 1960s, Andrei Amalrik explained the difference between *belaia* and *chernaia zavist'* (white and black envy) in Russia: "Many peasants find someone else's success more painful than their own failure. . . . when the average Russian sees that he is living less well than his neighbor, he will concentrate not on trying to do better for himself but rather on trying to bring his neighbor down to his level." See Amalrik, *Will the Soviet Union Survive Until 1984?* [no translator listed] (New York: Perennial Library/Harper and Row, 1971) 35. That this had not changed a quarter of a century later can be seen, for example, from stories about the dangers faced by Russia's new family farms from vandalism or arson by "jealous neighbors who believed that they had not received their due." See Anders Åslund, *How Russia Became a Market Economy* (Washington, D.C.: The Brookings Institution, 1995), 260.

46. Valentin Sorokin, "Svoi chuzhie," *Nash sovremennik* 9 (1989): 170.

47. Vladimir Chivilikhin, "Fragmenty iz roman-esse *Pamiat',*" in *Doroga: Iz arkhiva pisatelia* (Moscow: Sovremennik, 1989), 395–96.

48. Solzhenitsyn, *The Oak and the Calf,* 465.

49. Ibid., 471.

50. Iurii Olesha, *Ni dnia bez strochki* (Moscow: Sovetskaia Rossiia, 1965), 68, 175.

51. In J. A. E. Curtis, *Manuscripts Don't Burn: Mikhail Bulgakov, A Life in Letters* (Woodstock, N.Y.: The Overlook Press, 1992), 131.

52. Of course, the writer's vulnerability to travel restrictions was not limited to the Soviet period; one need only remember Pushkin who was never able to travel outside Russia.

53. Donald Fanger quotes Semen Vengerov's 1911 essay "The Fascination of Russian Literature" on success as a minor theme in Russian fiction as compared to its prominent place in Western literature. See Fanger, "On the Russianness of the Nineteenth-Century Novel," in *Art and Culture in Nineteenth-Century Russia,* ed. by Theofanis George Stavrou (Bloomington: Indiana University Press, 1983), 42. Aleksandr Ageev complains about the "barbarian" mentality which sees *bol'* (pain) and *terpenie* (patience) as positive and which claims that the poverty of Russia is its true wealth. See Ageev, "Varvarskaia lira: Ocherki 'patriotícheskoi' poezii," *Znamia* 1 (1991): 2.

54. Zamyatin, *A Soviet Heretic,* 32–33.

55. "Sobesednik na pominke (Vladimir Soloukhin v besede s korrespondentom 'LG' Lianoi Polukhinoi)," *Literaturnaia gazeta* 48 (Nov. 25, 1992): 5. In *The Oak and the Calf,* Solzhenitsyn constantly judges other people in terms of their endurance.

56. Václav Havel, *Open Letters: Selected Writings 1965–1990,* ed. by Paul Wilson, trans. by Paul Wilson, A. G. Brainy (New York: Vintage, 1992), 283.

57. Documents Nos. 10 and 28 in *The Solzhenitsyn Files,* ed. by Michael Scammell, trans. supervised by C. Fitzpatrick (Chicago: edition q, 1995).

58. Abram Tertz (Andrei Sinyavsky), "The Literary Process in Russia," trans. by Michael Glenny, in *Kontinent,* 77–78.

59. Abram Tertz [Andrei Sinyavsky], *A Voice from the Chorus,* trans. by Kyril Fitzlyon and Max Hayward (New York: Bantam, 1978), 128. The book was reissued by Yale University Press in 1995, with a new preface by the author and a reprinted essay by Max Hayward.

60. Bulgakov, in Curtis, *Manuscripts Don't Burn,* 141.
61. Stephen Cohen, "Introduction: Bukharin's Fate," in Nikolai Bukharin, *How It All Began,* trans. by George Shriver (New York: Columbia University Press, 1998), vii.
62. Cohen. "Introduction: Bukharin's Fate," 7–28.
63. Shentalinsky, *Arrested Voices: Resurrecting the Disappeared Writers of the Soviet Regime,* trans. by John Crowfoot, introd. by Robert Conquest (New York: The Free Press, 1996), 285.
64. For example, Yuri Miloslavsky recalled how all the different kinds of available literature (Socialist Realist—like Pikul; anomalous—like Voznesenskii's poetry; and *samizdat*—like Nabokov) were perceived and discussed by the intelligentsia as one continuous text. See his article: "Estetika realisticheskogo razocharovaniia," *Literaturnaia gazeta,* July 15, 1992: 4.
65. Alexander Solzhenitsyn, *Nobel Lecture,* trans. by F. D. Reeve (New York: Farrar, Straus and Giroux, 1974).
66. This is from Sosnora's June 1967 letter to the Secretariat of the Writers' Union, which was published in Roy Medvedev's *Politicheskii dnevnik,* and reprinted in *An End to Silence: Uncensored Opinion in the Soviet Union,* trans. by George Saunders, ed. and introd. by Stephen Cohen (New York: W. W. Norton, 1982), 252–54. John and Carol Garrard mention five levels of editorial oversight before the manuscript went to Glavlit. See *Inside the Soviet Writers' Union* (New York: Free Press/Macmillan, 1990), 175.
67. As noted in John Bayley, "Anna of all the Russias," *New York Review of Books* 40, no. 9 (May 13, 1993): 25–27. The photograph to which Bayley refers was included in *The Complete Poems of Anna Akhmatova, Updated and Expanded Edition,* trans. by Judith Hemschemeyer, ed. by Roberta Reeder (Somerville, Mass.: Zephyr Press, 1990).
68. Solzhenitsyn, *The Oak and the Calf,* 107–8.
69. Ibid., 103–5.
70. It makes up part of Curtis's *Manuscripts Don't Burn,* a memoir-compilation of various documents by, to, and about Bulgakov.
71. Solzhenitsyn, *The Oak and the Calf,* 8. It is ironic that while Solzhenitsyn lived to return to Russia in 1994, the publisher who planned two dozen volumes of the author's works suspended production in 1995 after just one book, citing lack of financial backing and reader interest.
72. Tertz, "The Literary Process," 90.
73. "Razbrosannym v pyli po magazinam / (Gde ikh nikto ne bral i ne beret!) / Moim stikham, kak dragotsennym vinam, / Nastanet svoi chered." The translation comes from Janet M. King, "Tsvetaeva," *Handbook of Russian Literature,* ed. by Victor Terras (New Haven: Yale University Press, 1985), 485–87. The poem begins with the words "Moim stikham" and was written in 1913. In 1931, in response to a questionnaire from the émigré journal *Chisla* 5 (1931) asking for Tsvetaeva's thoughts about her writing, she quoted this last stanza and called it the formula for her fate as a writer and as a person. The poem appeared in volume two of the controversial almanac *Literaturnaia Moskva* in 1956. The Russian text and notes come from Marina Tsvetaeva, *Izbrannye proizvedeniia,* ed. by A. Efron and A. Saakaiants (Moscow: Sovetskii pisatel', 1965), 57, 732.
74. Tertz, "The Literary Process," 82–83.

75. The epigraph is from David Remnick, "Letter from Moscow: Exit the Saints," *New Yorker* 71, no. 21 (July 18, 1994): 50.

76. Sergei Chuprinin, "Normal'nyi khod," *Znamia* 10 (1991), 222, 230. Trans. by Deming Brown in *Russian Studies in Literature* 29, no. 1 (Winter 1992–93).

77. "I u tekh, kto probilsia, starye rany noiut v nepogode. . . . spustia desiatiletiia posle mytarstv, v obespechennoi nagradami i tirazhami zrelosti." Chuprinin, "Normal'nyi khod," 230.

78. Viacheslav Kuritsyn, "Postmodernizm: Novaia pervobytnaia kul'tura," *Novyi mir* 2 (1992): 226.

79. Cited in Remnick, "Letter from Moscow," 57.

CHAPTER 6. THE END OF SOVIET LITERATURE AND THE LAST DANGEROUS TEXT...

1. The epigraph—"Ot tekh vremen kliuchi eshche lezhat"—is from Andrei Voznesensky, "The Thief of Memories," trans. by F. D. Reeve, in *An Arrow in the Wall*, ed. by W. J. Smith and F. D. Reeve (New York: Henry Holt, 1987), 237–39.

The philosopher Nikolai Berdyaev saw that among Russians "everything takes on a religious character . . . everything was appraised and assessed according to categories of orthodoxy and heresy." See *The Russian Idea*, trans. by R. M. French (Boston: Beacon Press, 1962), 27. The parallel to contemporary notions of Islamic and anti-Islamic literature was frequently mentioned by ultranationalists.

2. Viktor Erofeev, "Pominki po sovetskoi literature," *Literaturnaia gazeta*, July 4, 1990: 8.

3. A. N. Nikoliukin, "'Ne v izgnanii, a v poslanii': missiia literatury," in *Kul'turnoe nasledie rossiiskoi emigratsii 1917–1940*, Book 2, ed. by E. P. Chelyshev, D. M. Shakhovskoi (Moscow: "Nasledie," 1994), 6–16.

4. "Kakomu d'iavolu, kakomu psu v ugodu, / Kakim koshmarnym obuiannyi snom, / Narod, bezumstvuia, ubil svoiu svobodu, / I dazhe ne ubil—zasek knutom?" As cited in Nikoliukin, "'Ne v izgnanii'," 6.

5. Cited ibid., 8.

6. Alexander Zholkovsky, "Mandelstam's *Egyptian Stamp*: A Study in *Envy*?" *Slavic and East European Journal* 38, no. 2 (Summer 1994): 224–44.

7. Evgenii Dobrenko, "Sovetskaia mnogonatsional'naia kak oblast' semeinikh tain," *Literaturnoe obozrenie* 11 (1990): 52–54.

8. Nikoliukin, "'Ne v izgnanii'," 8.

9. This collective letter appeared in the *samizdat* journal *Politicheskii dnevnik* 64 (January 1970). It was reprinted in *An End to Silence: Uncensored Opinion in the Soviet Union*, trans. George Saunders. ed. and introd. by Stephen Cohen (New York: W. W. Norton, 1982), 180.

10. Iurii Lotman and Boris Uspenskii, "New Aspects in the Study of Early Russian Culture," trans. by N. F. C. Owen, in *The Semiotics of Russian Culture*, ed. by Ann Shukman, Michigan Slavic Contributions 11 (Ann Arbor: University of Michigan Press, 1984), 38.

11. Robert Conquest, "Tvardovsky and *Novy Mir*," in *Tyrants and Typewriters: Communiqués from the Struggle for Truth* (Lexington, Mass.: Lexington Books, 1989), 82–85.

12. Zamyatin said that critics in the 1920s behaved like an engineer he knew, for whom all

music fell into two categories. "On the one hand, 'God Save the Tsar' (*Bozhe-tsaria khrani*) on the other, everything else; if people got up, it meant that the music belonged to the first category; if they didn't, it belonged to the second—to the non-'God Save the Tsar' (*ne-Bozhe-tsaria*) category. This is the only kind of response heard by the writer today." Yevgeny Zamyatin, "The New Russian Prose," trans. by Mirra Ginsburg, in *A Soviet Heretic* (Chicago: University of Chicago Press, 1975), 92. The essay was written in 1923. The original title is "Novaia russkaia proza" and it can be found in Evgenii Zamiatin, *Litsa* (New York: Inter-Language Literary Associates, 1967), 193.

13. Valentin Kurbatov, "Iz dnevnika kritika," *Moskva* 1 (1992): 9. Kurbatov puts the *netendentsioznye pisateli* (e.g. Sasha Sokolov) together with *metaliteratory*, e.g. Vladimir Sorokin.

14. Boris Groys unintentionally provided the right wing with ammunition for this attack, although they developed the argument on their own. See Groys, *The Total Art of Stalinism: Avant-Garde, Esthetic Dictatorship, and Beyond*, trans. by Charles Rougle (Princeton: Princeton University Press, 1992). The "neo-Bolshevist" label is used by the Right to designate the forces, both non-Russian cosmopolitans and turncoat Russians, that destroyed Old Russia while making the Revolution. At the same time "Communists" was being used positively to designate Russians who restored the Great Russian state under Stalin, and whose work was undone by cosmopolitans and "false Russians" after 1985.

15. Irena Corten, *Vocabulary of Soviet Society and Culture: A Selected Guide to Russian Words, Ideas, and Expressions of the Post-Stalin Era, 1953-1991* (Durham: Duke University Press, 1992), 131.

16. Chuprinin, "Normal'nyi khod," *Znamia* 10 (1991): 233. See also: Iakov Krotov, "Sovok kak religioznyi tip," in *Razmyshleniia o raznom* (Moscow: Irina, 1992), 3–20; and M. Lipovetskii, "Sovok-bliuz: Shestidesiatniki segodnia," *Znamia* 9 (1991): 226–36. Corten, *Vocabulary of Soviet Society and Culture*, 134–35, says that *sovdepovskaia* was synonymous with *sovkovaia*.

17. Critic Lev Anninsky has said that schoolboy poems to Stalin were common in the early fifties and that he wrote one himself (interview with the author in Moscow, October 1992).

18. Vladimir Zviniatskovskii, "Partiinaia literatura bez partiinoi organizatsii," *Znamia* 2 (1992): 226.

19. A. Chagin, "Protivorechivaia tselostnost'," in Chelyshev and Shakhovskoi, *Kul'turnoe nasledie rossiiskoi emigratsii 1917–1940*, Book 2, 17–24.

20. Ibid., 19.

21. From Donald Fanger's comments for "Central European Writers as a Social Force," panel discussion in "Intellectuals and Social Change in Central and Eastern Europe," *Partisan Review* 4 (1992): 662.

22. Kurbatov, "Iz dnevnika kritika," 8.

23. A. Turkov, "Lgut karty, kogda oni perekraivaiutsia v ugodu okololiteraturnym interesam," *Izvestiia*, Oct. 16, 1990: 3.

24. Roman Jakobson, "On a Generation That Squandered Its Poets," in *My Futurist Years*, ed. by Bengt Jagenfeldt and Stephen Rudy, trans. by Stephen Rudy (New York: Marsilio Publishers, 1997), 209–45.

25. V. Korosteleva, *Pravda*, Oct. 13, 1990.

26. The first comparison is from Ia. Gordon, "Chto pozadi?" *Literaturnaia gazeta* 39 (Sept. 26, 1990): 5; the second is from Boris Mozhaev, ibid., 49 (Dec. 11, 1991): 2.

27. Turkov, "Lgut karty," 3.

28. I. Tolstoi, "Literaturnaia voina v Leningrade," *Russkaia mysl'*, May 11, 1990: 10.

29. Iurii Kashuk, "Nishi biotsenoza," *Literaturnaia gazeta*, Oct. 10, 1990: 4.

30. Ibid., 4.

31. Erofeev, "Pominki po sovetskoi literature," 8.

32. Vladimir Kolesnikov, "Plutarkhi i arkhipluty," *Den'*, May 31, 1992: 5.

33. The term "anti-urban" was proposed by M. Zolotusskii and quoted by Natal'ia Ivanova in "Russkii vopros," *Znamia* 1 (1992): 198. Ivanova blames this development on the anti-cosmopolitan campaign of the late 1940s, on Village Prose of the sixties and seventies, and on critics who allied themselves with rural writers. She also refers to this group as *pozhilaia gvardiia*, a play on *Molodaia gvardiia*, the journal which was most closely linked with National Bolshevism and neo-Stalinism. See N. Ivanova, "Pozhilaia gvardiia," *Sintaksis* 26 (1989): 203–9.

34. "Anekdoty" (signed by "Otdel literatury"), *Ogonek* 52 (Dec. 24, 1988): 14.

35. From Andrei Voznesenskii's 1960 poem "Krony i korni" ("Leaves and Roots"), ostensibly dedicated to Tolstoy, but seen as referring to Boris Pasternak. The original lines are: "No moshchno pod zemlei / Vorochaiutsia korni / Koriavoi piaternei." The translation by Stanley Kunitz is included in Andrey Voznesensky, *Antiworlds and "The Fifth Ace,"* ed. by Patricia Blake and Max Hayward (Garden City, N.Y.: Anchor, 1967), 120–23.

36. Thomas Seifrid uses this term in "Getting Across: Border-Consciousness in Soviet and Emigré Literature," in *Slavic and East European Journal* 38, no. 2 (Summer 1994): 245–60.

37. J. A. E. Curtis, *Manuscripts Don't Burn: Mikhail Bulgakov, A Life in Letters and Diaries* (Woodstock, N.Y.: Overlook Press, 1992), 248.

38. Ibid., 130–31.

39. Porvalas' sviaz' planety. / Aukat' ustaiu. / Voprosy bez otvetov. / Otvety v pustotu. / Svelo. Svelo. Svelo. / S toboi. S toboi. S toboi. / Allo. Allo. Allo. / Otboi. Otboi. Otboi. The poem was first published in *Kurortnaia gazeta* (Sept. 28, 1971), and then in *Novyi mir* in 1973. This translation is by Richard Wilbur in Andrei Voznesensky, *An Arrow in the Wall: Selected Poetry and Prose*, ed. by William J. Smith and F. D. Reeve (New York: Henry Holt, 1987), 110–13, 333nn.

40. Abram Tertz (Andrei Sinyavsky), "The Literary Process in Russia," trans. by Michael Glenny, in *Kontinent* (Garden City, N.Y.: Anchor Books, 1976), 107.

41. The epigraph is from Mikhail Bulgakov, *The Master and Margarita*, trans. by Dianna Burgin and Katherine T. O'Connor (New York: Vintage, 1996), 323.

42. Vladimir Bukovsky, *To Build a Castle—My Life as a Dissenter*, trans. by Michael Scammell (New York: Viking, 1979), 378.

43. Ibid., 292–93.

44. Alexander Herzen, *My Past and Thoughts*, trans. by Constance Garnett, rev. by H. Higgens, introd. by Isaiah Berlin, abridged with preface and notes by Dwight Macdon-

ald (Berkeley: University of California Press, 1991), 117–20. The student was forced into the army and died of consumption ten years later.

45. George F. Kennan, *The Marquis de Custine and His "Russia in 1839"* (Princeton: Princeton University Press, 1971), vii. See also Chap. 6, "The Reaction to 'Russia in 1839'," 95–117.

46. Alexander Herzen, *My Past and Thoughts,* trans. by Constance Garnett, abridged by Dwight Macdonald (Berkeley: University of California Press, 1991), 534. Isaiah Berlin mentions this as well in his introduction, xxxii.

47. *Meyers Konversations-Lexikon,* as cited in Marianna Tax Choldin, *A Fence Around the Empire: Russian Censorship of Western Ideas under the Tsars* (Durham: Duke University Press, 1985), 173.

48. Vitaly Shentalinsky, *Arrested Voices: Resurrecting the Disappeared Writers of the Soviet Regime,* trans. by John Crowfoot, introd. by Robert Conquest (New York: The Free Press, 1996), 80–81. The Russian edition is *Raby svobody, v literaturnykh arkhivakh KGB* (Moscow: "Parus," 1995), 172–75.

49. Vitalii Shentalinskii, "Master glazami GPU: Za kulisami zhizni Mikhaila Bulgakova," Parts 1 and 2, *Novyi mir* 10 and 11 (1997): 167–85, 182–98. Unless otherwise noted, the rest of this and the following paragraph summarize the material and Shentalinsky's observations in these two articles. Shentalinsky is unsure as to why the dossier only goes up to 1936, but assumes the remaining years were covered as well.

50. Curtis, *Manuscripts Don't Burn,* 75.

51. Shentalinsky, *Arrested Voices,* 73.

52. Ibid., 80–81.

53. Document numbers in the text refer to *The Solzhenitsyn Files,* ed. and introd. by Michael Scammell, trans. supervised by Catherine Fitzpatrick (Chicago: edition q, 1995). There is a Russian edition: *"Kremlevskii samosud": Sekretnye dokumenty Politburo o pisatele A. Solzhenitsyne,* ed. by A. Korotkov, S. Mel'chin, V. Denisov (Moscow: "Rodina"/edition q, 1994).

54. Stephen Lovell and Rosalind Marsh, "Culture and Crisis: The Intelligentsia and Literature after 1953," in *Russian Cultural Studies: An Introduction,* ed. by Catriona Kelly and David Shepherd (Oxford: Oxford University Press, 1998), 69.

55. Herzen, *My Past and Thoughts,* 652.

56. Jeffrey Brooks, *When Russia Learned to Read: Literacy and Popular Literature, 1861–1917* (Princeton: Princeton University Press, 1985).

57. Ewa M. Thompson, *Understanding Russia: The Holy Fool in Russian Culture* (New York: University Press of America, 1987), 31.

58. Ibid., 36.

59. Sergei Bulgakov, "Heroism and Asceticism: Reflections on the Religious Nature of the Russian Intelligentsia," in *Landmarks: A Collection of Russian Essays on the Russian Intelligentsia,* trans. by Marian Schwarz, ed. by Boris Shragin and Albert Todd (New York: Karz Howard, 1977), 53–55.

60. Victor Erofeyev, "The Possessed" (a review of Edvard Radzinsky, *The Rasputin File*), trans. by Jamey Gambrell, *New York Review of Books* 48, no. 5 (March 29, 2001): 12.

61. Thompson, *Understanding Russia,* 6, 37–38.

62. Ibid., 40. In 1997, one of the most celebrated holy figures in St. Petersburg was Ksenya Blazhennaia, an eighteenth-century *iurodivaia* canonized in the millennium year of 1988, whose gravesite attracted hundreds each day. See John Varoli in *St. Petersburg Times,* Nov. 24, 1997. Ksenya has been made the patron saint of St. Petersburg University, and students visit her statue with petitions for success in examinations.

63. Vladimir Voinovich, "Skurlatsky, Man of Letters," in *In Plain Russian,* trans. by Richard Lourie (New York: Farrar, Straus and Giroux, 1979), 226–27.

64. Brooks, *When Russia Learned to Read,* 25–27.

65. Ibid., 111.

66. Aleksandr I. Solzhenitsyn, *Letter to the Soviet Leaders,* trans. by Hilary Sternberg (New York: Perennial/Harper and Row, 1975), 53.

67. Michael Nelson, *War of the Black Heavens: The Battles of Western Broadcasting in the Cold War* (Syracuse: Syracuse University Press, 1997), 165.

68. Lovell and Marsh, "Culture and Crisis," 78.

69. V. Kardin (whose full name and patronymic are Emil' Vladimirovich), "Sekret Uspekha," first published in *Voprosy literatury* 5 (1986), and reprinted in V. Kardin, *Gde zaryta sobaka* (Moscow: Sovetskii pisatel', 1991), 253–92.

70. Said at a November 3, 1998, Moscow discussion in which I took part that included Rasputin, Gennadii Gusev (deputy editor of *Nash sovremennik*), Dmitrii Mamleev (of the Russian Peace Foundation),and Librarian of Congress James H. Billington.

71. Igor Zakharov, "Bookworm: Old Dogs Can Learn New Tricks of the Trade," *Moscow Times,* May 23, 1998; reposted on *Johnson's Russia List* 2192 (May 24, 1998).

72. "'Samyi chitaiushchii v mire narod,' otkryv dlia sebia Solzhenitsyna, Grossmana, Platonova, Ven. Erofeev, Brodskogo, Nabokova, otniud' ne otkazalsia ot knig, uslovno govoria, Pikulia. A vskore otdal im predpochtenie. Velikoe blago massovoi gramotnosti, rasshirenie sfery tsivilizatsii pri posredtsve radio, televideniia, dostavka na dom iskusstva . . . ne priveli i ne mogli privesti k uglubleniiu kul'turnogo sloia. . . . Literatura ne obrela svoego—pust' dazhe skromnogo—mesta v obnovivsheisia zhizni, i koe-kto uzhe tshchitsia ubedit': ei zdes' i delat' nechego." V. Kardin, "Troe na kacheliakh," *Voprosy literatury,* May–June 1997: 50–51.

73. In *Literaturnaia gazeta* 27 (July 5, 1995): 1.

74. Stephen Lovell, *The Russian Reading Revolution: Print Culture in the Soviet and Post-Soviet Eras* (London: Macmillan, 2000), 76.

75. Mentioned in: *Johnson's Russia List* 4232 (April 7, 2000), *Transitions Online* (www.tol.cz) for April 2000; Sophia Kornenko, "Resuscitating Russian," ibid., April 2000, about the new Council for the Russian Language organized by Putin on January 17, 2000, which included Valentin Rasputin and education leaders.

76. Stanislav Rassadin, "Legenda o velikom chitatele," *Strana i mir* 6 (Nov.–Dec. 1990): 135.

77. Lovell, *The Russian Reading Revolution,* 21–22.

78. From "Dear Dr. Husák," dated April 1975, in Václav Havel, *Open Letters: Selected Writings 1965–1990,* trans. by Paul Wilson and A. G. Brainy, ed. by Paul Wilson (New York: Vintage, 1992), 70.

79. Kardin, "Troe na kacheliakh," 50–51.

80. Sophie Labroschini, "Russia: Publishers Say Business Looking Better and Better," *Johnson's Russia List* 4666 (Dec. 3, 2000); the story was originally broadcast by RFE/RL on Dec. 1, 2000. See also Denis Maternovsky, "Fewer Books but a Whole Lot More to Read About," *Moscow Times,* June 6, 2003; reposted on *Johnson's Russia List* 7212 (June 6, 2003).

81. Donald Fanger, "Russian Writing in America," in *Intellectuals and Social Change in Central and Eastern Europe, Partisan Review* 4 (1992): 658.

82. Havel, *Open Letters,* 150–57.

83. Bukovsky, *To Build a Castle,* 213, 228–31.

84. Ibid., 277.

85. P. V. Annenkov, *The Extraordinary Decade: Literary Memoirs,* trans. by Irwin Titunik, ed. by Arthur Mendel (Ann Arbor: University of Michigan Press, 1968), 135.

86. Peter Yakovlevich Chaadayev, *Philosophical Letters and Apology of a Madman,* trans. and introd. by Mary-Barbara Zeldin (Knoxville: University of Tennessee, 1969), 40. This is from the first philosophical letter, the only one published during Chaadayev's lifetime.

87. Tertz, "The Literary Process in Russia," 105.

88. "Solzhenitsyn and the World," in Conquest, *Tyrants and Typewriters,* 104.

89. The three colloquia on Russian national identity were held in June 1998 at the New Jerusalem Monastery outside of Moscow, in November 1998 at the American Center in Tomsk, and in December 1999 at the Institute for World Economy and International Relations (RAS) in Moscow. They were funded by a Carnegie Foundation grant for the "Project on Russian Political Leaders," and convened by Librarian of Congress Dr. James Billington. Translated and annotated transcripts of the proceedings were prepared by Kathleen Parthé, and issued by the Library of Congress. An on-line version was issued in February 2003: www.loc.gov/about/welcome/speeches/russianperspectives/index.html

90. Vladimir Shlapentokh, *Soviet Intellectuals and Political Power: The Post-Stalin Era* (Princeton: Princeton University Press, 1990), 66.

91. Igor' Chubais, from the *Report on the Third Colloquium on Russian National Identity at the Turn of the Millenium,* Dec. 3, 1999, in Moscow; in the on-line pdf version, *http://www.loc.gov/about/welcome/speeches/russianperspectives/index.html,* this can be found on 90.

92. Lovell and Marsh, "Culture and Crisis," 76. They refer to ten groups discussed by Mikhail Zolotonosov.

93. See: Sergei Chuprinin, "Normal'nyi khod," *Znamia* 10 (1991); and Donald Fanger's contribution to "Central European Writers as a Social Force," *Partisan Review* 4 (1992): 639–55.

94. Andrei Vasilevskii, in "Kritiki o kritike," a critics' roundtable published in *Voprosy literatury,* Nov.–Dec. 1996: 43.

95. Kardin, "Troe na kacheliakh," 69–71.

96. W. Gareth Jones, "Politics," in *The Cambridge Companion to the Classic Russian Novel,* ed. by Malcolm Jones and Robin Feuer Miller (Cambridge: Cambridge University Press, 1998), 63–64. Plekhanov suggested compiling such a volume to the radical writer Stepniak.

97. Choldin, *A Fence Around the Empire,* especially chaps. 3 and 4.

98. Ibid., 104.

99. Ibid., 58–59, 111–12, 84.

100. Ibid., 74, 69.

101. Ibid., 57. 61.

102. Ibid., chapters 4 and 5, especially 74, 114–15.

103. Anna Dostoevsky, *Dostoevsky: Reminiscences,* trans. and ed. by B. Stillman (New York: Liveright, 1975), 125–26, 297.

104. L. Rozenblum, "Zhizn' Dostoevskogo v kontekste Rossiiskoi istorii," *Voprosy literatury,* March–April 2000: 340.

105. V. Tvardovskaia, "Romanovy chitali Dostoevskogo . . . ," a review of Igor' Volgin, *Koleblias' nad bezdnoi: Dostoevskii i imperatorskii dom,* in *Znamia* 10 (2000): 229.

106. Rozenblum, "Zhizn' Dostoevskogo," 339.

107. *Letopis' zhizni i tvorchestva F. M. Dostoevskogo 1821–1881,* vol. 3 (1875–1881), ed. by N. M. Budanova, G. M. Fridlender (St. Petersburg: "Akademicheskii proekt," 1995), 145. The *Letopis'* records a visit to the heir and his wife at the Anichkov Palace on December 16, 1880, but not the earlier Winter Palace visit (512–13). At the Anichkov, Dostoevsky was said to have behaved in his customary manner, leaving when he felt the conversation had gone on long enough so he could head over to the university to talk to law students.

108. Richard Wortman, *Scenarios of Power: Myth and Ceremony in Russian Monarchy,* vol. 2 (Princeton: Princeton University Press, 2000), 190–91. When Alexander III died in 1894, it was said that he had loved Russian literature, especially the works of Dostoevsky and Alexander Ostrovsky (303).

109. Anna Dostoevsky, *Dostoevsky,* 297–99.

110. Ibid., 298–300.

111. Tvardovskaia, "Romanovy chitali Dostoevskogo," 230–31.

112. Rozenblum, "Zhizn' Dostoevskogo," 340.

113. *Letopis' zhizni,* vol. 3, 550–55.

114. Anna Dostoevsky, *Dostoevsky,* 299–300.

115. Victor Terras, *A History of Russian Literature* (New Haven: Yale University Press, 1991), 384.

116. Vladimir Nabokov, *Speak Memory,* rev. ed. (New York: Putnam, 1966), 174–75

117. Benson Bobrick, *The Life and Reign of Ivan the Terrible* (New York: Paragon, 1989), 196.

118. These poems are juxtaposed in *The Literature of Eighteenth-Century Russia,* ed., trans., introd., and notes by Harold Segel, vol. 2 (New York: Dutton, 1967), 308–10.

119. A. S. Pushkin, *Sobranie sochinenii v shesti tomakh,* vol. 1, ed. D. D. Blagoi (Moscow: Biblioteka "Ogonek," 1969), 425. Blagoi's annotations indicate that in order for the poem to be published, Zhukovskii changed the bold line to "Chto prelest'iu zhivoi stikhov ia byl polezen" ("That with the lively charm of my verses I was useful"). In the manuscript version Pushkin had been even bolder: "Chto vsled Radishchevu vosslavil ia svobodu" ("That I followed Radishchev's path in celebrating freedom").

120. Annenkov, *The Extraordinary Decade,* 214.

121. V. G. Belinsky, "A Survey of Russian Literature in 1847," in *Selected Philosophical Works,* no trans. listed (Moscow: Foreign Languages Publishing House, 1956), 421–519.

122. As cited in Jones, "Politics," 64.

123. Tvardovskaia, "Romanovy chitali Dostoevskogo," 231.

124. Cited in a "Letter from Lidia Chukovskaya," in the Appendix to *On Trial: The Soviet State versus "Abram Tertz" and "Nikolai Arzhak,"* trans., ed., and introd. by Max Hayward, rev. and enlarged ed. (New York: Harper and Row, 1967), 288–89.

125. Zamyatin, "Alexander Blok," in *A Soviet Heretic,* 215.

126. "Letter from Lidia Chukovskaya," 288. The letter is addressed primarily to the Rostov-on-Don Section of the Union of Writers and Mikhail Sholokhov, whose call for a stiffer sentence for Sinyavsky and Daniel outraged Chukovskaya and many others.

127. Mark Steinberg, "Introduction" to Maxim Gorky, *Untimely Thoughts: Essays on Revolution, Culture and the Bolsheviks 1917–1918,* trans. by Herman Ermolaev, rev. ed. (New Haven: Yale University Press, 1995), xxii. Steinberg refers to Shklovsky's comments in *A Sentimental Journey.*

128. Aleksandr Solzhenitsyn, *The Gulag Archipelago 1918–1956,* vols. 3–4, trans. by Thomas Whitney (New York: Harper Perennial, 1975), 523.

129. "Letter of 63 Moscow Writers," in Sinyavsky, *On Trial,* 284–86.

130. "Pardons No Substitute for Justice," an editorial in the *Moscow Times,* Dec. 9, 2000. See also: Patrick Tyler, "Russian Panel May Urge Release of American Jailed as Spy," *New York Times,* Dec. 8, 2000, and, by the same journalist, "Russian Chief Plans Pardon of American Jailed as Spy," ibid., Dec. 10, 2000. The commission's sixteen members were predominantly intellectuals. Under Putin, the Justice Ministry began to take the commission's work less seriously, and it was eventually dissolved.

131. Lovell and Marsh, "Culture and Crisis," 56.

132. Ibid., 72.

133. Conquest, "Yevgeny Yevtushenko," in *Tyrants and Typewriters,* 65–78.

134. The first term comes from Lotman and Uspenskii, "New Aspects in the Study of Early Russian Culture," 38. The second is from David Joravsky, "Glasnost Theater," *New York Review of Books,* Nov. 10, 1988: 34.

135. Edward J. Brown, *Russian Literature since the Revolution,* rev. ed. (Cambridge, Mass.: Harvard University Press, 1982), 180–81, 185.

136. Robert Darnton, *Forbidden Best-Sellers of Pre-Revolutionary France* (New York: W. W. Norton, 1996), xvii.

137. Ibid., 20, 21, 232, 239–40.

138. As reported by Iurii Trifonov: "Gertsen govoril o pisateliakh: my ne vrachi, my bol'." From "Voobrazit' beskonechnost'," a 1977 interview with *Literaturnoe obozreniie* which is reprinted in Trifonov's *Kak slovo nashe otzovetsia* (Moscow: "Sovetskaia Rossiia," 1985), 281.

139. "Valentin Rasputin," an interview with Elizabeth Rich, trans. by Laura Weeks, *South Central Review* 12, no. 3–4 (Fall/Winter 1995): 64.

140. Igor' Chubais, in *Third Colloquium on Russian National Identity,* pdf version, 89.

141. *The Solzhenitsyn Files,* 9.

142. Sosnora's letter was printed in *Politicheskii dnevnik,* and reprinted in *An End to Silence,* 252–54.

143. In David Remnick, *Resurrection* (New York: Vintage/Random, 1998), 155.

144 Aleksandr Solzhenitsyn, *The Nobel Lecture,* trans. by F. D. Reeve (New York: Farrar, Straus and Giroux, 1974),, 29.

145. "Dlia takogo proizvedeniia, kak 'Krasnoe koleso,' kotoroe pisalos' 23 goda, nastoia-shchego, dostoinogo ego chitatelia v Rossii poka net." As quoted in Lev Pirogov, "Khozhdenie v narod," *Literaturnaia gazeta* 24 (June 14, 2000).

146. Lev Pirogov, "Khozhdenie v narod," *Literaturnaia gazeta* 24 (2000).

147. Arkady Ostrovsky, "An Astute Observer of Russia's Soul: The Noted Award-Winning Director's Productions Manage to Encapsulate the Country's History Better than Any History Book," *Financial Times,* May 10, 2000; reposted on *Johnson's Russia* List 4294 (May 11, 2000). (Report on the award to Lev Dodin of the European Theater Prize for tracing "the roots and consequences of Communism.") Twenty years earlier he did a controversial dramatization of Abramov's *Home* and *Brothers and Sisters* that was seen to emphasize the decline of the nation, and in 1992 he did a ten-hour production of Dostoevsky's *Demons* about the evil that exists no matter what the political system. At the time the article was written, his most recent production had been a dramatization of Platonov's *Chevengur.*

148. Eduard Ponarin, "Alexander Solzhenitsyn as a Mirror of the Russian Counter-Revolution," Memo no. 150, Program on New Approaches to Russian Security, Policy Memo Series (http://www.fas.harvard.edu/ponars).

149. RFE/RL Newsline, September 22, 2000; and "Solzhenitsyn Comments on Meeting with Putin," a translation of an article from the Sept. 26, 2000, issue of *Rossiiskaia gazeta* which appeared in *Johnson's Russia List,* Oct. 3, 2000.

150. "Solzhenitsyn Comments."

151. Yelena Dikun, "Solzhenitsyn Has Banished Chubais from the Country," from *Obshchaia gazeta,* Sept. 28, 2000, as translated for *Johnson's Russia List* 4554 (Oct. 3, 2000).

152. The Putin visit did not mark the end of the story of Solzhenitsyn and Russian state power; in December 2000 Solzhenitsyn, Chubais, and a host of other prominent figures criticized Putin's decision to revive the Soviet anthem, albeit with new words (*Jamestown Monitor,* Dec. 6, 2000). In May 2002, Solzhenitsyn lambasted Putin for his failure to punish those who—with Yeltsin's permission—stole so much from the country in the 1990s. See an AP report for May 31, reposted on *Johnson's Russia List,* June 1, 2002.

153. This is one of the three epigraphs at the beginning of Alexander Pushkin's *The Captain's Daughter.*

154. Vladimir Kirgizov, "Vse proshche," *Nezavisimaia gazeta,* literary supplement, July 2, 1997.

155. *Ogonek,* nos. 31, 33, and 35 (1999). For the comments on textbooks by Iasen N. Zasurskii, see Vladimir Poliakov, "Byt' russkim chelovekom, ne prochitav 'Mumu'?" *Literaturnaia gazeta* 31–32 (Aug. 8–14, 2001). The illustration that accompanies the article, in which Mumu is being dropped in the water with a stack of books tied to one paw, shows the less-than-solemn attitude of the editors of *Literaturnaia gazeta.*

156. Anne Appelbaum, "Inside the Gulag," a review article, *New York Review of Books,* June 15, 2000: 33–35.

AFTERWORD

1. Vladimir Bondarenko, "'Rossiia—Strana slova'," *Zavtra* 17 (April 1996), and his "Real'-naia literatura," published in *Zavtra* 51 (Dec. 1995) four months earlier.

2. Memoirs of the period from the mid-1950s through the mid-1980s provide frequent illustrations of the capacity for nonmandated collective behavior among people who went to the same school or who worked together. A Spanish professor who grew up in Russia remembered how her father—on the eve of his degree defense in Moscow—was told that the rules had changed and his dissertation on Spanish had to be translated into Russian. The problem was solved by fifty Spanish-speaking Russians, under the direction of linguist Igor Melchuk, who produced an acceptable translation in two weeks. See: Elena Vidal', "'V Rossii ukhabov net'," an interview conducted by Valentina Chemberdzhi, *Druzhba narodov* 6 (1999): 151. Having met Melchuk in 1975 and having participated in winter hikes he organized for young Russian linguists (whom he was prevented from teaching officially), I saw—as did many others who studied in Russia—the strong bonds that allowed the intelligentsia not just to circumvent government constraints, but to lead interesting professional lives marked by warm personal relationships.

3. Vladimir Shlapentokh, *Public and Private Life of the Soviet People: Changing Values in Post-Stalin Russia* (New York: Oxford University Press, 1989), 133.

4. From Alena Ledneva, *Russia's Economy of Favours: Blat, Networking and Informal Exchange* (Cambridge: Cambridge University Press, 1998), unattributed note in front matter.

5. Shlapentokh, *Public and Private Life*, 176.

6. Ibid., 227.

7. Alexander Herzen, *My Past and Thoughts*, trans. by Constance Garnett, rev. by Humphrey Higgins, ed. and abridged by Dwight Macdonald (Berkeley: University of California Press, 1982), 294.

8. Ibid., 297.

9. Ibid., 641.

10. V. G. Belinsky, "Thoughts and Notes on Russian Literature," in *Selected Philosophical Works*, no. trans. listed (Moscow: Foreign Languages Publishing House, 1956), 360–62.

11. Igor' Volgin, *Koleblias' nad bezdnoi: Dostoevskii i imperatorskii dom*, as cited in L. Rozenblium, "Zhizn' Dostoevskogo v kontekste Rossiiskoi istorii," *Voprosy literatury*, March–April 2000, 338.

12. John Lloyd, *Rebirth of a Nation: An Anatomy of Russia* (London: Michael Joseph, 1998), 395.

13. Susan Costanzo, "Reclaiming the Stage: Amateur Theater-Studio Audiences in the Late Soviet Era," *Slavic Review* 57, no. 2 (Summer 1998): 418, 421.

14. Shlapentokh, *Public and Private Life*, 133.

15. Aleksandr Solzhenitsyn, *Invisible Allies*, trans. by Alexis Klimoff and Michael Nicholson (Washington, D.C.: Counterpoint, 1995). Solzhenitsyn waited to publish this material until he was sure that no harm would come to his benefactors. Ironically, the original text, *Nevidimki*, appeared in the last two issues of *Novyi mir* published before the dissolution of the USSR at the end of December 1991.

16. Shlapentokh, *Public and Private Life,* 198.

17. Ibid., 134.

18. Vladimir Bukovsky, *To Build a Castle—My Life as a Dissenter,* trans. by Michael Scammell (New York: Viking, 1979), 354. Shlapentokh confirms that the Soviet population was comparatively well-informed (*Public and Private Life,* 146).

19. Ibid., 231, 143–45, 250, 276, 351.

20. Václav Havel, *Open Letters: Selected Writings 1965–1990,* ed. by Paul Wilson, trans. by Paul Wilson and A. G. Brain (New York: Vintage Books, 1992), 148. The citations from Havel in the rest of this paragraph come from 148–58, 178.

21. Ol'ga Pashkova, "Samizdat byl v kazhdom intelligentskim dome" (an interview with former dissident Viacheslav Bakhmin), *Segodnia* 281 (Dec. 11, 1999). An article on the state of government and private publishing in 2003 indicates a reduction in the number of copies but a rise in the number of titles. It would be worthwhile to explore links between the vitality of private publishing a dozen years after the end of the Soviet Union and both the *samizdat* tradition and the private publishing houses that existed through the 1920s. See Denis Maternovsky, "Fewer Books but a Whole Lot More to Read About," *Moscow Times,* June 6, 2003.

22. Michael Meerson-Aksenov, "The Dissident Movement and Samizdat," in *The Political, Social, and Religious Thought of Russian "Samizdat"—An Anthology,* trans. by Nicholas Lupin, ed. by Michael Meerson-Akenov (Belmont, Mass.: Nordland, 1977), 37–38.

23. Pavel Basinskii, "Otdushina," *Literaturnaia gazeta* 27 (July 4–10, 2001).

24. *Za Glinku! Protiv vozvrata k sovetskomu gimnu: Sbornik materialov,* ed. by M. Chudakova, A. Kurilkin, E. Toddes (Moscow: Shkola "Iazyka russkoi kul'tury," 2000), 46; see also 76–78, 82, 104, 106–107.

25. Sophie Lambroschini, "New Russian Media Document Gives Cause for Concern," *RFE/RL Newsline* 4, no. 179 (Sept. 15, 2000).

26. Galina Chermenskaya, "After the Battle," *The Jamestown Foundation Prism* 7, no. 5 (May 2001),

27. Andrew Solomon, "Young Russia's Defiant Decadence," *New York Times Magazine,* July 18, 1993.

28. *Jamestown Foundation Monitor* 7, no. 79 (April 24, 2001).

29. Pashkova, "Samizdat."

30. Vladimir Poliakov, "Byt' russkim chelovekom, ne prochitav 'Mumu'?" (an interview with Iasen Zasurskii), *Literaturnaia gazeta* 31–32 (Aug. 8–14, 2001).

31. From the *First Colloquium on Russian National Identity,* June 11–12, 1998, New Jerusalem Monastery, Istra, Russian Federation, prepared by James Billington and Kathleen Parthé. All three colloquia were issued on-line in February 2003: www.loc.gov/about/welcome/speeches/russianperspectives/index/html. In the pdf version, these comments can be found on 23, 28, 29.

32. From the *Third Colloquium on Russian National* Identity, Dec. 3, 1999, Institute for World Economy and International Relations (RAS), Moscow, Russian Federation, prepared by James Billington and Kathleen Parthé. In the on-line pdf version cited above, note 31, see 89.

33. See, for example: Viktor Shenderovich, *Kukly* (Moscow: Vagrius, 1996).

34. Petr Vail, "O vkuse i sprose," *Nezavisimaia gazeta—Ex Libris,* Sept. 15, 1997.

35. Igor' Kuznetsov, "Zolotaia lavka pisatelei," *Literaturnaia gazeta* 7 (Feb. 16, 2000).

36. Richard Balmforth, "Moscow Literary Site Saved after Residents Protest," an April 1, 2003 Reuters report reposted on *Johnson's Russia List* 7126 (April 1, 2003).

37. That was the title of the original. The English version is *Homeo Zapiens,* trans. by Andrew Bromfield (New York: Viking, 2002).

38. Maksim Pavlov, "Generation 'P' ili 'P' forever?" *Znamia* 12 (1999): 207.

39. Alla Latynina, "Bessmertnyi bol'noi," *Literaturnaia gazeta* 31–32 (Aug. 11, 1999): 9.

40. Ibid., 9. There was also a plea to show a traditional Russian measure of moral and social restraint in the language and the topics appearing in print. See: Gennadii Mikhailov, "'Nepechatnoe slovo': sushchestvuet li ono segodnya v Rossii? (Po materialam publikatsii 90-kh godov)," *Nash sovremennik* 2 (2002): 242–47.

41. William Scott Green, "The Hebrew Scriptures in Rabbinic Judaism," a separate chapter in Jacob Neusner, *Rabbinic Judaism: Structure and System* (Minneapolis: Fortress Press, 1995), 32.

Index

7, 207; and canon, 109, 120–21, 128, 161; and saintly poets, 110; as literary subject, 126–27; and righteousness, 146; and suffering, 150. *See also* Russianness (*russkost'*)

Etkind, Efim, 195

Fadeev, Alexander, 164
Faith texts, 53–54
Fanger, Donald, 7, 67, 181, 240n12, 252n53, 255n21
Fedotov, G. P., 115
Fet, Afanasy, 92, 108
Feuer, Kathryn, 18
Figes, Orlando, 222n26
Figner, Vera, 58, 65
Fletcher, Giles, 25–27
Florensky, Pavel, 136
Folklore, 23–26, 114, 115, 117, 135, 137, 147, 149
Fonvizin, Denis, 32
Foreign Censorship Committee, x, 37, 40–41, 55, 189, 190
Frank, Joseph, 20, 37, 38, 39
French Revolution, 200
Fukuyama, Francis, 49

Gannibal, Abram, 104, 111, 241n23
Genis, Alexander, 55
Gippius, Zinaida, 162
Glasnost years: and Russian culture, xv; and literary-political nexus, xv, 3, 48, 106, 160; and national identity, 9; and writer-state relations, 49–50; and Village Prose, 83–85, 140, 141–42; and canon, 106, 165; and writers' deaths, 114; and righteousness, 140–46, 147; and suffering, 152; and resurfacing of texts, 157
Glinka, Mikhail, 34, 214
Glushkova, Tatyana, 116–17, 126, 129, 247n94
Godlove, Terry, 219n7
Gogol, Nikolai: and responsibility of talent,

7, 221–22n25; and national identity, 9, 216; and Belinsky, 34, 56, 188; biography of, 58; and territoriality, 103; and Russianness, 108; death of, 114; and righteousness, 146; characters of, 185; *Selected Passage from a Correspondence with Friends*, 188; and police informers, 210; *Dead Souls*, 216
Goldfaden, Abraham, *Shulammite*, 60
Goncharov, Ivan, 9, 58, 82, 103, 184–85, 188, 189; *Oblomov*, 20, 149; "Oblomov's Dream," 97
Gorbachev, Mikhail: and literary freedom, xiv, 3; and "one-text" phenomenon, 12, 13; and *shestidesiatniki*, 48; and nationalists, 85, 88; and Sinyavsky, 202; and negative revelations in print, 214. *See also* Glasnost years
Gorenshtein, Fridrikh, 166
Gorky, Maxim, 22, 113, 118, 149, 194, 194–95, 216
Gosizdat (officially published works): and state ideology, x; and "one-text" phenomenon, 12, 13, 14; and censorship, 17; and quality of writing, 19; and Solovki prison camp, 45; and Village Prose, 81, 91; and writers' reputations, 100; and collective life, 156, 211; as Soviet literature, 164; and networking, 210
Graphomania, 35, 62–64
Green, William Scott, xviii, 222n33, 223–24nn48, 59, 231n11, 239nn6, 7, 265n41
Griboyedov, Alexander, 35, 197; *Woe from Wit*, 31, 33
Grossman, Vasily, 146, 180; *Everything Flows*, 20; *Life and Fate*, 20, 153, 157
Groys, Boris, 255n14
Gumilev, Nikolai, 22, 43, 113, 207

Ha-Am, Ahad, 41
Haraszti, Miklos, 19, 21
Havel, Václav, 83, 153, 181, 182–83, 209, 213

process, 130, 169; and righteousness, 133, 134, 137, 148; and literary criticism, 161–62. *See also* Ultranationalism

Nekrasov, Nikolai, 39, 194

Nepomnyashchy, C. T., xviii, 230nn3, 187, 234nn75, 76

Networking, 209–10

Neusner, Jacob, ix–x

Nevsky, Alexander, 111, 116

New Russians, 215

Nexus. *See* Literary-political nexus

Nicholas I (tsar): and censorship, x, 31, 40, 174; and state's attitude towards texts, 23, 28, 30, 31, 33, 34; and Fletcher, 27; and writer-state relations, 193

Nicholas II (tsar), 192, 194, 243nn49, 57

Nikolaeva, Galina: *Harvest,* 76; "The Manager of the Machine-Tractor Station and the Chief Agronomist," 138

Nikon, Patriarch, 27–28

Nobel Prize in literature, 7, 11, 123, 155, 201

Novikov, Nikolai, 16, 30, 31, 187, 197

Novikov, Vladimir, 11

Novyi mir (journal): and Russian classics, 11; and censorship, 17, 46; and Solzhenitsyn, 46, 49, 92, 100, 137, 153; and nationalism, 78; and collectivization, 86; and Village Prose, 90; translated selections from, 164

October 1993 crisis, 71, 72, 87, 88, 202, 208

Odoevsky, Vladimir, 188

Officially published works (*gosizdat*). See *Gosizdat* (officially published works)

Okudzhava, Bulat, 22, 195, 220n6

Old Believers: persecution of, 28–29; and unrest, 37; and Bulgakov, 57; and territoriality, 102; and *derevenshchiki,* 125; and Avvakum, 133; and righteousness, 136, 137, 139; and Russian God, 146; literacy of, 179

Olesha, Yuri: *No Day without a Line,* 151; *Envy,* 163

"One-text" phenomenon, 12–15, 63, 161, 186–88, 210

Orthodox Church: intercessional role of, ix; values of, 3; and political thought, 6; and national identity, 9, 11; and faith narratives, 14; and literary-political nexus, 24, 26–29, 34–35; and censorship, 34–35, 42; and orthography, 45; and Sinyavsky, 68, 70; and Khrushchev, 78; and Krupin, 89; and corrected versions of holy texts, 102; and intercession of righteous dead, 114, 115, 119; and martyrdom, 115; and knowledge, 117; and writers' deaths, 119; and nationalism, 122; and modernism, 124; and Russianness, 125, 127; and Avvakum, 133; and righteousness, 135; and suffering, 152; and advisory role to tsar, 192–93; and spiritual collectivity, 209

Orthography, 44, 45

Ostrovsky, Alexander, 58; *The Storm,* 177

Others: as outside national text, 15; Sinyavsky as not an "other," 47–48; demonization of, 72; and Zamyatin, 73–74; and Village Prose, 84; Jews as, 104, 108, 109, 127–28; and nationalism, 107–8, 109; and writers' deaths, 116; and Russianness, 121–22, 124, 129, 246–47n94; and Zyuganov, 208

Ovechkin, Valentin, 83, 96; "District Routine," 12, 76

Pale of Settlement, 8, 41

Pamphlets, 37–38, 39

Pamyat, 85, 86, 87, 88

Paraliterary space: and "one-text" phenomenon, 12; and repressive measures, 46; and literary criticism, 52, 54, 169, 231n13; and "Flaming Revolutionaries," 58; and graphomania, 63; and Sinyavsky and Tertz, 66–74; and saintly poets, 110; and ethnicity, 118; enemies in, 168; as danger zone, 173; texts in, 173, 176; and permitted anomalies, 197; and Solzhenitsyn, 201